# THE EARLY ILLUSTRATED BOOK

EDITED BY SANDRA HINDMAN

LIBRARY OF CONGRESS ※ WASHINGTON ※ 1982

# THE EARLY ILLUSTRATED BOOK

## ESSAYS IN HONOR OF LESSING J. ROSENWALD

*Library of Congress Cataloging in Publication Data*
*Main entry under title:*

*The Early illustrated book.*

*Includes bibliographical references and index.*
*1. Illustrated books—Congresses. 2. Rosenwald, Lessing J. (Lessing Julius), 1891–1979.*
*I. Rosenwald, Lessing J. (Lessing Julius), 1891–1979. II. Hindman, Sandra, 1944– .*
*Z1023.E18 1982 096'.1 82–600192*
*ISBN 0–8444–0398–9 AACR2*

# CONTENTS

## PART TWO
## LANDSCAPE AND THE EARLY ILLUSTRATED BOOK



## PART THREE
## THE ILLUSTRATION OF VERGIL IN PRINTED BOOKS

# LIST OF COLOR PLATES

# FOREWORD

In May 1980 the Library of Congress paid honor to one of its greatest benefactors, Lessing J. Rosenwald, who had died at his home in Jenkintown, Pennsylvania, the previous year. The tribute took the form of an interdisciplinary symposium that focused on the scholarly potential of the magnificent collection of illustrated books Mr. Rosenwald presented, beginning in 1943, to the Library. The Center for the Book in the Library of Congress, the symposium's principal sponsor, is pleased to make a collection of essays that derive from papers presented at that conference available to a wide audience of scholars, librarians, and booklovers.

In addition to the participants whose essays are here presented, the Center for the Book is grateful to Sandra Hindman for shaping the papers into a book and to William Matheson, chief of the Rare Book and Special Collections Division, for his help in organizing the meeting. Thanks also go to Lois Fern for her index and to Margery Maier for her assistance in preparing the manuscript for publication.

Proposed by Librarian of Congress Daniel J. Boorstin and established by Act of Congress in 1977, the Center for the Book exists to "keep the book flourishing" by stimulating interest in books, reading, and the printed word. The center works closely with organizations outside the Library of Congress to increase the public's book awareness, to promote reading, and to stimulate the study of books. It pursues these goals primarily by bringing together members of the book, educational, and business communities for symposia and projects. The center's major interests include the educational and cultural role of the book, both nationally and internationally, the history of books and printing, and the future of the book and the printed word.

The center's programs also address authorship and writing, the printing, publishing, and preservation of books, the use of books and printed materials, and literacy. The Center for the Book's symposia and publications are supported by tax-deductible gifts from individuals and organizations. This volume would not be possible without such support, for which we are grateful.

Additional support for the present volume came from the Clapp Publication Fund, which was established in honor of Verner W. Clapp, Chief Assistant Librarian of Congress, upon his retirement in 1956 after a long and distinguished career in the Library. This fund was recently enhanced by a publication fund that had been established by Mr. Rosenwald, and hence its use here is particularly fitting.

JOHN Y. COLE
*Executive Director*
*Center for the Book*

# AN APPRECIATION

## LESSING J. ROSENWALD: THE COLLECTOR AND HIS COLLECTION

When the symposium of which this volume is a record was first conceived in December 1978, Lessing J. Rosenwald, the donor of the Library of Congress's greatest rare book collection, was approaching his eighty-eighth birthday. He responded enthusiastically to the idea of a conference bringing together scholars from many disciplines to discuss the illustrated book—the focus of his magnificent collection—and to point out new avenues in its study. In May 1979 he welcomed Ruth Mortimer and this writer to the Alverthorpe Gallery, his private gallery in Jenkintown, Pennsylvania. Miss Mortimer wished to see parts of the collection in order to select the grouping of books which would best serve as the theme of the symposium session she had been asked to organize. In two highly regarded catalogs she had described the sixteenth-century French and Italian portions of a related collection in the Department of Printing and Graphic Arts at Harvard. Mr. Rosenwald was clearly delighted to have such a perceptive visitor and brought out some of his favorites as well as specific titles his visitor asked to see. When he died shortly after this visit, on June 24, 1979, from complications following a fall, the symposium intended to honor him had to be dedicated to his memory.

Lessing Rosenwald was born in Chicago, Illinois, on February 10, 1891. He was bitten by the collecting bug in his middle thirties at the time he was managing the Philadelphia branch of Sears Roebuck, the mail order firm his father, Julius Rosenwald, had played such an instrumental role in forming and making into one of the great success stories of modern times. Starting out in 1926 as a collector of prints, Mr. Rosenwald by 1928 had added books to his collecting scope. In retrospect there was a certain inevitability in his moving from collecting the separate fifteenth-century woodcut to collecting books from that period containing examples of the woodcutter's art. He made his first major book purchases—a group of well-known German illustrated incunabula in superlative condition—from A. S. W. Rosenbach in 1928, moving on to a spectacular burst of buying in 1929 and 1930 that left him sorely overextended when the effects of the Depression began to be felt. By 1932 his collecting had slowed to a standstill, gradually to be resumed in 1935, at a time when great bargains were to be had. He resigned from the position of chairman of the board of Sears Roebuck in 1939 at the age of forty-eight to devote himself to the cultural and philanthropic interests with which his name will forever be associated. Shortly before his retirement he built a private gallery referred to earlier and hired as its curator Elizabeth Mongan, who came with strong recommendations from Paul Sachs, codirector of the Fogg Museum at Harvard. These two friends and advisers, the rare book dealer A. S. W. Rosenbach, Frederick R. Goff, chief of the Rare Book Division at the Library of Congress from 1945 to 1972, and his beloved wife, Edith, are the five people to whom he expressed the greatest indebtedness in his privately printed *Recollections of a Collector* (1976).

When Mr. Rosenwald made his first gift to the Library of Congress in 1943, he had been collecting for less than a third of the fifty years he was to devote to this activity. By the terms of an agreement between himself and the Library he was able during his lifetime to keep physical possession of the books he gave to the nation. From this first gift until his death, books moved back and forth between Jenkintown and Washington in response to requests from scholars, for exhibits, and for cataloging. In making his gift this early, he ensured that his books would be used, an essential point for a man who said on one occasion that a print not seen might as well not have been created.

In contrast to collectors who do everything possible to avoid showing their books and firmly believe the oft-quoted remark that a rare book loses five dollars of its value every time it is opened, he encouraged students to handle his books, including young children whose teachers so regularly brought groups to the Alverthorpe Gallery. The bindings of his works were, of course, sturdy and the paper of a quality that collectors of twentieth-century books can only marvel at. Though he wanted his books to be seen and used, he took necessary precautions, making sure that they did not remain in exhibits so long that they might suffer, that they were kept in specially made morocco slipcases, that they were worked on only by the best restoration binders, and that they stayed in the superb condition for which the collection was famed.

Lessing Rosenwald was not a man who wrote often or at length about his motivations for collecting. His precepts remained constant throughout his life, led off by the one he voiced most frequently: "Collect the best quality of anything that you can obtain." By giving his book collection to the Library of Congress and his print collection to the National Gallery of Art only fifteen years after he had begun to form them, he put another conviction into action: the belief that a collector has a responsibility to make his collection available to others.

In choosing the Library of Congress as the recipient of his books, he found a splendid way of thanking the country that had brought him the means to form the collection. Throughout his longstanding association with the Library he demonstrated deep affection for it and constant concern for its welfare. As a member of the Librarian's Council, launched by Archibald MacLeish in 1942, he participated in the meetings of this group of outside observers assigned the task of studying the Library's operations and activities and making recommendations for their improvement. In making his first gift a year afterward he surely hoped to set an example for other American collectors and in later years lamented that the national library of the United States, unlike the national libraries of England and France, had not been the recipient of the collections he felt it deserved and did not have the money needed for the purchase of rare books.

After Archibald MacLeish's resignation, Mr. Rosenwald continued to work with MacLeish's successor, Librarian of Congress Luther Evans, writing him in 1947: "The National Library deserves and demands the strongest rare book collection that it can possibly build." As if inspired to accomplish this singlehandedly, in the three-year period from 1945 to 1947 he bought some of the greatest books in his collection, reaching a level of activity that prompted A. S. W. Rosenbach to observe in the introduction to a Library of Congress exhibit of recent additions to the Rosenwald Collection that "no other library in this country, or abroad, has received during this period a collection comparable to it."

In this period Mr. Rosenwald is reported to have spent close to a million dollars, acquiring books that ten times that amount would not buy thirty-five years later. By the 1950s there was a tapering off in collecting, rounded off by a conscious slowing down in the 1960s and 1970s. I believe that some of the excitement and the pleasure of the chase fell away when "Doc" Rosenbach, the flamboyant rare book dealer and close friend, died in 1952. And yet at all times Mr. Rosenwald bought widely from other dealers—William H. Schab, the Robinsons, H. P. Kraus, Pierre Berès, Georges Heilbrun, and many, many others, contradicting the widespread impression that Rosenbach was his sole source. Though some of the greatest and most expensive books came from Rosenbach, particularly in the bursts of activity in the late 1920s and mid-1940s, the files show that an amazingly wide range of dealers provided him with books over the years.

When he died in 1979, Mr. Rosenwald had given the Library the more than twenty-six hundred books described in the catalog of the collection published by the Library of Congress in 1978, approximately five thousand reference books, and a number of other books eventually to be described in a supplement to the 1978 catalog. In October 1979 the books in the published catalog were moved from Jenkintown to Washington, and in June 1980 the reference books and the books not previously given made their way as well. Shortly afterward the Alverthorpe Gallery closed and several of its employees came to Washington to join the collections at the Library of Congress and the National Gallery of Art. By the provisions of the original indenture, which set the pattern for all Mr. Rosenwald's gifts, the Library is encouraged to dispose of duplicates from the collection when another copy, as good or better than the one in the Rosenwald Collection, is available in another Library of Congress collection. Given the quality of the Rosenwald books, there can be no tremendous outflow of duplicates, but there will be continuing possibilities for adding to the collection.

So far we have identified three constant themes in Mr. Rosenwald's relations with the Library of Congress—his commitment to the idea of its potential greatness, his interest in seeing that potential realized, and his conviction that his books could play an important part in that realization. Awareness of this passionate interest in seeing the Library fulfill its potential and a deep sense of gratitude led John Cole, executive director of the Center for the Book, and me, in my capacity as chief of the Rare Book and Special Collections Division, to organize a symposium. Although Mr. Rosenwald's books had been featured in exhibits and greatly admired as physical objects, they were, as we viewed the matter, seen by too many people as precious objects, a rich man's baubles, with only incidental relevance to the 1980s. To suggest the tremendous intellectual potential of the collection, we asked three organizers, representing varying disciplines, to plan sessions around themes exemplified in the Rosenwald Collection. In these sessions the organizers were urged to extend the interdisciplinary approach by consciously seeking speakers representing diverse approaches and specializations. Additional participants were invited in an observer capacity from other fields that might be expected to respond to the Rosenwald Collection. A total of forty people gathered for this invitational seminar on May 30–31, 1980. The papers were sometimes summarized and sometimes delivered in fuller form. Following the symposium, in response to the discussion, the speakers reworked their papers in varying degrees for inclusion in this volume. From the outset a publication was intended, and every effort has been made to ensure that it is worthy of the man whose memory it honors and whose collection it celebrates.

The discussions at the symposium and the papers in this volume make it clear that the eye-opener for the largest number of participants was the richness and untapped potential of the Arenberg Collection, purchased en bloc by Mr. Rosenwald from the antiquarian book dealer William H. Schab in 1955. James Marrow, at the time professor in the Department of the History of Art at Yale University and observer at the symposium, commented that there were specialists in Dutch and Flemish art present who were seeing these illustrations for the first time. Mr. Rosenwald, who almost invariably bought individual rarities, not collections, made an exception in acquiring the 160 Dutch and Flemish fifteenth- and sixteenth-century books from the library of the dukes of Arenberg. Undoubtedly his determining that more than thirty of the Arenberg books were unique influenced his decision. The clinching fact must surely have been his awareness that the Arenberg books had for more than half a century been inaccessible to scholars. In 1884 in *The Woodcutters of the Netherlands in the Fifteenth Century*, William Martin Conway described his frustrations in trying to examine the Arenberg books. Marie Kronenberg in many places recounted her repeated rebuffs in trying to gain access to the Arenberg books, which she desperately wished to include in *Nederlandsche Bibliographie van 1500 tot 1540*.

Within the first year of his buying the collection, Mr. Rosenwald proposed that he send the books to Belgium and the Netherlands. Marie Kronenberg wrote to warn him that the peculiar circumstances of the sale of the collection (the duke of Arenberg had served in the German army during the first World War, had had his property confiscated, and had succeeded in getting the book collection out of Belgium) made it risky to send the collection to the Low Countries. By 1960, working closely with the Dutch and Belgian governments, Mr. Rosenwald felt comfortable in lending the books for exhibition in the two countries. Even today there are uncertainties about just what was disposed of by the Arenberg heirs in the mid-1950s. In her article about the dispersal of the Arenberg Collection in *Het Boek*, volume 33 (1958–59), Marie Kronenberg tells of her shock in seeing books clearly from the Arenberg Collection suddenly appearing in catalogs of Lathrop Harper, H. P. Kraus, and other rare book dealers. Harvard lent three of the books it had acquired in this period to Mr. Rosenwald for the exhibit in Belgium and the Netherlands. We can be certain that Mr. Rosenwald purchased the largest part of the Arenberg Collection, a corpus so important that, following the symposium, James Marrow wrote to John Cole to say that the Library of Congress could make no more important use of this Rosenwald Collection than to organize and sponsor a publication of the illustrations in the Rosenwald books from the Low Countries.

In the spring of 1980, at the time that final plans were being made for the symposium, Paul Needham, curator of rare books and bindings at the Pierpont Morgan Library, in examining one of the best known books in the Rosenwald Collection, a volume containing four separate works printed by William Caxton, England's first printer, in a binding by John Reynes, discovered an unknown fifth Caxton imprint, an Indulgence, in the vellum strips used by the binder to guard the signatures. Mr. Rosenwald loved this volume and would have taken the keenest interest in this discovery. The Center for the Book has commissioned Mr. Needham to describe his findings in a monograph to be published by the Library. The Indulgence exemplifies one kind of discovery to be made in the Rosenwald Collection. The papers in this volume suggest the broad range of approaches to which the collection lends itself so admirably. The Library of Congress invites you to acquaint yourself with the riches of the collection and to help it build on the noble foundation created by this great donor.

WILLIAM MATHESON
*Chief, Rare Book and Special Collections Division*

# THE EARLY ILLUSTRATED BOOK

SANDRA HINDMAN

# PROBING THE ROSENWALD COLLECTION

Lessing J. Rosenwald's self-professed specialty was "the illustrated book . . . from the fifteenth century up to modern times,"[1] a designation readily confirmed by an overview of the collection. Of the more than twenty-six hundred separately described entries in the recently published catalog of the Rosenwald Collection, the vast majority are illustrated.[2] Deviations from this interest are accounted for either by extenuating circumstances, such as the purchase of an entire collection like the Arenberg library, or by special interests, such as in typography and calligraphy, subjects closely allied, in any case, with illustration.[3] Within the broad chronological spectrum covered by Rosenwald's books, quantitatively and qualitatively important groups cluster around the fifteenth and sixteenth centuries and the eighteenth through twentieth centuries.

Eighteen illuminated manuscripts, most dating from the fifteenth and early sixteenth centuries, buttress the collection of printed books. Also dating largely from the fifteenth century is the outstanding group of ten blockbooks, books which were among the earliest purchases by Rosenwald, who had already amassed an extraordinarily important collection of prints (some of which dated from the same era as the blockbooks).[4] The period of early printing is represented, in part, by Dutch and Belgian books from the Arenberg Collection, which were purchased as a group in 1956. Italian illustrators, especially from the last decade of the fifteenth century, are similarly well-represented, since they were among Rosenwald's favorites. The next high point in the collection begins in the eighteenth century, although a number of significant works date from the seventeenth century, especially on subjects Rosenwald liked, such as science (especially botany and astronomy) and culture (for instance, the history of architecture, dance, and chess). Exceptional eighteenth-century editions include many imprints with original drawings by such artists as Prud'hon, Gabrielle de Saint-Aubin, and Gravelot. Of special continuing interest is one of the most complete, extant William Blake collections, which includes many unique items such as drawings, proofs, and plates, as well as books.[5] Finally, twentieth-century monuments of printing include an extensive sampling of livres d'artiste executed by an extraordinary cast of important modern painters: Matisse, Chagall, Rouault, Picasso, Braque, Bonnard, Dufy, Miro, and Toulouse-Lautrec.

Such a rich collection obviously could prompt numerous research projects on a great variety of topics. The papers contained in this volume focus primarily, although not exclusively, on scholarly problems that concern the earlier period of the history of printing, namely the fifteenth and sixteenth centuries. Even within this limited time period, the essays explore from the points of view of scholars of diverse disciplines only a few of the possible subjects of study: (1) problems related to fifteenth- and sixteenth-century Dutch and Belgian books (that is, the Arenberg portion of the collection), (2) landscape and the illustrated book, and (3) the illustration of Vergil's works. Many other equally interesting and important subjects figure scarcely or not at all: Blake illustrations, the livres d'artiste, French romantic drawings and engravings, and so forth. In this introduction I will attempt to situate the subjects treated in the eleven essays making up this book within the complete collection and within scholarship in general. That is, I will summarize for each of the three parts of the volume the nature and degree of its treatment of a segment of the Rosenwald Collection, showing, too, how even these portions of the collection can command additional study. I will further endeavor to elaborate the broader scholarly context for the papers, in order to show how they—singly and together—have contributed to key intellectual issues. This volume is only the beginning. It will, I hope, continue to stimulate many other investigations that further draw on the bountiful resources of the Rosenwald Collection.

The Arenberg books, so-called because they derive from the library of the dukes of Arenberg, make up only a fraction of the total Rosenwald Collection, approximately 170 out of 2,600 items. Acquired in 1956, the collection includes printed books of the fifteenth through sixteenth centuries representing the output of nearly every major Dutch and Belgian press. Only about half the volumes contain illustrations, but unadorned copies often include decoration and rubrication done by hand. This fact alone could have justified the purchase of a collection that comprised so many unillustrated exemplars. Other special features, however, also contribute to the value of the collection and more than sanction the purchase. Many copies of the Arenberg books are unique, and some are even the only extant examples of books that were never reedited. Nine of these unique copies date from the incunable period, and a surprising twenty-one copies originated in the sixteenth century.[6] Nearly all the Arenberg books are in pristine condition, perhaps partly because the dukes of Arenberg rarely permitted their books to be viewed, but surely also owing to their shrewd and careful collecting. Many reveal unexpected data on the circumstances and nature of their production and ownership. For example, they often possess handsome original bindings, informative manuscript notes, and careful professional hand-coloring. Added to the blockbooks and to eight or ten Dutch and Flemish specimens that already formed part of Rosenwald's collection before this purchase in 1956,[7] the Arenberg books thus constitute an exceptional source for research.

Despite the unquestioned importance of the collection, scholars have probed only slightly beneath its surface. Two exhibition catalogs survey the books, citing skeletal bibliographical data and including textual summaries and artistic attributions. The first of these publications, its text written by Frederick Goff in 1958, includes 180 items, each with brief entries and well-chosen reproductions of woodcuts, often from the unique copies.[8] The second, more extensive catalog, unfortunately now difficult to obtain, represented the combined editorial efforts of W. Post, R. Penninck, and E. Indestege, all at the Bibliothèque royale in Brussels, which cosponsored the exhibition in 1960 with the Museum Meermanno-Westreenianum in The Hague.[9] Among the various edition and facsimile projects involving Rosenwald books, only one has focused on an Arenberg book, the edition by Elly Cockx-Indestege of the first Belgian cookbook anonymously illustrated with a delightful woodcut of a fat, tired cook surrounded by his pots and pans.[10] Scholars can study another Rosenwald-Arenberg book, one that is not unique, however, in another edition by Luc Indestege: the so-called Ludolphus of Saxony, *Tboek vanden leven ons heeren Iesu Christi*, published in 1487 in Antwerp by Gerard Leeu.[11]

Scrutiny of the 1958 and 1960 catalogs—and of the holdings themselves—discloses certain highlights within the Dutch and Belgian collection. Among fifteenth-century imprints, nearly every major illustrator originally isolated by Conway and Schretlen[12] appears, excepting Colard Mansion's Bruges Woodcutter and Arend de Keysere's Ghent Woodcutter, whose editions are extraordinarily rare. Surely one of the densest concentrations of illustrated imprints is that of Jacob Bellaert's press in Haarlem, established by 1483 and operative only until 1486, when Bellaert presumably merged with Gerard Leeu in Gouda.[13] The Rosenwald Collection includes half of the twelve or thirteen issues from this press, all illustrated by a gifted anonymous woodcutter dubbed the Bellaert Master. Not only is the number of Bellaert imprints noteworthy, but the fresh, careful coloring and immaculate condition of the books further distinguish them. The more mechanical style of the prolific Gouda Woodcutter is also recognizable in a number of Rosenwald imprints.[14]

The collection provides as well an unusual opportunity to study hand-colored woodcuts attributed to the Netherlandish painter, the Master of the Virgo inter virgines, who worked in Delft first for Jacob van der Meer and later for Christian Snellaert, who took over the former's press.[15] Three distinct issues of the popular *Epistolen ende evangelien* contain the same cycle of woodcuts by this Delft woodcutter, and the cycle also reappears in Ludolphus of Saxony's *Leven ons heren*.

Additionally a copy, unrecorded elsewhere, of the 1488 edition of *Die vier uterste* includes five woodcuts by the same artist. Like the Bellaert books, all these copies display hand-coloring, which varies considerably from one volume to the next. Other woodcutters whose work can be studied in the collection include the Utrecht, Antwerp, Leyden, Zwolle, and Louvain woodcutters, as well as Jacob Cornelis.[16] The essays that follow analyze artistic contributions by the Bellaert Master and the Utrecht Woodcutter and illustrate prints by the Antwerp and Gouda Woodcutters.

Fifteenth-century unillustrated Dutch and Belgian books pose other equally interesting problems for the scholar. An unusually large number of books represent the presses of Johannes of Westphalia in Louvain and the Brothers of the Common Life in Brussels.[17] Although few issues from these presses received pictures, rubricators and decorators adorned many copies with initials and penscrolls. Codicological investigation of these copies, the results of which would be compared with similar investigations of other copies now in other collections, could elucidate procedures of rubrication and decoration in early printing shops, thereby permitting comparisons with production methods used for manuscripts. Some interesting unedited texts may be read only in unique copies in the Rosenwald Collection. An example is *Dit boecxken leert hoe men mach voghelen vanghen metten handen*, "the only complete copy known of the earliest Dutch book devoted to hunting and fishing."[18]

The fifteenth-century portion of the Arenberg library is perhaps richest, however, in the data it provides on the history of illustration, the subject of two of the four essays included in part one of the volume. Diane Scillia, in "The Master of the London Passional: Johann Veldener's 'Utrecht Cutter,'" identifies the woodcutter with an artist previously known only as an illuminator, the Passional Master, who worked in Utrecht between 1470 and 1480. She further expands the attributions to this woodcutter-miniaturist, whose palette she recognized in the Rosenwald copy of one of Veldener's imprints, the *Fasciculus temporum*. In addition, one of the Passional Master's collaborators, "Master B," also worked in both media, for Scillia has recognized his style in woodcuts in the *Fasciculus* and the *Speculum humanae salvationis*, of which he may have been the designer. This link between the *Speculum* and Utrecht manuscript illumination suggests that the proposal of Utrecht as a home for the Netherlandish blockbooks deserves close scrutiny. In his essay entitled "The Bellaert Master and *De proprietatibus rerum*," James Snyder likewise reiterates connections between Haarlem and early blockbook production, noting as well the Bellaert Master's relationship to panel painters. Snyder's principal focus, on the Bartholomaeus edition published by Bellaert in 1485, allows him to consider an extraordinarily innovative and little-known series of full-page, hand-colored woodcuts by the Bellaert Master. His comparison between this series and a contemporary one in a book published in Lyons led him to conclude that, although the Bellaert Master had access to a related prototype, he often deviated from it, "especially in the treatment of flora, fauna, and landscape."

Both papers thus extend our knowledge of the artistic activity of two important northern Netherlandish centers, Utrecht and Haarlem. Because Scillia and Snyder have used securely dated and localized documents—that is, printed books—it is now possible to speak with more confidence and in greater detail of local stylistic characteristics. Following their examples, manuscript and panel painting specialists investigating other locales may find important documentary evidence in printed books. Additionally, Scillia and Snyder both confirm that eclecticism characterizes artistic production in the North, at least in the 1480s. Both have convincingly redefined artistic careers to include works in several media. If they and others are right that these artists worked in a variety of media, modern specialists will need to broaden their field of vision to document the extraordinary degree of interchange that characterized the work of these craftsmen.

If Scillia's and Snyder's papers recommend methodologies for tackling certain problems in the history of illustration, they also point to further issues. Differences in scale and technique between manuscripts, woodcuts, and paintings make difficult, if not suspect, the ordinary methods of connoisseurship. Neither paper explores fully the question of the use of models, a working procedure which could, in itself, account for the affinities both scholars suggested between artists of diverse media.[19] Such an explanation would obviate the need for accepting shared identities. Model-sharing could also account for the apparently contradictory conclusions that Utrecht and Haarlem were both centers of the same blockbook production.

In the third essay, "The Genesis Woodcuts of a Dutch Adaptation of the *Vita Christi*," Barabra Lane also focuses on Flemish book production in the 1480s but from a different perspective, that of the relationship between pictures and texts. Lane's concentration on two imprints of an adaptation of Ludolphus of Saxony's *Vita Christi*, published in Antwerp and Delft, led her to conclude that the Dutch text was only a liberal paraphrase of Ludolphus's tract, considerably amplified or abbreviated in places by the anonymous author-translator. Her subsequent examination of the extensive Genesis cycle that adorns these copies revealed that its woodcuts often drew unusual pictorial details from the colloquial and personalized text. At the same time, certain features of the woodcuts derived from somewhat earlier biblical iconographies established in the Netherlands for the densely illustrated First History Bibles. Lane's careful analysis thus provides a case study of the relationship between artistic innovation inspired by a newly translated text and artistic tradition in the adaptation of preexistent models from related texts.[20] In the woodcuts of the *Vita Christi*, Lane has perceived a predominant eschewal of convention, something which characterizes much other fifteenth-century Dutch illustration as well. Such freedom of interpretation is in line with the "personal tone of much of the literature of the Devotio Moderna."

Like the incunables, sixteenth-century books from the Arenberg library can contribute to the resolution of a number of pictorial and textual issues. Less well studied than their fifteenth-century counterparts, sixteenth-century graphic artists, especially those active in Antwerp, are well represented in the Rosenwald Collection. Early sixteenth-century imprints permit scholars to trace the repeated reuse of blocks designed decades before, such as those by the Master of Bellaert or Jacob Cornelis.[21]

Sixteenth-century artists of whom the collection particularly encourages study include the Master of the Delbecq-Schreiber Passion, whose vigorous style is represented in no less than ten books from the collection, and the virtually unknown Master of Thomas van der Noot, whose woodcuts appear in four books.[22] Numerous books containing fine illustrations date from the period around mid-century. These include two exceptionally choice and rare Plantin imprints with excellent engraved illustrations cut by Jan and Hieronymus Wierix and Pieter Huys after drawings by Pieter van der Borcht.[23] One of these, a Book of Hours, includes engraved marginalia on each page and suggests comparison with other printed Horae by Adriaen van Liesvelt and Henrick Peetersen.[24] Examples by the latter incorporate dotted woodcuts, a technique more common in Germany. Other artists include the printer Josse Lambrecht, Jan Swart, Pieter Coecke van Aalst, Cornelis Galle, and Marcus Gheeraerts, the last an engraver from Bruges represented in two interesting collections of moralized fables.[25]

The sixteenth-century books also constitute a repository of little-known textual material. The Netherlandish prototype of the popular novel, the *volksboek*, exists in three or four different examples in the collection, several of which are unique. They include the stories *Margarieten van Limborch*, *Peeter van Provencen*, and *Turias ende Floreta*, the last two forbidden by ecclesiastical authorities presumably because of the amorous exploits of the protagonists.[26] Banned in 1540 because they expressed sentiments of the Reformation were copies of the important rederijker plays entitled *Spelen van zinne . . . binnen Ghendt*, originally published in Antwerp in 1539 by Josse Lambrecht, who also contributed an engraving of the open-air theater at which the plays were performed.[27] Yet another rederijker play, one by Matthijs de Castelein entitled *Pyramus ende Thisbe*, [28] exists in a unique copy in the Rosenwald Collection. Scholars can investigate sixteenth-century attitudes toward women in other unedited treatises, including the satiric *Evangelien van den Spinrock*, in which women exchange, while spinning, their views on religion, marriage, and family life.[29] Finally, mirrors of everyday life in the sixteenth century, which could serve to formulate a social history of the period, include books—some illustrated and some not—on cooking, currency, and medicine and pharmacology, among which at least ten imprints treat subjects allied to the practice of medicine.[30]

The last essay in part one focuses on sixteenth-century textual traditions, as exemplified by two Rosenwald Collection imprints and their literary analogues. In "*The Ship of Fools* and the Idea of Folly in Sixteenth-Century Netherlandish Literature," Keith Moxey investigates the literary context for Sebastian Brant's work, of which two among the three sixteenth-century Flemish translations exist in the Rosenwald Collection. Moxey first cites and assesses a substantial and little-known body of Flemish literature which he considers to include counterparts of *The Ship of Fools*. Among these works are *De Blauwe Schuit* (*The Blue Boat*), *Van den Langhen Waghen* (*Concerning the Long Wagon*), *Van de bonte Kapkens* (*Concerning the Gay Caps*), *Den Rechten Weg nae't Gasthuys* (*The Right Way to the Poorhouse*), *Schip van Sint Reynuut* (*St. Empty's Ship*), *Vanden, x, esels* (*Concerning the Ten*

*Donkeys*), and *De Eed van Meester Oom met vier ooren* (*The Oath of Master Uncle with Four Ears*). Moxey thus sets the popularity of *The Ship of Fools* against a background of texts which he characterizes as an already well-established chorus of moralizing poetry. He then suggests that the popularity of this literary genre among authors of an artisanal class background was a manifestation of the popular impact of the troubling spiritual issues posed by the Reformation. Moxey's study thus not only uncovers an extensive literary field of interest to the textual scholar but endeavors to explain that genre within a social-historical context. At the same time, the art historian will find in "*The Ship of Fools* and the Idea of Folly" an invaluable inventory of comic notions which quickly found their way into sixteenth-century paintings and prints.

I have dealt at such length with the Arenberg portion of the Rosenwald Collection because its research potentials are perhaps the least realized of all those in the collection, but other sections of it suggest different investigations. One is the group of fifteenth- and sixteenth-century books from German presses which provided the basis for three essays in part two on landscape and the illustrated book. Indeed, this portion of the collection coincides with the emergence and full flowering of landscape representation as an artistic genre at the end of the fifteenth century, a phenomenon still inadequately explained or analyzed for northern Europe. The essays presented in part two considerably advance our understanding of landscape with special reference to its appearance and use in the German illustrated book.

Whereas the emergence of landscape painting as a genre in Italy, including its theoretical context and historical progress, has been treated in some detail, studies on the northern landscape are still sporadic and disjunctive. Scholars often cite the preeminence of Haarlem as a fifteenth-century center of landscape, following the testimony of Carel van Mander (1604), a Haarlem artist and biographer of Netherlandish painters.[31] Indeed, Snyder found that the earliest use of the word *landscap* ("landscape") in an artistic context occurred in a contract for a Haarlem triptych where landscapes were to provide the backgrounds for religious scenes.[32] A Dutch exhibition of cityscapes called attention to another Haarlem painting, perhaps by the Master of Bellaert, in which a view of a town square pushes prominently into the foreground to provide an urban setting for Christ before Pilate.[33] The Master of Bellaert surely was a craftsman unusually capable of depicting the natural world, as he did in the woodcuts of Bartholomaeus Anglicus's *De proprietatibus rerum* discussed in this volume by Snyder. Taken together, such accounts on the one hand support the notion of a significant Haarlem contribution to the northern landscape, equally manifest in graphic and painted media and including city as well as country views. On the other hand, in all the extant works except woodcuts of the *Proprieteyten* landscape remains merely a backdrop, analogous to a stage setting, for more salient events.

Friedländer expounded the customary view that landscape painting asserted its individuality, its "separateness," from allied figural scenes only once a market for landscapes had developed.[34] Implicit in Friedländer's interpretation was a belief that such landscapes grew directly out of other subject genres until nature itself dominated the entire compositional space, a reasoning questioned by Gombrich. Gombrich held that the practice of landscape painting necessarily postdated its conceptualization in artistic theory. He called attention to Vitruvius, who divided stage design into three modes of which the third, or satyric, category demanded landscape scenery.[35] Focusing as they have on "high" art, what Gombrich and others have not considered is whether the medium of book illustration made any special contribution to the formulation of landscape in the North. Nor have they considered the social-historical impetus—apart from Friedländer's assumption of an appropriate patronage—which still may have spurred the practice of landscape, even if the concept of landscape predated its execution. Nor have scholars sorted out and discussed separately the diverse manifestations of the early landscape, a genre which from an early date comprised landscapes, cityscapes, and topographic views, including maps.

Charles Talbot's essay, "Topography as Landscape in Early Printed Books," directly addresses some of these issues. Initially drawing on an important article by Rainer Gruenter,[36] as well as on Gombrich's essay discussed above, Talbot asks whether the medieval German meaning of the word *landschaft* as "regio" or "territorium" might explain the content of some woodblock landscapes. The sixteenth century understood the regio or landschaft to be a "geographic area defined by political boundaries," and it was precisely in this sense that many printed books first incorporated landscapes. Talbot suggests that, although woodcut landscapes may have occurred first as diagramatic schemae of the regio, the very compositional field occupied by the landscape transformed the prints through their engagement with the viewer. According to Talbot, these scenes accentuate a panoramic background from which human activity was excluded and to which the spectator related as though to the world of the traveler. Talbot's thesis provides a compelling argument that explains the existence and proliferation of certain types of landscapes, especially in books. Because woodcut landscapes were so plentiful at the time when landscape painting was initially practiced, scholars of painting should necessarily consider this evidence, which is associated with the medium of the book and thus is linked to texts which partially explain the pictures.

The impulse to record empirically this material world is also Karen Pearson's subject in "The Multimedia Approach to Landscape in German Renaissance Geography Books." Pearson traces the development of the descriptive geography book that incorporated the diverse media of literature, cartography, and art, and she concludes that this genre "had assumed mature form by the mid-sixteenth century." Scientific advances coupled with national self-consciousness helped spur the progress of geography books, of which Pearson analyzes three key examples: Hartmann Schedel's *Liber chronicarum* (1493), Conrad Celtes's *Quatuor libri amorum* (1502), and Sebastian Münster's *Cosmographia* (1550). An initial dichotomy between "a scientific approach to cartography and the pictorial approach of the views," apparent in the *Liber chronicarum* and the *Quatuor libri amorum*, is resolved only in the *Cosmographia* by the incorporation of medium-scale regional maps alongside urban townscapes and small-scale maps. In the *Cosmographia* a modern cartographic vocabulary, with indicators of scale and orientation, also appeared for the first time. Other important distinctions emerge as well from a full examination of these books. Whereas the editors of the *Liber chronicarum* conceived it after the model of a medieval world chronicle in which biblical exegesis was coeval with modern history, the *Cosmographia* contained an entire section on the regions of Europe. Both in textual and pictorial terms, it characterized the terrain, plants, animals, activities, and dress proper to each locale. Historians of printing will also note that the three books simultaneously chart a transition from Gothic to humanistic typefaces. The font in the *Cosmographia* even further enhances the book's "modernity."

Like Talbot's, Pearson's study has a number of implications for the study of landscape. It, too, makes clear that the art historian seeking to understand landscape must now consult printed books, since they provide an interrelated pictorial and textual context for interpreting man's perception of his physical environment. The historian of early modern Europe will likewise be interested to learn that advances in geography, as recorded in books, coincide with a heightened historical self-consciousness of the German past and present.[37] Although landscape imagery in early printed books reflects an empiricism not always present in painted and engraved counterparts, juxtaposition of the woodcuts with engravings and paintings might be revealing nonetheless. Silver, for example, has viewed Danube School painting partially as an attempt to romanticize the German wilderness, seen by humanist writers as an ideal alternative to the corruption of court and city.[38] Underlying these images, he has signaled, as does Pearson, humanist endeavors to search for a German past, which authors like Celtes resurrected, mingling description and myth. Analogues of these painted and engraved romanticized visions do exist in some printed books, especially those associated with Albrecht Dürer and artists of the court of Emperor Maximilian I, so well-represented in the Rosenwald Collection.[39] In this context, the plain, unembellished woodcuts in the "topographic" category contrast sharply with the lusciously colored prints in the "idealized" category, at least in the Rosenwald Collection exemplars.

To understand both the emergence and success of the phenomenon of landscape, it is essential to provide also a social-historical context. Whether landscapes were empirical statements of topographic individuality or symbol-laden natural havens from a turbulent world, complex motivations must have furthered their execution. The birth of landscape in Germany corresponds with a period of rising populations both in city and country, a factor which presumably provoked a greater awareness of the physical constraints on everyday life.[40] The increase in the depictions of cityscapes such as appear in the Nuremberg Chronicle are surely partially statements of the social and economic growth of an urban Europe, as much as they are records of the artistic patrimony of its architecture.[41] Artists working in the towns executed countryscapes as townspeople formulated the articles of the Peasants' War.[42] Both facts suggest that the barrier between town and country may have lessened by the sixteenth century. The economic causes of the peasant insurrection itself testify to a keen awareness of the terrain, which parallels the awareness that accompanies the execution of landscapes. Lists of peasant grievances focused in part on the legitimate use of the land by its tenants, who increasingly saw their rights violated by lords who hawked, hunted, fished, and gathered wood in fields and forests previously reserved for the poorer classes. In short, the production of landscapes first occurred in a period of considerable social-historical ferment, which may have given rise to diverse motivations underlying their creation: for example, was landscaping an effort to hold onto the past, by faithfully recording a geographic heritage, or was it an attempt to shape the future, by fabricating an imaginary environment?

A grip on the past and a vision of the future both characterize early written and pictured descriptions of the New World. The third essay on landscape, J. H. Parry's "Depicting a New World," contributes a revealing interpretation of these records of newly discovered lands. After observing that "close and fruitful collaboration" between artists and explorers existed in the late eighteenth and early nineteenth centuries, Parry seeks to uncover the artist-explorer relationship during the earlier Golden Age of discovery. His examination of journals of discovery shows the explorers to be fundamentally practical, "more interested in the works of man than in the works of nature; more interested in cultivated fields than in forests; more interested in the uses of things than in what they looked like." The accounts contained in the journals imply a perceptual insensitivity to the actual beauties of the land which is paralleled by the relative absence of accurately observed and reproduced portraits of the New World.[43] Parry found that only at the end of the sixteenth century, in watercolors by John White and Jacques le Moyne, was there an awareness of and interest in the visual documentation of discovery.

His conclusions thus modify another popularly held view, that the dearth of early depictions of the New World was due to man's inability to portray the strangeness of its marvels which he, nonetheless, acutely perceived with wonderment.[44] Instead, some early pictures rendered the Americas with buildings and terrain that belonged to a European past and present, and others fashioned a mythical paradise, at once unfamiliar but comforting. Parry's essay also calls attention to the phenomena of travel and exploration that surely influenced the growth of landscape, as much as did rising urban populations, the Peasants' War, and national self-consciousness.

Once developed, the topographic landscape representing Europe or the New World experienced a vogue that extended as far as China, as James Cahill convincingly demonstrates. In an essay entitled "Late Ming Landscape Albums and European Printed Books," he investigates European sources for three landscape albums painted by Chang Hung between 1627 and 1639. An introductory survey of the development of topographic landscape painting from the tenth-century Sung through the Ming dynasties prefaces his detailed study of Chang Hung's landscapes. This survey explicates the essentially nonrepresentational goals of pre-Ming landscapes, most of which are noticeably conventionalized.[45] Many of these early pictures "evoke without really describing" a locale, and their expressed dual aim was to describe a place and to convey its impact. On the other hand, albums by Chang Hung parallel both the aims and techniques of European prints, such as those in Braun and Hogenberg's *Civitates orbis terrarum* (Cologne, 1572), which by this time were known in China through western missionaries. In one inscription Chang Hung stated that he recorded a trip just as he "had seen" it. Examination of the accompanying album leaves shows that he adopted as well European stylistic formulas, such as an elevated, bird's-eye view and a descriptive, nonconventional style.

Cahill's conclusions, that these pictures are "both descriptions and visual metaphors for the act of penetrating and observing a new region," could apply as well to western landscapes, especially those considered by Parry. Talbot and Pearson have treated topographic landscapes primarily as description, but a metaphoric and symbolic content also characterize some of their examples. Indeed, a fuller understanding of early landscapes might emerge through a careful assessment of the relative relationship in individual examples between description, symbol, and metaphor, evaluated within a broad historical context. Landscape gradually shed its symbolic justification, as religious iconography was elsewhere discarded. At the same time, it began to embrace new categories—the picturesque, the sublime, the singular—which were, in themselves, metaphors for different conceits. The evolving perfection of the topographic landscape, primarily manifest in sixteenth-century printed books, was an important stage in this development of the modern landscape.

The final section of this volume includes three essays on the subject of "Vergil and the Illustrated Book." A brief survey of the historical and critical context for the illustration of Vergil up to the initial years of printing will make it apparent that early modern illustrations of Vergil depart significantly from ancient and medieval traditions, a deviation which necessitates the development of alternative critical strategies to understand fully later books of Vergilian texts.

All of Vergil's texts were illustrated in antiquity, according to Weitzmann's study on the illumination of ancient books.[46] Two extant Roman manuscripts, known as the Vatican Vergil and the Vergilius Romanus and dating from the fourth and fifth or sixth centuries respectively, testify to the illustration in classical times of the *Aeneid*, the *Eclogues*, and the *Georgics*.[47] Although both of these include full-page miniatures, a type of illustration apparently unknown in the Greek world, Greek manuscripts of other texts supplied the pictorial models. Weitzmann's investigations also imply that the *Eclogues* may have been adorned with several miniatures per poem.[48] Despite the disfavor Vergilian works experienced during the

Middle Ages, the persistence of ancient pictorial traditions was strong. In a tenth-century Italian manuscript of the *Aeneid* now in Naples, the few marginal illustrations remain typical of late classical art.[49]

Roman illustrations of Vergil's works, especially the *Aeneid*, share common pictorial concerns. Miniatures in the Vatican Vergil and the Vergilius Romanus for the most part illustrate a single narrative moment, with only a few figures, a sparse setting, and a minimum of implied action. For example, the Council of the Gods appears twice in similar form in the Vergilius Romanus.[50] Both miniatures show one god—Neptune and Jupiter, respectively—seated in the center, flanked by four figures, two on each side. Posed beneath a rainbow, indicative of the heavens, and a sun and moon, all appear either in direct frontal or sharp profile position. Pictures illustrating both the *Eclogues* and *Georgics* were apparently nonnarrative in these manuscripts. They show shepherds amid their flocks in bucolic landscapes, evoking the pastoral mood rather than supplying the subject matter proper of the poems.[51] Ancient miniatures of Vergilian texts in general convey a simple monumentality which the later Middle Ages and early modern period radically transformed.

By the end of the Middle Ages, at least from the thirteenth century onward, illustrations to Vergil's works no longer directly reflect models from ancient book illumination. Later epic poems and prose accounts, even when they paraphrased Vergil, used the verbal language of courtly romance. The language was mirrored in the heraldic accents of their pictures, such as those in a Middle High German *Eneide* cited by Weitzmann.[52] From the thirteenth through fifteenth centuries, Vergil was accessible to readers primarily through other popular texts built on his writings: for example, the *Roman des sept sages*, *L'Image du monde*, *Renart contrefait*, and the *Gesta romanorum*.[53] A glance at the pictures in these texts demonstrates that they, too, depart significantly from the classical past. Regular production of Vergil in Latin resumed only in the latter half of the fifteenth century in many printed books and isolated manuscripts, which, taken together, clearly suggest a revival of interest in the original, rather than the reworked, writings by Vergil.

One interesting question about this body of material concerns the reinvention of pictorial cycles to satisfy new needs and interests. Two solutions are apparent in fifteenth-century manuscripts of the *Aeneid* and the *Eclogues*, some of which recall classical versions while others remain entirely distinct from them. Several manuscripts include miniatures which distill the essential narrative content of the *Aeneid*. One example is a turn-of-the-century French codex of Vergil's collected works, now in Dijon.[54] The subjects of the full-page miniatures adorning the Dijon manuscript often approximate those in the Vergilius Romanus, and this is also the case with a copy of Vergil's *Opera* produced in Germany and now in the Vatican. Of the single miniatures that preface each book of the *Aeneid*, those of the Banquet of Dido, Iris and Turnus, and the Council of the Gods share subjects and general compositions with their classical counterparts.[55] Only the form used to present these subjects—the historical initial—betrays a thoroughly medieval conception. Another Vergil manuscript in The Hague, associated with the style of Vrelant, is more densely illustrated since it includes, prefacing each book of the *Aeneid*, full-page miniatures divided into three registers, each displaying at least one episode.[56] For example, the frontispiece for Book Five shows the burning of Carthage, the arrival of the ships of Aeneas in Italy, the storm at sea, Aeneas and Anchises in prayer, and the Roman games authorized by Aeneas. This fuller cycle synopsizes a complete narrative in scenic form, instead of capsuling the story in a single image as earlier manuscripts had done.

A comparable multiplicity of illustrations characterizes an early printed edition of Vergil's works, that by Sebastian Brant published by Johann Grüninger at Strasbourg in 1502. In the first essay in part three, entitled "Illustration as Interpretation in Brant's and Dryden's Editions of Vergil," Eleanor Leach compares the pictures and texts in Brant's edition with those in the seventeenth-century edition of Dryden's translation, published in 1697. Through a careful analysis of the prints that accompany the *Eclogues* and the *Aeneid* in both editions, Leach distinguishes essential differences between the two books that enable her to assert that "illustration assumes the role of interpretation" in both instances. She notes that Brant's illustrations elaborate the narrative, and sometimes even the accompanying commentaries, with a completeness absent almost entirely in the later edition. The use of a bird's-eye topographic landscape in most of the Brant woodcuts provides an adequately spacious setting for the numerous episodes. At the same time, these landscapes articulate a sense of the topographical or geographical range of certain passages. On the other hand, the engravings in the Dryden edition serve a different function, since they ostensibly play a primarily decorative role, eschewing narrative altogether. They focus on action at dramatic moments in time, situating that action against staged settings. The divergent conceptualizations of the hero, Aeneas, in each book further differentiates them. As interpreted in pictorial terms, Brant's conventionalized hero recalls a nonspecific mythic antiquity, whereas Dryden's Aeneas is truly ennobled, in line with the "theoretical ideas of the epic."

Read against the background of the history of the illustration of Vergil, Leach's study adds to that survey by examining in such detail two important books. But Leach also contributes to two questions that concern late medieval and early modern illustrated books in a more general sense: first, who initiated the creation of new pictorial cycles and what was the process involved; and, second, once those cycles were created, what role did pictures play in illustrated books? Following earlier studies, Leach cites the supposition that Brant gave his artists master sketches from which to work, a hypothesis which her own essay substantiates by uncovering instances of the inclusion of unusual detail that came from the commentaries as well as the text.[57] Leach further evaluates the woodcuts as subtle interpretive glosses on the commentaries and text, for which they supplied a complex and intelligent reading most likely due to the editor himself. This view modifies another interpretation that accepts at face value Brant's own words in the colophon where he stated that:

"With illustrations Brant wishes, and with his pictured page, / To bring him [Vergil] to unlettered folk and rustics of all age."[58] Leach's argument for considerable editorial intervention in the planning of a new cycle gathers additional strength from even a cursory comparison of Brant's woodcuts with those of earlier cycles from which they differ.

Similar comparative studies of the illustration of Vergil could originate with other material in the Rosenwald Collection, as is clear from Ruth Mortimer's bibliographic survey included in this volume. Mortimer's essay, "Vergıl in the Rosenwald Collection," examines texts and illustrations in seventeen Vergilian editions of the *Aeneid*, the *Eclogues*, and the *Georgics* that date from the fifteenth through the twentieth centuries. The essay can be read with various bibliographic surveys published in 1930 at the time of the Vergil bimillenium that are, nonetheless, still useful.[59] Focusing on specific volumes, Mortimer pinpoints changes in technique over the centuries, from woodcuts to copper engravings to lithographs. She also notes some phenomena crucial to any consideration of the relationship between text and illustration, such as the reuse of "successful" woodblocks in other editions, a practice that may have induced a widening conceptual gap between words and pictures. For books in the baroque period, which customarily included engravings printed separately from the text, Mortimer does indeed call attention to a material and spiritual separation of illustrations from their texts. Finally, for the modern era, Mortimer recognizes the predominance of editions of the *Eclogues* and *Georgics*, instead of the *Aeneid*, as people were "interested less in national origins, epic, and the daily life of the gods than in an escape into a supposedly idyllic country life." An assessment of various livres d'artiste leads Mortimer to conclude that "the artist expands the text as the poet expands the limits of language."

In this context, it is appropriate that an illustrated essay by an artist concludes the volume. Elfriede Abbe reveals how an artist looks at the *Georgics*. Illustrated with twenty-four of her own wood engravings designed to capture the properties of specific plants, Abbe's essay also explains her process of creation. She discusses the shared role of bibliographic investigations and nature studies of the plants themselves. And she concludes with charming descriptions of those regions in Italy familiar to Vergil and described in the *Georgics*, thereby lending a contemporary actuality to the study of Vergil and the illustrated book. Taken together, Mortimer's and Abbe's studies, focusing in part on the modern era, can serve as prolegomena to further investigations of the Rosenwald Collection, investigations that might center on the modern illustrated book.

At the same time, the Rosenwald Collection continues to offer the scholar a fertile field for additional research on the early illustrated book; its surface has been only slightly probed. Study of other aspects of the collection might well include diverse inquiries, for example, on the placement of the blockbook in the early history of printing, or the artistic interchange between woodcuts in Italian incunables and paintings and prints produced in fifteenth-century Italy, or the history of treatises on calligraphy and typefaces, or the interrelationship between Rosenwald's outstanding print collection given to the National Gallery of Art and his book collection in the Library of Congress. It is inevitable that the Rosenwald Collection, though it was amassed in little over half a century, will profitably yield results to many generations of curious scholars.

# NOTES

*I gratefully acknowledge the assistance of John Cole and William Matheson of the Library of Congress for continuing help with intellectual and administrative matters, Kathleen Hunt of the Rare Book and Special Collections Division of the Library of Congress for overseeing the enormous operation of obtaining the photographs, Larry Silver and Kurt Weitzmann for permission to refer to unpublished material, and Cecelia Gallagher and Margery Maier for typing. This project was concluded while I was a fellow at the Center for Advanced Study in the Visual Arts, National Gallery of Art, Washington, D.C. I thank all the contributors for the stimulating essays that provoked considerable thought.*

1. Lessing J. Rosenwald, "The Mirror of the Collector," *Quarterly Journal of the Library of Congress* 22 (1965):160.

2. All items are cataloged in Library of Congress, *The Lessing J. Rosenwald Collection: A Catalogue of the Gifts of Lessing J. Rosenwald to the Library of Congress, 1943 to 1975* (Washington: Library of Congress, 1977). A recent overview of the collection, with many illustrations, is William Matheson, "Lessing J. Rosenwald, 'A Splendidly Generous Man'," *Quarterly Journal of the Library of Congress* 37 (1980):2–24. See also two recent Library of Congress exhibition catalogs: *Treasures from the Lessing J. Rosenwald Collection: An Exhibit Honoring Mr. Rosenwald's Eighty-second Birthday* (Washington: Library of Congress, 1973) and *Printed on Vellum: An Exhibition at the Library of Congress* (Washington: Library of Congress, 1977).

3. See *Rosenwald Collection*, pp. 164–65; Frederick Goff, "The Gift of Lessing J. Rosenwald to the Library of Congress: A Bibliographer's Survey of the Collection from the 15th through the 18th Century," *Quarterly Journal of the Library of Congress* 22 (1965):170–93; and Carl Zigrosser, "So Wide a Net; a Curator's View of the Lessing J. Rosenwald Collection, 17th to the 20th Century," ibid., pp. 194–205.

4. On the acquisition of his prints, see especially Lessing J. Rosenwald, "Reminiscences of a Print Collector," *American Scholar* 42 (1973):620–35. See the recent exhibition catalog by Ruth Fine on diverse aspects of Rosenwald's print collection, *Lessing J. Rosenwald: Tribute to a Collector* (Washington: National Gallery of Art, 1982).

5. Ruth Fine [Lehrer], "Blake Material in the Lessing J. Rosenwald Collection; a Checklist," *Blake Newsletter* 9, no. 35 (1975–76):60–85.

6. See especially Goff, "The Gift," pp. 170–71, for an identification of the unique copies.

7. These are described in detail by Frederick Goff, "Early Belgian Books in the Rosenwald Collection of the Library of Congress," *De Gulden Passer* 25 (1947):246–56.

8. Library of Congress, *Early Printed Books of the Low Countries from the Lessing J. Rosenwald Collection; an Exhibition in the Library of Congress, April 2, 1958, to August 31, 1958* (Washington: Library of Congress, 1958).

9. Lessing J. Rosenwald, *Livres anciens des Pays-Bas; la Collection Lessing J. Rosenwald provenant de la Bibliothèque d'Arenberg* ([Brussels]: Bibliothèque royale de Belgique, [1960]).

10. Gerardus Vorselman, *Eenen nyeuwen coock boeck; kookboek samengesteld door Gheeraert Vorselman en gedrukt te Antwerpen in 1560*, ed. Elly Cockx-Indestege (Wiesbaden: G. Pressler, 1971).

11. Ludolphus of Saxony, *Tboek vanden leven ons heeren Iesu Christi* (*Geeraert Leeu: Antwerpen, 1487*): *Facsimile-druk van de houtsneden*, ed. Luc Indestege, Vereeniging der Antwerpsche Bibliophielen, 2d ed., 3d ser. (Antwerp: De Nederlandsche Boekhandel, 1952).

12. William Martin Conway, *The Woodcutters of the Netherlands in the Fifteenth Century* (Cambridge: University Press, 1884; reprint ed., Hildesheim: Georg Olms; Nieuwkoop: De Graaf, 1970), and M. J. Schretlen, *Dutch and Flemish Woodcuts of the Fifteenth Century* (London: E. Benn, 1925; reprint ed., New York: Hacker Art Books, 1969).

13. See Conway, *The Woodcutters*, pp. 60–87; Schretlen, *Dutch and Flemish Woodcuts*, pp. 23–29, 33–35; and, on the publishing house, the detailed exhibition catalog from Brussels, Bibliothèque royale, *Le Cinquième Centenaire de l'imprimerie dans les anciens Pays-Bas* (Brussels: Bibliothèque royale Albert 1er, 1973), pp. 282–83. Bellaert imprints in the Rosenwald Collection are nos. 482, 485, 487, 488, 489, 490, and 491.

14. Rosenwald Collection, nos. 475, 476, 480, 545, and 547.

15. Conway, *The Woodcutters*, pp. 112–26; Schretlen, *Dutch and Flemish Woodcuts*, pp. 38–42; *Le Cinquième Centenaire*, pp. 262–69; and imprints from the Rosenwald Collection, nos. 492, 496, 497, and 499.

16. Conway, *The Woodcutters*, p. 20; Schretlen, *Dutch and Flemish Woodcuts*, p. 30 and passim. Rosenwald Collection volumes by these artists are nos. 474 (Utrecht), 540 (Antwerp), 509 and 510 (Leiden), 507 (Zwolle), 474 and 543 (Louvain), and 493 (Cornelis).

17. Books published by Johannes of Westphalia in the Rosenwald Collection are nos. 512, 518, 520, 524, 525, 528, 530, 532, 533, 534, and 536, and those published by the Brothers of the Common Life are Rosenwald Collection, nos. 515, 517, 519, 521, and 522.

18. Library of Congress, *Early Printed Books of the Low Countries*, p. 17.

19. A convenient summary on models is by James Douglas Farquhar, "The Manuscript as a Book," in *Pen to Press: Illustrated Manuscripts and Printed Books in the First Century of Printing* (College Park: Art Dept., University of Maryland, 1977), pp. 78–79, 94–95 (nn. 97, 99).

20. Pictorial innovation and tradition is discussed by Kurt Weitzmann, "The Art of Ancient and Medieval Book Illumination," to be published in the proceedings of the Conference on Manuscript Studies, Osaka, Japan, in press.

21. By the Master of Bellaert, Rosenwald Collection, nos. 1110, 1111, 1114, 1125, 1130, 1136, and 1175; and by Jacob Cornelis, nos. 1104 and 1145.

22. The classic studies remain Wilhelm Molsdorf, *Die niederländische Holzschnitt-Passion Delbecq-Schreiber*, 2 vols. (Strasbourg: Heitz, 1908–12), vol. 2, *Die vollständige Folge und ihre deutschen Kopien*, ed. Gustav Gugenbauer. Rosenwald Collection imprints by the Master of the Delbecq-Schreiber Passion are nos. 1112, 1119, 1120, 1132, 1136, 1140, 1144, 1145, 1147, and 1149 and by the Master of Thomas van Noot, nos. 1127, 1129, 1131, and 1139.

23. Rosenwald Collection, nos. 1193 and 1194.

24. Rosenwald Collection, nos. 549 and 1167.

25. Works by these artists are in the following imprints in the Rosenwald Collection: nos. 1156 (Lambrecht), 1159 (Swart), 1170 and 1207 (Coecke van Aalst), 1453 and 1455 (Galle), and 1189 and 1203 (Gheeraerts).

26. The classic studies on this material are: Luc Debaene, *De Nederlandse volksboeken; ontstaan de geschiedenis van de nederlandse prozaromans, gedrukt tussen 1475 en 1540* (Antwerp: De Vlijt, 1951) and Emile H. van Heurck, *Les Livres populaires flamands* (Anvers: J.-E. Buschmann, 1931). Rosenwald Collection imprints are nos. 1134, 1180, and 1188.

27. Rosenwald Collection, no. 1157.

28. Rosenwald Collection, no. 1160.

29. Rosenwald Collection, no. 1172.

30. On cooking, Rosenwald Collection, no. 1185; on currency, no. 1155; and on medicine, nos. 1122, 1139, 1150, 1156, 1159, 1176, 1177, 1178, 1179, and 1182.

31. Carel van Mander, *Het Schilder-boek* (Haarlem, 1604).

32. See note 8, p. 62.

33. Discussed and illustrated in Amsterdam, Historisch Museum and Toronto, Art Gallery of Ontario, *Opkomst en bloei van het Noord-nederlandse stadsgezicht in de 17de eeuw/The Dutch Cityscape in the 17th Century and Its Sources* (Amsterdam, [1977]), pp. 76–77, and M. J. Schretlen, "Een Haarlemsch stadgezicht uit de 15de eeuw. 'De meester van Bellaert,'" *Oud-Holland* 47 (1930): 122–29.

34. Max J. Friedländer, *Landscape, Portrait, Still-life: Their Origin and Development*, trans. R. F. C. Hull (Oxford: B. Cassirer, [1949]), pp. 16–17, 46–47.

35. Ernst H. Gombrich, "Renaissance Artistic Theory and the Development of Landscape

Painting," *Gazette des Beaux-Arts* 41 (1953):335–60, republished in *Norm and Form*, Studies in the Art of the Renaissance 1 (London: Phaidon, 1966), pp. 107–21, especially pp. 118–21.

36. Rainer Gruenter, "Landschaft: Bemerkungen zur Wort- und Bedeutungsgeschichte," *Germanisch-Romanische Monatsschrift* 3 (1953):110–20, republished in A. Ritter, ed., *Landschaft und Raum in der Erzählkunst* (Darmstadt: Wissenschafliche Buchgesellschaft, 1975), pp. 192–207.

37. The relationship between geography and historiography is discussed by Gerald Strauss, *Sixteenth-Century Germany: Its Topography and Topographers* (Madison: University of Wisconsin Press, 1959).

38. Larry Silver, "Forest Primeval: Wilderness Images in Early German Art," *Art Quarterly*, in press.

39. For example, twenty-seven Rosenwald Collection imprints contain woodcuts attributed to Dürer, of which the hand-painted *Salus anime* (no. 596), printed on vellum, is of exceptional interest. Maximilian's court imprints include the *Theuerdank* (no. 634).

40. A contribution to sixteenth-century urban history is Bernd Moeller, *Imperial Cities and the Reformation: Three Essays*, ed. and trans. H. C. Erik Midelfort and Mark U. Edwards, Jr. (Philadelphia: Fortress Press, 1972).

41. This is the view presented by Jean Wirth, "La Représentation de la ville dans la gravure d'illustration," in the exhibition catalog *La Ville au Moyen Age: Gravure allemande du XVe siècle* (Geneva: Cabinet des estampes, Musée d'art et d'histoire, [1974]), pp. 15–30.

42. This collaboration is noted by Moeller, *Imperial Cities*, pp. 55–56. Grievances drawn up by Territorial Diet of Württemberg (1514) and the articles of the peasants of Stühlingen and Lupfen (1525) are translated and published in Gerald Strauss, *Manifestations of Discontent in Germany on the Eve of the Reformation; a Collection of Documents* (Bloomington: Indiana University Press, [1971]), pp. 150–66.

43. See also the catalog of images, which confirms Parry's observations, by William C. Sturtevant, "First Visual Images of Native America," in *First Images of America: The Impact of the New World on the Old*, ed. Fredi Chiappelli with Michael J. B. Allen and Robert L. Benson, 2 vols. (Berkeley: University of California Press, 1976), 1:417–54.

44. See Hugh Honour, *The European Vision of America: A Special Exhibition to Honor the Bicentennial of the United States* (Cleveland: Cleveland Museum of Art, 1975), p. 1. The exhibition was organized by the Cleveland Museum of Art with the collaboration of the National Gallery of Art, Washington, and the Réunion des musées nationaux, Paris.

45. A useful summary of early Chinese philosophy of landscape appears in Michael Sullivan, *The Birth of Landscape Painting in China*, 2 vols. (Berkeley: University of California Press, 1962–80), 1:165–67.

46. Kurt Weitzmann, *Ancient Book Illumination*, Martin Classical Lectures, vol. 16 (Cambridge: Published for Oberlin College and the Dept. of Art & Archaeology of Princeton University by Harvard University Press, 1959), pp. 28–29, 59–62, 89–93.

47. Facsimiles and studies are Erwin Rosenthal, *The Illuminations of the Vergilius Romanus (Cod. Vat. Lat. 3867); a Stylistic and Iconographical Analysis* (Dietikon-Zurich: Urs Graf-Verlag, 1972), and Johannes de Wit, *Die Miniaturen des Vergilius Vaticanus* (Amsterdam: Swets & Zeitlinger, 1959).

48. Weitzmann, *Ancient Book Illumination*, p. 90.

49. Bib. nac., Cod. Olim Vienna 58. See ibid., pp. 61, 91, 119; figs. 70, 100, 128; and Pierre Courcelle, "La Tradition antique dans les miniatures inédites d'un Virgile de Naples," *Mélanges d'archéologie et d'histoire* 61 (1939):249–79.

50. *Aeneid* 10. 1 ff. and 5. 799 ff. For a discussion of the illustration of the Council of the Gods, see Rosenthal, *Illuminations of the Vergilius Romanus*, pp. 48, 49, pls. VI and VII.

51. Ibid., p. 75, pl. XV; p. 77, pl. XVI; p. 34, pl. II; p. 37, pl. III; p. 40, pl. IV.

52. Weitzmann, *Ancient Book Illumination*, pp. 61–62.

53. Domenico P. A. Comparetti, *Vergil in the Middle Ages*, trans. E. F. M. Benecke (1908; reprint ed., Hamden, Conn.: Archon Books, 1966), pp. 239–48, 302–8, and passim.

54. Dijon, Bib. mun., Ms. 493. Discussed and illustrated by C. Oursel, "Les manuscrits à miniatures de la bibliothèque à Dijon," *Bulletin de la Société française de reproductions de manuscrits à peintures* 7 (1923):5–33, especially pp. 30–33, pls. XVI–XVIII. On the illustration of Vergil in many manuscripts produced in Paris around 1400 by an artistic workshop headed by the so-called "Roman Texts Master," see Millard Meiss, *French Painting in the Time of Jean de Berry: The Limbourgs and*

*Their Contemporaries*, 2 vols. (London: Thames and Hudson, 1974), 1:55–61; 2: figs. 226–52.

55. Vatican, Cod. Pal. 1693. The passages referred to are *Aeneid* 4. 77, 9. 2 ff., and 10. 1 ff. See J. Courcelle-Ladmirant, "Les miniatures inédites d'un Virgile du XVe siècle conservé à la Bibliothèque Vaticane," *Bulletin de l'Institut historique belge de Rome* 25 (1949):145–58, especially pl. V, fig. 1, and pl. VI, fig. 2.

56. The Hague, Kon. Bib., Ms. 76 E 21. Discussed and illustrated by A. W. Byvanck, "Aanteekeningen over handschriften met miniaturen. V. Vlaamsche miniaturen in Nederland," *Oudheidkundig Jaarboek*, 3d ser., 6 (1926):177–96, especially p. 191 and pl. 7.

57. Especially Gilbert R. Redgrave, "The Illustrated Books of Sebastian Brandt," in *Bibliographica*, 3 vols. (London: K. Paul, Trench, Trübner and Co., 1895–97; reprint ed., Westport, Conn.: Greenwood Reprint Corp., 1970), 2:47–60.

58. Quoted from the partial facsimile edited by Anna Cox Brinton: Sebastian Brant, *Descensus Averno; Fourteen Woodcuts Reproduced from Sebastian Brant's Virgil, Strassburg, MDII* (Stanford University, Calif.: Stanford University Press; London: H. Milford, Oxford University Press, 1930).

59. Newberry Library, *Virgil: An Exhibition of Early Editions and Facsimiles of Manuscripts Commemorating the Two-thousandth Anniversary of His Birth, 70 B.C.–1930 A.D.* (Chicago, 1930); and New York Public Library, *Bimillennium: Vergilianum LXX A.C.–A.D. MCMXXX: A Vergilian Exhibition, List of Books and Manuscripts*, with an introductory essay by Charles Knapp (New York, 1930).

# PART ✠ ONE

# FIFTEENTH- AND SIXTEENTH-CENTURY DUTCH AND FLEMISH BOOKS

DIANE G. SCILLIA

# THE MASTER OF THE LONDON PASSIONAL: JOHANN VELDENER'S "UTRECHT CUTTER"

Johann Veldener, a native of the Diocese of Würzburg, set up a printing press at Louvain in 1473.[1] One of his earliest publications was Werner Rolewinck's *Fasciculus temporum*, a chronicle of world history from the creation up to the present.[2] Veldener's Louvain edition of the *Fasciculus* appeared December 29, 1475, and was modeled on the first edition published by Arnold Ther Hoern at Cologne the previous year.[3] Veldener even included a set of illustrations that followed those decorating the Cologne original. In his colophon, he proudly states that he took the greatest care and expense in having these images made.[4]

When Veldener moved to Utrecht in 1478 and established his press in that city, he had already planned a Dutch translation of the *Fasciculus*. The demand for the book was so great that thirty-three printings of it in five different languages took place between 1474 and 1500,[5] making it one of the first "best-sellers." Veldener's Dutch edition was published on February 14, 1480.[6] In it he reprinted many of the woodcuts commissioned for his earlier Louvain edition and he added eight others newly designed to enliven the historical accounts.

Arthur Hind points to two of the woodblocks added to the Dutch *Fasciculus* as being particularly interesting: the St. Peter at the Gate of Heaven (fig. 10) and the large *G* with accompanying border on the page facing the frontispiece (pl. 1).[7] In addition, Veldener's printer's mark (pl. 1)—made for his Utrecht press—is illus-

FIGURE 1. Passional Master, The Finding of Moses. The Hague Bible, The Hague, Koninklijke Bibliotheek, Ms. 78 D 39, fol. 47. Courtesy Koninklijke Bibliotheek.

trated in some general works on early printing. The remaining five blocks commissioned at Utrecht received little attention from Hind and other scholars. Hind noted only that they derived from the illustrations in that "other compendium of universal history, the *Rudimentum Novitiorum* that Lucas Brandis published at Lübeck in 1475."[8]

M. J. Schretlen recognized that the woodblocks added to the Utrecht *Fasciculus* were designed by the same artist responsible for the blocks illustrating Otto von Passau's *Boeck des Gulden Throens*, which was published at Utrecht in March 1480.[9] This designer has received the inaccurate and misleading name of "Veldener's Utrecht Cutter." The name is inaccurate because although he was the designer of the *Fasciculus* blocks he may not have been the actual cutter. It is misleading because this designer did not work exclusively for Johann Veldener. Nevertheless, I shall use the name "Utrecht Cutter" to avoid confusion.

The blocks designed by the Utrecht Cutter for the Dutch *Fasciculus* and for the von Passau text have a vitality and charm often lacking in more polished illustrations. Aside from their technical accomplishments, these woodblocks have merited little attention from art historians.[10] Schretlen held that the woodcuts decorating Veldener's 1475 Louvain *Fasciculus* were of little consequence in the larger development of the woodcut in the Low Countries.[11] Although he leveled no such pejorative criticism at the eight additional Utrecht blocks of 1480, the significance of these later blocks and the identity of their designer have gone unnoticed.

These woodcuts are significant as they give evidence to a close working relationship between Utrecht miniaturists and printing, for the *Fasciculus* blocks derive from models and compositions found in the circle of the Master of Evert van Soudenbalch, a miniaturist active at Utrecht between 1460 and 1470. Moreover, all but one of the woodblocks of 1480 were designed by a single manuscript illuminator known as the Master of the London Passional.[12]

The name Master of the London Passional is one of convenience and is the most common in current literature. The decoration of the so-called London *Passional* of 1465–70 led Byvanck to isolate and to characterize the hallmarks of our artist and to give him that name.[13] He began his career as a peripheral member, a miniaturist and border worker, in the circle of the Soudenbalch Master. As Hoogewerff and Vermeeren both note, he was largely responsible for the illustrations in the second volume of the important Bible of Evert van Soudenbalch of 1460–65.[14] Later, he was chief miniaturist of the Hague Bible of 1465–70 (fig. 1), which, unlike the other manuscripts produced by the Soudenbalch circle, was written on paper.[15]

L. M. J. Delaissé called the Passional Master "perhaps the most prolific miniaturist active at Utrecht around 1460."[16] He identified the Passional Master's hand in the painted historiated initials and borders in the "Hours of Mary van Vronensteyn" of 1460.[17] Borders and miniatures by the Passional Master appear in many small manuscript prayerbooks, some of which can be dated as late as 1475 to 1480.[18] It is clear that the Passional Master directed a large and successful stable of coworkers.

Our Master has two alternate ad hoc names—Delaissé's "Master C in the Hours of Mary van Vronensteyn" and Hoogewerff's "Meester der Vederwolken." Hoogewerff's name for the artist indicates a veritable hallmark of the Master. Vederwolken are cirrus clouds and these same feathery cloud forms float through the intense blue skies of his illuminations (fig. 1). Under these balmy skies energetic knights and armored foot soldiers march to battle and spritely little figures build cities and reap harvests. His women have a shy grace in their awkward and passive postures. Yet, male or female, all of the Passional Master's figures suffer from the stylistic malady of swollen eyelids.

The Passional Master was not a great artist. His style is homely and inelegant but at the same time vigorous and decorative. It has a piquant quality missing in the

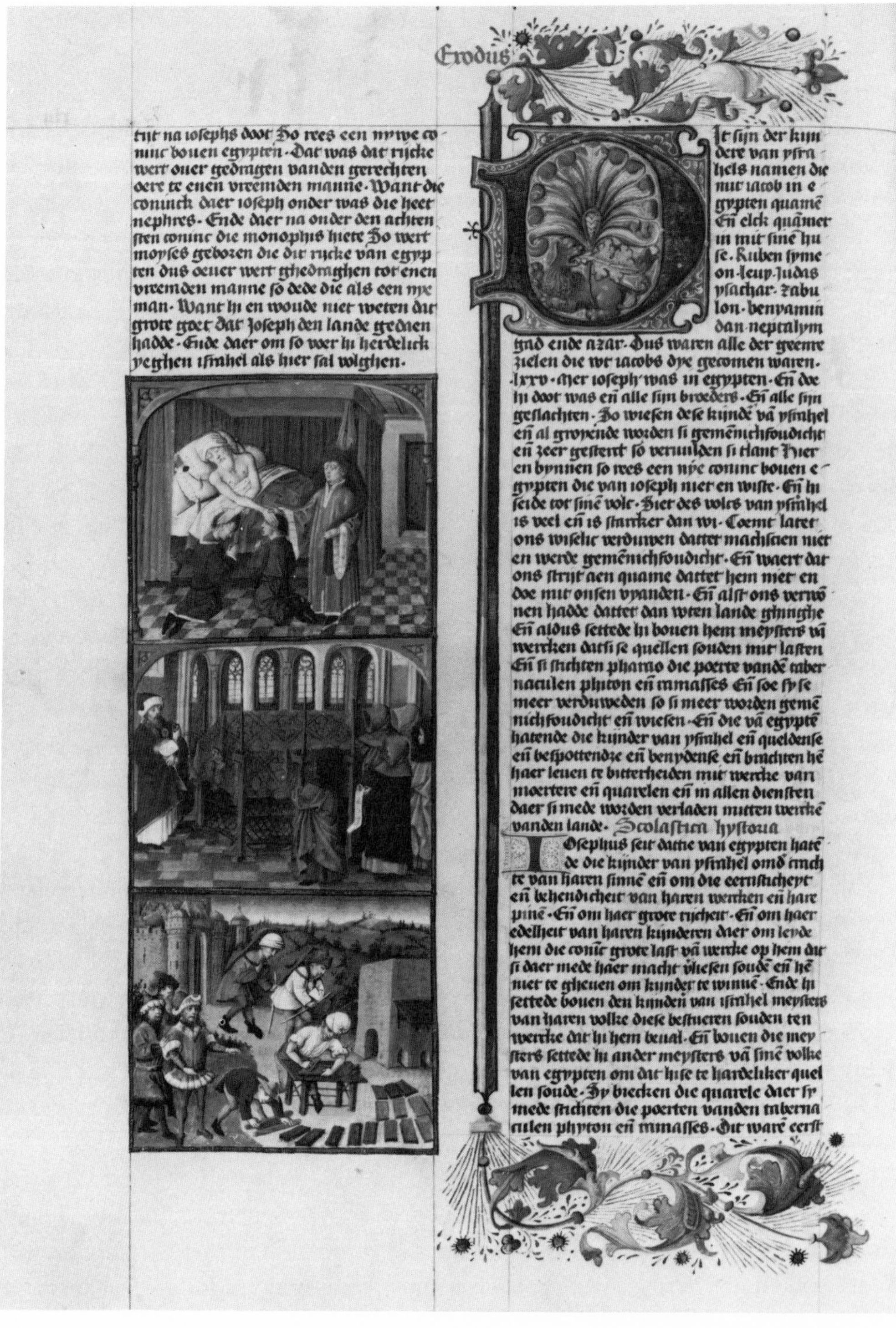

FIGURE 2. Soudenbalch Master, The Israelites Making Bricks. Bible of Evert van Soudenbalch, Vienna, Österreichische Nationalbibliothek, Cod. 2771, fol. 49v. Courtesy Österreichische Nationalbibliothek.

FIGURE 3. Master of the Providence Crucifixion, The Crucifixion with the Two Thieves. Providence, Rhode Island School of Design, Museum of Art. Courtesy of the Rhode Island School of Design.

more refined and beautiful miniatures of the Soudenbalch Master (fig. 2). The bearded Elder is, perhaps, the Passional Master's most typical figure type (figs. 1 and 6). He is stocky and squarely built, standing usually in some attitude of authority. He often wears a turban, a crown, or some fashionable hat, and his large hands and long fingers convey his meaning expressively. He has an extensive wardrobe—his robes and gowns take any number of forms—but his pose changes only slightly. Here he faces the viewer, there he is turned three-quarters to the left or three-quarters to the right.

There are other stylistic characteristics of the Passional Master. In his miniatures (fig. 1), he uses staggered, overlapping hillocks to divide the foreground from the background. Through this simplified landscape a winding path or road often leads to a handsome city that all but obscures the horizon. This typical city can be found in almost all the miniatures from his hand and, interestingly enough, in the Crucifixion panel at the Museum of Art of the Rhode Island School of Design (fig. 3).[19] With the exception of the cirrus clouds, all of these motifs—the walled city, the characteristic landscape, the figure types with their strangely swollen eyes—appear in the woodcuts made for the Dutch *Fasciculus* of 1480.

That Utrecht miniaturists, and especially the Passional Master, used patterns

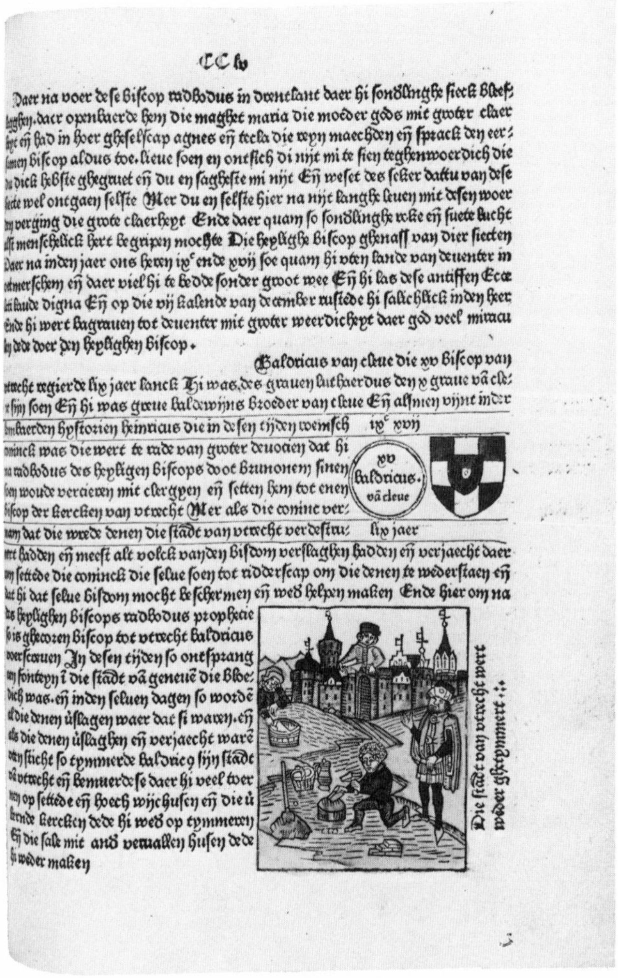

FIGURE 4. "Utrecht Cutter," Rebuilding of Utrecht. Werner Rolevinck, *Fasciculus temporum* (Utrecht: Jan Veldener, 1480), Rosenwald Collection, no. 474.

FIGURE 5. "Utrecht Cutter," Jerusalem Rebuilt. Werner Rolevinck, *Fasciculus temporum* (Utrecht: Jan Veldener, 1480), Rosenwald Collection, no. 474.

or models has long been suspected.[20] The Passional Master's reliance on contemporary woodcuts was first published by Hoogewerff, who demonstrated how the artist freely based his miniature of Anian and Jeroboam's Wife in the Soudenbalch Bible on a woodcut in the second edition of the *Exercitium super pater noster*, printed near Brussels around 1450–60.[21] Recently, M. Smeyers and Robert Koch have shown that the Passional Master based several miniatures in the "Vronensteyn Hours" and in the Soudenbalch Bible on woodcuts from the *Biblia pauperum*.[22] Koch further noted that the Passional Master's use of bias hatched lines for internal modeling in these and other miniatures may result from the direct influence of the woodcuts. None of the three advanced the likelihood that the Passional Master designed woodblocks himself.

The additional woodblocks illustrating the Dutch *Fasciculus* of 1480 show a blending of elements from earlier manuscript and woodcut compositions. Moreover, as noted above, they exhibit the stylistic hallmarks of the Passional Master. These compositions, until now, were discussed only in the context of contemporary woodcuts. Equally fruitful, however, is a comparison with contemporary manuscript illumination. Specifically, the designer of the *Fasciculus* cuts, the Utrecht Cutter (who I propose is identical to the Passional Master) most probably drew figures and motifs from the miniatures of the Soudenbalch group and from the woodcuts of the 1470–75 edition of the *Speculum humanae salvationis.*[23] For example, for his Rebuilding of Utrecht in the *Fasciculus* (fig. 4), the Utrecht Cutter turned to the Soudenbalch Master's Israelites Making Bricks in the Soudenbalch Bible (fig. 2) and borrowed the major figure, the standing Elder, and the ensemble of city walls. The proportional relationship of the figure to the architecture is similar as well. The Utrecht Cutter has simplified the miniature landscape in a now recognized manner, and the stocky figures in the woodcut have the blocky physical proportions and the swollen eyes we have come to associate with the style of the Passional Master.

In his Jerusalem Rebuilt (fig. 5), the Utrecht Cutter varied the composition. The landscape is comparable to that of his earlier cut, but the Elder is now on the left and wears a long robe. In one of the laborers in the foreground, the Utrecht Cutter repeats the awkward David in the Passional Master's David Buying the Threshing Floor of Arauna in the Soudenbalch Bible (fig. 6).[24]

FIGURE 6. Passional Master, David Buying the Threshing Floor of Arauna. Bible of Evert van Soudenbalch, Vienna, Österreichische Nationalbibliothek, Cod. 2771, fol. 189. Courtesy Österreichische Nationalbibliothek.

FIGURE 7. "Utrecht Cutter," Ninevah Destroyed.
Werner Rolevinck, *Fasciculus temporum*
(Utrecht: Jan Veldener, 1480), Rosenwald Collection, no. 474.

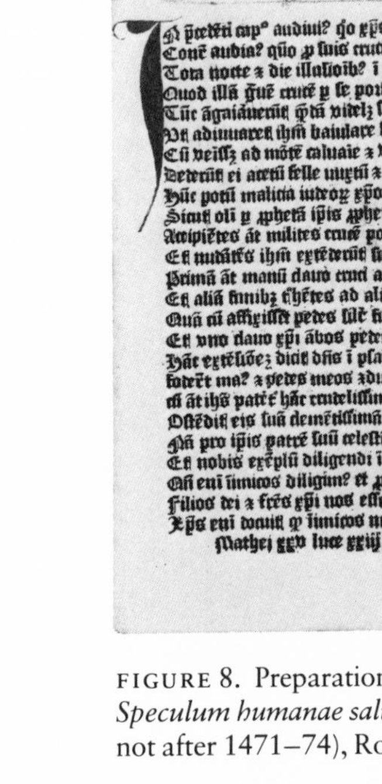

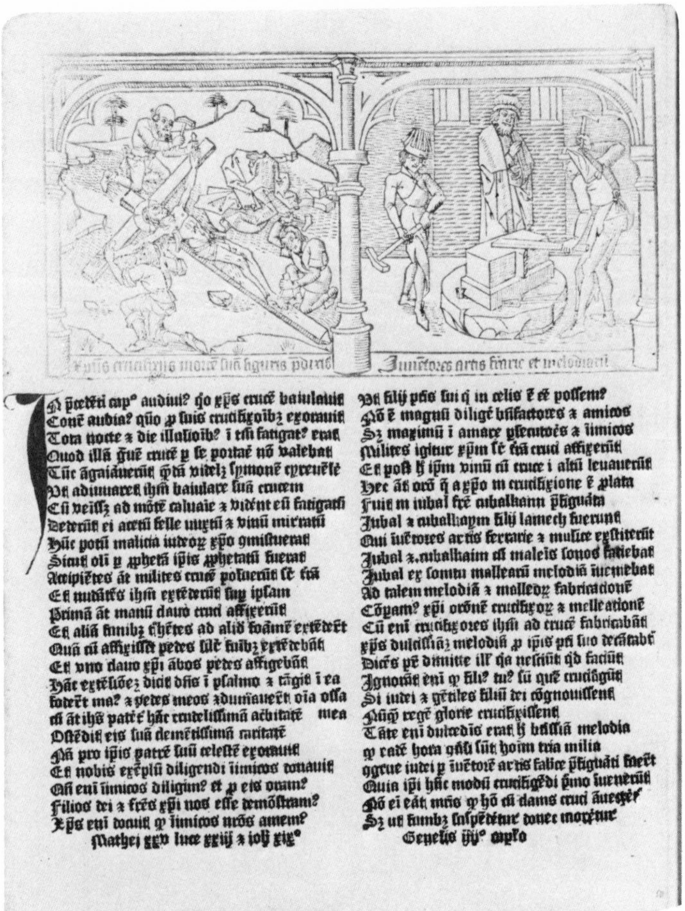

FIGURE 8. Preparation of the Cross and Building of the Ark.
*Speculum humanae salvationis* (Utrecht: Printer of the Speculum, not after 1471–74), Rosenwald Collection, no. 458.

FIGURE 9. "Utrecht Cutter," Destruction of Babylon.
Werner Rolevinck, *Fasciculus temporum*
(Utrecht: Jan Veldener, 1480), Rosenwald Collection, no. 474.

The Utrecht Cutter was slightly more eclectic in his scenes of the sieges and destruction of cities. In Nineveh Destroyed (fig. 7), several of his figures repeat poses of armored figures in the borders in the "Hours of Gysbrecht van Brederode" of ca. 1460.[25] This manuscript was also illuminated by members of the Soudenbalch group. The style of the Utrecht Cutter's armor is itself very like that seen in miniatures in the "Vronensteyn Hours," the Hague Bible, and in panels painted at Utrecht around 1470. The kneeling cannoneer in the foreground of the woodcut has a slightly different pedigree. He appeared earlier, without armor, but in courtly dress, in the Christ before Pilate in the "Vronensteyn Hours," and in the guise of an executioner in the Preparation of the Cross from the *Speculum humanae salvationis* (fig. 8).

For his Destruction of Babylon (fig. 9), the Utrecht Cutter again combined figures borrowed from both miniatures and woodcuts. The crossbowman in the foreground of the Babylon scene derives from the workman with the hammer in the background of David Buying the Threshing Floor of Arauna (fig. 6). Most curious is the fact that both figures have one foot obscured. The kneeling cannoneer at the far left of the *Fasciculus* woodcut echoes the kneeling man in the Gathering of Manna from the *Speculum humanae salvationis* (fig. 19), to whom I shall return shortly. A final comparison can be made between the soldier carrying the ladder in the woodcut and the soldier standing with his back to us at the foot of the cross in the Crucifixion panel (fig. 3).

Hind called the St. Peter at the Gate of Heaven (fig. 10) the most attractive of the Utrecht Cutter's compositions.[26] In this cut, the designer combined woodcut and miniature motifs once again. The great hexagonal tower of Heaven with double stairway stems from the *Speculum* block of the Wise and Foolish Virgins (fig. 11).[27] For his musicmaking angels in the arches above St. Peter, the Utrecht Cutter may

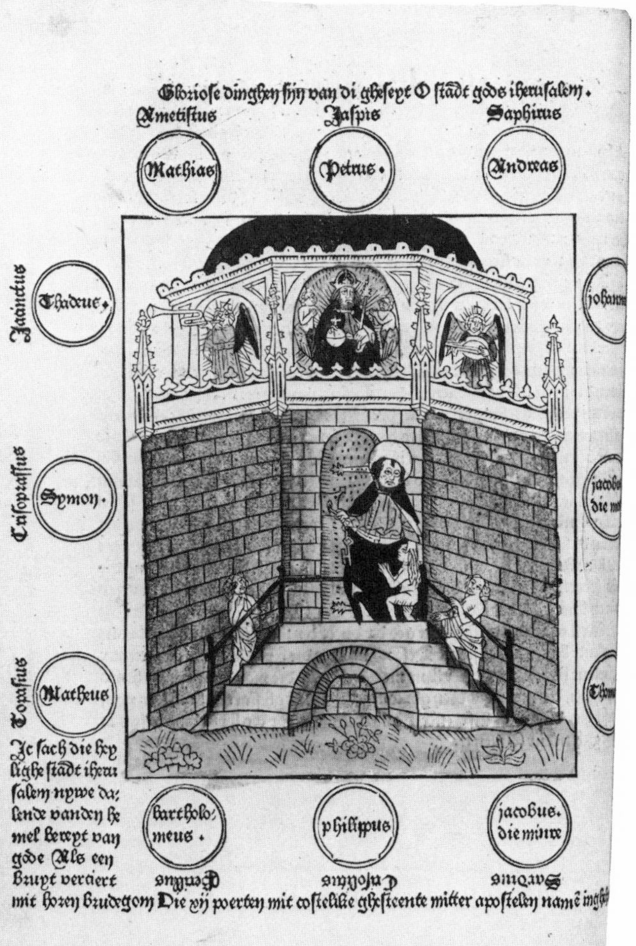


FIGURE 10. "Utrecht Cutter," St. Peter at the Gate of Heaven. Werner Rolevinck, *Fasciculus temporum* (Utrecht: Jan Veldener, 1480), Rosenwald Collection, no. 474.

FIGURE 11. Wise and Foolish Virgins. *Speculum humanae salvationis* (Utrecht: Printer of the Speculum, not after 1471–74), Rosenwald Collection, no. 458.

have turned to a miniature, or one very like it, by the Soudenbalch Master in a Book of Hours of 1460–70 formerly owned by Hans P. Kraus.[28]

Even purely decorative elements, such as the large *G* and the borders, continue types found in the manuscripts of the Soudenbalch group. In particular, the high curving bow of the large *G* and the curled foliage decorating the sides of the letter are identical to those in the *G* with the Annunciation in the "Vronensteyn Hours" (fig. 12). The woodcut borders of the *Fasciculus* (pl. 1 and fig. 15) follow the format of the "Brederode Hours" borders, although they are unpopulated and there are slight differences in the actual drawing of the foliage forms, which in the manu-

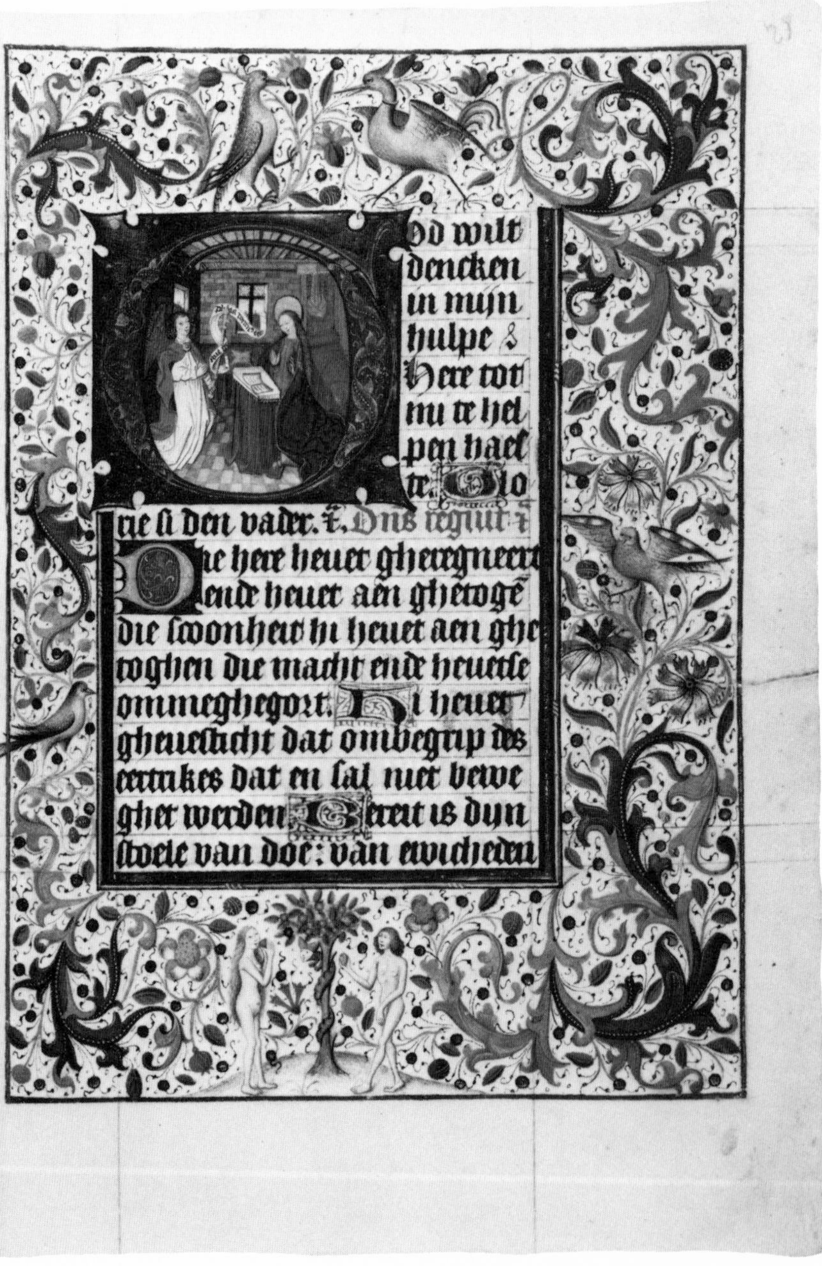

FIGURE 12. Master B, Letter *G* with the Annunciation. "Book of Hours of Mary van Vronensteyn," Brussels, Bibliothèque royale, Ms. II 7619, fol. 28. Copyright Bibliothèque royale Albert 1er.

PLATE 1. Frontispiece and Facing Page with *G* and Border.
Werner Rolevinck, *Fasciculus temporum* (Utrecht: Jan Veldener, 1480),
Rosenwald Collection, no. 474.

PLATE 2. Printer's Mark of Jacob Bellaert.
Jacobus Palladinus de Theramo, *Consolatio peccatorum, seu Processus Belial* (Haarlem: Jacob Bellaert, 1484), Rosenwald Collection, no. 482.

FIGURE 13. Master W with a Key, Large Coat of Arms of Charles the Bold. From Max Lehrs, *Late Gothic Engravings of Germany & the Netherlands* (New York: Dover Publications, 1969), fig. 460. Copyright © 1969 by Dover Publications, Inc.

CCC xxx

Hier Eyndet dat boeck datmen hiet fasciculus temporum in houdende die Cro
nijcken van ouden tijden Als van dat die werlt eerst ghescapen is Ende van dat
Adam ende Eua eerst ghemaect worden totter ghebuert xpristi toe Ende voert vā
allen Paeusen ende Keyseren die nader ghebuert xpristi ghewe̅est hebben tot noch
toe Ende daer nae Cortelick besluytende mit die Cronijcken der coninghen van
vranckrijck . van Enghelant Ende van die hertoghen van brabant . Ende van
die Biscoppen van Utrecht Eñ van die Greuen van vlaenderen . van hollant . vā
zeelant . van henegouwen . van Ghelre . van Cleue . tot huden op den dach toe
Hy my volmaect jan veldenar woennende tutrecht opten dam Int jaer ons heren M CCCC lxxx op sinte valentijns dach op die vastelauont etc̄ .

FIGURE 14. "Utrecht Cutter," Colophon, with Johann Veldener's Printer's Mark. Werner Rolevinck, *Fasciculus temporum* (Utrecht: Jan Veldener, 1480), Rosenwald Collection, no. 474.

script are fleshier. The exotic flower shapes so prominent in the woodcut borders can be found in the painted borders of the "Vronensteyn Hours."[29]

The Utrecht Cutter borrowed from contemporary engravings as well. Veldener's printer's mark (pl. 1 and fig. 14) is a variation of the engraved Large Coat of Arms of Charles the Bold by Master W with a Key (fig. 13).[30] The Utrecht Cutter probably made his adaptation of the engraved ducal arms at Johann Veldener's request. In the woodcut, the two heraldic lions are reversed, but they mirror their engraved counterparts, with one minor exception. In the printer's mark, the Utrecht Cutter moved the forepaw of the lion on the right so that it copied his partner's.[31] The two heraldic beasts in the woodcut suffer from the same affliction of the eyes that affects all of the Passional Master's figures.

The consistent stylistic similarities with the miniatures of the Passional Master found in all of the blocks by the Utrecht Cutter indicate that Veldener's designer

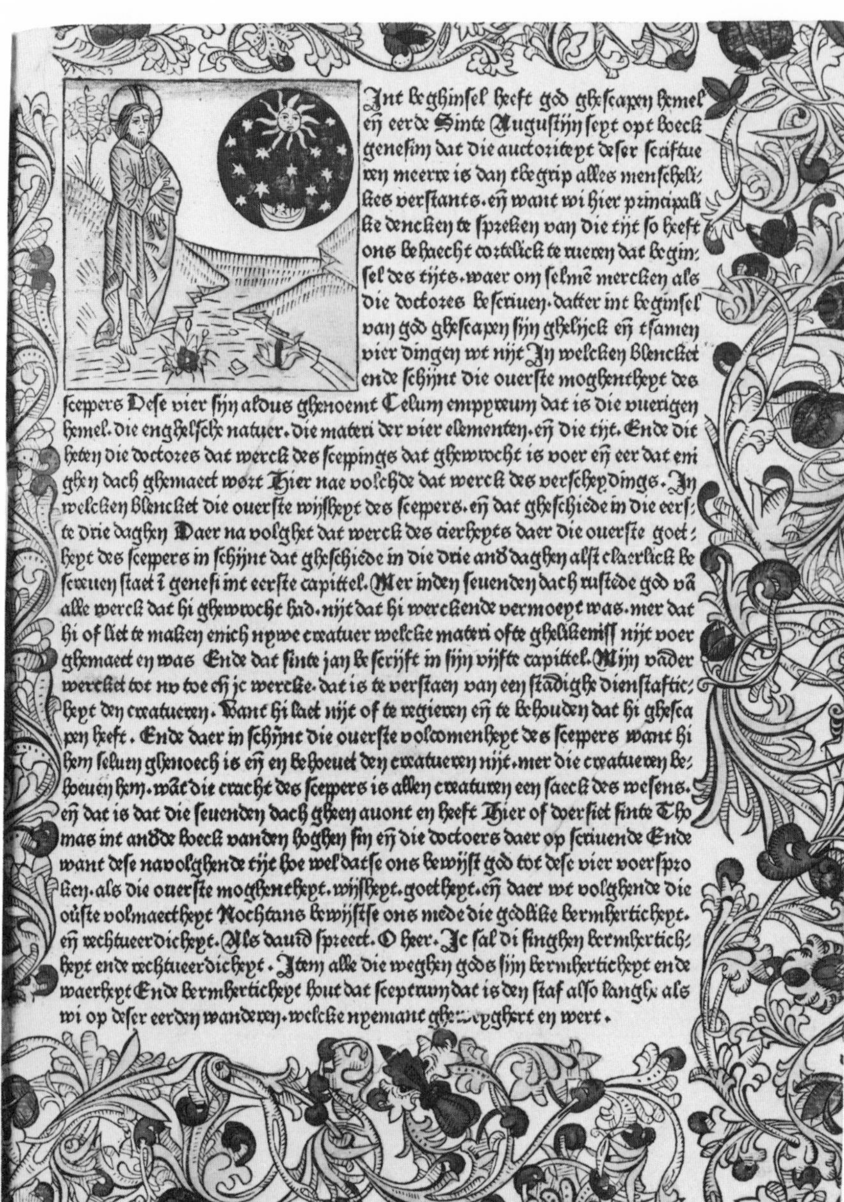
Int beghinsel heeft god ghescapen hemel
eñ eerde Sinte Augustijn seyt opt boeck
genesim dat die auctoriteyt deser scriftue
ren meerre is dan thegrip alles menscheli-
kes verstants. eñ want wi hier principali
ke dencken te spreken van die tijt so heeft
ons behaecht cortelick te ruren dat beginsel des tijts. waer om selmē mercken als
die doctores bescriuen. datter int beginsel
van god ghescapen sijn ghelijck eñ tsamen
vier dingen wt niet In welcken blencket
ende schijnt die ouerste moghentheyt des
sceppers Dese vier sijn aldus ghenoemt Celum empyreum dat is die vuerigen
hemel. die enghelsche natuer. die materi der vier elementen. eñ die tijt. Ende dit
heten die doctores dat werck des sceppings dat ghewrocht is voer eñ eer dat eni
ghen dach ghemaect wort Hier nae volchde dat werck des verscheydings. In
welcken blencket die ouerste wijsheyt des sceppers. eñ dat gheschiede in die eerste drie daghen Daer na volghet dat werck des cierheyts daer die ouerste goetheyt des sceppers in schijnt dat gheschiede in die drie and' daghen alst claerlick be
screuen staet ī genesi int eerste capittel. Mer inden seuenden dach rustede god vā
alle werck dat hi ghewrocht had. niet dat hi werckende vermoeyt was. mer dat
hi of liet te maken enich nywe creatuer welcke materi ofte ghelikenisse niet voer
ghemaect en was Ende dat sinte jan bescrijft in sijn vijfte capittel. Mijn vader
werket tot nv toe eñ ic wercke. dat is te verstaen van een stadighe dienstaftic-
heyt den creatueren. Want hi laet niet of te regieren eñ te behouden dat hi ghesca
pen heeft. Ende daer in schijnt die ouerste volcomenheyt des sceppers want hi
hem seluen ghenoech is eñ en behoeuet den creatueren niet. mer die creatueren be-
hoeuen hem. wāt die cracht des sceppers is allen creaturen een saeck des wesens.
eñ dat is dat die seuenden dach gheen auont en heeft Hier of doersiet sinte Tho
mas int and'de boeck vanden hoghen sin eñ die doctoers daer op scriuende Ende
want dese navolghende tijt hoe wel datse ons bewijst god tot dese vier voerspro
ken. als die ouerste moghentheyt. wijsheyt. goetheyt. eñ daer wt volghende die
ouste volmaectheyt Nochtans bewijstse ons mede die godlike bermhertichheyt.
eñ rechtueerdicheyt. Als dauid spreect. O heer. Ic sal di singhen bermhertichheyt ende rechtueerdicheyt. Item alle die weghen gods sijn bermherticheyt ende
waerheyt Ende bermherticheyt hout dat sceptrum dat is den staf also langhe als
wi op deser eerden wanderen. welcke nyemant ghe[illegible]yghert en wert.

FIGURE 15. Master B (here attributed to), The Creation. Werner Rolevinck, *Fasciculus temporum* (Utrecht: Jan Veldener, 1480), Rosenwald Collection, no. 474.

was no simple copiest but was in fact the miniaturist himself. Even the single additional block in the *Fasciculus* of 1480 that the Passional Master or the Utrecht Cutter did not design supports this identification. The Creation on folio 1 (fig. 15) is by a coworker. Significantly, this artist can be identified with the very same person who collaborated with the Passional Master on several manuscripts. One such joint effort can be found on folio 85 in Ms. Douce 381 at the Bodleian Library at Oxford, where the miniature is by the coworker, whom Delaissé identified as "Master B in the Vronensteyn Hours," and the border is by the Passional Master or "Master C in the Vronensteyn Hours."[32] The styles of both artists are very similar, but Master B is, perhaps, the more accomplished of the two. Delaissé describes Master B as being especially fond of details in both landscapes and interiors but adds that his figures are uninteresting and weakly drawn.[33] The kneeling David from the "Vronensteyn Hours" (fig. 16) serves as an excellent comparison to the Creation (fig. 15). The same

FIGURE 16. Master B, Letter *H* with David at Prayer. "Book of Hours of Mary van Vronensteyn," Brussels, Bibliothèque royale, Ms. II 7619, fol. 139. Copyright Bibliothèque royale Albert 1er.

FIGURE 17. Master B (here attributed to), Crucifixion. From the Prologue, *Spieghel onser behoudenisse* (*Speculum humanae salvationis*) (Culemborg: Johann Veldener, 1483), New York, Pierpont Morgan Library. Courtesy of the Trustees of the Pierpont Morgan Library.

plants dot the foreground of this miniature and of the woodcut. Moreover, the physiognomy of David corresponds with that of the Creator. The two figures could be identical twins.

In 1483, Johann Veldener moved to Culemborg and reprinted the blocks to the *Speculum humanae salvationis*.[34] Where the original woodblocks illustrating this text were cut and printed remains a matter of dispute among scholars. The arguments in favor of Utrecht as the site of first publication are as convincing as those put forth in favor of Haarlem. Master B's Creation in the Dutch *Fasciculus* may provide a key to resolving at least part of this lively debate.

The proportions of the figures and the types depicted in several of the original *Speculum* woodcuts, such as the Crucifixion (fig. 17), which Veldener reused as the prologue to his Culemborg printing, echo those found in Master B's miniatures (fig. 16) and in the Creation of 1480 (fig. 15). Master B's role as one of the designers of

FIGURE 18. Gathering of Manna. *Speculum humanae salvationis* (Utrecht: Printer of the Speculum, not after 1471–74), Rosenwald Collection, no. 458.

FIGURE 19. Passional Master, Ruth and Boas. The Hague Bible, The Hague, Koninklijke Bibliotheek, Ms. 78 D 39, fol. 166v. Courtesy Koninklijke Bibliotheek.

the *Speculum* illustrations corresponds to his role as one of the illuminators of the "Vronensteyn Hours," for he was responsible for only a limited number of the *Speculum* cuts and was not the primary master. Neither Master B nor the Utrecht Cutter made the move to Culemborg with Veldener, and new illustrations by the two do not appear among Veldener's later printings.

Folio 1 of the Rosenwald copy of the *Fasciculus* (fig. 15) is the only folio, save those on which appear the printer's mark and page facing the frontispiece (pl. 1), that is graced with a border. The carefully painted Creation and its richly illuminated borders imitate contemporary manuscript decoration. Unlike other incunabula in which the woodcuts were carelessly colored-in, the Rosenwald *Fasciculus* may have been painted by a professional. The washes of color do not obscure the lines of the woodcut and darker shadings have been applied carefully in the draperies of almost all the figures (figs. 4 and 15). Bright blue, red, and orange pigments and transparent washes of apple green, pale blue, gray, brown, and lavender recall the palette of the "Vronensteyn Hours," the Soudenbalch Bible, the "Brederode Hours," and other manuscripts illuminated by the Soudenbalch Master and his coworkers.[35] Such a close working relationship between miniaturists and the designers of woodcuts is further suggested by additional evidence.

In 1925, Schretlen proposed that the woodcuts illustrating the *Speculum humanae salvationis* and another blockbook, the *Canticum canticorum*, may have been designed by miniaturists, specifically by the Soudenbalch Master.[36] At least one of the miniaturists of the Soudenbalch group also designed cuts in the *Speculum*, and the Utrecht Cutter undoubtedly drew upon the *Speculum* woodcuts for his blocks in the *Fasciculus* of 1480.

Two further examples will underscore the nature of the Utrecht Cutter's ties to the designers of the blockbooks. The standing Elder and the artisan bending over in the foreground of the Soudenbalch Master's Israelites Making Bricks in the Soudenbalch Bible (fig. 2) were the prototypes for figures in the *Speculum* woodcut of the Gathering of Manna (fig. 18). In his Rebuilding of Utrecht (fig. 4), the Utrecht Cutter had taken the Elder and the city walls from the Soudenbalch Master's miniature. However, he also included in his scene of Utrecht being rebuilt the kneeling figure at the far right in the *Speculum* cut of the Gathering of Manna (fig. 18).

The second example is more problematic. In the Passional Master's Ruth and Boas in the Hague Bible of 1465–70 (fig. 19), a figure carrying sheaves of wheat on his back parallels a figure in one of the cuts from the contemporaneous *Canticum canticorum*.[37] One cannot be certain whether the miniature or the woodcut came first. The Passional Master and the designer of the *Canticum* may both have drawn upon a common source, perhaps the *Biblia pauperum* or a related manuscript.

Carl Bühler and others, and especially those scholars who took part in the "Pen to Press" symposium at Baltimore and College Park in 1977, stress the intimate kinship between fifteenth-century manuscripts and early printed books.[38] Judging from the woodblocks added to Johann Veldener's Dutch edition of the *Fasciculus temporum* and their handsome illumination, the Master of the London Passional (Veldener's Utrecht Cutter) and Master B in the "Vronensteyn Hours" made the transition easily from one form of book illustration to another.

## NOTES

*I am grateful to the staff of the Alverthorpe Library at Jenkintown, Pennsylvania, to the staff of the Rare Book and Special Collections Division of the Library of Congress, and to the staff of the Rare Book Room at the Mariam Coffin Canaday Library at Bryn Mawr College, Bryn Mawr, Pennsylvania, for their generous assistance during my research on the* Fasciculus *woodcuts.*

1. For Johann Veldener (active 1473–87), see *Allgemeine deutsche Biographie* 56 vols. (Berlin: Duncker & Humblot, 1967–71), 39:571–72, and Ferdinand Geldner, *Die deutschen Inkunabeldrucker; ein Handbuch der deutschen Buchdrucker des XV. Jahrhunderts nach Druckorten*, 2 vols. (Stuttgart: A. Hiersemann, 1968–70), vol. 2, *Die fremden Sprachgebiete* (1970), pp. 319, 323–25, and 338–40.

2. A copy of the *Fasciculus temporum* (Louvain, 1475) is in the Lessing J. Rosenwald Collection, no. 513. For Werner Rolewinck (1425–1502), a Carthusian monk and author of the *Fasciculus*, see *Allgemeine deutsche Biographie*, vol. 29, pp. 72–73. A copy of Arnold Ther Hoern's "editio princeps" of the *Fasciculus* is in the Marjorie Walter Goodhart Medieval Library at Bryn Mawr College

(Rare Book Room, fR 246). For Ther Hoern, see Geldner, *Die deutschen Incunabeldrucker*, vol. 1, *Das deutsche Sprachgebiet* (1968), pp. 89–92.

3. Arthur M. Hind, *An Introduction to a History of Woodcut, with a Detailed Survey of Work Done in the Fifteenth Century*, 2 vols. (London: Constable and Co., 1935; reprint ed., New York: Dover Publications, 1963), 2:560. Also see Elizabeth Mongan and Edwin Wolf, 2nd, *The First Printers and Their Books: A Catalogue of an Exhibition Commemorating the Five Hundredth Anniversary of the Invention of Printing* (Philadelphia: The Free Library of Philadelphia, 1940), no. 52 (Rosenwald Collection, no. 474), and Geldner, *Die fremden Sprachgebiete*, pp. 323–25, figs. 132 and 133.

4. Geldner, *Die fremden Sprachgebiete*, fig. 133, reproduces the complete text of the colophon.

5. Carl Bühler, "The Fasciculus Temporum and Morgan Ms. 801," *Speculum* 28 (1952): 182–83.

6. Like other vernacular editions of the *Fasciculus*, Veldener's Dutch edition of 1480 was an augmented translation. He added local material to Rolewinck's text. Veldener's Louvain edition more closely followed Rolewinck's original and contained only seventy-two leaves of text. The colophon of the Utrecht edition of 1480, which appears on folio 330 (cccxxx), clearly outlines its contents:

> Hier Eyndet dat Boeck dat men hiet fasciculus Temporum in houdende die Cronijchen van ouden tijden Als van dat die werlt eerst ghescapen is Ende van dat Adam ende Eva eerft ghemaect worden totter gheboert xpristi toe Ende voert van allen Paeusen ende keyseren die nander gheboert xpristi gheweest hebben tot noch toe Ende daer nae Corttelich Beslutende mit die Cronijchen der coninghen van vranchrijck, van Enghelant Ende van die hertoghen van Brabant. Ende van die Biscoppen van Utrecht Ende van die Graven van Vlaenderen. van hollant, van zeelant. van henegouwen. van Ghelre. van Cleve, tot huden op den dach toe By my volmaect jan veldener woennende tutrecht opten dam Int jaer ons heren MCCCCLXXX op sinte valentijns dach op die vastelavont ( )c.

7. Hind, *History of Woodcut*, p. 560; Mongan and Wolf, *The First Printers*, no. 52, includes the printer's mark as noteworthy. The major woodcuts illustrating the *Fasciculus temporum* (Utrecht: Jan Veldener, 1480) are as follows:

a. frontispiece (printer's mark)
b. large *G* and borders, cropped along upper margin in Rosenwald Collection, no. 474
c. The Creation and borders, cropped along upper, lower, and side margins in Rosenwald Collection, no. 474, on folio 1 (j)
d. The Building of Rome, on folio 32 (xxxij)
e. Nineveh Destroyed, on folio 35 (xxxv)
f. The Destruction of Babylon, on folio 38 verso ($\text{xxxviij}_v$)
g. Jerusalem Rebuilt, on folio 44 (xliiij)
h. St. Peter at the Gate of Heaven, on folio 71 verso ($\text{lxxj}_v$)
i. Christ Blessing, on folio 75 verso ($\text{lxxv}_v$), reused from the Louvain, 1475 edition
j. The Rebuilding of London, on folio 220 (ccxx), repeat of Jerusalem Rebuilt
k. Utrecht Destroyed, on folio 253 verso ($\text{ccliij}_v$), repeat of the Destruction of Babylon
l. The Rebuilding of Utrecht, on folio 255 (cclv), repeat of the Building of Rome
m. colophon (printer's mark), on folio 330 (cccxxx), repeat of the frontispiece.

8. Hind, *History of Woodcut*, p. 560.

9. M. J. Schretlen, *Dutch and Flemish Woodcuts of the Fifteenth Century* (London: E. Benn, 1925; reprint ed., New York: Hacker Art Books, 1969), p. 32; and Hind, *History of Woodcut*, p. 562.

10. Jan Willem Holtrop, *Monuments typographiques des Pays-Bas au quinzième siècle: Collection de fac-simile d'après les originaux conservés à la Bibliothèque royale de La Haye et ailleurs* (The Hague: M. Nijhoff, 1868), pls. 40–42, reproduces some of the series. Schretlen, *Dutch and Flemish Woodcuts*, pl. 41D, illustrates one of the von Passau illustrations, and Hind, *History of Woodcut*, pp. 562–63, discusses the technical achievements of this remarkable set of illustrations.

11. Schretlen, *Dutch and Flemish Woodcuts*, p. 48.

12. M. Smeyers, "De invloed der blokboekeditie van de *Biblia pauperum* op het getijdenboek van Maria van Vronensteyn," *Bijdragen tot de geschiedenis van de grafische kunst op gedragen aan Prof. Dr. Louis Lebeers* (Antwerp: Vereeniging van de Antwerpsche Bibliophielen, 1975), pp. 307–25; and Robert A. Koch, "New Criteria for Dating the Netherlandish *Biblia pauperum* Blockbook," *Studies in Late Medieval and Renaissance Painting in Honor of Millard Meiss*, ed. Irving Lavin and John Plummer, 2 vols. (New York: New York University Press, 1977), 1:283–89, for the most recent

bibliographies on the Passional Master. For the Master of Evert van Soudenbalch, see L. M. J. Delaissé, *A Century of Dutch Manuscript Illumination*, California Studies in the History of Art, 5 (Berkeley: University of California Press, 1968), pp. 41–48.

13. See P. H. J. Vermeeren, "Het Passyonael van den Heyligen in het Brits Museum te Londen (Ms. Add. 18,162)," *Het Boek* 33 (1959):193–210, for earlier bibliography.

14. G. J. Hoogewerff, *De noord-nederlandsche schilderkunst*, 5 vols. (The Hague: M. Nijhoff, 1936–47), 1:538; and P. H. J. Vermeeren, "De Nederlandse Historiebijbel der Oosternrijkse National Bibliotheek, Codex 2771 en 2772," *Het Boek* 32 (1955):101–39. Vienna, Nationalbibliothek, *Die Illuminierte Handschriften und Inkunabeln der Österreichischen Nationalbibliothek*, ed. Otto Pächt (Vienna: Verlag der Österreichischen Akademie der Wissenschaften, 1974–), vol. 3, pp. 43–85 and pls. 80–261, gives the most recent bibliography on this manuscript. Also see Sandra Hindman, *Text and Image in Fifteenth-Century Illustrated Dutch Bibles*, Verzameling van Middelnederlandse bijbelteksten: Miscellanea; vol. 1 (Leiden: Brill, 1977), for its place at the end of a series of large illuminated Dutch History Bibles.

15. A. W. Byvanck and G. J. Hoogewerff, trans. E. P. van den Berghe, *La Miniature hollandaise et les manuscrits illustrés du XIVe au XVIe siècle aux Pays-Bas septentrionaux* (The Hague: M. Nijhoff, 1922–26), no. 110, pls. 52, 118–20; and A. W. Byvanck, *La Miniature dans les Pays-Bas septentrionaux,* trans. Adrienne Haye (Paris: Les Editions d'art et d'histoire, 1937), p. 88 f. and pls. 87–88. See the catalog of the Bibliothèque royale, *Noordnederlandse Miniaturen: De Gouden Eeuw der Boekverluchting in de Noordelijke Nederlanden* (Brussels, 1971), no. 35, for the second volume of the Hague Bible (Ghent, Bibliotheek der Rijksuniversiteit, Ms. 632), which is dated 1468.

16. Delaissé, *A Century of Dutch Manuscript Illumination*, p. 72.

17. For a bibliography, see Bibliothèque royale, *Noordnederlandse Miniaturen*, no. 40. The first owner of this manuscript was Jan van Amerongen and his name sometimes appears in the literature. For the related "Prayerbook" (Liège, Bibliothèque de l'Université, Ms. Wittert 34) and "Hours of Gysbrecht van Brederode" (Liège, Bibliothèque de l'Université, Ms. Wittert 13), see Bibliothèque royale, *Noordnederlandse Miniaturen*, nos. 41 and 42.

18. Brussels, Bibliothèque royale, Ms. 10,761 (see Bibliothèque royale, *Noordnederlandse Miniaturen*, no. 46) and Brussels, Bibliothèque royale, Ms. IV 194 (see Delaissé, *A Century of Dutch Manuscript Illumination*, fig. 128) are examples of these later manuscripts.

19. David G. Carter, "The Providence Crucifixion: Its Place and Meaning for Dutch 15th Century Painting," *Bulletin of the Rhode Island School of Design* 48 (May 1962):1–40. I wish to thank David Carter for generously bringing my attention to Korine Hazelset's study *Een schilderij centraal: Het Utrechtse Kruisigingdrieluik en de aanblik van de hostie. Eerste tentoonstelling in een reeks van zes in samenwerking met het Kunsthistorisch Instituut Rijksuniversiteit Utrecht* (Utrecht: Het Centraal Museum, 1979).

20. Ferdinand Winkler, "Zwei miniaturen aus der frühzeit der hollandischer Malerei und die Heures des Turin," *Jahrbuch der Kunsthistorisch Sammlungen der allerhochsten Kaiserhauses* 23 (1915):324–33, first suggested the use of patternbooks by artists in the Soudenbalch group. Robert G. Calkins, "Parallels between Incunabula and Manuscripts from the Circle of the Master of Catherine of Cleves," *Oud Holland* 92 (1978):137–60, demonstrated how miniature compositions were used by the designers of the blockbooks and vice versa.

21. Hoogewerff, *De noord-nederlandsche schilderkunst*, 1:538– 40, figs. 298–99.

22. Smeyers, "De invloed," pp. 307–25, and Koch, "New Criteria," pp. 285–87. In addition, Avril Henry, "The Forty-Page Block Book *Biblia pauperum*: Schreiber Editions One and Eight Reconsidered," *Oud Holland* 95 (1981):127–50, reexamines some of the problems associated with the *Biblia pauperum* illustrations and the miniatures given to Utrecht artists. I thank Sandra Hindman for bringing my attention to Dr. Henry's article.

23. See Mongan and Wolf, *The First Printers*, no. 4 (Rosenwald Collection, no. 458). Another copy of the *Speculum humanae salvationis* is in the J. Pierpont Morgan Library in New York (PML 90680). See *Treasures from the Pierpont Morgan Library; Fiftieth Anniversary Exhibition, 1957* (New York, 1957), no. 46. The date of the earliest edition is generally accepted as ca. 1470–75. See William Martin Conway, *The Woodcutters of the Netherlands in the Fifteenth Century* (Cambridge: University Press, 1884), pp. 12 and 334. See Koch, "New Criteria," p. 284, and Calkins, "Parallels," pp. 150–53, for additional bibliographies.

24. Hoogewerff, *De noord-nederlandsche schilderkunst*, fig. 320.

25. Delaissé, *A Century of Dutch Manuscript Illumination*, fig. 105.

26. Hind, *History of Woodcut*, p. 560.

27. This composition may also derive from that of the Foolish Virgins in the earlier *Biblia*

*pauperum*; see Elisabeth Soltész, *Biblia pauperum* (Budapest, 1967), pl. 20. The stemma of a specific composition such as that of the Wise and Foolish Virgins is not always clear, but the kinship between compositions in the *Biblia pauperum* and the *Speculum humanae salvationis* deserves further study.

28. Delaissé, *A Century of Dutch Manuscript Illumination*, 54 and fig. 99.

29. Hoogewerff, *De noord-nederlandsche schilderkunst*, fig. 320, and Delaissé, *A Century of Dutch Manuscript Illumination*, fig. 105. The borders of a Dutch "Prayerbook" (Brussels, Bibliothèque royale, Ms. IV 216) attributed to "Utrecht(?), around 1490," contain similar fanlike leaves. See Bibliothèque royale, *Noordnederlandse Miniaturen*, no. 53.

30. This engraver, also known as Master W with an Anchor and Master W.A., was probably active at Bruges between 1465 and 1485. Charles the Bold, duke of Burgundy, died in the Battle of Nancy in 1477.

31. Master W with a Key's Large Coat of Arms of Charles the Bold was a popular model for printer's marks. Gerard Leeuw's mark in Nicolaus Pergamensus, *Dialogus creaturarum moralisatus* (Gouda, June 3, 1480)—see Mongan and Wolf, *The First Printers*, no. 53 (Rosenwald Collection, no. 475) and Library of Congress, *Early Printed Books of the Low Countries from the Lessing J. Rosenwald Collection; an Exhibition in the Library of Congress, April 2, 1958, to August 31, 1958* (Washington: Library of Congress, 1958), cat. no. 26—and Johannes Snell's mark in Maynus de Mayneriis, *Dialogus creaturarum* (Stockholm, December 20, 1483)—see Geldner, *Die fremden Sprachgebiete*, fig. 150—both derive from Master W with a Key's engraving. Snell's mark follows Leeuw's (and the engraved original) in varying the placing of the lions' paws on the shield. Snell included, however, the two small coats of arms hanging from a branch in the lower margin that were based on Veldener's device (fig. 17).

32. Otto Pächt and J. J. G. Alexander, *Illuminated Manuscripts in the Bodleian Library, Oxford*, 3 vols. (Oxford: Clarendon Press, 1966–73), vol. 1, *German, Dutch, Flemish, French, and Spanish Schools*, no. 246; and Delaissé, *A Century of Dutch Manuscript Illumination*, p. 72 and fig. 109.

33. L. M. J. Delaissé, "Le Livre d'Heures de Mary de Vronensteyn, chef-d'oeuvre d'un atelier d'Utrecht, achevé en 1460," *Scriptorium* 3 (1949): 230–45, and Delaissé, *A Century of Dutch Manuscript Illumination*, pp. 48–50.

34. M. F. A. G. Campbell, *Annales de la typographie néerlandaise au XVe siècle* (The Hague: M. Nijhoff, 1878), no. 1573; and Conway, *Woodcutters of the Netherlands*, iii, F.; and Geldner, *Die fremden Sprachgebiete*, pp. 338–39.

35. In the Soudenbalch Bible and in the "Vronensteyn Hours," the Passional Master's miniatures are marked by the use of earth brown, ocher, and deep blue pigments. His borders in the "Brederode Hours," however, are warmer and brighter in color, with red and orange contrasting with apple green and pale blue. It is this warmer, more colorful, palette that is found in the borders of the Rosenwald *Fasciculus* (Rosenwald Collection, no. 474). Even with this warmer palette, the illuminator falls back on deep blue, ocher, and earth brown as major color chords in the small scenes decorating the text. The copy of the *Fasciculus temporum* (Utrecht: Jan Veldener, 1480) in the Marjorie Walter Goodhart Medieval Library at Bryn Mawr College (Rare Book Room, fR 270) is also painted. Here, the illuminator used the more somber palette, although he colored the bricks of the tower of Heaven in the St. Peter at the Gate of Heaven (folio 71v) so they alternate red, blue, and yellow. The smaller cuts, however, are less garish, more reserved in their contrasts. So are the borders. Earth brown, apple green, and lavender predominate. Brilliant red, yellow, and blue appear only in the painted shields throughout the text and in the St. Peter at the Gate of Heaven. The Passional Master probably directed the illumination of both copies of the *Fasciculus*, and the differences in the respective color schemes may reflect the normal range of variation within one miniaturist's immediate circle.

36. Schretlen, *Dutch and Flemish Woodcuts*, pp. 9–10, 19–20. More recently, Gloria Konig Fiero, "Devotional Illumination in Early Netherlandish Manuscripts: A Study of the Grisaille Miniatures in Thirteen Related Fifteenth Century Dutch Books of Hours" (Ph.D. diss., Florida State University, 1970), discusses the reappearance of compositions from the grisaille manuscripts in later Netherlandish manuscripts and woodcuts. Some of the *Speculum* and *Canticum* woodcuts and some of the miniature compositions used by the Soudenbalch Master and his coworkers may continue this earlier tradition as well.

37. For the *Canticum canticorum*, see *Treasures from the Pierpont Morgan Library*, no. 44.

38. See Carl Bühler, *The Fifteenth Century Book* (Philadelphia, 1960), passim, and Sandra Hindman and James Douglas Farquhar, *Pen to Press: Illustrated Manuscripts and Printed Books in the First Century of Printing* (College Park: Art Dept., University of Maryland, 1977), for a bibliography.

JAMES SNYDER

# THE BELLAERT MASTER AND *DE PROPRIETATIBUS RERUM*

Among the fifty-two books printed in Holland in the fifteenth century listed in the catalog of the Lessing J. Rosenwald Collection, six published in Haarlem are of special interest to the art historian. They are the books issued by Jacobus Bellaert between 1484 and 1486 that are illustrated with some of the most progressive woodcuts of the period in the Netherlands.[1]

Nothing is known of Bellaert's activity before he set up his shop in Haarlem. He must have known Gerard Leeu of Gouda, because in his first publication, the *Lyden ons Heeren*, dated 10 December 1483, he used type and woodcuts formerly employed by Leeu.[2] He entrusted the design of his printer's device, a griffin holding a shield enframed by a canopy of ornate tendrils from which hangs the coat of arms of Haarlem, to a local artist (pl. 2). Bellaert then employed the Haarlem designer and his shop to illustrate his subsequent editions:

1. Jacobus Palladinus de Theramo, *Consolatio peccatorum, seu Processus Belial (Der sonderen troest)*, 15 February 1484. Rosenwald Collection, no. 482.

2. Otto von Passau, *Die vierundzwanzig Alten, oder Der goldne Thron (Boec des gulden throens of der xxiiij. ouden)*, 25 October 1484. Rosenwald Collection, no. 485.

3. [Raoul Lefèvre], *Le Roman de Jason et Medée (Histoire van den vromen ridder Iason)*, before 5 May 1485. Rosenwald Collection, no. 490.

4. Raoul Lefèvre, *Le Recueil des histoires de Troyes (Vergaderinge der historien van Troy)*, 5 May 1485. Rosenwald Collection, no. 487.

5. Bartholomaeus Anglicus, *De proprietatibus rerum* (*Boeck van de proprieteyten der dinghen*), 24 December 1485. Rosenwald Collection, no. 488.

6. Guillaume de Deguilleville, *Le Pélerinage de vie humaine* (*Boeck van den pelgherym*), 20 August 1486. Rosenwald Collection, no. 491.

With the exception of the last publication, the *Book of the Pilgrimage of Human Life*, the style of the illustrations is consistent enough to assign their designs to one master and his shop. They are extremely pictorial for the woodcut medium. Elaborate architectural sets and deep, rocky landscapes appear in many compositions as colorful stages for the numerous narrative episodes linked together or conflated in a fashion that is typical of the Haarlem painters of the period. The delicate hatching and shading, characteristic of the woodcuts in the *Speculum humanae salvationis*, usually dated between 1470 and 1475 and attributed to Haarlem or Utrecht,[3] are elaborated even further in many of the Bellaert illustrations, particularly in the varieties of sketchy modeling lines that produce a truly painterly effect. For the first time floating clouds fill the blank skies, and delight in rendering complex landscapes is everywhere evident. This unusual interest in landscape, as well as the meticulous cataloging of the varieties of flora and fauna, characterizes the marvelous cuts in the *Boeck van de proprieteyten der dinghen*, one of the most engaging nature books illustrated in the fifteenth century.[4]

Written about 1260, *De proprietatibus rerum* was immediately popular as a handbook for the clergy, and by the fourteenth century it had been translated into French, Spanish, Dutch, German, and English. The author, Bartholomaeus Anglicus, was an English Franciscan and teacher of the Grey Friars who traveled extensively and served for a time as professor of theology at the University of Paris.[5]

There are a number of unusual aspects of Bellaert's edition of Bartholomaeus's text which clearly mark it as a special publication. First, it is the only publication by Bellaert in which all of the illustrations are full-page frontispieces for the individual books, some serving for two books and conflated in a rather ingenious manner with several isolated pictorial motifs depicted within a broad, unifying landscape. It was thus designed to be a sumptuous special edition. Second, Bellaert designed a new font for the text. In his earlier publications, he used a type set borrowed from Gerard Leeu of Gouda, but here Bellaert introduced a new font, which was only recently recognized by Hellinga, that again indicates that the book was a special production.[6] Third, the *Boeck van de proprieteyten der dinghen* was issued on Christmas Eve—the title page states "op Kerstavont, 1485"—which indicates that it might have had some special market. Interestingly, there is no dedication picture and no coat of arms to associate it with a patron. Thus, it was very likely a deluxe book comparable to a modern Christmas edition.

Bartholomaeus's lengthy treatise is divided into some eighteen books that conform roughly to the tradition of moralizing natural histories. It begins with a discussion of the nature of God and the orders of angels much derived from the Celestial Hierarchies of Dionysius the Areopagite. It then describes the nature of the elements—earth, fire, water, air—and the humors or temperaments of man, following, more or less, the Aristotelian theories on such matters that were still popular in the mid-thirteenth century. The text then is divided into sections on the corporeal and ethereal nature of man, astronomy, the seasons of the year, geography, physiology, physics, chemistry, and, finally, natural history, including the stones of the fields. Bartholomaeus's sources are obvious in most instances and have been cataloged. They include, besides Dionysius and Aristotle, Pliny, Isidor of Seville, various Arabic scientists, and the standard works on the Physiologus, Herbarium, and Lapidarium.[7]

The eleven full-page woodcuts are some of the most beautiful and unusual in Bellaert's oeuvre. Here the designer had the opportunity to give full rein to his love for landscapes and animals, and the resulting illustrations are truly exceptional in the history of nature studies at such an early date. In some illustrations he seems to follow the text quite carefully, as he does with Bartholomaeus's rather simplistic discussion of God, the universe, and man. But when it comes to cataloging the varieties of plants, animals, fishes, and birds, he breaks with tradition. He discards the convention of displaying them as multi-vignettes or single motifs, following one after the other in the text, and instead sprinkles the flora and fauna quite naturally in a panoramic landscape so that they all live in harmony on one page. The impetus for such an outright interest in landscape can be attributed to the prevailing taste of the Haarlemers and, for that reason, these illustrations deserve a special chapter of their own in the history of Dutch landscape painting in general.[8]

One obvious question is raised here. To what extent are these illustrations original in the medieval sense of the word? Did our designer have access to a number of different illustrated nature books and manuscripts from which he rather freely culled the varieties of life to be depicted in his pictures, where he could then place them randomly in landscapes? Or, in keeping with the practice of other illustrators of the day, did he have a basic cycle to follow where the conflation had already occurred? This is difficult to answer, since few illustrated editions of *De proprietatibus rerum* are cataloged for comparative study. The answer can be found in part, however, in another illustrated Bartholomaeus in the Rosenwald Collection, the French translation published by Johannes Siber in Lyons sometime after 26 January 1486, where in a similar fashion illustrations introduce the various books of the treatise.[9] The Lyons edition cannot depend on the Bellaert book for a number of reasons, to be discussed below, but it seems to preserve in a more mechanical and slavish fashion the archetypal sequence of illustrations established in some earlier Bartholomaeus. The Master of Bellaert no doubt had a related model to follow, but his departures from the standard nature book conventions for such illustrations are truly startling and provocative. The frontispiece for the Prologue and Book One, God the Father Enthroned in the Heavens (fig. 1), is a rather traditional representation at first sight. It displays the hieratic portrayal of God the Father enthroned

FIGURE 1.
God the Father Enthroned in the Heavens.
Bartholomaeus Anglicus, *De proprietatibus rerum* (*Boeck van de proprieteyten der dinghen*) (Haarlem: Jacob Bellaert, 24 December 1485), Rosenwald Collection, no. 488.

within a radiant aureole of three circles that gradually diminish in brightness. This is achieved in a simple but effective manner by increasing the number of radial lines in the circles as we move out from the blank center that surrounds the deity to the utter blackness of the corners of the page. The gradual increase in the density of the needlelike lines that radiate from the One produces an image of pure light dissolving in the darker recesses of his creation, an effect achieved by painters by changing the color scheme from an intense yellow in the center (pure light, pure being) through a rainbow spectrum of colors to the deep blue-blacks of the further umbra. The text tells us: "The light of the Father, from which emerges all of the best things and illuminates the good done by man in the world, both conceals the profound with the darkness and brings the concealed into light."

The same illustration in the Lyons edition features a representation of the Trinity without the gradations in luminosity. God the Father, the Dove, and the crucified Christ in His arms appear on the central axis surrounded by four angels, a rather conventional representation of the Trinity in late Gothic art. For his image of God the Father, the Bellaert designer chose to follow instead a type often found in

North-Netherlandish Bibles with frontispieces for the books of Genesis, where God appears enthroned above illustrations of the six days of creation. In fact, Bellaert's image so closely resembles the enthroned deity holding a scepter and an orb in the frontispiece of a Utrecht Bible in Vienna, ca. 1470, that one scholar has attributed both figures to the same artist.[10]

God the Father Enthroned and the Fall of the Rebel Angels (fig. 2) illustrates Book Two, which defines the hierarchies of the angels (nine orders following the division of Dionysius the Areopagite) and describes the fall of the rebel angels. The illustration in the Lyons edition has three registers, each with three angels. In the lowest zone, the regular angels carry musical instruments; the middle register features three archangels dressed as warriors; and the topmost threesome, the seraphim, are provided with two sets of wings to cover their bodies. The Bellaert illustrator

FIGURE 2. God the Father Enthroned and the Fall of the Rebel Angels. Bartholomaeus Anglicus, *De proprietatibus rerum* *(Boeck van de proprieteyten der dinghen)* (Haarlem: Jacob Bellaert, 24 December 1485), Rosenwald Collection, no. 488.

chose rather to depict the fall of the rebel angels. He repeated the figure of the enthroned God the Father in his glory of three luminous circles of light surrounded by a scalloped border representing the first heaven above the barren mountains and waters of the earth. Two angels genuflect before Him, holding their hands out in gestures of adoration. From the wavy clouds, three demons plunge downward. A fourth demon, his tail just visible, disappears into the sea in the lower center.

The Spiritual and Corporeal Man (fig. 3) serves as a frontispiece for Books Three and Four, lengthy discussions of the dual nature of man. Man is first described as formed of base matter but enlivened by a divine spark, a soul, which distinguishes him from the lower beasts on the ladder of being. In both the Lyons and Haarlem editions, the "spiritual" man is illustrated with the creation of man as related in Genesis. In the former book the nude form of Adam reclines in the traditional sleeping pose to the lower right, while God the Father appears in the upper left dispatching the soul in the form of a tiny infant to quicken and infuse man's earthy being. In the Bellaert illustration an alternative episode is depicted. In the upper half of the woodcut, within the walled Garden of Eden with its towered gateways and bastions, appears the creation of Eve from the side of Adam, who is depicted in the same reclining posture amid the verdant meadows of Eden as he takes in the scene in the Lyons edition.

Book Four deals with the "earthly" man. Here the corporeal aspects of his being are discussed in terms of his anatomy, his temperaments or humors, and his other human qualities. This is illustrated in two woodcuts in the Lyons book. The first is a diagram of a circular earth surrounded by bands of air, sea, and fire, each appropriately labeled: earth is cold and dry; air is hot and humid; water is cold and humid; and fire is hot and dry. Following the four humors is another illustration with five doctors performing a dissection of a corpse stretched out on a table. They cut open the stomach of their specimen.

Departing from the text in this instance, the Bellaert designer placed a figure of a nude man in the lower half of the illustration, standing frontally with his arms apart in the fashion of the familiar Zodiacal Man.[11] Traditionally, this figure was sometimes combined with inscriptions of the four humors, as it is in the "Très Riches Heures," and the signs of the zodiac, which indicated their dominance over the parts of the body. The Bellaert Master, however, remained true to his earthly approach to such matters by eliminating the four humors and the zodiac signs and placing the figure in a barren landscape below the verdant Garden of Eden raised on a plateau and separated from the world outside by a river into which two of the four rivers of paradise flow. In place of the vertical line of the zodiac signs, the illustrator opened the body, revealing the organs and viscera that constitute man's corporeal makeup. The details of viscera are amazingly depicted, with the ribs, tendons, muscles, stomach, and intestines, all of which are described in the text, all delineated.

FIGURE 3. The Spiritual and Corporeal Man. Bartholomaeus Anglicus, *De proprietatibus rerum* (*Boeck van de proprieteyten der dinghen*) (Haarlem: Jacob Bellaert, 24 December 1485), Rosenwald Collection, no. 488.

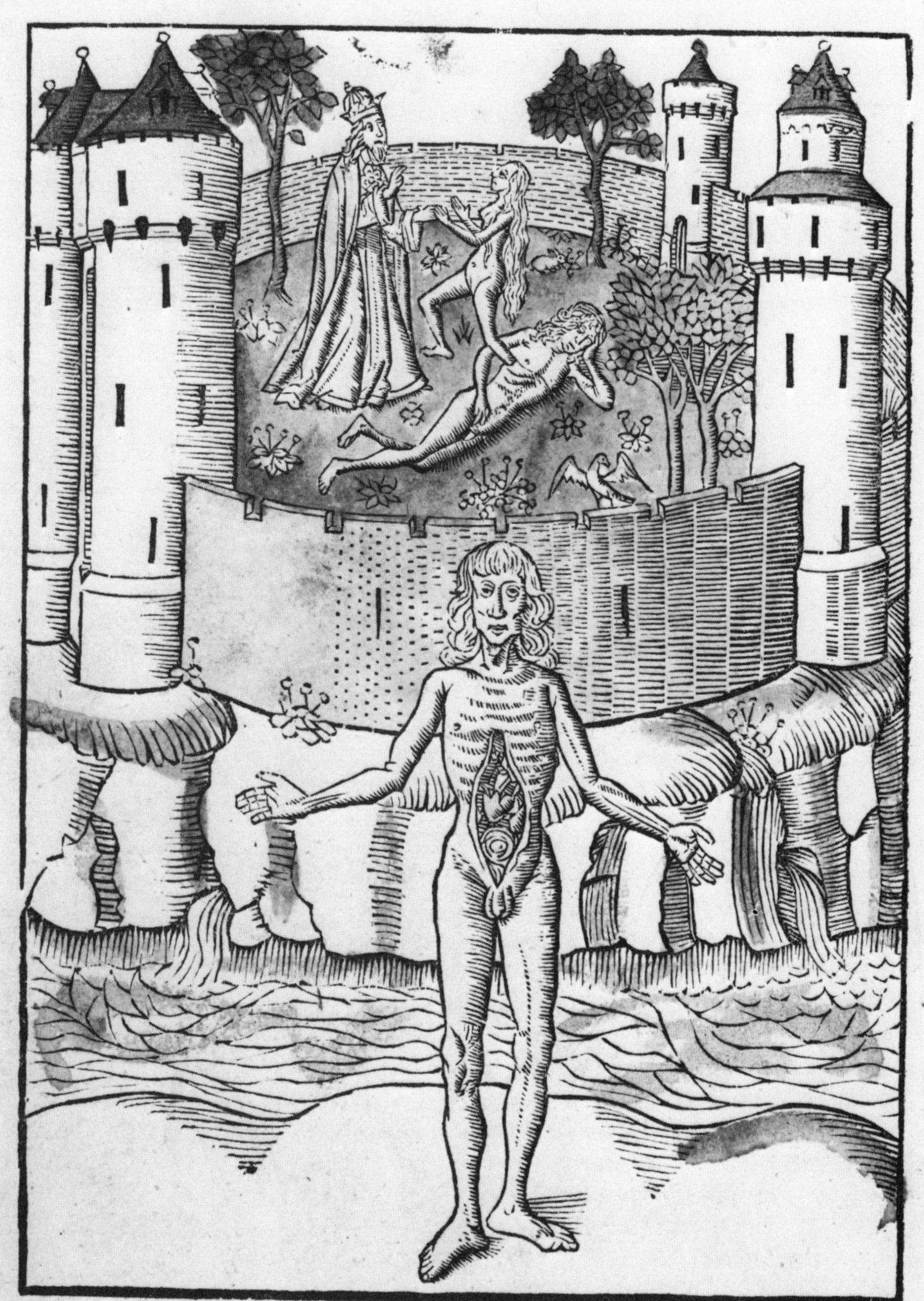

The Ages of Man and Infirmities (fig. 4), the fourth frontispiece, serves as the illustration for Book Six, on the ages of man, and Book Seven, on sickness and medicines. In the Lyons Bartholomaeus the two books are illustrated separately. For Book Six the Lyons illustrator presents the traditional lineup of the Seven Ages of Man, from cradle to old age, within a domestic interior (fig. 5). In the Bellaert woodcut a similar group of seven figures (augmented by an eighth, a skeleton) are placed diagonally in a rolling landscape. On the far left, infans, seated on the ground holding a flower, appears. Puerica, astride a pole and pointing a windmill lance, mocks a joust, and adolescens hunts birds with bow and arrow. Iuvens, a young dandy with a falcon on his wrist, stands with hand on hip before a group of three older men, of which the heavily draped man with his back turned to us probably represents senex. The third age in the Lyons edition, puerica, appears in reverse as the second age of man in the Bellaert woodcut.[12]

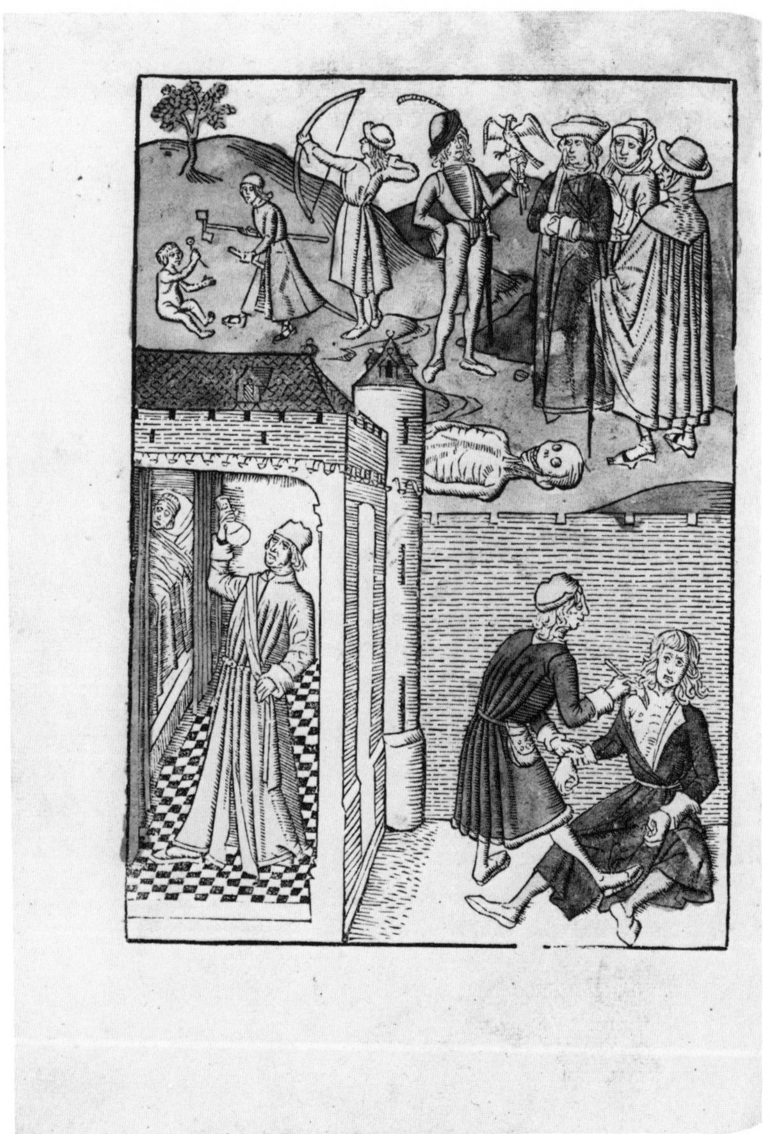

FIGURE 4. The Ages of Man and Infirmities. Bartholomaeus Anglicus, *De proprietatibus rerum* (*Boeck van de proprieteyten der dinghen*) (Haarlem: Jacob Bellaert, 24 December 1485), Rosenwald Collection, no. 488.

PLATE 3. The Birds. Bartholomaeus Anglicus, *De proprietatibus rerum* (*Boeck van den proprieteyten der dinghen*) (Haarlem: Jacob Bellaert, 1485), Rosenwald Collection, no. 488.

PLATE 4. God with Adam and Eve in the Garden of Paradise.
*Tboeck vanden leuen Ons Heeren Ihesu Christi* (Antwerp: Gerard Leeu, 1487), Rosenwald Collection, no. 540.

FIGURE 5. Ages of Man. Bartholomaeus Anglicus, *De proprietatibus rerum* (Lyons: Johannes Siber, after 26 January 1486), Rosenwald Collection, no. 394.

Below the seven figures in the Haarlem frontispiece appears the illustration for Book Seven, on sickness and medicine. In an open court to the right, one practitioner applies a scalpel to a shoulder wound on a young man seated against a wall. His patient has a slight grimace on his face. In the lower left, within an open room, stands another doctor, of higher status no doubt, wearing a full-length cloak and a scholar's beret or cap. He holds up a urine flask to check its color, one of the most common methods of diagnosis in medieval medicine. His patient lies in a bed to the left, wrapped tightly in sheets. This latter scene appears much the same in the Lyons illustration for Book Seven, but the accompanying illustration is not one of treatment of a wound, but rather of an interior of an apothecary shop with the proprietor seated at a table before his shop that is outfitted with shelves of medicine jars. That the apothecary scene was originally in the cycle is attested to by a woodcut illustration in another edition of Bartholomaeus, the *Libro de proprietatibus rerum* published by Heinrich Mayer in 1494 in Toulouse for Spanish export.[13] Its woodcuts are crudely cut, but the design for De las enfermedades clearly depends on a common model. It therefore appears that the Bellaert illustrator took the liberty here to introduce a new scene in the cycle.

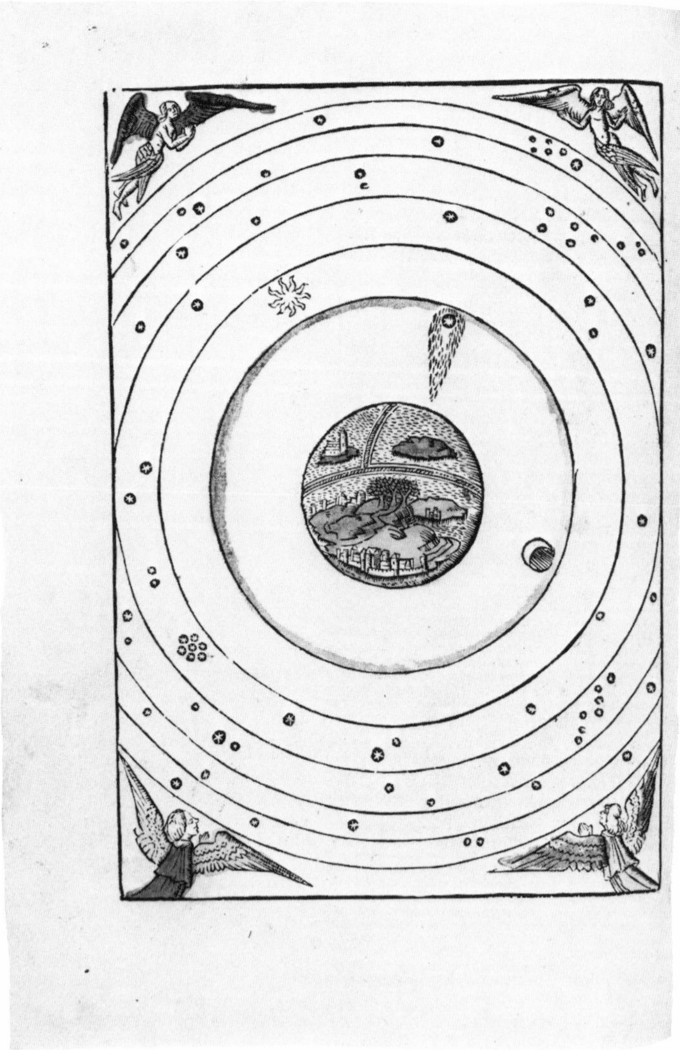

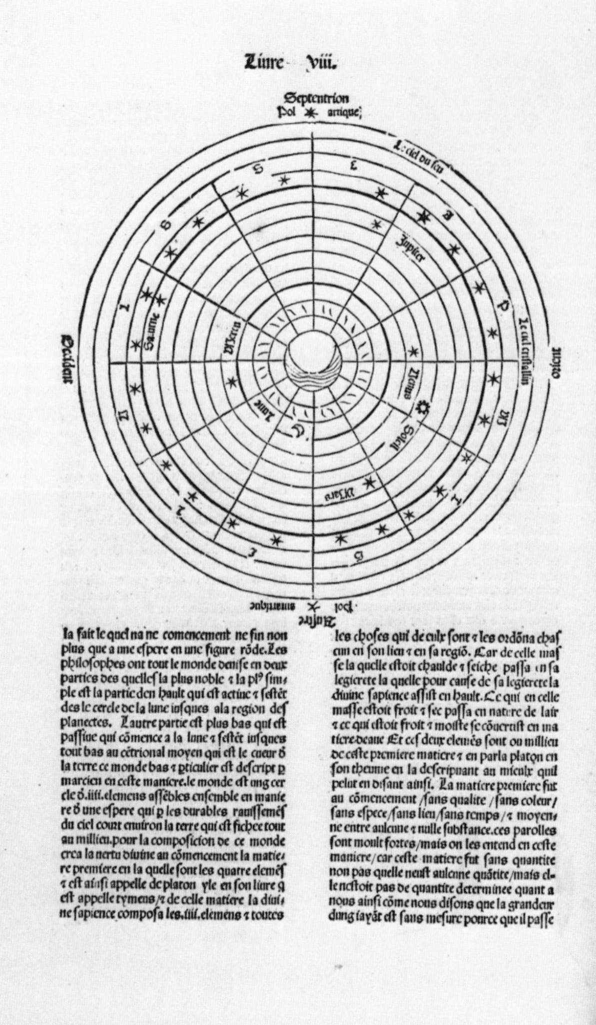

Liure viii.

Septentrion
Pol ⁎ artique

la fait le quel na ne comencement ne fin non plus que a une espere en une figure rōde. Les philosophes ont tout le monde deuise en deux parties des quelles la plus noble ⁊ la pl⁹ simple est la partie den hault qui est actiue ⁊ sestēt des le cercle de la lune iusques a la region des planectes. Lautre partie est plus bas qui est passiue qui cōmence a la lune ⁊ sestēt iusques tout bas au cētrional moyen qui est le cueur ꝺ la terre ce monde bas ⁊ pticulier est descript p marcien en ceste maniere. le monde est ung cercle ꝺ .iiii. elemens assēbles ensemble en maniere ꝺ une espere qui p les durables rauissemēs du ciel court enuiron la terre qui est fichee tout au millieu. pour la composicion de ce monde crea la uertu diuine au cōmencement la matiere premiere en la quelle sont les quatre elemēs ⁊ est ainsi appelle de platon yle en son liure q est appelle tymeus / ⁊ de celle matiere la diuine sapience composa les. iiii. elemens ⁊ toutes les choses qui de eulx sont ⁊ les ordōna chascun en son lieu ⁊ en sa regiō. Car de celle masse la quelle estoit chaulde ⁊ seiche passa en sa legierete la quelle pour cause de sa legierete la diuine sapience assist en hault. Ce qui en celle masse estoit froit ⁊ sec passa en nature de lair ⁊ ce qui estoit froit ⁊ moiste se cōuertist en matiere deaue Et ces deux elemēs sont ou millieu de ceste premiere matiere ⁊ en parla platon en son theume en la descripuant au mieulx quil peut en disant ainsi. La matiere premiere fut au cōmencement / sans qualite / sans coleur / sans espece / sans lieu / sans temps / ⁊ moyenne entre aulcune ⁊ nulle substance. ces parolles sont moult fortes / mais on les entend en ceste maniere / car ceste matiere fut sans quantite non pas quelle neust aulcune quātite / mais elle nestoit pas de quantite determinee quant a nous ainsi cōme nous disons que la grandeur dung iayāt est sans mesure pource que il passe

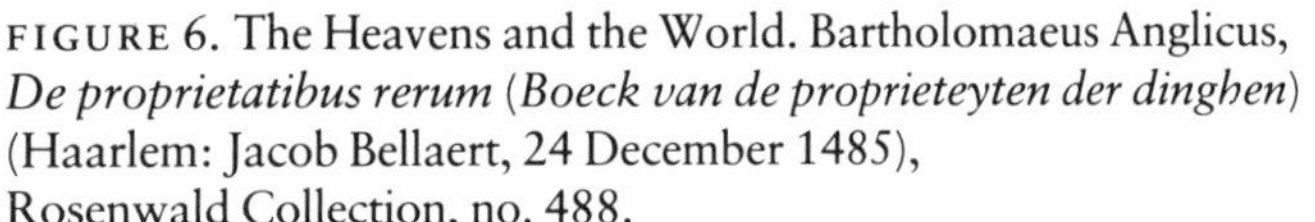

FIGURE 6. The Heavens and the World. Bartholomaeus Anglicus, *De proprietatibus rerum* (*Boeck van de proprieteyten der dinghen*) (Haarlem: Jacob Bellaert, 24 December 1485), Rosenwald Collection, no. 488.

FIGURE 7. The Heavens and the World. Bartholomaeus Anglicus, *De proprietatibus rerum* (Lyons: Johannes Siber, after 26 January 1486), Rosenwald Collection, no. 394.

The Heavens and the World (fig. 6) illustrates cosmology, discussed in Book Eight, with a marvelous diagram of the heavens, seven in all, encircling the Earth, which is represented by a trisected orb with three islands in choppy seas: Europe, Asia, and Africa. The corresponding illustration in the Lyons book is much simplified, having thirteen concentric circles about an Earth that is simply divided in half for land and sea (fig. 7). The Haarlem universe is much more pictorial. The inner heaven is slightly darker in color and contains the moon in quarter phase and a bright cometlike North Star rotating about the globe. The flared sun appears in the second circle, and, in keeping with the Ptolemaic concept of the universe, the other circles are dotted by various clusters of stars and planets. The Big Dipper in the top right crosses the fourth and fifth circles. Finally, in the seventh zone, the four corners of the woodcut, heavenly creatures appear: two angels in the lower corners, two seraphim in the upper.

Book Nine is devoted to the divisions of the times of the year. The Divisions of Time (fig. 8) illustrates the subject. The Lyons woodcut is more complete in terms of illustrating the text, displaying a large circle of the zodiac with inner compartments marked off by the spokes of the wheel of time and containing illustrations of the twelve labors of the months. The Bellaert artist preferred to expand the labors themselves with an eye-catching depiction of the twelve labors neatly composed within small circles arranged in four rows. Although there are a number of variations on the individual labors, they generally follow the same pattern, with a man at banquet in January, an old man before a fire in February, a young courtier falconing in May, a peasant picking grapes in September, and a farmer slaughtering a pig in December.[14]

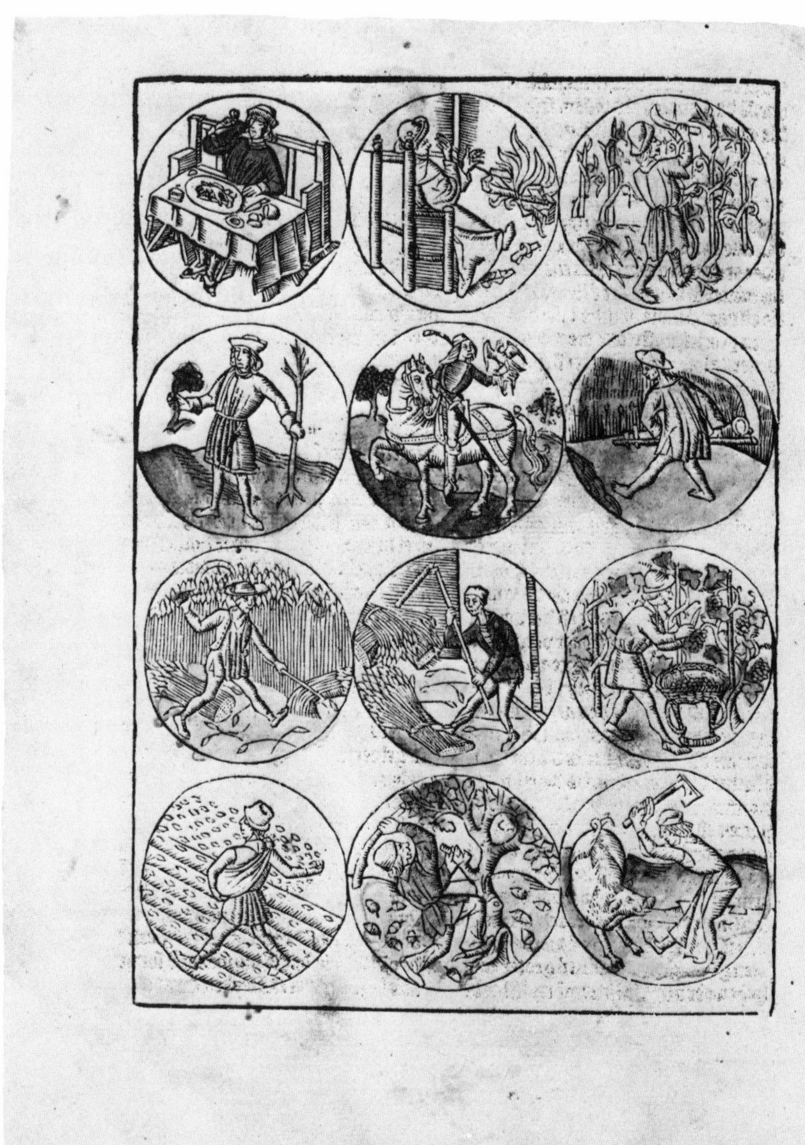

FIGURE 8.
The Divisions of Time.
Bartholomaeus Anglicus,
*De proprietatibus rerum*
(*Boeck van de proprieteyten der dinghen*)
(Haarlem: Jacob Bellaert,
24 December 1485),
Rosenwald Collection, no. 488.

The Birds (pl. 3) illustrates Book Twelve, which describes the creatures of the air, and presents a colorful landscape filled with a variety of winged creatures. For some reason, Books Ten and Eleven, on matter and form and the properties of the air, were not provided with illustrations in the Bellaert edition, although schematic diagrams do appear for them in the Lyons book. The picture for Book Twelve in the Lyons Bartholomaeus presents the conventional representation (fig. 9) where individual studies of birds (such as we find them in the *Dialogus creaturarum* printed by Leeu in Gouda in 1480) are brought together and scattered about a simple landscape composed of overlapping coulisses indicated by lines. In the upper center, the phoenix sits atop its pyre to be consumed by the fire of its nest, a symbol of Christ's resurrection. The pelican, a symbol of Christ's sacrifice, plucking at its breast to feed its young with its own blood, is perched on a nest in the upper right. The owl, an evil bird of darkness according to medieval thought, occupies the central position and is besieged by smaller birds of virtue in the daytime.

At first sight, the Bellaert page would seem to be a more sophisticated variation on the model, but it is not so simple. For one thing, the religious associations are lacking entirely. The phoenix does not destroy itself, and the owl rests peacefully under a tree in the upper right. Pelicans wade the shore seeking food, and the other birds cavort in a quite natural fashion. The eagle, who has "principality among the fowls" according to Bartholomaeus, is perched high in a tree in the upper part of the frontispiece. The swans swim in consort in the lower left, one drake between two

Liure Xii

FIGURE 9. The Birds. Bartholomaeus Anglicus, *De proprietatibus rerum* (Lyons: Johannes Siber, after 26 January 1486), Rosenwald Collection, no. 394.

FIGURE 10. The Fishes. Bartholomaeus Anglicus, *De proprietatibus rerum* (*Boeck van de proprieteyten der dinghen*) (Haarlem: Jacob Bellaert, 24 December 1485), Rosenwald Collection, no. 488.

females, in courtship as Bartholomaeus describes them: "When a swan is seeking the female in love, he attracts her by twisting his neck and beckoning her toward him." The cranes, lower right, are "family" birds, according to Bartholomaeus, birds that love their own kind only. The conspicuous griffin, middle left, introduced as some heraldic beast, is depicted just as the text describes: "It is four-footed, likened unto an eagle in its foreparts, heads, and wings, and in the other part, it resembles a lion." A number of lesser species can be identified easily, including water birds such as mallards, coots, pipers, and herons. The proud rooster of the barnyard appears on the shore, and a number of smaller varieties, quails, pigeons, ravens, swallows, sparrows, and finches, seek out food along the rushes and in the meadows.

The Master of Bellaert obviously took great delight in recording all of these varieties, and he placed them in a comforting landscape with meadows, trees, and a broad pond with rushes and reeds growing along its banks. In no other illustrated book of birds of this period do we find such a natural aviary provided for the winged creatures.[15]

The Lyons illustration for Book Thirteen, on the waters and the fish in them, is merely a circular earth surrounded and dissected by wavy bands indicating the seas and rivers, whereas the Bellaert frontispiece, The Fishes (fig. 10), shows again one of those fascinating habitats, a huge aquarium of sorts, where the waters are truly

"graceful and beautiful" (displaying "sierheyt," as the Dutch text informs us). Its undulating lines suggest the depths of the sea and white-crested waves. Against this graceful design the variety of fish are placed in profile (what other view could describe a fish?), and many of them can be easily identified.

Here again, it appears that the illustrator had the text in mind when he designed the page. For instance, Bartholomaeus begins his discussion of the fish with the following: "There is a great fish in the sea, called Bellua, that forces water out of its jaws that has a sweet smelling vapor, and other fish sense the smell and follow after him and enter into his jaws following the smell, and he swallows them and is thus nourished." The Bellua is a sturgeon of the Black Sea (Beluga) and Bartholomaeus's source here was one Jorath, the Syriac writer of *De animalibus*. Certainly the huge fish at the top of the page is meant to be the Bellua swallowing up one of its victims. A number of fish that the artist had seen firsthand can be identified. Below the Bellua swim a sturgeon with a humped back, a dolphin, swordfish, skate, sea bass, carp, flounder, and, along the bottom, the trout, the pike, and an eel. To the middle left is a sea lion, and just opposite is a larger species, a whale or dolphin. The varieties of both saltwater and freshwater fish are drawn with amazing accuracy when compared to most early representations of fish in which they all have the same profile, differing only in size.

The Earth and Its Divisions (fig. 11) is the remarkable frontispiece for Books Fourteen and Fifteen. It anticipates the vast global panoramas characteristic of sixteenth-century Netherlandish landscapes. In it, we look across a deep vista organized into layers of landscape with a meandering river and seas separating the rolling land masses into many coulisses stacked one behind the other. In the immediate foreground is a great walled city, perhaps inspired by the woodcut illustrations in Breydenbach's *Peregrinationes*,[16] with a two-towered gateway, a domed temple, and a towered church squeezed between various domestic buildings. Is this meant to be Jerusalem? Beyond are other villages, some just visible behind the hillocks, others nestled in harbors or perched on hilltops. The winding river flows into a broad sea where a number of islands with dwellings are visible. Tiny ships sail among the isles. As in the panoramic frontispiece for *Der sonderen troest*,[17] the Bellaert designer added floating clouds to complete his vision of a vast landscape, and aside from the discrepancies in the sizes of swans, trees, and birds, the diminution in scale is remarkably convincing. One senses not only the depth and breadth of his landscape but also its vibrancy and texture filtered through a slight atmosphere.

This frontispiece is all the more surprising and engaging when compared to the illustrations of the same chapters in the other Bartholomaeus books. The Lyons edition has an illustration for each book in which Earth is merely indicated by a representation of roughly hewn rocks, and the divisions of the Earth are depicted as

FIGURE 11. The Earth and its Divisions.
Bartholomaeus Anglicus, *De proprietatibus rerum*
(*Boeck van de proprieteyten der dinghen*)
(Haarlem: Jacob Bellaert, 24 December 1485), Rosenwald Collection, no. 488.

linear partitions in a simple circle-globe surrounded by a band of water (fig. 12). The Bellaert landscape, on the other hand, introduces us to a wholly new mode of pictorial thinking and representation of landscape that anticipates the mannerist panoramas of Patinir and later generations of Antwerp painters.

Costly Stones and Plants (fig. 13) illustrates Books Seventeen and Eighteen, which deal with the identification and mining of precious stones and types of trees and plants. Again, the Lyons illustrator provided an illustration for each book. Book Seventeen begins with a picture of miners digging the earth and wading the streams in search of stones, a rather common illustration in books on mining. A simple groundline with five trees and a few schematic plants illustrates the second topic. Once again, the Bellaert Master expands the illustration into a refreshing view of meadowlands, with a sparkling stream meandering through a verdant pasture. The five trees of the Lyons woodcut appear in the background in the same generalized form to represent what Bartholomaeus describes as "woods," or trees that grow in wild places, many without fruit, where wild beasts and fowl live and feed on the herbs and grasses that grow about them.

The stones and gems, described in Book Seventeen, are barely discernible, though they can be found, here and there, scattered about the banks of the stream in the foreground and snuggled amid the "grace and beauty of the earth" (*sierheyt en*

Liure XV

FIGURE 12. The Earth and Its Divisions. Bartholomaeus Anglicus, *De proprietatibus rerum* (Lyons: Johannes Siber, after 26 January 1486), Rosenwald Collection, no. 394.

FIGURE 13. Costly Stones and Plants.
Bartholomaeus Anglicus, *De proprietatibus rerum*
(*Boeck van de proprieteyten der dinghen*)
(Haarlem: Jacob Bellaert, 24 December 1485), Rosenwald Collection, no. 488.

*scoenheit der eerde*). Apparently our designer did not plan to include Book Seventeen in this frontispiece originally, since the flora fill the carpetlike pasture. Some plants can be identified—dandelions, violets, daisies, and so on—but, for the most part, the plants are rendered in the conventional shapes that one often finds in illustrated herbals and nature books of the later middle ages. However summary his treatment of the individual species may appear, his foremost intention, to render convincingly and sympathetically a passage of nature, a meadow spangled with plants and flowers, is marvelously accomplished. Even the tiny blades of grass add to the allover pattern of a miraflores decoration without detracting from the charming view of a stretch of land that gently recedes to softly undulating mounds with trees on the horizon.

FIGURE 14. Animals. Bartholomaeus Anglicus, *De proprietatibus rerum* (*Boeck van de proprieteyten der dinghen*) (Haarlem: Jacob Bellaert, 24 December 1485), Rosenwald Collection, no. 488.

Animals (fig. 14) is the frontispiece for Book Eighteen, the final section of the natural history. It is devoted to the animals, and, in many respects, it is the most interesting illustration in Bartholomaeus's treatise. The conventional representation, such as that in the Lyons edition, features a circle of animals about two deer in the center: (reading clockwise from top right) a rabbit, goat, boar, lamb, cat, horse, and bear. They resemble simple profile cutouts mounted against a flat, schematic foil of hills (fig. 15). The Bellaert edition, on the other hand, has all the naturalism of an open-air zoo. About the hart, which occupies the center as in the Lyons book, a parade of animals appears that would be a credit to Noah. Serpents, lizards, hedgehogs, monkeys, toads, squirrels, mice, rabbits, foxes, martins, and other smaller species are sprinkled among the other animals that seem to be characterized in part by the text. To the upper left are two alert dogs, one a whippet and the other a hound, which, according to Bartholomaeus, "know their names and love their masters." Below, prancing before two bovines, is an elegant horse: "Horses are joyful in the fields . . . and are mindful of the trumpets that call forth battle."

Opposite is the slovenly donkey, resting: "The ass is fair of shape and of disposition while he is young and tender; but the older donkey is . . . a melancholic beast (that is, cold and dry), and is therefore sluggish and slow . . . nevertheless he bears his burdens." The bear in the upper right is busy as "he licks and sucks his own feet for the tasty juice in them." Below the bear are the heraldic griffin and unicorn, the only imaginary beasts in the print.

In general, the naturalism in the rendering of the animals is truly surprising for the period. They are not all shown in profile. The crocodile in the lower right is boldly foreshortened, with his menacing jaws prepared for prey: "If he finds a man by the edge of the water or a cliff, he attacks him, then he weeps on him (hence the expression, 'crocodile tears'), and then swallows him whole." Two camels, a dromedary and a two-humped Bactrian, in the lower left might well have been studied firsthand, but by far the most astonishing beast of all is the huge elephant that dominates the composition in the lower right. The elephant does not appear in the Lyons Bartholomaeus, although it is one of the most important animals discussed in the book, but representations of the big beast do appear in the 1480 Gouda *Dialogus creaturarum* printed by Leeu, mentioned above, where it is depicted as some stuffed toy along with the other animals (fig. 16).

FIGURE 15. Animals. Bartholomaeus Anglicus, *De proprietatibus rerum* (Lyons: Johannes Siber, after 26 January 1486), Rosenwald Collection, no. 394.

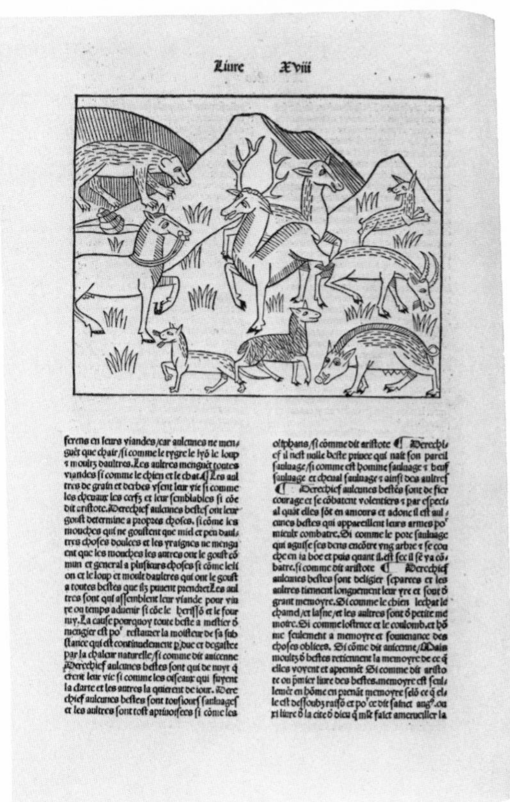

Liure XViii

FIGURE 16. Elephant and Other Animals. *Dialogus creaturarum* (Gouda: Gerard Leeu, 3 June 1480), Rosenwald Collection, no. 475.

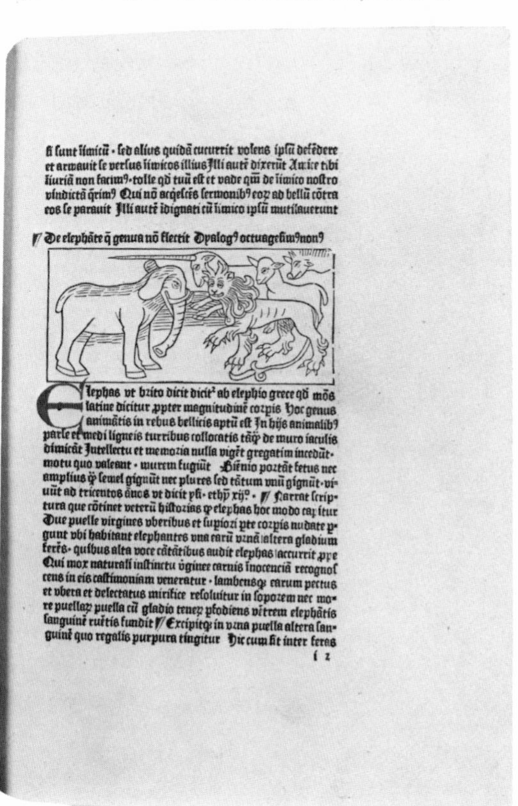

Where did our Haarlem artist find such an exotic model? There can be no doubt that the elephant here was based on some direct knowledge of the beast. Had the Bellaert Master actually seen an elephant? It seems very likely. In the *Cronycke van Hollandt*, printed in 1517 by J. Seversoen, it is recorded that in the year 1484 "a living elephant was conducted around Holland from town to town, to the great profit of its master . . . it drowned near Muiden when embarking for Utrecht."[18] A year later, ca. 1485–86, a similarly realistic elephant suddenly appeared as a handsome printer's mark in books published in Gouda by the printer G.D. (Gotfridus de Os?) (fig. 17). It would seem, therefore, that the Gouda and the Haarlem pachyderms, both appearing a year after the event, were inspired by the "living elephant" led "round Holland from town to town."[19]

In conclusion, we might say that the magnificent elephant in the Bellaert print is a fitting tribute to Bartholomaeus Anglicus. One of our best sources for the life of Bartholomaeus is the Parma Chronicles of Salimbene degli Adami, written about 1287.[20] Salimbene tells us that Bartholomaeus was for a time professor of theology at the University of Paris, where "he lectured on the whole Bible." The lecture that Salimbene best remembered was one based on the nature of the elephant as described in *De proprietatibus rerum*. There Bartholomaeus relates that "Among all the beasts the elephant is of highest virtue . . . they are of good wit and learn easily." But they are weary of man and withdraw to the woods when they encounter him. To capture the elephant, Bartholomaeus continues, the Ethiopians would send two beautiful young maidens into the open fields, "all naked and bare with their hair let down." There the two would sing a sensuous love song. The elephant, a gentle and loving creature, would be attracted to their song of enchantment and amble out from his hiding place, and after being lulled to sleep by the sweet refrains, he would be taken by the hunters who waited nearby. It is interesting to note that in the Bellaert print a hissing serpent, the archetypal symbol of woman's temptation, is placed directly at the feet of the elephant.[21]

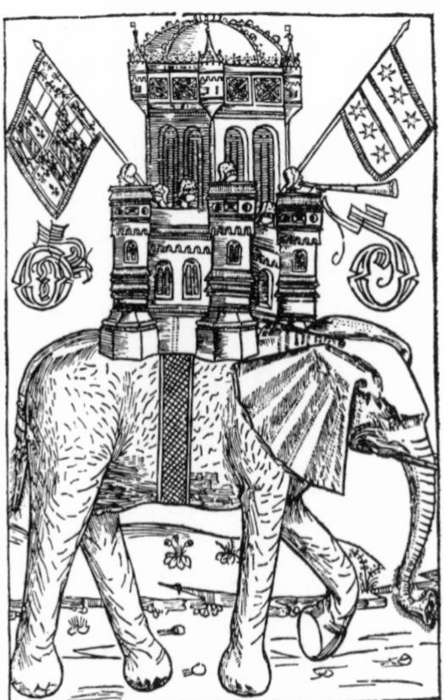

FIGURE 17. Mark of the Printer G. D., with Elephant. Gouda: G. D. (Gotfridus de Os?), ca. 1485–86. From Arthur M. Hind, *An Introduction to a History of Woodcut* (New York: Dover Publications, 1963), vol. 2, fig. 342.

The colorful illustrations in the Haarlem book *On the Properties of Things* represent the finest works of Bellaert's chief designer. We have seen how these remarkable illustrations follow earlier picture cycles in general, but it is also apparent that the models have been transformed into original designs that reflect the tastes of the patrons of Haarlem, especially in the treatment of flora, fauna, and landscape. To be sure, a number of different hands and models must be reckoned with in Bellaert's vast production of illustrated books, but his foremost artist clearly belonged to the circle of distinguished painters in Haarlem, a fact that indicates the importance the illustrated book had attained in early Dutch art.

## NOTES

1. Library of Congress, *The Lessing J. Rosenwald Collection: A Catalog of the Gifts of Lessing J. Rosenwald to the Library of Congress, 1943 to 1975* (Washington: Library of Congress, 1977), pp. 89–98, nos. 482, 485, 487, 488, 490, 491. References to the books in the British Museum catalogs; in Marinus F. A. G. Campbell, *Annales de la typographie néerlandaise au XVe siècle* (The Hague: M. Nijhoff, 1864); in Ludwig F. T. Hain, *Repertorium bibliographicum* 7 (Stuttgart: J. G. Cotta, 1826–38); in Wilhelm Ludwig Schreiber, *Manuel de l'amateur de la gravure sur bois et sur métal au XVe siècle* (Berlin: A. Cohn, 1891–1911), and so forth, are conveniently listed below each entry.

For a useful catalog of the Bellaert woodcuts, see Bernard F. Reilly, "Bellaert Incunabula in the Lessing J. Rosenwald Collection" (M.A. thesis, Bryn Mawr College, 1974).

2. M. J. Schretlen, *Dutch and Flemish Woodcuts of the Fifteenth Century* (London: E. Benn, 1925), p. 22; Arthur M. Hind, *An Introduction to a History of Woodcut*, 2 vols. (New York: Dover Publications, 1963), 1:566, 574; William Martin Conway, *The Woodcutters of the Netherlands in the Fifteenth Century* (Cambridge: University Press, 1884), pp. 60, 222 ff.

3. Schretlen, *Dutch and Flemish Woodcuts*, pp. 7–20. For arguments for the date and localization of the *Speculum humanae salvationis*, see Conway, *Woodcutters of the Netherlands*; Amsterdam, Rijks-Museum, *Middeleeuwse kunst der noordelijke Nederlanden*, 150 jaar Rijksmuseum jubileumtentoonstelling, 28 juni/28 september 1958 (Amsterdam, 1958), p. 168; and Robert A. Koch, "New Criteria for Dating the Netherlandish *Biblia pauperum* Blockbook," in *Studies in Late Medieval and Renaissance Painting in Honor of Millard Meiss*, ed. Irving Lavin and John Plummer, 2 vols. (New York: New York University Press, 1977), 1:283–89. Avril Henry's forthcoming monograph on the *Speculum* artists locates the shop in Utrecht.

4. The relationships between the Bellaert illustrations and North-Netherlandish painting have led to considerable speculation and controversy over the identity of the "Master of Bellaert." Schretlen, *Dutch and Flemish Woodcuts*, pp. 5, 49 ff., suggests that the designer was the teacher of Jacob Cornelisz van Oostsanen, and that he might be identified as the artist of the *Speculum humanae salvationis* and the miniaturist of a Dutch Bible of 1474 in the British Museum (no. 16,951). Wilhelm Valentiner, in "Aelbert van Ouwater," *Art Quarterly* 6 (1943):74–91, identified the Master of Bellaert as Ouwater, but confused Ouwater with another Haarlem painter, the Master of the Tiburtine Sibyl—see James Snyder, "The Early Haarlem School of Painting—I," *Art Bulletin* 42 (1960):53–55. A note of caution should be taken here in identifying the artist or artists of the Bellaert illustrations. See Sandra Hindman and James Douglas Farquhar, *Pen to Press: Illustrated Manuscripts and Printed Books in the First Century of Printing* (College Park: Art Dept., University of Maryland, 1977), p. 116: "the vast production ascribed to the Haarlem Woodcutter is simply not by one hand, nor even designs of a single artist."

5. Robert Steele, ed., *Mediaeval Lore from Bartholomew Anglicus* (London, 1905), pp. 4–8, 182.

6. Lotte and Wytze Hellinga, *The Fifteenth-Century Printing Types of the Low Countries*, trans. D. A. S. Reid, 2 vols. (Amsterdam: M. Hertzberger, 1966), 1:73 ff.

7. Steele, *Mediaeval Lore*, pp. 173–80.

8. Interest in landscape was not just the particular concern of the painters of Haarlem but was apparently favored by the patrons as well. A unique document, *een boekje van 1490 op een los stuk papier* ("a record of 1490 on a loose piece of paper") (see A. Weissman, "Gegevens omtrent Bouw en Inrichting van de Sint Bavokerk te Haarlem," *Oud-Holland* 33 [1915], pp. 69–70), records a commission for an altarpiece in which the usual concerns—the quality of the pigments, positions of the figures, and so on—were not specified, but the use of landscape (*landscap*) was: "The first panel where the angel announces to the shepherds must have a landscape . . . the other panel where Our Lord is circumcised must be placed in a temple of the appropriate type. And the third panel where Our Lord is presented with gifts from the three holy kings must be set in a house in Bethlehem in a landscape. And the fourth panel where Our Lord is presented in the temple should be painted with a temple appropriate for the story. The fifth panel where Herod orders the massacre of the innocents must be placed in a landscape. And where Mary travels to Egypt that too must be placed in a landscape of the proper type. And where Our Lord sits in the middle of the doctors that should be made decoratively in a temple. And where Saint John baptizes Our Lord must be painted according to fashion in the air and landscape." (My translation.) To my knowledge this is the earliest occurrence of the term *landscape* in the context of art.

9. *Le Propriétaire des choses* (*De proprietatibus rerum*) (Lyons, 1486). Siber's cuts were adapted from those in an earlier Lyons edition, 1482, printed by Matthais Huss. See Library of Congress, *Lessing J. Rosenwald Collection*, p. 78, no. 394.

10. Schretlen, *Dutch and Flemish Woodcuts*, p. 26.

11. See especially H. Bober, "The Zodiacal Miniature of the 'Très Riches Heures' of the Duke of Berry; Its Sources and Meaning," *Journal of the Warburg and Courtauld Institutes* 11 (1948), pp. 1–34.

12. Raimond van Marle, *Iconographie de l'art profane au Moyen-Âge et à la Renaissance et la décoration des demeures*, 2 vols. (The Hague: M. Nijhoff, 1931), 2:155 ff.

13. Hind, *History of Woodcut*, p. 620.

14. James Carson Webster, *The Labors of the Months in Antique and Mediaeval Art to the End of the Twelfth Century* (Evanston and Chicago: Northwestern University, 1938), pp. 66 ff.; van Marle, *Iconographie de l'art profane*, 1:373 ff.

15. Compare, for instance, those in the Gouda editions of the *Dialogus creaturarum* published by Gerard Leeu in 1480 and 1482 in the Rosenwald Collection, nos. 475 and 480.

16. Library of Congress, *Lessing J. Rosenwald Collection*, p. 30, no. 116.

17. For an illustration of the frontispiece of *Der sonderen troest*, see Hindman and Farquhar, *Pen to Press*, p. 171, pl. 2.

18. Quoted in Hind, *History of Woodcut*, p. 586.

19. A very similar elephant appears in the left panel of Bosch's *Garden of Earthly Delights*. Phyllis W. Lehmann, *Cyriacus of Ancona's Egyptian Visit and its Reflections in Gentile Bellini and Hieronymus Bosch* (Locust Valley, N.Y.: J. J. Augustin, 1977), pp. 15 ff., finds the source for Bosch's elephant and giraffe in the scene in Eden in the illustrated editions of Cyriacus's Egyptian diary and concludes that Bosch must have traveled to Venice or North Italy before he executed his painting. In fact, the elephant in the *Garden of Earthly Delights* is closer to the one in our woodcut. The giraffe, on the other hand, does have a remarkable resemblance to the one in the Cyriacus manuscripts.

20. Steele, *Mediaeval Lore*, p. 6.

21. The standard bestiary relates the following: "Now the Elephant and his wife represent Adam and Eve. For when they were pleasing to God, before their provocation in the flesh, they knew nothing about copulation nor had any knowledge of sin. When, however, the wife ate of the Tree of Knowledge, which is what Mandragora means, and gave one of the fruits to her man, she was immediately made a wanderer and they had to clear out of Paradise on account of it." See Terence Hanbury White, *The Book of Beasts, Being a Translation from a Latin Bestiary of the Twelfth Century* (New York: Putnam's, 1960), p. 27.

BARBARA G. LANE

# THE GENESIS WOODCUTS OF A DUTCH ADAPTATION OF THE *VITA CHRISTI*

The Rosenwald Collection includes five editions of a Dutch meditational treatise on the life of Christ that has been virtually ignored by modern scholars. *Tboeck vanden leven Jhesu Christi* was first published by Gerard Leeu in Antwerp, in 1487, with 146 woodcuts.[1] Just one year later, it appeared in two separate versions in Delft and Antwerp,[2] and at least eight subsequent editions from 1495 to 1536 attest to its tremendous popularity.[3] Considerations of its innovative illustrations are curiously rare, however, and investigations of its text are nonexistent.

This study will concentrate on the two earliest Rosenwald copies, whose woodcuts are brilliantly hand-colored: the first edition of 1487 and the 1488 publication by Christian Snellaert in Delft. All of the later editions of the book reuse the blocks of one or the other of these. Since many of these woodcuts have similar but reversed compositions, as in the first scene after the title page (figs. 1 and 2), scholars have concentrated their attention on the question of which set of illustrations influenced the other. Conway was the first to propose that the Delft blocks were copied from the cuts of the 1487 edition.[4] In 1925, however, Schretlen pointed out that if the Delft cuts also dated in 1487, they could have served as the models for the Antwerp blocks.[5]

Support for Schretlen's hypothesis occurs in the opening woodcut of Man and Scripture in the Delft edition (fig. 2). This block must have been executed at least as early as 1487, since it was used for the title page of Van der Meer's publication of the

FIGURE 2. Man and Scripture.
*Een notabel boec vandē leuen Ons Heerē Ihesu Christi*
(Delft: [Jacob Jacobszoen van der Meer or Christian Snellaert], 1488), Rosenwald Collection, no. 496.

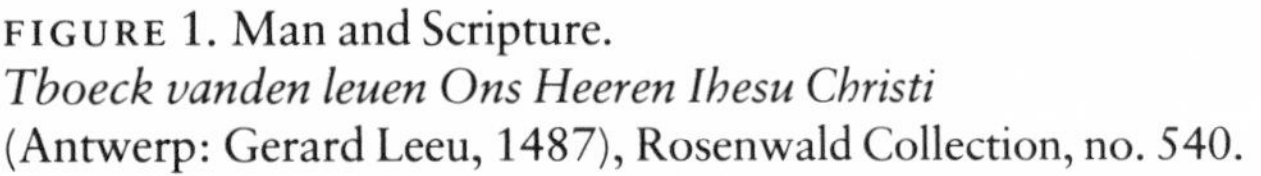

FIGURE 1. Man and Scripture.
*Tboeck vanden leuen Ons Heeren Ihesu Christi*
(Antwerp: Gerard Leeu, 1487), Rosenwald Collection, no. 540.

*Passionael* in that year. Later editions of this Dutch translation of Jacobus de Varagine's *Golden Legend*, for example the Delft version of 1499–1500 (fig. 3),[6] continued to use this block. No inscriptions identify the figures of this woodcut in any edition of the *Passionael*, since no mention of either of them occurs in its text. The entire Dutch treatise on the life of Christ, however, is written as a dialogue between Man and Scripture, and so the figures are clearly labeled in its opening scene. This block, therefore, must have been invented for the text under consideration here, which we want now to give the attention it deserves.

The prologue of *Tboeck vanden leven Jhesu Christi* informs the reader that it was translated from the book by the "devout and learned" Ludolphus the Carthusian. On the basis of this reference, apparently, it has always been cataloged as a Dutch translation of the fourteenth-century *Vita Christi*. Ludolphus's erudite treatment of Christ's life is preserved today in over 230 manuscripts.[7] It was first published in Latin in 1472 in Cologne,[8] and the numerous editions and translations

FIGURE 3. Title Page. [Jacobus de Varagine], *Legenda aurea sanctorum sive Lombardica historia* (*Passionael het winter stuck. Datmen heet die gulden legende*) (Delft: Hendrik Eckert, August 1499–1500), Rosenwald Collection, no. 508.

throughout Europe suggest that it was one of the most popular meditational treatises of the late Middle Ages and Renaissance.[9]

A comparison of the Dutch and Latin texts, however, reveals some curious discrepancies. Ludolphus's *Vita Christi* is more formal in tone, and it is not a dialogue. It contains extensive quotations of specific sources, moreover, that occur nowhere in the Dutch book.[10] Although the subjects of the 175 chapters in the Dutch version generally correspond to the 181 chapters of the *Vita Christi*, only the concluding prayers of each chapter can be called "free translations" of the Latin.[11] Indeed, a mere glance at the dimensions of the Dutch editions in comparison to any Latin version reveals that they are less than half the size of Ludolphus's exceedingly wordy treatise.[12]

Apparently, therefore, the Dutch text is not the literal translation of Ludolphus that it claims to be. Although its general structure may derive from the *Vita Christi*, it retains only a loose dependence on the content of its Latin prototype. Ludolphus's name, in fact, never appears on the title page of any of the Dutch versions. As early as the second Antwerp edition of 1488, moreover, and in all of the later editions, the title was expanded with an explanation of how the text had been

FIGURE 4. Genesis Page. Bible of Evert van Soudenbalch, Vienna, Österreichische Nationalbibliothek, Cod. 2771, fol. 10. Courtesy Österreichische Nationalbibliothek.

corrected and improved with additional material.[13] Whereas Ludolphus's name appears in the table of contents of the two earliest editions, it mysteriously disappears in all of the later versions. Only in the prologue does the reference to Ludolphus consistently occur. No evidence remains to indicate whether a translation of Ludolphus was originally intended when the prologue was first written, and then never completed, or whether his name was merely evoked as a means of ensuring the success of the publication. In any event, the new title page of the later editions reveals an awareness on the part of the publishers that the Dutch version was not exactly the translation described in the prologue.

It is curious, however, that this discrepancy has not been recognized in more recent times. In 1854, Willem Moll included a list of nine editions of our book in his study on Johannes Brugman and briefly described the pronounced differences between the Dutch and Latin texts. He praised the Dutch Life of Christ, in fact, as one of the most original productions of its type in the period.[14] Unfortunately, however, Moll's own text was also in Dutch, and it apparently failed to change the established practice of classifying the Dutch book as a translation of Ludolphus.

Since catalogers rarely have time to read all of the books that they must record, of course, one can hardly blame them for relying on the information provided in the prologue. On the other hand, one wonders how many scholars who examined the woodcuts considered carefully the text that they illustrate. This study will concentrate on one unusual set of woodcuts to demonstrate that a full understanding of the meaning of the scenes depicted is impossible without an actual reading of their remarkably colloquial and original text.

Significant textual differences distinguish the second chapters of the Dutch and Latin versions of the *Vita Christi*. Chapter 2 of Ludolphus's *Vita Christi* consists of only seven columns of text. The Dutch version expands this chapter into thirty-five columns. Whereas the Latin text begins with an account of Lucifer's fall and God's decision to redeem the human race from Eve's sin, the Dutch chapter dwells at length on the first six days of Creation and the story of Adam and Eve.

The five Genesis woodcuts that illustrate the first part of chapter 2 include imagery unparalleled in books devoted to the life of Christ. In this period, in fact, Creation cycles are curiously rare in general,[15] although the Dutch History Bibles often include miniatures of each of the days of Creation on their opening pages of Genesis (fig. 4).[16] More extensive cycles of the Fall of Man occur in some of the earlier Dutch Bibles, which include precedents for the subjects of three of the woodcuts here: the Creation of Eve, the Temptation, and the Expulsion.[17] These three events also appear on the Paradise panels of several of Bosch's triptychs. The left wing of the Haywain Triptych, for instance, depicts them from back to front, in a single landscape, and they appear in reverse order on the corresponding wing of the Vienna Triptych of the Last Judgment.[18] No Creation cycles of the period, however, parallel the unusual imagery of the first, second, and fourth scenes in the Dutch cycle.

In the first woodcut of chapter 2 (figs. 5 and 6), a series of densely populated concentric circles surround the Creation of Eve. Beyond the last of these circles looms the Creator, with personifications of the four winds. This complicated scene is one of a number of woodcuts in the Dutch books that derive from the Cologne Bible, published by Heinrich Quentell about 1478–79.[19] The German woodcut (fig. 7) introducing the Book of Genesis also includes three circles around the central Creation scene. The innermost of these circles in all three images depicts fish in a patternized body of water. A band of clouds around the water contains the sun, moon, and stars. In the final circles, praying angels radiate outward, forming a decorative pattern with their wings. The text that accompanies these complex illustrations clarifies their meaning.

The early portion of chapter 2 includes the type of description of the spheres of the universe that occurs more frequently in treatises on nature than in books dealing with the life of Christ. The cosmology of the Dutch text corresponds to the late medieval interpretation of the Ptolemaic system of the universe. It derives ultimately from Plato's *Timaeus*, with its Pythagorean arrangement of the four elements.[20] Numerous encyclopedists, such as the seventh-century Isidore of Seville, transmitted this cosmology to medieval thought.[21]

Hijr beghynt Genesis dat erste boeck der
vyff boeckere Moysi. Dat erste capittel ys
van der geschyppenis der werlt vnde aller creaturen vnde de wercke der sees daghe

In dem anbegynne schoep
god hemmel vnde erden·
Mer de erde was leddych
vñ de dustermisse weren vp
deme anclate des affgron-
des dat ys vp deme ange
sichte der elementen do vn
uerscheiden. vnde der geist
godes wart gevoert bouen
de watere· Vñ god de sprak
dat licht werde: vñ dat licht ward: vñ got de
sach dat licht dat dat gud was· vnde he deide
dat licht vā der dustermisse· vñ dat licht nom

de he den dach· vñ de dustermisse de nacht· vñ
der auent vnde morgen wart een dach· Vnde
got de sprak: dat firmamēt werde i dem midde
le der watē vñ he schedde de watē vā dē wate
ren Vñ god makede dat firmamēt: vñ delde de
watere de dat werē vnder dem firmament vā
dē de dat werē bauē dem firmament vñ dat ge
schach also· Vñ got nomde dat firmament dē
hēmel vñ dat wart der auent vñ de morghen
de ander dach Vñ god sprack euer De watere
de vnder dem hemele sint werden vergaddert
an eene stede· vñ erschyne de drticheit· vnde
dat geschach also· vñ god hete de drticheyt
dat ertrijke· vñ de vergaderinge der watere he
te he dat meer· vñ got sach dat dat gud was
Vnde he sprack· De erde groye groyende krut
vñ dat saet make· vñ holt dat appel drage nae
syme kunne· des saet sij in eme sulues vpp der

*above:*
FIGURE 7. Creation of Eve.
Cologne Bible (Cologne: H. Quentell, 1478–79),
New York, Pierpont Morgan Library, ChL ff251.
Courtesy of the Trustees of the Pierpont Morgan Library.

*opposite page, left:*
FIGURE 5. Creation of Eve. *Tboeck vanden leuen Ons Heeren Ihesu Christi*
(Antwerp: Gerard Leeu, 1487), Rosenwald Collection, no. 540.

*opposite page, right:*
FIGURE 6. Creation of Eve. *Een notabel boec vandē leuen Ons Heerē Ihesu Christi*
(Delft: [Jacob Jacobszoen van der Meer or Christian Snellaert], 1488),
Rosenwald Collection, no. 496.

FIGURE 8. Cosmos. Bible of Evert van Soudenbalch, Vienna, Österreichische Nationalbibliothek, Cod. 2771, fol. 9. Courtesy Österreichische Nationalbibliothek.

Two examples will serve to illustrate the diversity of diagrams of the cosmos in the fifteenth century: a frontispiece of a Dutch History Bible in Vienna of 1450–60 (fig. 8)[22] and a more clearly labeled diagram in Hartmann Schedel's *Nuremberg Chronicle*, published by Anton Koberger in Latin and German editions in 1493.[23] The woodcut on folio V verso of Schedel's comprehensive history of the world illustrates the seventh day of Creation (fig. 9).[24] In both diagrams, the central Earth is surrounded by water, air, and fire. These four elements are followed by the circles of the then-recognized seven planets: the moon, Mercury, Venus, the sun, Mars, Jupiter, and Saturn. Next comes the firmament of fixed stars, with the signs of the zodiac, which is the last ring in the Dutch miniature. The Nuremberg diagram also includes the medieval additions of the invisible crystalline sphere and the outermost "primum mobile," which was thought to control the movement of the universe. Finally, the Lord and his angels dwell in the highest heaven, or "Empyrium."[25]

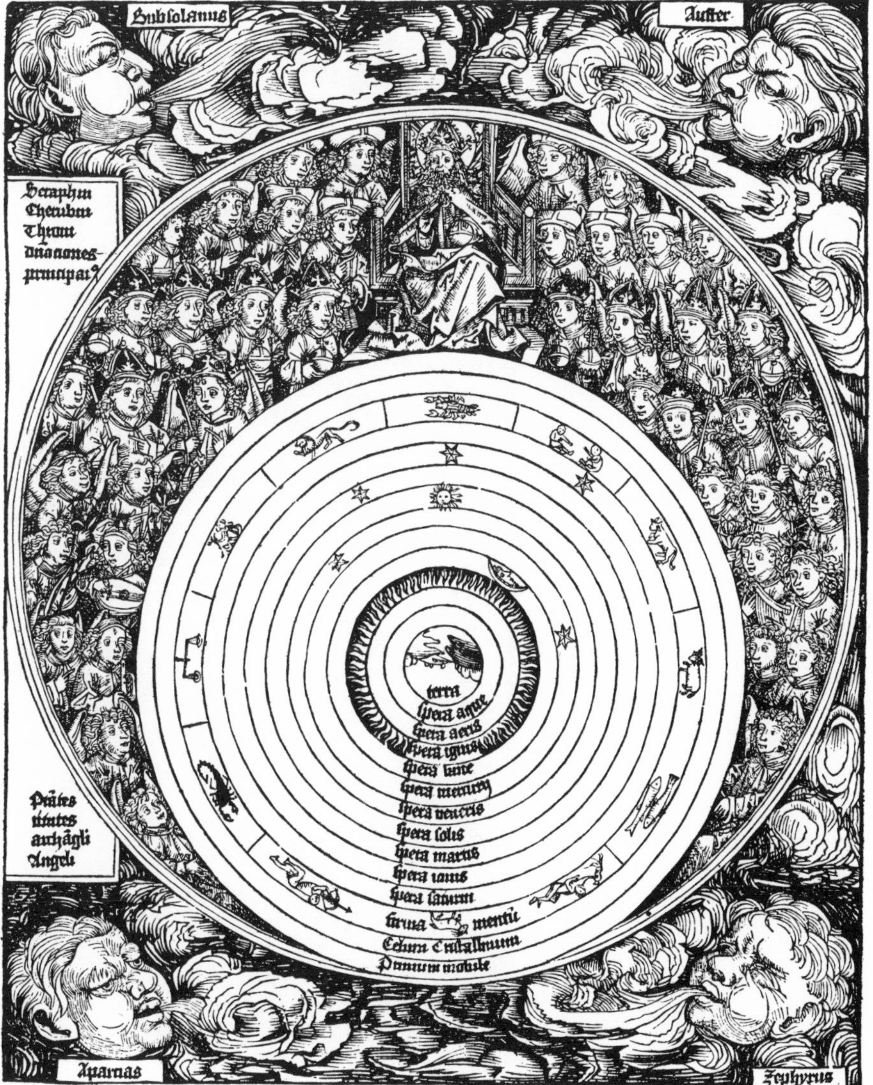


FIGURE 9. Cosmos. Hartmann Schedel, *Liber chronicarum* (Nuremberg: Anton Koberger, 12 July 1493), Rosenwald Collection, no. 163.

The publisher of the *Nuremberg Chronicle*, Anton Koberger, owned the blocks of the Cologne Bible and used them in his own Nuremberg Bible of 1483.[26] If the Cologne woodcut (fig. 7) influenced the Nuremberg diagram, as has been suggested,[27] then it, too, must signify the cosmos. Both images place angels and the Creator in the outer circle and personifications of the four winds in the corners. The four winds appear often in earlier cosmological diagrams, as in a schematized miniature in a German treatise on the universe of about 1295 in Munich (fig. 10).[28] Here, the winds fill the spaces between clearly labeled personifications of the four elements, around a square that encloses the spheres of the universe.

FIGURE 10. Cosmos. Thomas of Cantimpré, "De naturis rerum," Munich, Bayerische Staatsbibliothek, Clm. 2655, fol. 105. Courtesy Bayerische Staatsbibliothek.

FIGURE 11. Cosmos. *Symbolum apostolicum* (ca. 1450–60), Vienna, Österreichische Nationalbibliothek, Incunable II. D. 42. Courtesy Österreichische Nationalbibliothek.

It has been suggested that the image in the Cologne Bible may derive from the first page of the *Symbolum apostolicum*, a blockbook of about 1450–60 preserved in three unique editions (in Vienna, Heidelberg, and Munich).[29] Inscriptions of the names of the seven planets appear in the innermost ring of the first edition, in Vienna (fig. 11). These labels seem to identify the heavenly bodies in the middle circle, although there is an unidentified eighth star. Since only seven angels appear in the outer ring, however, the inscriptions may also allude to the seven planetary spheres.[30]

In the Cologne Bible, the individual spheres were compressed into a design that would not overpower the central Creation of Eve. Its outer circle of angels may signify all of the outer rings of the universe, which encompass the four elements in the center. Here (fig. 7), as in the Dutch woodcuts (figs. 5 and 6), the inner circles must correspond to earth, water, air, and fire, although air and fire seem to intermingle in the ring of clouds and stars. This graphic convention is not as illogical as it may seem at first, since, after all, Plato's Timaeus states that stars are made of fire.[31]

N dem anbegynne schop got hyemel vnd erde. Vnd de veer Elementen
Alse water Fure. Lucht vnd erde De weren vmscheden. Vnd got mackede
In dem hyemel teyn kore der engel In dem teynde kore was Lucyfer der
schoneste Engel. Vnd was dar Inne nicht eyne stunde. wente he verhoff
sick Jegen synen schypper Vnd wolde gelick wesen godde dem herren. Do
qwam go[illegible] vnd stottede one dat he strumpelde. vnd vel in de affgrunt der
helle. O wy armen mynschen. was de Duuel in dem hyemel. vnd was
de aller Schoneste vnde konde dar Inne nicht blyuen vormyddelst syner
hoffart Vnd vel dar vt mit allen synen gesellen hyr vmb wel de hoffart
in dem hymel nicht wesen. wede sick hyr in ertrick vorheuet de schal dort
vornyddert werden. Vnd valt den wech den lucyfer vel. Got de schopp

FIGURE 12. Creation of Eve. [Konrad Bote], *Cronecken der Sassen* (Mainz: Peter Schoeffer, 1492), Rosenwald Collection, no. 157.

The stars, of course, may also allude to the planets, as in the blockbook. This may also be true in some later condensations of the Cologne Bible woodcut, which omit the outer ring completely. In the *Cronecken der Sassen*, published in Mainz by Peter Schoeffer in 1492, for instance, only two circles surround the large Creation of Eve in the center (fig. 12).[32] The reference to the four elements in the text immediately below the illustration, however, confirms its cosmic intent, as does the description of the universe in the Dutch book. The diversity of such images suggests that any similar circular diagram with the Earth at the center would be understood as a symbol of the cosmos, no matter how abbreviated its details were.

FIGURE 13. God with Adam and Eve in the Garden of Paradise. *Tboeck vanden leuen Ons Heeren Ihesu Christi* (Antwerp: Gerard Leeu, 1487), Rosenwald Collection, no. 540.

FIGURE 14. God with Adam and Eve in the Garden of Paradise. *Een notabel boec vandē leuen Ons Heerē Ihesu Christi* (Delft: [Jacob Jacobszoen van der Meer or Christian Snellaert], 1488), Rosenwald Collection, no. 496.

Scriptura·
Siet hier mēsche:die ghedaente
eñ sceppenisse:so na als ic dat
ramen can:eñ hoort die vclaringhe
daer of· ¶ Indē dach als god die he
mel eñ aerdē was makēde:so maec-
te hi oec int oest eynde vā aertrijke
een wtgenomē plaetse:vol vā al dz
dē mēsche luste eñ genoechte in brē-
ghē soude moghē:ghenoemt:dz aert

In the second large woodcut of the Genesis cycle (fig. 13 or pl. 4 and fig. 14), Adam and Eve step through a resplendent Gothic portal into Eden, where God gestures toward the "tree of the knowledge of good and evil." An elaborate, stepped fountain rises grandly in the center of this verdant garden, and the four rivers of Paradise, each specifically labeled in the 1487 block, issue from heads in its foreground wall. In the Rosenwald copies of these two early editions, the brilliant coloring of these scenes almost blinds the viewer to their iconographic complexity.

A search for visual parallels for this unusual combination of motifs reveals only isolated examples that include just one or two of the details of the woodcuts. In

FIGURE 15. Paradise. "Très Riches Heures du duc de Berry," Chantilly, Musée Condé, Ms. 65, fol. 25v. Photo Giraudon.

the Paradise miniature of the Limbourgs' "Très Riches Heures du duc de Berry" of about 1415–16 in Chantilly (fig. 15),[33] for instance, four consecutive events of the story occur in a circular walled garden that is dominated by an elaborate architectural font. In the same period, scenes of the Marriage of Adam and Eve often appear in an enclosed garden, with one or more of the rivers of Paradise. In a miniature of about 1420 in Paris, for instance, the rivers surge through openings in the low wall (fig. 16).[34] In some of the Creation cycles of the Dutch History Bibles, too, the four rivers of Paradise flow from an architectural structure. In one of these miniatures, the ecclesiastical form of this structure seems to foreshadow the Eucharistic meaning of the Dutch woodcuts of Adam and Eve.[35]

FIGURE 16. Marriage of Adam and Eve. "Les Antiquités judaïques," Paris, Bibliothèque nationale, Ms. fr. 247, fol. 3. Phot. Bibl. nat. Paris.

Only one additional woodcut of the story occurs in the Cologne Bible. In it, the Temptation and Expulsion are combined in a single scene (fig. 17).[36] These two subjects also occur in the later *Nuremberg Chronicle*, although here four rivers spring from a single fountain.[37] The left wing of Bosch's Garden of Delights Triptych also includes a fountain in the middle ground.[38] Even here, however, in a painting that probably dates within ten or twenty years of the Dutch book, the scene does not parallel the specific imagery of the woodcuts.

The Dutch text closely follows Genesis 2:10 in its statement that a beautiful river arose in Paradise and separated into four additional rivers. Its description of the Physon, however, strays from the biblical source; the text erroneously relates that the name of this river derives from its Hebrew meaning of abundance, since it has so many fish. The 1487 woodcut (fig. 13) indicates the artist's dependence on this section of the text, for only this river is "full of fish."

According to the text, the main river watered the garden and enriched it. Genesis 2:6 describes a "fons" that irrigated the face of the earth, and medieval exegesis interpreted this as a baptismal fountain of life. Several features of the Dutch woodcuts suggest that their towering fountains signify baptismal fonts.

First of all, a peacock perches on the edge of each of the fountains. As discussed by Underwood some years ago, Carolingian images of the Fountain of Life include peacocks because of their baptismal symbolism.[39] In the early ninth-century Gospels of St. Medard de Soissons, for instance, paired peacocks flank the canopy of the architectural font (fig. 18).[40] The loss of the peacock's feathers every fall and their regrowth every spring parallels the rebirth and resurrection symbolism of baptism. Through this sacrament, the sins of the catechumen are buried in the font, in imitation of Christ's death, and the rebirth of the new man after baptism intentionally alludes to the resurrection of Christ.

The harts in such Carolingian images have a similar connection to baptism. Although the deerlike creatures in the Delft block (fig. 14) are somewhat ambiguous, a clearly portrayed hart appears behind the Lord in the 1487 cut (fig. 13). Psalm 42:1

FIGURE 17. Temptation and Expulsion. Cologne Bible (Cologne: H. Quentell, 1478–79), New York, Pierpont Morgan Library, ChL ff251. Courtesy of the Trustees of the Pierpont Morgan Library.

FIGURE 18. Fountain of Life. Gospels of St. Medard de Soissons, Paris, Bibliothèque nationale, Ms. lat. 8850, fol. 6v. Phot. Bibl. nat. Paris.

reads, "As the hart panteth after the water brooks, so panteth my soul after thee, O God." A reference to this analogy occurs in the traditional blessing of the baptismal font on Holy Saturday: "Almighty everlasting God, look mercifully on the devotion of thy people who are born anew, who pant, as the hart, after the fountain of thy waters: and mercifully grant, that the thirst of their faith may, by the mystery of baptism, sanctify their souls and bodies."[41]

The monumental portal through which Adam and Eve pass in the Dutch woodcuts may also have a sacramental intent, for baptism was often described as the entrance to Paradise. According to St. Thomas Aquinas, for instance, "Baptism opens the gates of the kingdom of heaven to the baptized in so far as it incorporates him into the Passion of Christ."[42] Paradise, of course, also alludes to the Church, which represents the kingdom of heaven on earth, and its rivers correspond to the four Gospels that spread the New Law. St. Cyprian's summary of this symbolism perhaps best clarifies the meaning of the Dutch woodcuts: "Ecclesia, setting forth the likeness of Paradise, includes within her walls fruit-bearing trees [which] she waters with four rivers, that is, with the four Gospels wherewith, by a celestial inundation, she bestows the grace of saving baptism."[43]

In the Dutch book, the prayer that immediately precedes the beginning of this chapter pleads for a cleansing from sin that can only be accomplished in baptism: "Thou who didst make me, remake and reform me, for I am stained and corrupted with sins; through thy great mercy, make my poor soul safe." This prayer, which is a simplified version of the concluding prayer of chapter 1 in Ludolphus's *Vita Christi*,[44] appears twice in the later editions of the Dutch book, as if to underscore the baptismal symbolism of the woodcuts.

FIGURE 19. Temptation.
*Tboeck vanden leuen Ons Heeren Ihesu Christi*
(Antwerp: Gerard Leeu, 1487),
Rosenwald Collection, no. 540.

FIGURE 20. Temptation.
*Een notabel boec vandē leuen Ons Heerē Ihesu Christi*
(Delft: [Jacob Jacobszoen van der Meer or
Christian Snellaert], 1488), Rosenwald Collection, no. 496.

FIGURE 21. The Lord Admonishes Adam and Eve.
*Tboeck vanden leuen Ons Heeren Ihesu Christi*
(Antwerp: Gerard Leeu, 1487),
Rosenwald Collection, no. 540.

FIGURE 22. The Lord Admonishes Adam and Eve.
*Een notabel boec vandē leuen Ons Heerē Ihesu Christi*
(Delft: [Jacob Jacobszoen van der Meer or
Christian Snellaert], 1488), Rosenwald Collection, no. 496.

FIGURE 23. Expulsion.
*Tboeck vanden leuen Ons Heeren Ihesu Christi*
(Antwerp: Gerard Leeu, 1487),
Rosenwald Collection, no. 540.

FIGURE 24. Expulsion. *Een notabel boec vandē leuen Ons Heerē Ihesu Christi*
(Delft: [Jacob Jacobszoen van der Meer or Christian Snellaert], 1488),
Rosenwald Collection, no. 496.

The remaining three woodcuts of the Genesis cycle illustrate the story of the Fall of Man. The 1487 and 1488 versions of the rather traditional Temptation (figs. 19 and 20) resemble the Temptation miniatures in the Dutch History Bibles as well as the woodcut of this subject in the Cologne Bible (fig. 17). There is no parallel in any of these sources, however, for the scene of the Lord's reprimands to Adam and Eve (figs. 21 and 22). Inscribed scrolls in the 1487 cut (fig. 21) clarify the action: God asks Adam where he is hiding, Adam places the blame on Eve, and Eve demurely declares that the serpent made her do it. Whereas similar inscriptions occasionally appear in other renderings of this subject, there are no precedents for the fountains in the Dutch images. Since these fountains echo the shapes of their predecessors in the large Paradise woodcuts (fig. 13 or pl. 4 and fig. 14), they must convey a similar sacramental meaning. The Lord seems to gesture toward them, in fact, as the remedy for original sin. The final woodcut of the Expulsion (figs. 23 and 24) provides one last link between the pictures and their text, which states that Adam and Eve were expelled from Paradise by an angel with a "fiery sword." This passage is depicted literally in both the 1487 and 1488 versions, in which the angel's sword bursts into flame. Although the artist may have known similar flaming swords in some of the Dutch History Bibles,[45] he seems to have adapted them here to the text at hand.

Further investigation of this prolifically illustrated book may reveal similar connections between its text and woodcuts beyond chapter 2. As in the Dutch History Bibles recently investigated by Sandra Hindman, only a knowledge of the text can explain the original iconography of the scenes.[46] Although parallels for many of the individual motifs of these woodcuts occur in earlier sources, the cuts for the Life of Christ reveal the artist's desire to illustrate the devotional spirit of the book as well as its actual descriptions of events.

The meditational character of this unjustly ignored, intimate book corresponds to the personal tone of much of the literature of the Devotio Moderna.[47] As James Marrow noted, the increased use of the vernacular in this period encouraged the pious to write their own accounts of Christ's life as a means of expressing their devotion.[48] This Dutch book, which appeared in at least eleven editions in less than fifty years, seems to have been one of the most successful of these personal interpretations. Its extraordinary popularity must have resulted from its appealing, colloquial text, its spirited, original illustrations, and its alleged association with Ludolphus's renowned *Vita Christi.*

## NOTES

1. Marinus F. A. G. Campbell, *Annales de la typographie néerlandaise au XVe siècle* (The Hague: M. Nijhoff, 1874), no. 1181 (hereafter cited as Campbell). For the Rosenwald Collection copy, see Library of Congress, *The Lessing J. Rosenwald Collection: A Catalog of the Gifts of Lessing J. Rosenwald to the Library of Congress, 1943 to 1975* (Washington: Library of Congress, 1977), p. 103, no. 540. See the facsimile of the woodcuts by Luc Indestege, *Tboeck vanden leven ons Heeren Iesu Christi (Geeraert Leeu, Antwerpen, 1487)*, Vereeniging der Antwerpsche Bibliophielen, 2d ed., 3d ser. (Antwerp, 1952).

2. Campbell 1182 (Delft: Christian Snellaert, 1488) and 1183 (Antwerp: Claes Leeu, 1488). For the Delft edition, see Library of Congress, *Lessing J. Rosenwald Collection*, p. 96, no. 496.

3. The following editions are recorded:
   a. 1495, Zwolle, Pieter van Os (Campbell 1184)
   b. 1499, Zwolle, Pieter van Os (Campbell 1185; Rosenwald Collection, no. 507)
   c. 1503, Antwerp, H. Eckert van Homberch (Wouter Nijhoff and Maria E. Kronenberg, *Nederlandsche bibliographie van 1500 tot 1540*, 3 vols. in 7 [The Hague: M. Nijhoff, 1923–66], no. 1407 [hereafter cited as Nijhoff and Kronenberg]; Rosenwald Collection, no. 1112)
   d. 1510, Antwerp, A. van Berghen (Nijhoff and Kronenberg 1408)
   e. 1512, Antwerp, H. Eckert van Homberch (Nijhoff and Kronenberg 1409; Rosenwald Collection, no. 1125)
   f. 1521, Antwerp, H. Eckert van Homberch (Nijhoff and Kronenberg 1410)
   g. 1521, Antwerp, Claes de Grave (Nijhoff and Kronenberg 1411)
   h. 1536, Antwerp, Claes de Grave (Nijhoff and Kronenberg 1412)

Mistakes in colophons led some authors to list other editions: e.g., Willem Moll, *Johannes Brugman en het godsdienstig leven onzer vaderen in de vijftiende eeuw*, 2 vols. (Amsterdam: G. Portielie & Zoon, 1854), 2: 272, listed editions in Zwolle of 1515 and 1519 that are identical with the 1495 and 1499 editions mentioned above. See Nijhoff and Kronenberg 0835 and 0836.

4. William Martin Conway, *The Woodcutters of the Netherlands in the Fifteenth Century* (Cambridge: University Press, 1884), p. 279.

5. M. J. Schretlen, *Dutch and Flemish Woodcuts of the Fifteenth Century* (London: E. Benn, 1925), p. 41. Schretlen concluded that the Delft blocks, which he attributed to the "Master of the Virgin among the Virgins," were "very coarsely copied" by the Antwerp artist. Arthur M. Hind, in *An*

*Introduction to a History of Woodcut*, 2 vols. (London: Constable and Co., 1935; reprint ed., New York: Dover Publications, 1963), 2:571, admitted that the Delft cuts often displayed greater originality than the blocks of the 1487 editions, which he believed to have been executed by three different artists. Compare F. W. H. Hollstein, *Dutch and Flemish Etchings, Engravings, and Woodcuts, ca. 1450–1700*, 22 vols. (Amsterdam: M. Hertzberger, 1949–80), 12:200, who listed both sets of woodcuts, as well as seven later editions of the book, as works by the "Master of the Virgin among the Virgins."

6. Rosenwald Collection, no. 508; Campbell 1767 (H. Eckert van Homberch). See also Rosenwald Collection, no. 1136 (Antwerp: H. Eckert van Homberch, 1516) and Nijhoff and Kronenberg 1195. Conway, *Woodcutters of the Netherlands*, p. 277, lists the Delft cut of Man and Scripture as one of the illustrations made for the 1487 *Passionael* (Campbell 1763).

7. I am grateful to Mr. Roger Wieck for supplying me with this information. According to Mr. Wieck, who is preparing a dissertation on illustrated Ludolphus manuscripts, only fifteen of these manuscripts are illuminated.

8. Mary Immaculate Bodenstedt, *The Vita Christi of Ludolphus the Carthusian*, The Catholic University of America, Studies in Medieval and Renaissance Latin Language and Literature, vol. 16 (Washington: The Catholic University of America Press, 1944), p. 19, with references to specific copies listed in n. 97, p. 19.

9. Ibid., pp. 19–23, cites over sixty Latin editions after 1472 and many translations in various languages. For the influence and popularity of the *Vita Christi*, see ibid., pp. 53–92, and Charles Abbott Conway, *The Vita Christi of Ludolph of Saxony and Late Medieval Devotion Centred on the Incarnation: A Descriptive Analysis*, Analecta Cartusiana, 34 (Salzburg: Institut für Englische Sprache und Literatur, Universität Salzburg, 1976), pp. 1–2.

10. The most complete treatment of Ludolphus's sources occurs in Bodenstedt, *Vita Christi*, pp. 24–52.

11. Ludolphus's concluding prayers have been published and translated by Sister Mary Immaculate Bodenstedt, *Praying the Life of Christ: First English Translation of the Prayers Concluding the 181 Chapters of the Vita Christi of Ludolphus the Carthusian*, Analecta Cartusiana, 15 (Salzburg: Institut für Englische Sprache und Literatur, Universität Salzburg, 1973).

12. The 1487 and 1488 editions, for instance, are approximately 26 by 19 cm, in comparison to the Strasbourg edition of 1474 at the Pierpont Morgan Library that measures 37 by 30 cm. The Dutch texts are 5 cm thick, moreover, as opposed to the 10-cm thickness of the 1474 Latin version.

13. The title page of the work cataloged as Ludolphus de Saxonia, *Vita Christi* (Zwolle: Pieter van Os, 1499), Rosenwald Collection, no. 507, for instance, reads: "Dat booc vanden leuen Ons Liefs Here Ih̃u Cristi derdeweruen gheprint, ghecorrigeert eñ merckelijc verbetert met addicien van sconen moralen ende gheesteliken leringhen en deuoten meditacien. . . ." For the 1488 Antwerp title page with similar wording, see *Catalogue of Books Printed in the XVth Century Now in the British Museum*, 10 vols. in 11 (London, 1908–71), part 9, *Holland and Belgium* (London, 1967; lithographic reprint of the 1962 edition), p. 198.

14. Moll, *Johannes Brugman*, 2:44–45 and 272–74. For the editions, see n. 3 above.

15. The most extensive series of Adam and Eve scenes occur earlier in the Middle Ages, in the works of art that belong to the "Cotton Genesis" group, so-called from the severely mutilated sixth-century Greek manuscript at the British Museum (Ms. Cotton Otho B. VI). The earliest extant examples to derive from this tradition occur in full-page frontispieces to Genesis in the large Carolingian Bibles produced at Tours (see Herbert L. Kessler, "Hic Homo Formatur: The Genesis Frontispieces of the Carolingian Bibles," *Art Bulletin* 53 [1971]: 143–60). For the Cotton Genesis recension in general, see Kurt Weitzmann, "Observations on the Cotton Genesis Fragments," in *Late Classical and Mediaeval Studies in Honor of Albert Mathias Friend, Jr.*, ed. Kurt Weitzmann (Princeton, N.J.: Princeton University Press, 1955), pp. 112–31 and Rosalie B. Green, "The Adam and Eve Cycle in the Hortus Deliciarum," ibid., pp. 340–47.

16. Such as Ms. 2771, of about 1450–60, in the Nationalbibliothek, Vienna, fol. 10 (fig. 4). See Vienna, Nationalbibliothek, *Die illuminierten Handschriften und Inkunabeln der Österreichischen Nationalbibliothek*, ed. Otto Pächt (Vienna: Verlag der Österreichischen Akademie der Wissenschaften, 1974–), vol. 3, *Holländische Schule* (Vienna, 1975), p. 50, pl. V. Similar Creation pages occur, e.g., in London, British Library Add. ms. 15410, fol. 10, ca. 1440 (Alexander Willem Byvanck and G. J. Hoogewerff, *La Miniature hollandaise et les manuscrits illustrés du XIVe au XVIe siècle aux Pays-Bas septentrionaux* (The Hague: M. Nijhoff, 1922–26), no. 60; Amsterdam, Koninklijk Oudheidkundig Genootschap, fol. 1 (ibid., no. 61, pl. 112, ca. 1445); and The Hague, Koninklijke Bibliotheek, Ms. 78 D 39, fol. Hv., ca. 1468 (ibid., no. 110, pl. 52).

17. E.g., London, British Library, Add. ms. 38122, fols. 9v, 13v, and 15v; London, British Library, Add. ms. 16951, fols. 14, 19, and 20; London, British Library, Add. ms. 10043, fols. 6v, 7v, and 8v; and The Hague, Koninklijke Bibliotheek, Ms. 78 D 38, fols. 7v, 8v, and 9v. I am grateful to Sandra Hindman for this information.

18. For the two versions of the Haywain at the Prado and the Escorial, see Max J. Friedländer, *Early Netherlandish Painting*, trans. H. Norden from *Die Altniederländische Malerei*, published 1924–37, 11 vols. (New York: Praeger, 1967–74), vol. 5 (1969), no. 111, pls. 103–6. For the Last Judgment Triptych at the Gemäldegalerie der Akademie der Bildenden Künste, see ibid., no. 85, pls. 66–68.

19. Conway, *Woodcutters of the Netherlands*, p. 229, noted that many of the 1487 cuts were copied from the Cologne Bible, although he did not specify which ones. For Quentell's Bible, see especially Hind, *History of Woodcut*, 1:358–62, and James Strachan, *Early Bible Illustrations: A Short Study Based on Some Fifteenth and Early Sixteenth Century Printed Texts* (Cambridge: University Press, 1957), pp. 11–15.

20. The most comprehensive treatment of medieval cosmology occurs in S. K. Heninger, Jr., *The Cosmographical Glass: Renaissance Diagrams of the Universe* (San Marino, Calif.: Huntington Library, 1977). See also Ellen Judith Beer, *Die Rose der Kathedrale von Lausanne, und der kosmologische Bilderkreis des Mittelalters* (Bern: Benteli Verlag, 1952), pp. 18–32, and H. Holländer, "Weltall, Weltbild," in *Lexikon der christlichen Ikonographie*, ed. Engelbert Kirschbaum et al., vol. 4 (Freiburg im Breisgau, 1972), pp. 498–509.

21. See, for example, Isidore's *Etymologiarum* 13 (Jacques Paul Migne, ed., *Patrologiae latina*, vol. 82, cols. 471–96) and *De natura rerum*, especially chaps. 9 and 11 (ibid., vol. 83, cols. 977–78 and 979–82). The writings of later encyclopedists were equally important; e.g., Bede, *De natura rerum*, especially chaps. 3–11 (ibid., vol. 90, cols. 192–208).

22. Vienna, Nationalbibliothek, Ms. 2771, fol. 9 (Vienna, Nationalbibliothek, *Holländische Schule*, pp. 49–50, pl. IV).

23. Rosenwald Collection, nos. 163 and 166. Ludwig F. T. Hain, *Repertorium Bibliographicum . . .*, 2 vols. in 4 (Stuttgart: J. G. Cotta, 1826–38), nos. 14508 and 14510 (hereafter cited as Hain). For this major publication, see the study by Adrian Wilson, *The Making of the Nuremberg Chronicle* (Amsterdam: Nico Israel, 1977).

24. For this complicated diagram, see Rudolf Bernoulli, "Das Weltallbild in Hartmann Schedels Weltchronik," in *Buch und Bucheinband: Aufsätze und graphische Blätter zum 60. Geburtstage von Hans Loubier* (Leipzig: K. W. Hiersemann, 1923), pp. 48–58.

25. The space occupied by the highest heaven in the Dutch miniature is identified as the Empyrium in the text on folio 10. On the Empyrium in general, see Robert Hughes, *Heaven and Hell in Western Art* (New York: Stein and Day, 1968), pp. 111–12.

26. Bernoulli, "Weltallbild," pp. 56–57, and Strachan, *Early Bible Illustrations*, p. 12.

27. Bernoulli, "Weltallbild," p. 56. The influence of the Cologne woodcut continued for several decades, as indicated by variations of it in many later books (e.g., the Lübeck Bible, published by Steffen Arndes in 1494; Rosenwald Collection, no. 168, Hain 3143).

28. Thomas of Cantimpré, *De naturis rerum*, Munich, Staatsbibliothek, Clm. 2655, fol. 105. For this diagram, see Beer, *Die Rose*, pp. 22–23, fig. 54, and Anna C. Esmeijer, *Divina Quaternitas; a Preliminary Study in the Method and Application of Visual Exegesis* (Amsterdam: Gorcum, 1978), pp. 102–4, fig. 84b.

29. Bernoulli, "Weltallbild," p. 57, with the woodcut from the second edition in Heidelberg reproduced as fig.3. For the first edition in Vienna (National Library, Incunable II.D. 42), see Ottokar Smital's introduction in *Symbolum Apostolicum. A Facsimile after the Unique Copy in the Vienna National Library* (Paris: Pegasus Press, 1927). For the second edition in the University Library in Heidelberg, see Paul Kristeller, *Decalogus, Septimania Poenalis, Symbolum Apostolicum*, Graphische Gesellschaft 4. Veröffentlichung (Berlin: B. Cassirer, 1907), pls. XVII–XXV, and for the third edition in the State Library in Munich, see Paul Kristeller, *Symbolum Apostolicum: Blockbuch-Unicum der K. Hof- und Staatsbibliothek zu München*, Graphische Gesellschaft 23. Veröffentlichung (Berlin: B. Cassirer, 1917).

30. Cf. Bernoulli, "Weltallbild," p. 55. It is notable, however, that only seven stars appear in the middle ring in both the Munich edition (Kristeller, *Symbolum Apostolicum*, pl. 1) and the Heidelberg edition, which does not include the labels (Kristeller, *Decalogus*, pl. XVII).

31. Plato, *Timaeus*, 40a. *Plato, with an English Translation*, vol. 7, trans. Robert Gregg Bury (1929; reprint ed., Cambridge, Mass.: Harvard University Press, 1961–), p. 85.

32. Rosenwald Collection, no. 157; Hain 4990.

33. Musée Condé, Ms. 65, fol. 25v. For this manuscript, see Millard Meiss, *French Painting in the Time of Jean de Berry: The Limbourgs and Their Contemporaries*, 2 vols. (New York: G. Braziller, 1974), pp. 143–224 and 308–24.

34. See ibid., p. 343, where this miniature, "Les Antiquités judaïques" (Paris, Bibliothèque nationale, ms. fr. 247, fol. 3), is attributed to the "Harvard Hannibal Master." The other eleven large miniatures in this manuscript were executed by Jean Fouquet. According to Meiss, p. 44, this type of scene originated in the Boucicaut workshop. See also, for instance, the similar miniature of about 1415 in a French translation of Bartholomaeus Anglicus in Cambridge, Fitzwilliam Museum, Ms. 251, fol. 16, reproduced in color in Millard Meiss, *French Painting in the Time of Jean de Berry: The Boucicaut Master* (London: Phaidon, 1968), fig. 457.

35. London, British Library, Add. ms. 16951, fol. 17. The rivers issue from the towers of a palace in the illustration in a Bible in Munich, Bayerische Staatsbibliothek, Cod. Germ. 1102, fol. 7, and from the doors of a castle in a Bible in The Hague, Koninklijke Bibliotheek, ms. 78 D 38, fol. 7. I am grateful to Sandra Hindman for this information.

36. This woodcut, however, seems to have been the model for an additional scene in the 1499 edition of the *Leven van Christi*, Rosenwald Collection, no. 507, and this scene was in turn used in some of the later editions.

37. Folio VII. For the symbolism of the trees in this woodcut, see R. A. Koch, "Martin Schongauer's Dragon Tree," *Tribute to Wolfgang Stechow, Print Review* 5 (1976):115–16, with the Nuremberg woodcut reproduced as fig. 2.

38. Madrid, Museo del Prado (Friedländer, *Early Netherlandish Painting*, 5, no. 110, pls. 100–102).

39. Paul A. Underwood, "The Fountain of Life in Manuscripts of the Gospels," *Dumbarton Oaks Papers* 5 (1950):88.

40. Paris, Bibliothèque nationale, ms. lat. 8850, fol. 6v. For this miniature see ibid., pp. 46–53, fig. 26.

41. For the similar wording in the modern missal, see *Roman Missal in Latin and English* (New York: Benziger Brothers, 1910), p. 543. Compare Underwood, who traces this prayer to the sixth century, "Fountain of Life," p. 52.

42. "Baptismus intantum aperit baptizato januam regni caelestis, inquantum incorporat eum passioni Christi." *Summa theologiae* 3a. 69. 7. Saint Thomas Aquinas, *Summa theologiae* (London: Blackfriars, 1964–), vol. 57, Latin text and English trans. James Justin Cunningham (London, 1975), p. 142. Compare Barbara G. Lane, "Rogier's Saint John and Miraflores Altarpieces Reconsidered," *Art Bulletin* 60 (1978):670–71, and J. Daniélou, *Sacramentum futuri; études sur les origines de la typologie biblique* (Paris: Beauchesne, 1950), pp. 16–17.

43. "Ecclesia paradisi instar exprimens arbores frugiferas intra muros suos intus inclusit . . . has arbores rigat quattuor fluminibus id est evangeliis quattuor, quibus baptismi gratiam salutari et caelesti inundatione largitur." *Epistulae* 73, chap. 10. *Corpus Scriptorum Ecclesiasticorum Latinorum* (Vienna: C. Geroldi filium, 1866–), vol. 3, ed. Guilelmus Hartel, pt. 2 (1868), p. 785. Compare Underwood, "Fountain of Life," p. 73, and Daniélou, *Sacramentum futuri*, p. 17.

44. Bodenstedt, *Praying the Life of Christ*, p. 1, transcribes the Latin with a translation: "Qui me fecisti, refice infectum vitiis; qui me formasti, reforma corruptum peccatis; ut secundum magnam tuam misericordiam salves animam meam miseram." ("Thou who didst make me, restore me for I am stained with vices; thou who didst form me, fashion me over again for I am corrupted by sins. Then through thy great mercy salvation will dawn for my wretched soul.") The Dutch prayer in the 1487 edition reads: "Die mij gescapen hebīte: wilt mij hermaken eñ reformeren die met sondē besmet eñ ghecorrūpeert ben, op dattu nae dijn groote ontfermherticheijt salich makes mijn arme ziele."

45. For example, the Dutch History Bibles in London, British Library, Add. ms. 10043, fol. 8v. and The Hague, Koninklijke Bibliotheek, Ms. 78 D 38, fol. 9v. I am grateful to Sandra Hindman for this reference.

46. Sandra Hindman, *Text and Image in Fifteenth-Century Illustrated Dutch Bibles*, Verzameling van Middelnederlandse bijbeleksten: Miscellanea; vol. 1 (Leiden: Brill, 1977), passim.

47. For this movement, see Regnerus R. Post, *The Modern Devotion: Confrontation with Reformation and Humanism* (Leiden: E. J. Brill, 1968). The meditational character of Ludolphus's own text may, of course, also account in part for its popularity.

48. James H. Marrow, *Passion Iconography in Northern European Art of the Late Middle Ages and Early Renaissance: A Study of the Transformation of Sacred Metaphor into Descriptive Narrative* (Kortrijk, Belgium: Van Ghemmert Pub. Co., 1979), pp. 21–22.

KEITH P. F. MOXEY

# *THE SHIP OF FOOLS* AND THE IDEA OF FOLLY IN SIXTEENTH-CENTURY NETHERLANDISH LITERATURE

Among the books given to the Library of Congress by Lessing J. Rosenwald are two sixteenth-century Flemish translations of *The Ship of Fools* by Sebastian Brant. Following its publication in Basel in 1494, this work went on to become one of the most successful published works of the age. At least twelve German editions appeared before Brant's death in 1521.[1] Its translation into Latin by Jacob Locher in 1497 made the book accessible to an international audience, for it was this translation on which subsequent French, English, and Flemish translations were based. The Flemish translation of *The Ship of Fools* was first published in 1500 by a Flemish printer living in Paris called Guyot Marchand (originally Guide Coopman). John Sinnema has shown that although it is largely based on Locher's Latin translation, it also contains references to earlier French and German editions.[2] Editions of Marchand's translation appeared in Antwerp in 1504, 1548, and 1584. The books given to the Library by Mr. Rosenwald are examples of the editions of 1548 and 1584 (figs. 1 and 2).[3] The woodcuts in both books are copies of those that illustrated the German edition of 1494, together with additional cuts added to the Locher translation.

The intent of this paper is to sketch the literary context in which the Flemish translation of Brant's book first appeared, showing that Brant's work corresponded to a preexistent literary genre of moralizing or didactic poetry and defining the character of the Flemish productions so as to be able to demonstrate the ways in which they differ from Brant's work as well as the extent to which they were indebted to it.[4] The extraordinary popularity of this moralizing literature poses fascinating questions for our understanding of Netherlandish culture of this period. Why were these poems so popular? What social function did they serve? Although an attempt to provide definitive answers to such questions is beyond the scope of this essay, such questions can at least be formulated and considered in this context.

The idea of folly as the organizing principle of a moralizing poem was already familiar in the Netherlands before the publication of *The Ship of Fools*. Jacob van Oestvoren's *De Blauwe Schuit* (*The Blue Boat*) which was written in Flanders or Brabant early in the fifteenth century depends on this idea.[5] Oestvoren's poem was inspired by a medieval literary tradition known as the estates satires in which the social abuses committed by each class and profession are cataloged and criticized in what was meant to serve as a call for social cooperation and unity in the fulfillment of God's plan for mankind.[6] Oestvoren's "Blue Boat" is the name of a mock "guild" of the type associated with the celebration of carnival. Membership in this guild is dependent upon the extent to which one's actions are subject to the vagaries of folly. Those termed worthy of inclusion, for example, are nobles who fail to live within their means, men who waste their money on women and drink, monks who lead a luxurious life and who embezzle the funds of their monasteries, nuns who are unchaste, women who marry old men and old men who marry young women, and,

Der sotten schip

oft dat Narren schip

FIGURE 1. Title Page. Sebastian Brant, *Der sotten schip, oft, Dat Narrenschip* (Antwerp: M. Ancxt, 1548), Rosenwald Collection, no. 1169.

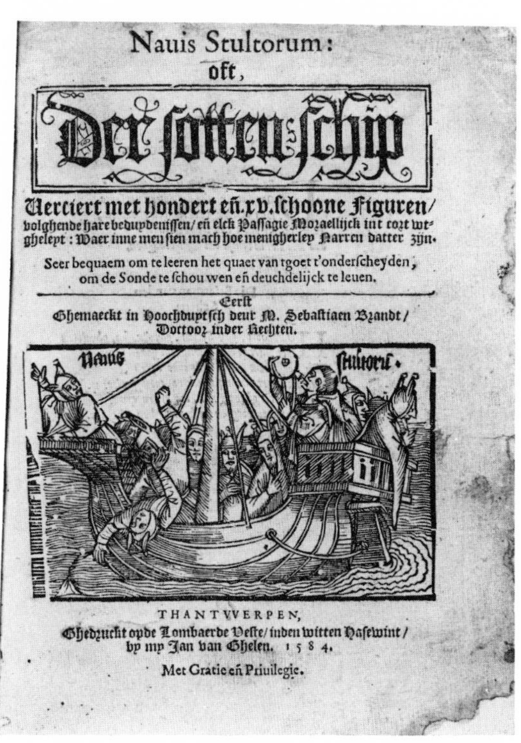

Nauis Stultorum:

oft,

Der sotten schip

Verciert met hondert eñ.xv.schoone Figuren/ volghende hare bedupdenissen/ eñ elck Passagie Morаellijck int cort wtghelept: Waer inne men sien mach hoe menigherley Narren datter zijn.

Seer bequaem om te leeren het quaet van tgoet t'onderscheyden, om de Sonde te schouwen eñ deuchdelijck te leuen.

Eerst Ghemaeckt in Hoochduptsch deur M. Sebastiaen Brandt/ Doctoor inder Rechten.



THANTVVERPEN,

Ghedruckt opde Lombaerde Veste/ inden witten Hasewint/ by mp Jan van Ghelen. 1584.

Met Gratie eñ Priuilegie.

FIGURE 2. Title Page. Sebastian Brant, *Nauis stultorum, oft, Der sotten schip* (Antwerp: J. van Ghelen, 1584), Rosenwald Collection, no. 1206.

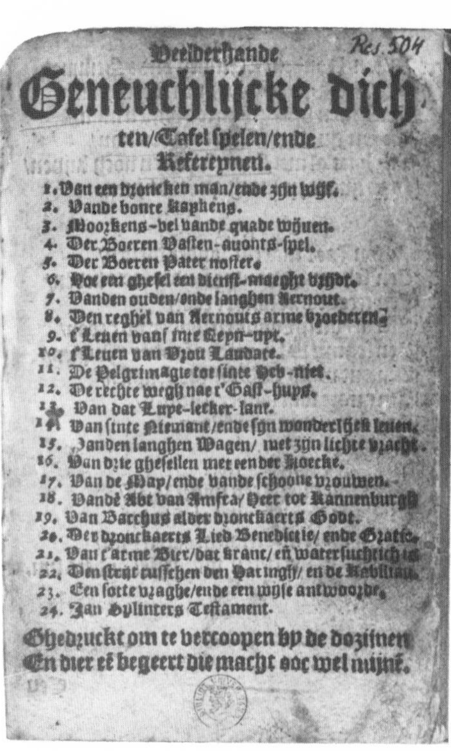
Res. 504

Veelderhande
Geneuchlijcke dich
ten/Tafel ſpelen/ende
Refereynen.
1. Van een droncken man/ende zijn wijf.
2. Vande bonte Kapkens.
3. Moorkens-vel vande quade wijuen.
4. Der Boeren Vasten-auonts-ſpel.
5. Der Boeren Pater noster.
6. Hoe een ghesel een dienst-maeght vrijdt.
7. Vanden ouden/ende langhen Aernout.
8. Den reghel van Aernouts arme broederen.
9. t'Leuen vans ſinte Reyn-uyt.
10. t'Leuen van Vrou Laudate.
11. De Pelgrimagie tot ſinte Heb-niet.
12. De rechte wegh nae t'Gast-huys.
13. Van dat Luye-lecker-lant.
14. Van ſinte Niemant/ende ſijn wonderlijck leuen.
15. Vanden langhen Wagen/ met zijn lichte vracht.
16. Van drie ghesellen met een der Hoercke.
17. Van de Map/ende vande ſchoone vrouwen.
18. Vandē Abt van Amfra/Heer tot Kannenburgh
19. Van Bacchus alder dronckaerts Godt.
20. Der dronckaerts Lied Benedicitie/ ende Gratie.
21. Van t'arme Bier/dat krant/eñ watersuchtich is
22. Den strijt tusschen den Haringh/ en de Kabilliau.
23. Een sotte vraghe/ende een wijse antwoorde.
24. Jan Splinters Testament.

Ghedruckt om te vercoopen by de dozijnen
En dier eē begeert die macht ooc wel nijnē.

FIGURE 3. Title Page.
*Veelderhande Geneuchlijcke Dichten* (Antwerp, 1600), Ghent, Universiteits Bibliotheek, Res. 504. Courtesy Universiteits Bibliotheek.

lastly, youths who spend their time in taverns, dancing and gambling when they should be at home. The criterion for membership in the "guild" is defined as follows:

> Now someone might ask if he wished to come into the guild, whether he should fulfill all the requirements specified above. We would have to answer in the following terms: The candidate should look inside himself and observe the conduct of his life and social intercourse, his habits and all other aspects of the routine that he is accustomed to perform on a daily basis. If he finds more indications that incline him to wisdom—to wisdom, that is, rather than to folly—then he cannot become a member of our guild. But he who sees in himself more similarities with the type of conduct described above than could permit the pursuit of a virtuous life, and which rule his behavior as well as cause him financial loss, then this man must come aboard our ship and become a member of our guild.[7]

The treatment of folly in *The Ship of Fools* differs significantly from that of *The Blue Boat*. Not only is Brant's list of objectionable kinds of behavior far longer, but the tone of criticism is quite distinct. Gone is the lighthearted attitude of the composer of the parodic guild. Brant is not content simply to list the varieties of moral failure but instead subjects them to a detailed analysis and condemns them at length, bringing to bear the full force of his considerable biblical and humanistic learning. The list of those reprimanded is encyclopedic. Rather than restrict himself to the criticism of representatives of the various estates and occupations, Brant deals with moral issues affecting all members of society. The list is an inventory of morally questionable activities that range from the serious to the downright petty, from examples of the seven deadly sins to those who buy more books than they can read or who fail to obey their doctor's orders. The book thus transcends the tradition of the estates satires and becomes a moral critique of the human condition rather than of the social structure.[8]

Reflections of *The Blue Boat* and possibly of *The Ship of Fools* as well can be found in several of the poems included in the collection known as the *Veelderhande Geneuchlijcke Dichten* (*Assorted Pleasant Poems*) (fig. 3).[9] The first preserved edition of this collection is that published in Antwerp in 1600, but since some of the poems are known to have been in circulation considerably earlier, it is thought likely that there was an early sixteenth-century edition that has been lost.[10] One of these poems, entitled *Van den Langhen Waghen ende van zijn licht-gheladen Vracht van alderhande volcxken* (*Concerning the Long Wagon and Its Lightweight Freight Consisting of Various Types of People*)[11] substitutes transport on a wagon for membership in a guild as a metaphor of folly. The poem resembles *The Blue Boat* in consisting of a list of morally questionable activities that in this case qualify one for passage on the "Long Wagon." The passengers include prostitutes, priests, nuns, drunkards, quacks, beggars, and misers. By way of conclusion, the author invites anyone who considers himself qualified to come aboard and make himself comfortable. As the wagon sets off, the author remarks on the load's lack of weight. Despite the crowd of people, the load is so light that it threatens to blow away in the wind. The lightness of the load is clearly intended as a metaphor for the insignificance of those whose lives are marked by sinfulness or folly. Although the Flemish edition of *The Ship of Fools* neither mentions nor illustrates the idea of a wagon full of fools, it is possible that the anonymous author of *Van den Langhen Waghen* drew his inspiration from one of the German editions in which this idea is discussed in the prologue as well as illustrated on the title page.[12]

Another poem in the same collection, bearing the title *Van de bonte Kapkens diemen nu eerst nieus ghepracktiseert ende ghevonden heeft* (*Concerning the Gay Caps That Men Have Recently Invented and Begun to Wear*),[13] makes the sale of foolscaps an allegory of foolishness. The poem takes the form of a soliloquy, or rather a sales pitch, delivered by a peddler to an audience that includes the reader. The peddler praises the foolscaps, remarking on their bright colors, their snug fit, their warmth, and the fact that they are fitted with ears that can be flapped about so as to ring the bells on the ends. Disappointed by the lack of response, he tells the audience that he will take his wares elsewhere and offer them to those he knows will appreciate them. He then lists various types of people whose behavior is sinful and therefore, it is implied, foolish. He mentions men who patronize prostitutes, those who waste money on banquets, those who regard themselves higher than their station, those who are offended by the good fortune of others, those who are avaricious, those who sing before their sweethearts' windows, and others.

The foolscaps, which are the central symbol of folly on which the work depends, are a frequently cited symbol in *The Ship of Fools*. The motif is most prominent in the German editions, where they are mentioned in the prologue as well as in the poet's apology that concludes the work. In the former, Brant asserts:

> I cut a cap for every chap,
> But none of them will care a rap.
> And if I'd named and then apprised him,
> He'd say I had not recognized him.[14]

In the apology, Brant admits that,

> If men should scold me, saying:
> "Please O doctor, cure your own disease,
> For you are also foolish, odd—"
> I know it, I confess to God,
> Of Folly I was never free,
> I've joined the fool's fraternity.
> I pull the cap which I would fain doff,
> Yet my fool's cap will not come off.[15]

Another indication that the author of the *Gay Caps* was familiar with *The Ship of Fools* is his inclusion of those who serenade beneath their sweethearts' windows among the examples of foolish behavior. This action corresponds precisely with the contents of Brant's chapter 62, "Of Serenading at Night."[16]

The poem entitled *Den Rechten Weg nae 't Gasthuys* (*The Right Way to the Poorhouse*), belonging to the same collection, was first published in French at Lyons in 1502.[17] Like *The Blue Boat* the poem is a list of types of foolish behavior but this time it is carefully chosen with an eye for the financial losses such behavior may occasion. Among the various social types criticized in this manner are merchants who buy dear and sell cheap, gamblers who lose their money and their time, entertainers who spend their earnings as easily as they were obtained, people who go to sleep early and who wake up late, businessmen who have lost their goods and who are no longer trusted by investors, and those who live beyond their means.

In contrast to the French original as well as its English translation, the Dutch version of *The Right Way to the Poorhouse* concludes with the testament of the poorhouse owner, which specifies the types of people who may not, under any circumstances, be allowed into his institution. This prohibition, which seems to echo the list of those not permitted membership in *The Blue Boat*, includes people who do all things according to measure, who handle their affairs in such a way as always to make a profit, or who lead a sober life, as well as young men who prefer the church to the tavern and artisans who prefer to work rather than waste their money on drink.

According to W. G. Moore, *The Right Way to the Poorhouse* was strongly influenced by *The Ship of Fools*. He supports his view by pointing out several correspondences between the subject matter of the two works,[18] similarities which are so general, however, that they do not overcome this reader's impression that the two books are completely different in conception and purpose. It is possible that the author of *The Poorhouse* was aware of Brant's book, but the animating idea of *The Ship* is that folly is a moral deficiency, whereas that of *The Poorhouse* is that folly is economic irresponsibility. The essential messages of the works, therefore, are sufficiently distinct to suggest that any similarity between the two is the result of a common attitude toward certain moral failings.

The variety and the strength of imagination that characterizes the native tradition of moralizing poetry is demonstrated by the poem known as the *Schip van*

FIGURE 4. Aertgen van Leyden, *Het Schip van Sinte Reynuut*, woodcut, ca. 1530. Oxford, Ashmolean Museum of Art and Archaeology. Courtesy Photographic Service, Ashmolean Museum.

*Sint Reynuut* (*St. Empty's Ship*) (fig. 4), which accompanied a large woodcut illustrating the subject by Aertgen van Leyden published in Amsterdam about 1530.[19] St. Empty was a popular saint in Netherlandish literature of the sixteenth century. A poem entitled *'t Leven van Sinte Reynuut* (*The Life of St. Empty*) was included in the collection known as the *Assorted Pleasant Poems* and Mathijs de Casteleyn included a *Sermoen van Sente Reinhuut* (*St. Empty's Sermon*) in his *Konst van Rhetoriken* (*The Art of Poetry*) of 1548. In contrast to the other two poems, *St. Empty's Ship* belongs to the tradition of moralizing poetry we have been discussing. That is, it consists of a list of different social classes and occupations whose foolish behavior is regarded as morally reprehensible. The poem depends upon a pilgrimage metaphor: all those considered guilty of offense are thought qualified for a pilgrimage to St. Empty. St. Empty owes his name to his function as the patron saint of drinkers. It refers not only to their unquenchable thirst but to the consequences of their habit for their wallets.

As in the *Right Way to the Poorhouse*, foolish behavior is defined as that which leads to poverty and indigence. Among those thought worthy pilgrims are men who waste money on women, merchants who lose money, soldiers whose adventuring comes to nought, and monks, nuns, friars, and clerks who waste their money. Finally, entertainers, drunkards, prostitutes, pimps, painters, printers, and others are included in the list even though the nature of their transgressions is occasionally unspecified.

The woodcut inevitably recalls the frontispiece of the German editions of *The Ship of Fools* with its horse-drawn as well as its seafaring fools, though there is no exact correspondence of visual motifs. While the print is thoroughly original and most inventive and amusing in its satire of the actions of those obsessed by drink, it may be possible to discern echoes of the frontispiece of *The Ship of Fools* in the boats full of artisans and clerics carrying the implements of their trade at the center of the composition. They also recall the woodcut to chapter 48, "A Journeyman's Ship," in which representatives of the various trades are represented in boats.[20]

The closest parallel to *The Ship of Fools* in Netherlandish literature of the early sixteenth century is undoubtedly the book entitled *Vanden, x, esels* (*Concerning the Ten Donkeys*), which was published in Antwerp about 1530 and again in 1558 and 1580 (fig. 5).[21] According to the work itself it is a Flemish translation of an

FIGURE 5. Title Page, Detail. *Vanden, x, esels* (Antwerp: Jacob van Liesuelt, 1558). From *Het Volksboek Vanden, x, esels*, ed. A. van Elslander (Antwerp: De Sikkel, 1946).

English original. The translator is thought to have been the book's Flemish publisher, the printer Jan van Doesborch. In this case the poem does not depend on an allegory such as those which made foolishness a requirement for membership in a guild, a wagon ride, the possession of a foolscap, or entry to the poorhouse, but rather it depends upon a symbol—namely the equation of fools with donkeys. The use of the word *donkey* with the secondary meaning *fool* was well established both in the Netherlands and in Germany in the fifteenth and sixteenth centuries.[22] Brant, for example, made extensive use of this meaning of the word in *The Ship of Fools*.[23] The author of *The Ten Donkeys* claims to have enlisted the aid of a woman in choosing the ten men whose actions are most foolish and who are therefore worthy of growing ass's ears. His selection bears out this fiction, for most of the behavior criticized concerns relations between the sexes. He comments negatively on men who neglect their wives but patronize prostitutes, men who allow themselves to be dominated by their wives, men who suffer from unrequited love, men who own brothels, men who live off their wives' prostitution, men who are unreasonably jealous, merchants who speculate with the goods of others and risk bankruptcy, misers whose lives are dominated by avarice and whose fortunes are wasted by others after their deaths, men who boast of their success with women and display the gifts they have been given by them, and, finally, pimps who seduce young girls and lead them into prostitution. With only two exceptions the list is dominated by a sexual theme. In each case the men are characterized as foolish because of their failure to observe the ethical norms for sexual behavior.

The organization of the book, in which each of the moral failures is discussed in a separate chapter, is closely related to that of *The Ship of Fools*. In addition, each chapter is introduced by a distich in a way that resembles the lines of verse that precede the woodcuts and the text in Brant's book. Finally, the title page is illustrated with a woodcut divided into ten scenes, each of which represents one of the errors criticized in the text. Rudimentary and crude though these scenes may appear in comparison to the woodcuts that illustrate *The Ship of Fools*, they nevertheless provide visual emblems for the sins discussed in the text in a way that is analogous to the relation of text and image in Brant's book.

A poem that may betray the influence of *The Ship of Fools* was included in a collection assembled by Jan van Stijevoort in 1524.[24] The poem bears the refrain *Alle Sotten en draghen gheen bellen* ("All fools do not wear bells"), a line that bears a striking resemblance to the verse that introduces chapter 77 of the Dutch translation of Brant's book, which reads, *Hy is wel sot al draeght hy gheen bellen so wie hem laet vanden Esel quellen* ("Whoever allows himself to be plagued by the donkey [i.e., by folly], is a fool even though he doesn't wear bells").[25] Although Brant's chapter is mainly directed at men who are dominated by their wives or by their sensuality, the poem criticizes a variety of questionable traits including pride, anger, greed, and drunkenness.

Another poem in the same collection appears to have been inspired by *The Blue Boat*. The title is "Dees syn werdich in die gilde ghescreven" ("These Are

Erasme Roterodame
De la declamation des louenges de follie/stille facessieux et profitable pour congnoistre les erreurs et abuz du monde.

Stultorum numerus infinitus.

On les vend a Paris par Galliot du pre Marchant Libraire/demeurant sur le pont nostre dame a lenseigne de la Gallee/Et en la grād salle du palais au tiers pillier.

Auec priuilege



FIGURE 6. Title Page. Erasmus, *De la declamation des louenges de follie . . .* (Paris: Galliot du Pré, 1520), Oxford, Bodleian Library, Douce E.250. Courtesy of the Keeper, Department of Printed Books, Bodleian Library.

Worthy of Being Admitted to the Guild").[26] Its list of sins contains several echoes of those criticized in the earlier work. It includes those who fail to live within their means, widows who go drinking, wives who go out when their husbands are asleep, miserly parents, wasteful offspring, nuns who display their breasts, monks who forget their duties, maidens who are unchaste, clerics who chase women, dishonest merchants, drunkards, and many others.

The complex associations inherent in the concept of folly, an idea that was synonymous with madness and the license of carnival as well as with sinfulness, were brilliantly exploited by Erasmus in *The Praise of Folly* (fig. 6).[27] First published in Paris in 1511, the book went through thirty-six editions in cities throughout Europe before Erasmus's death in 1536.[28] Two editions based on the Latin original appeared in Antwerp in 1511 and 1512.

The first part of the book is an enormously witty ironic praise of folly spoken by none other than Dame Folly herself. By placing his praise of the idea of folly in the mouth of the personification of foolishness, Erasmus qualifies and compromises every statement he makes so as to rob it of its literal meaning. In the mouth of folly, foolishness becomes an indispensable positive force in human affairs. A force without which social intercourse would be impossible and without which the race could not reproduce, since it is the inspiration of human sexuality. Defining human nature as one part reason and five parts emotion and characterizing reason as divine and the emotions as foolish, Dame Folly asserts that human behavior must inevitably be under her control. Her position appears to be a philosophical recognition of the social release and institutional renewal brought about by the expression of the spirit of carnival as well as a sophisticated understanding of the contingent nature of human rationality. It is only on reflection that we realize that this attitude is expressed by none other than Dame Folly and that it must consequently be rejected as specious. Erasmus thus presents us with a fascinating paradox. By assembling the separate strands of the tradition of folly current in his time, the fool as the embodiment of the spirit of carnival on the one hand and as a symbol of sinfulness on the other, Erasmus created a figure whose statements could elicit both our approval and our disapproval.[29]

The second part of the book is more easily related to the type of literature we have been discussing. In it Erasmus examines the failings of different social classes and professions as well as morally questionable actions of all kinds. His attitude is closely related to that of the tradition of estates satires and there are unmistakable echoes of *The Ship of Fools*. By far the largest share of this analysis of professional sins is taken up with the lapses of the clergy, whose misguided and unethical activities he describes at length and with considerable satire.

*The Praise of Folly* differs significantly from the rest of the literature we have been discussing. Its structure depends upon an ancient literary model, that of the mock encomium, and its text is liberally sprinkled with references to ancient literature. The book is something of an "in joke" in which Erasmus tests the learning of his readers by references to unusual and esoteric sources. More than *The Ship of Fools* which also reflected the humanist erudition of its author, *The Praise of Folly* appears to be addressed to a relatively small audience of cultivated men. Whereas *The Ship of Fools* was rapidly translated into the vernacular, this process took longer in the case of *The Praise of Folly*.[30] It was translated into French and German in 1520, into Italian in 1539, and into English in 1549, but it was not published in Dutch until 1560.[31] It is of particular interest that the French translation, the one which might be assumed to have circulated most widely in the Netherlands, should have been subjected by its translator to a thoroughgoing moralization which served to remove its genial ambiguities and make it more like the tradition of estates satires to which *The Ship of Fools* belonged.[32] Moreover, this edition was provided with woodcuts from *The Ship of Fools*. Although these must have been well-nigh unintelligible in the context of Erasmus's work, they would have contributed to its didactic appearance by suggesting its contents were equivalent to those of the earlier work.

A poem whose irony may well have been inspired by *The Praise of Folly* is *De Eed van Meester Oom met vier ooren, Prince der dooren* (*The Oath of Master Uncle with Four Ears, the Prince of Fools*) (fig. 7).[33] It was written by Jan Colyns, the head of one of the Brussels dramatic societies as well as its official fool, in honor of a "Festival of Fools" held in Brussels in 1551 by the various dramatic societies of the cities and towns of Brabant.[34] A figure called the "Grijpier," meaning "grabber" or "taker," which is meant to be a pun on the word *griffier* or "clerk of court," addresses the King of Fools, asking his protection for a number of dubious moral types. The list of people is similar to that of *The Blue Boat* or those of the various poems of *The Assorted Pleasant Poems* collection. Starting with the clergy, the grabber requests royal protection for those who drink too much, those who borrow more than they can pay, nuns who leave the cloister, and monks who break their vows. Secondly, he recommends nobles who assert their chivalry on rented horses, braggarts without means, soldiers who would rather plunder than fight, and those who claim bravery yet show their rumps to the enemy. Thirdly, he seeks royal patronage for madams and whores, maidens who chase men, and women who weave with more than one spindle (that is, entertain more than one lover). They must, he says, at all costs be prevented from entering the poorhouse. Fourthly, the King's assistance is requested for those who spend today what they earn tomorrow and those who enjoy life outside the home but who do nothing but argue and fight within it. The fifth verse is the most closely related to the estates satires for it consists of a list of the ways in which different trades and professions cheat the public. Finally, the grabber recommends that the King set a good example to his subjects by going to bed late and rising late, frequenting taverns, and by exiling those who talk to the necessity of doing good works—unless they mean those performed in the whorehouse. The King is advised to be amorous but not too faithful, for whoever lives with only one woman leads a life of trouble. In conclusion the King is asked to swear to take care of all the rogues mentioned, and they in turn are asked to swear an oath of allegiance to him.

The poem depends upon a paradox similar to that which inspired *The Praise of Folly*. The plea for the protection of immoral behavior is ironic, because both the person to whom it is addressed, the King of Fools, as well as the petitioner, who is identified as an avaricious cheat on account of his name Grabber, are morally questionable individuals. Just as the reader cannot take Dame Folly's praise of folly seriously, we cannot accept this poem at face value either. The traditional list of foolish actions is inverted. Moral failure does not qualify one for membership in a guild of fools, for a ride on the long wagon, for a colorful cap, or for a trip to the poorhouse. Moral deficiency is in this case a virtue that entitles one to the protection of the King of Fools. Negative values are presented positively and can only be recognized for what they really are if one understands the irony that underlies the work as a whole.

Another poem which has been associated with *The Praise of Folly* is the *Leenhof der Gilden* (*The Feudal Property Court*) of Jan van den Berghe, which was

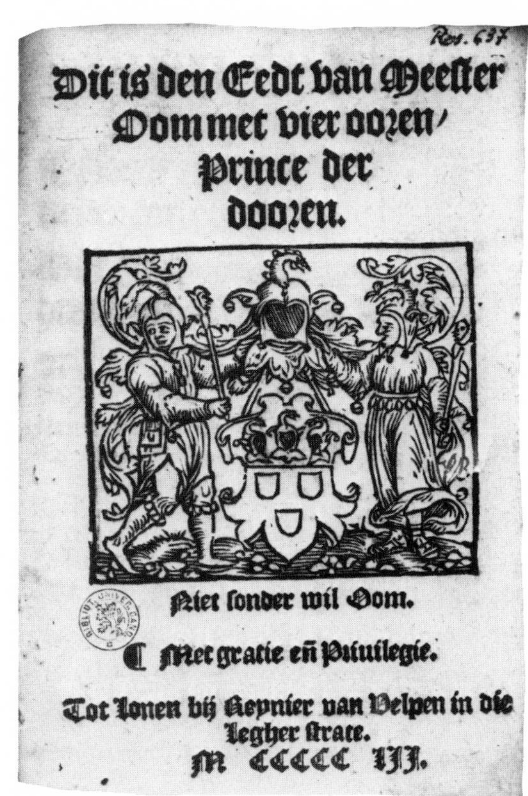


Dit is den Eedt van Meester Oom met vier ooren, Prince der dooren.

Niet sonder wil Oom.

Met gratie eñ Priuilegie.

Tot Louen bij Reynier van Uelpen in die Legher strate.
M CCCCC LII.

FIGURE 7. Title Page. Jan Colyns, *Dit is den Eedt van Meester Oom met vier ooren, Prince der dooren* (Louvain: Reynier van Velpen, 1552), Ghent, Universiteits Bibliotheek, Res. 637. Courtesy Universiteits Bibliotheek.

published in Antwerp in 1564.[35] The poem is a moral allegory which depends upon the description of an imaginary country or state carried out on the basis of its system of land ownership, a system that depends upon the operation of the feudal property court. The state's social classes, its estates, its cities, towns, and villages, and its inhabitants are all used as a means of criticizing moral transgressions. The poem consists of three parts. The first lists the abuses of the various inhabitants of the imaginary state, including the aristocracy, the clergy, the officials of the feudal property court, and the owners of feudal lands. Another describes and passes judgment upon the ways in which women abuse their husbands. A third warns against the abuses to which the feudal court is itself subject.

The allegory of *The Feudal Property Court* is carried out systematically and with considerable inventiveness. A striking change of mood between the first two and the third sections, however, robs the poem of its structural coherency. The first two are marked by a heavy-handed irony, but this element is missing from the account of some of the abuses to which feudal property transfers were susceptible.

Like *The Oath of Master Uncle*, *The Feudal Property Court* cannot be read literally. The satirical description of the kingdom and its inhabitants invites us to condemn their moral character. Similarly, the fact that women are rewarded for their vices is meant to strike the reader as paradoxical and unjust. Distant though the echoes of Erasmian wit may appear in these leaden ironies, it is possible that *The Praise of Folly* was the source of van den Berghe's inspiration. Confirmation of this interpretation is found in the author's introduction, where he stresses the light-hearted intention of the work, disclaiming responsibility for its contents by asserting that the poem was given to him in a tavern. This is an attitude that inevitably calls to mind Dame Folly's introduction to Erasmus's work.

Reviewing the moralizing poetry produced in the Netherlands in the first half of the sixteenth century in the light of the publication of Brant's *Ship of Fools*, several important questions deserve to be raised. First and foremost, what is the place of Brant's *Ship of Fools* in the context afforded by Netherlandish moralizing poetry? There is little doubt that Brant's book was the most thoroughgoing piece of moral instruction to use the concept of folly as its vehicle. Not only does Brant deal with a broader range of social types and moral situations but his advice is detailed and hard-hitting. Although the strength of Brant's criticism was tempered in the Flemish translation of the book as a consequence of its dependence on the Latin version of *The Ship of Fools* from which much original material was excluded, the work is still a very much more coherent moralization than the contemporary Flemish productions of the same kind. Flemish poems tend to be mere lists of offensive behavior rather than detailed commentaries on exemplary instances of such behavior. In contrast to *The Ship of Fools*, such poems as *The Blue Boat*, *The Gay Caps*, *The Long Wagon*, *St. Empty's Ship*, *The Oath of Master Uncle*, and *The Feudal Property Court* appear lighthearted and frivolous. The actions of the peddler in the *Gay Caps* prevent us from taking what he has to say very seriously. His attempt to hard sell his audience and his facetious descriptions of the appearance of the caps as well as of the benefits to be derived from wearing them all have a comic quality. Comedy also lies at the heart of the paradoxical *Oath of Master Uncle*. The irony of the poem delights and amuses us. The catalog of vices is hard to interpret as a serious indictment in view of the superficial and bantering tone of the work as a whole. Only the *Right Way to the Poorhouse*, *The Ten Donkeys*, and some portions of *The Feudal Property Court* deal with their subjects with an attitude anywhere near the sobriety that characterizes *The Ship of Fools*.

Brant's work, therefore, cannot be said to have decisively influenced the tradition of moralizing poetry in the Netherlands. Far from transforming the character of the native genre, *The Ship of Fools* added its own distinctive voice to what was an already well-established chorus. On the other hand, *The Ship* seems to have offered Netherlandish authors a repertoire of literary and visual ideas which they could incorporate in their own autonomous productions.

Erasmus's *Praise of Folly*, on the contrary, shares the lighthearted attitude toward moralizing that characterizes the Netherlandish poems. Yet its literary sophistication distinguishes it from the rest of this genre. There is no equivalent to the elegant and witty brilliance of its irony. The only echo of its central idea, the paradox of placing the praise of the morally unfit in the mouth of the immoral, is found in the *Oath of Master Uncle*.

Secondly, what is the function of the notion of folly as it is expressed in moralizing literature for Netherlandish culture as a whole? How do we account for the seemingly boundless popularity of these lists of social and moral transgressions—many of which resemble each other quite closely? One way of approaching these questions has been to examine the class composition of the authors and audience of these poems in order to determine whether class interests had anything to do with their content. Much of the information required to answer such a question is, however, unavailable to us. Many of the authors are anonymous so that we have no means of knowing their class background. Similarly, we have no insight into the class composition of their audience. In his recent work on *The Blue Boat*, Herman Pleij has argued that the social and moral criticism contained in moralizing poetry of this type represents the formation of a new middle class morality.[36] He regards such criticism as an attempt by a new social class to shape its own value structure. Pleij believes that the structure of the estates satires is transcended by the imposition of a single principle from which all other moral judgments are derived: this principle is the necessity for financial responsibility, a condition which is to be achieved by means of work. This is not the place to assess in detail Pleij's arguments concerning *The Blue Boat* and similar moralizing poems. Nonetheless, I think that two general points are worth making in this context. First, it is clear that certain poems are better suited to his argument than others. For example, although the importance of work as a canon of moral judgment is clear in such poems as *The Blue Boat*, *The Right Way to the Poorhouse*, and *St. Empty's Ship*, it is more difficult to accept the thesis that this is the moral ground on which the selection of items for the lists of morally reprehensible activities in such poems as *The Gay Caps* and *The Feudal Property Court* was based, and the work ethic seems to have singularly little to do with a book such as *The Ten Donkeys*. Second, the traditional character of these poems is at least as important as their innovative qualities. Not only do the poets spend their time castigating examples of the Seven Deadly Sins, but they do so within a structure inherited from the medieval estates satire. This tradition was continued not only in these works but in the dramatic productions of the period. Two anonymous Dutch plays, for example, dating from ca. 1559 and ca. 1564 respectively, deal with the moral shortcomings of the different classes and professions. This criticism, which was aimed at the powerful and wealthy as well as at artisans and common laborers, was a means of preaching the necessity for social order by emphasizing the essential unworthiness of all members of society.[37]

In light of the continuity with both earlier and contemporaneous estates satires that characterizes the values of the moralizing poems, it might be argued that rather than expressing the attitudes of a new social class, the popular moralizing poetry of folly might represent the active participation in a traditional culture by social groups that had heretofore played little or no role in its formulation. Moral issues that had previously been the province of clerical writers of didactic tracts had come to be considered the legitimate concern of the lay artisan. Increased participation in the affirmation of moral values could be seen as a function of a spiritually troubled age that witnessed the Reformation, one in which the character of human redemption was in the process of redefinition and in which the means by which religious beliefs should be given social manifestation were a matter of urgent debate and deep concern.

The medieval definition of folly as madness and the identification of madness with sin, together with its association with carnival and the licensed expression of socially threatening behavior, made it a rich and complex concept for the expression of moral ideas. Far from being restricted to the identification of a particular category of sinfulness, the idea was susceptible to interpretation in unique and personal ways, ways that would not violate a preexistent system of thought. Furthermore, its inherent ambiguity permitted its use in the expression of moral judgments of widely differing strength. If one emphasized the equation of sin and folly as Brant had done, the concept permitted moral statements of scathing intensity. If the notion was interpreted in its carnival aspect, it permitted the development of satirical, ironic, and even comic attitudes toward certain aspects of moral behavior. It appears that Flemish authors by and large exploited the new ways in which moral failing could be characterized. The idea of a guild, a ride on a long wagon, the right to a colorful cap, entry to the poorhouse, or citizenship in a kingdom all represent imaginative new variations on a fascinating and apparently inexhaustible theme. Whereas all of these poems set out to make explicit the ethical mores of the day, they do so in ways that were meant to intrigue and entertain as well as to admonish.

The idea of folly in Netherlandish literature of the first half of the sixteenth century seems to have served a double function. On the one hand it made manifest in new form the values of a traditional society, but on the other it profoundly altered their nature. The performance of a morally questionable action was no longer to be viewed as the transgression of a moral law but as a sign that one was susceptible to the influence of an entirely human weakness. The strength of the indictment did not depend upon the application of a preestablished religious principle but varied according to the individual author's interpretation of the notion of folly. It is perhaps the freedom with which moral issues could be discussed as a consequence of the introduction of this indefinite and flexible concept of moral value that accounts for the popularity of the idea of folly in moralizing literature of this period.

## NOTES

*I would like to thank fellow participants in the Rosenwald symposium for their suggestions and comments on this paper. Special thanks are due Walter Gibson and Sandra Hindman.*

1. See Sebastian Brant, *Narrenschiff*, ed. Friedrich Zarncke (Leipzig: G. Wigand, 1854), pp. lxxix ff.; Sebastian Brant, *The Ship of Fools*, trans. with intro. and commentary by Edwin H. Zeydel (New York: Columbia University Press, 1944), pp. 17 ff.

2. John Ralph Sinnema, "A Critical Study of the Dutch Translation of Sebastian Brant's *Narrenschiff*" (Ph.D. diss., University of Cincinnati, 1949) and "The German Source of the Middle Dutch 'Der zotten ende der narren scip,'" in *On Romanticism and the Art of Translation: Studies in Honor of Edwin Hermann Zeydel*, ed. Gottfried F. Merkel (Princeton: Published for the University of Cincinnati, Princeton University Press, 1956), pp. 233–54.

3. Sebastian Brant, *Der sotten schip, oft, dat Narrenschip* (Antwerp: Marien Ancxt, 1548), Rosenwald Collection, no. 1169; Sebastian Brant, *Navis stultorum oft Der sottenschip* (Antwerp: Jan van Ghelen, 1584), Rosenwald Collection, no. 1206.

4. The impact of *The Ship of Fools* in countries other than Germany has only been discussed in relation to France and England. See Dorothy O'Connor, "Notes on the Influence of Brant's *Narrenschiff* outside of Germany," *Modern Language Review* 20 (1925):64–70 and "Sébastien Brant en France au xvie siècle," *Revue de littérature comparée* 8 (1928):309–17. Also, W. G. Moore, "The Evolution of a Sixteenth-Century Satire," in *A Miscellany of Studies in Romance Languages & Literatures Presented to Leon E. Kastner*, ed. Mary Williams and James A. de Rothschild (Cambridge: W. Heffer & Sons, 1932), pp. 351–60.

5. For the most recent edition of the manuscript as well as for a thorough discussion of this work, see Herman Pleij, *Het gilde van de Blauwe Schuit Literatuur volksfeest en burgermoraal in de late middeleeuwen* (Amsterdam: Meulenhoff, 1979).

6. See Ruth Mohl, *The Three Estates in Medieval and Renaissance Literature* (New York: F. Ungar Pub. Co., 1962) and Wolfgang Heinemann, "Zur Ständedidaxe in der deutschen Literatur des 13–15 Jahrhunderts," *Beiträge zur Geschichte der deutschen Sprache und Literatur* 88 (1966):1–90; 89 (1967):290–403; 92 (1970):388–437.

7. Pleij, *Het gilde van de Blauwe Schuit*, p. 241. "Nu mocht een vraghen of hi wilde, / Die in dit ghilde comen woude, / Of hi al dese punten soude, / Moeten doen die sijn voerscreven. / Hierop will wi antwoert gheven: / Een mensche sal in hemselven gaen, / Ende sien sijn regiment aen, / Van sinen leven ende wandelinghen, / Van seden ende van alle dinghen, / Die hi daghelix plecht te hantieren. / Vint hi meer punten van manieren, / Dan hem meer ten wijsheit trecken, / Dan wijsheit die ter dwaesheit trecken, / So en is hi in onse ghilde niet. / Mer die in hemselven siet, / Meer punten dan hier staten voerscreven, / Dan wijselike mede te leven, / Die sinen staet meest regeren, / Ende sinen goede meest deeren, / Dese sullen in onse scute gaen, / Ende onse ghilde nemen aen." My translation.

8. For a valuable discussion of Brant's use of the concept of folly, see Barbara Könneker, *Wesen und Wandlung der Narrenidee im Zeitalter des Humanismus: Brant, Murner, Erasmus* (Wiesbaden: Steiner, 1966).

9. *Veelderhande geneuchlijcke dichten, tafelspelen ende refereynen* (Leiden, 1899; reprint ed., Utrecht: HES, 1972).

10. Gerrit Kalff, *Geschiedenis der Nederlandsche letterkunde in de 16. eeuw*, 2 vols. (Leiden: E. J. Brill, 1889), 1:101, n. 5.

11. *Veelderhande*, pp. 156–60.

12. Brant, *Ship of Fools*, pp. 55 and 57–58.

13. *Veelderhande*, pp. 15–20.

14. Brant, *Ship of Fools*, p. 59.

15. Ibid., p. 362.

16. Ibid., pp. 206–7.

17. *Veelderhande*, pp. 126–41. For the first edition, see Moore, "The Evolution," p. 351.

18. Moore, "The Evolution," pp. 351–53.

19. The poem and woodcut were published by C. P. Burger, Jr., "Nederlandsche Houtsneden 1500–1550: Het Schip van Sinte Reynuut," *Het Boek*, 2d ser., 20 (1931): 209–21, especially 211–20. The woodcut has been attributed to various artists. The attribution to Aertgen van Leyden is the most recent and the most convincing. See J. Bruyn, "Twee St. Antonius-Panelen en andere Werken van Aertgen van Leyden," *Nederlands Kunsthistorisch Jaarboek* 11 (1960):37–119, especially 103–6. (I am indebted to Christine Armstrong for this reference.)

20. Brant, *Ship of Fools*, pp. 55 and 172.

21. A. van Elslander, ed., *Het Volksboek Vanden, x, esels* (Antwerp: De Sikkel, 1946). For different opinions regarding the authorship and date of this work, see J. van Mierlo, "Kroniek van de Middelnederlandse Letteren," *Dietsche Warande en Belfort* (1949):368–75, and the same author's *Nieuwe Studien over Anna Bijns en Andere Opstellen* (Ghent: Drukkerij Erasmus, 1953), pp. 43 ff.

22. Jacob and Wilhelm Grimm, *Deutsches Wörterbuch*, 32 vols. (Leipzig: S. Hirzel, 1854–1965) vol. 3, col. 1155 ff., "Esel"; *Woordenboek der Nederlandsche Taal* (The Hague: M. Nijhoff, 1882–1949), 3: cols. 4328–29, "Ezel."

23. Brant, *Narrenschiff*, pp. xlvii–xlviii.

24. *Jan van Stijevoorts Refereinenbundel Anno MDXXIV*, ed. F. Lyna and W. van Eeghem, 2 vols. (Antwerp, 1930), 2:clxv.

25. Brant, *Der sotten schip*, chap. 73. The refrain also finds a parallel in the Flemish fifteenth-century proverb, "Bells need not be hung on a fool"; see *Proverbia Communia: A Fifteenth Century Collection of Dutch Proverbs*, ed. Richard Jente (Bloomington: Indiana University Press, 1947), no. 475. According to G. Degroote this poem was influenced by Erasmus's *Praise of Folly*; see "Erasmiana,"

in *De Nieuwe Taalgids* 41 (1948):145–55, and the same author's "Erasmus en de Rederijkers van de XVIe eeuw," *Revue belge de philologie et d'histoire* 29 (1951):389–420 and 1029–62. He offers no support for this suggestion. Like many of the other claims made for Erasmian influence in these articles, the only basis for a relationship appears to be that they deal with the common subject of folly. In light of the widespread character of this idea in the literature of the period, such grounds are clearly insufficient. For a critique of Degroote's suggestions regarding the Erasmian sources of this and other poems, see Dirk Coigneau, "Beschouwingen over de Refreinen in het Zotte uit de bundel van Jan van Styevoort," *Rederijkersstudien* 6 (1972):1–60, especially 56–60.

26. Jan van Stijevoorts, *Refereinenbundel*, 1:cxviii.

27. Desiderius Erasmus, *The Praise of Folly*, trans. Clarence H. Miller (New Haven: Yale University Press, 1979). For descriptions of the various dimensions of the concept of folly in this period, see Barbara Swain, *Fools and Folly during the Middle Ages and the Renaissance* (New York: Columbia University Press, 1932) and Enid Welsford, *The Fool: His Social and Literary History* (New York: Farrar & Rinehart, [1936]). The equation of the concept of folly as madness with the idea of sin is discussed by Penelope B. R. Doob, *Nebuchadnezzar's Children: Conventions of Madness in Middle English Literature* (New Haven: Yale University Press, 1974), chap. 1. The use of the idea of folly in carnival celebrations is described by Natalie Zemon Davis, "The Reasons of Misrule," in her book *Society and Culture in Early Modern France* (Stanford, Calif.: Stanford University Press, 1975), pp. 97–123.

28. Erasmus, *Praise of Folly*, p. xiii.

29. A brilliant analysis of the complexities of ambiguity developed by Erasmus in this text is found in Walter Kaiser, *Praisers of Folly: Erasmus, Rabelais, Shakespeare* (Cambridge: Harvard University Press, 1963).

30. The smaller readership that the delay in translation might imply should not be overstressed in view of the large sales volume of the Latin editions of the work; see Sandra Hindman and James Farquhar, *Pen to Press: Illustrated Manuscripts and Printed Books in the First Century of Printing* (College Park: Art Dept., University of Maryland, 1977), p. 190, n. 91.

31. *Bibliotheca Belgica: Bibliographie générale des Pays-Bas*, ed. M.-T. Langer, 6 vols. (Brussels: Cultur et Civilisation, 1964–70), vol. 2.

32. John G. Rechtien, "A 1520 French Translation of the Moria Encomium," *Renaissance Quarterly* 27 (1974):23–35.

33. R. H. Marijnissen, "De Eed van Meester Oom. Een Voorbeeld van Brabantse Jokkernij uit Bruegels Tijd," in *Pieter Bruegel und seine Welt*, ed. Otto von Simson and Matthias Winner (Berlin: Mann, 1979), pp. 51–61.

34. For a description of this festival, see W. van Eeghem, "Rhetores Bruxelliensis," *Revue belge de philologie et d'histoire* 15 (1936):47–78.

35. *Dichten en Spelen van Jan van den Berghe*, ed. C. Kruyskamp (The Hague: M. Nijhoff, 1950). Its relation to *The Praise of Folly* has been emphasized by G. Degroote, "Jan Vandenberghe, Erasmiaanse Geest en zijn, 'Leenhof der Gilden,'" in *Album Professor Dr. Frank Baur*, 2 vols. (Antwerp: Standaard-Boekhandel, 1948), 1:165–75.

36. See n. 5.

37. Benjamin Hendrik Erné, *Twee zestiende eeuwse spelen van de hel* (Groningen: Wolters, 1934).

# PART TWO

# LANDSCAPE AND THE EARLY ILLUSTRATED BOOK

## CHARLES TALBOT

# TOPOGRAPHY AS LANDSCAPE IN EARLY PRINTED BOOKS

Landscape, composed of an infinite variety of forms within a matrix of space, light, and atmosphere, requires the most pictorial means of representation. It is particularly the domain of painters and came into sudden prominence in European art with the work of Jan van Eyck and other early Netherlandish masters of pictorial illusion. In the Age of the Baroque when European art entered a distinctly "painterly" phase—to use Wölfflin's term—landscape was an inseparable part of this development. Given the close, natural alliance between painting and landscape, it is reasonable to expect that such a linear medium as woodcut would have little part to play in the history of landscape or in its emergence as a major, independent branch of painting. Yet because woodcut was the medium of book illustrations in the fifteenth century, it took on a special, if little recognized, role in establishing landscape's claim to a place of its own in art. The printed texts at that time did not call for illustrations of pure landscape in the sense of later landscape painting, but from the mid-1480s words and pictures in travel books and historical chronicles addressed a growing interest in the appearance of this world. Topographical views of near and distant places became so popular that publishers provided them whether they knew what some of the places looked like or not.

This was certainly the case with the *Nuremberg Chronicle* of 1493, the most profusely illustrated book of the fifteenth century. It contains fifty-three different views of cities and lands in Europe and around the Mediterranean. When available, drawings of the actual sites were used as the basis for the woodcuts; otherwise the artist was on his own. Most of the imaginary views were repeated to illustrate various places, some as often as six or seven, one even eleven times.[1] None but the most casual observer could have failed to notice what was going on. These déjà vus were clearly fictitious scenes. Although the frugal practice of repeating illustrations in the same book was common enough at the time, the mixing of imaginary scenes with real ones suggests that the appeal of these woodcuts derived as much from the pleasure of viewing landscape in pictures as it did from satisfying curiosity about actual places. Nevertheless, topographical illustrations—real or imaginary—in the *Nuremberg Chronicle* and in other books of the period offered contemporary observers a portrayal of landscape that was independent of narrative or devotional subject matter. Landscapes without such figural subjects did not appear in panel painting, to judge by surviving examples, until the second decade of the sixteenth century and probably not until the end of that decade. Despite the well-developed pictorial means to represent landscape in painting by the end of the fifteenth century, the traditional purposes of panel painting restricted landscape to the background. The woodcut book illustrations of topographical views clearly anticipate the day when landscape would be liberated in painting as an independent subject.

Whether the woodcuts contributed directly to that event is still an open question, but there are reasons for thinking they did. Albrecht Altdorfer's earliest landscape drawings from 1511 show a graphic style closely related to that which was developed for topographical landscapes in woodcut, and it is only to be expected that artists in Southern Germany who made the break to pure landscape would have had a special interest in the printed and illustrated literature of the time that dealt with topography.[2] However, a thorough consideration of the precedents for independent landscape painting obviously has to take more into account than book illustrations.

Woodcut illustrations, like the printed texts themselves, began in emulation of manuscripts. It has been well noted in the literature on fifteenth-century Netherlandish painting that manuscript illuminations prepared the way for naturalism in panel painting where landscapes as well as other spatial settings are concerned. In a recent publication Otto Pächt has brought to light some exceptionally interesting and beautiful examples of landscapes without figural subjects from French and Netherlandish manuscripts.[3] Two manuscripts of the "Livre des propriétés des choses," a translation by Jean Corbechon of Bartholomaeus Anglicus's *De proprietatibus rerum*, contain landscapes representing the four elements and the creation of the world that anticipate by some eighty years the appearance of pure landscape painting on panels. Pächt dates both these manuscripts around 1440, and he attributes the illuminations in one of them to Simon Marmion.[4] Of a later date, but still before the earliest topographical woodcuts, is the remarkable illumination in a manuscript of about 1470–80 from Bruges. Titled the "Trésor des histoires," the text includes a chapter on the "provinces du monde" in which this particular illumination is identified as a view of Flanders.[5]

A different sort of precedent for independent landscape (and this has also been noted by Pächt)[6] existed in panel painting itself. From at least the 1420s landscapes could be seen as separate views within their own frames by virtue of their appearing through windows portrayed as part of an interior scene. From the middle of the fifteenth century the interior with a window open onto a landscape became a popular setting for portraiture. The landscape view connected the figure with the wider world, while the window opening admitted light and air into the room. Although in retrospect it is easy enough to imagine how an artist might have thought of transferring the landscape view framed by a window to a whole panel, just as he might have considered that a landscape found evocative and beautiful in a manuscript could likewise stand as the subject for an independent picture, the traditions of panel painting clearly resisted this obvious step. There was still a conceptual gap to be bridged where both the thematic expectations of panel painting and the evaluation of landscape itself were concerned.

In a frequently cited essay, "The Renaissance Theory of Art and the Rise of Landscape," Ernst Gombrich addresses this very problem and seeks to explain what brought landscape into its own during the sixteenth century.[7] He distinguishes between the stylistic development of landscape, long since under way in the backgrounds of Netherlandish paintings, and the "institutional" aspect of the subject. He contends that with the authority of Pliny and Vitruvius, Renaissance artists and writers such as Alberti, Leonardo, and Lomazzo gave theoretical justification to landscape and thereby enabled it to become an independent genre, however inferior that genre might still be in the hierarchy of painting. Gombrich stresses his belief that theory must precede practice by asking rhetorically, "how could anyone demand landscape paintings unless the concept and even the word existed?"[8]

What Vitruvius says about the portrayal of landscape is a component of his theory on appropriate stage scenery for tragic, comic, and satyric theater. It is in the satyric category that "scenes are decorated with trees, caverns, mountains, and other rustic objects delineated in landscape style."[9] The Vitruvian classification may have been an important factor in the thinking of Alberti and others who accepted landscape within a system of stratified categories of art, but it would be curious if a theory on stage design were to have been instrumental in eliminating human actors from landscapes or other kinds of scenes. In any case the forests of Altdorfer or the fantastic valleys and promontories of Patinir would seem especially unlikely terrain in which to encounter the spirit of Vitruvius. Yet Gombrich is surely right that a certain conceptual basis underlay early landscape painting, even if the concept was not articulated in theory where Northern European art was concerned.

Perhaps it is also true that the demand for landscape paintings presupposes the existence of a word for them. The word, *landscape*, was in use already in Middle High German but not with the same meaning we are discussing. Only from the end of the fifteenth century does it turn up in the context of art. James Snyder has called attention to a contract from 1490 for an altarpiece in Haarlem that refers several times to a "landscap" as the necessary setting for the religious subjects.[10] Another

FIGURE 1. Erhard Reuwich, Corfu. Bernhard von Breydenbach, *Peregrinatio in Terram Sanctam* (Mainz: Erhard Reuwich, 1486), New Haven, Connecticut, Yale University, Beinecke Rare Book and Manuscript Library. Courtesy Beinecke Library.

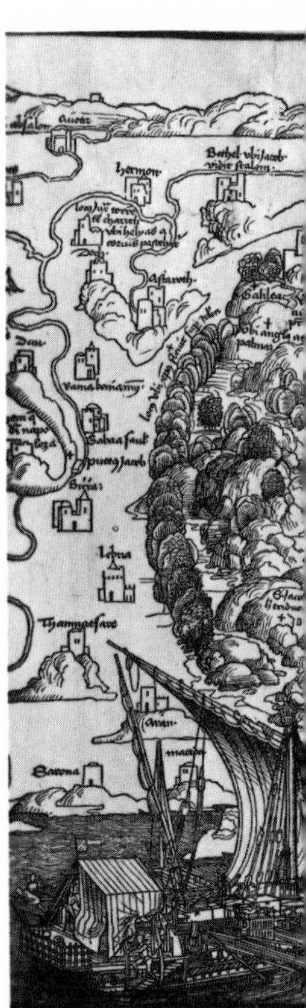

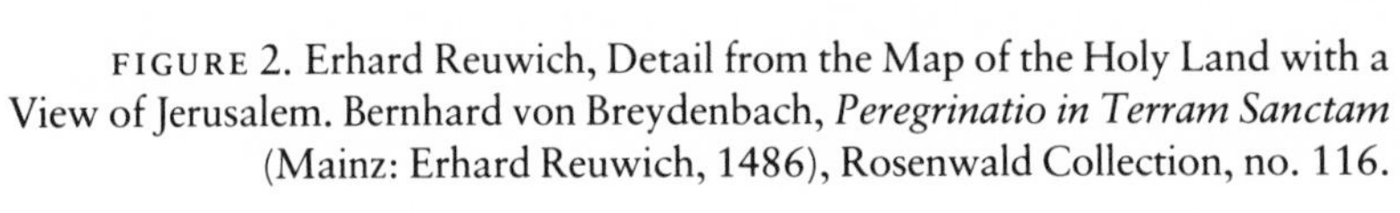

FIGURE 2. Erhard Reuwich, Detail from the Map of the Holy Land with a View of Jerusalem. Bernhard von Breydenbach, *Peregrinatio in Terram Sanctam* (Mainz: Erhard Reuwich, 1486), Rosenwald Collection, no. 116.

example of the same usage is found in a contract of 1518 for an altarpiece by Hans Herbst in Basel, where the text calls for "two saints on the stationary wings and the background must [be painted] with sky and landscape (hymel und landschafft)."[11] Then there is the famous passage of 1521 from Dürer's Netherlandish Journal in which the artist speaks of Joachim Patinir as the good landscape painter ("der gut landschafft mahler").[12] These early examples of the word used in the modern sense of landscape painting occur just at the time landscape itself is on the verge of gaining its independence in art.

What then, we may ask, was the connotation of *landschaft* before this time? Rainer Gruenter provides an answer in an article published in 1953, the same year in which Gombrich's essay first appeared.[13] The original meaning of *landschaft* or *lantschaft*, as it was spelled in its earliest form, was not a view of nature but rather a geographic area defined by political boundaries in the sense of the Latin *territorium* or *regio*. The word continued to be used in this sense long after it had also become a term with reference to art. If it is true, as Gombrich maintains, that language sanctioned the development of independent landscape painting, then it should be worth considering whether an evolution in the meaning of the word *landscape* finds any correspondence in art. This is where the topographical landscapes come back in.

In 1486 Bernhard von Breydenbach published from Mainz his *Peregrinatio in Terram Sanctam* with woodcut illustrations by Erhard Reuwich. Reuwich had ac-

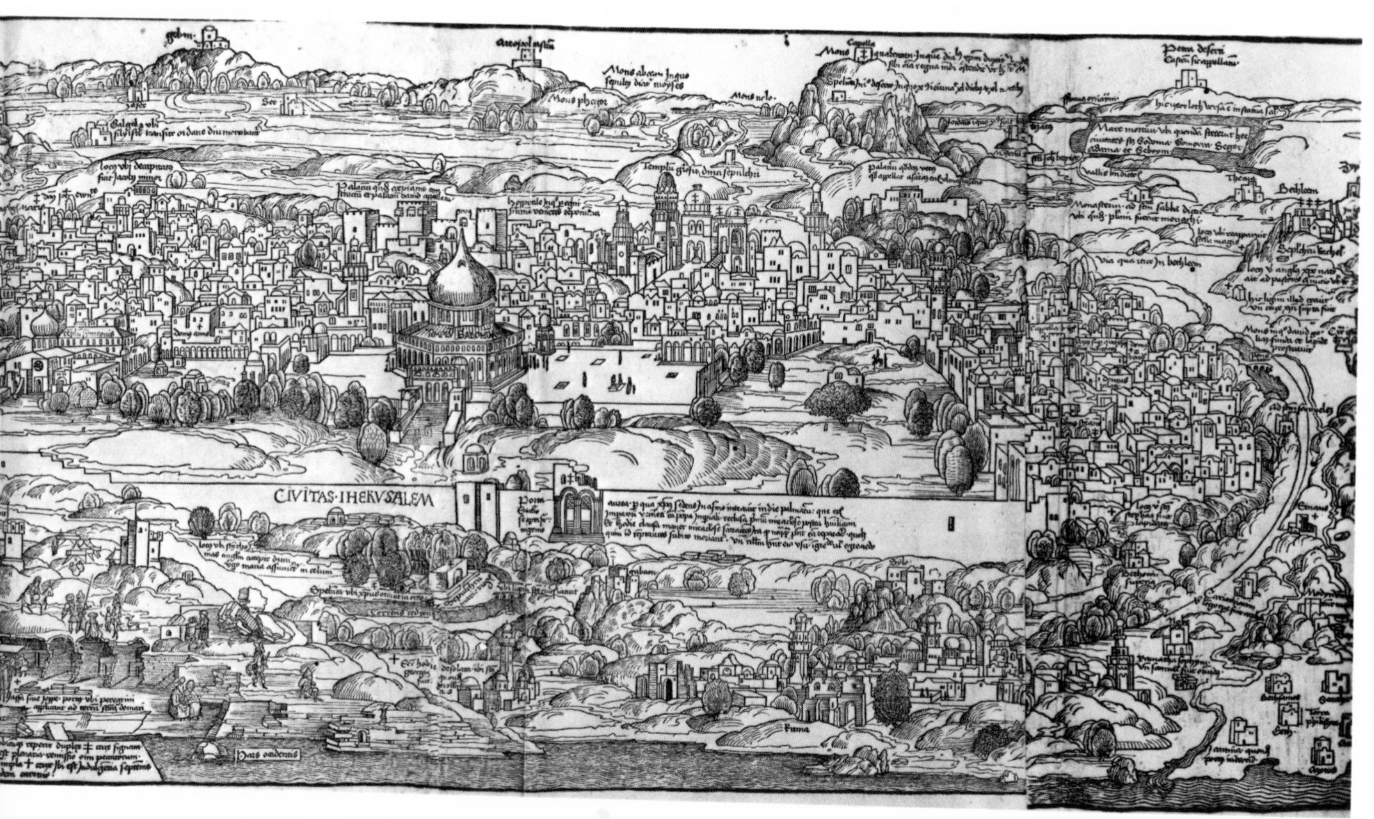

companied Breydenbach on a pilgrimage with the specific purpose of making drawings of Jerusalem and major cities along the way in preparation for the eventual woodcuts. Considering the state of the art before he started, Reuwich's woodcuts are remarkably vivid representations of the places he saw, and they set a standard for the rest of the century. He devised a graphic style that was informative, clear, and well suited to the medium. The illustrations show the cities as encountered by the artist arriving by ship. The view of Corfu (fig. 1), for example, is taken from far enough offshore so that the whole city fits into the picture. The harbor is full of activity with ships being loaded or getting under way. The pictorial interest of this lively cityscape is a notable achievement in itself, but Reuwich did not lose sight of the fact that he was expected to portray a specific place known by name. To that end a fantastic banderole flutters over the entire city proclaiming its identity. How easily the artist's mind moved between the pictorial, topographical, and even cartographic aspects of his subject can be observed in the foldout view of the Holy Land, where a scenic mode of representation converts into a map at the outskirts of Jerusalem (fig. 2). The map portrays landscape in its territorial sense, outlining its shape and most prominent features, while the topographical view is well on its way to becoming a pictorial landscape.

Another instance of a landscape in woodcut having been motivated by topographical concerns is the illustration identified as the Castle on the Gaisbühel (fig. 3) in Thomas Lirer's *Chronik von allen Königen und Kaisern*, called the *Swabian Chronicle*, which was published in Ulm by Dinckmut in 1486. In this case, however, the anonymous illustrator was no skilled topographical artist like Reuwich. The landscape looks like a conventionalized background with the usual foreground

*right:*
FIGURE 3. Castle on the "Gaisbühel." Thomas Lirer, *Chronik von allen Königen und Kaisern* (Ulm: Conrad Dinckmut, 1486), Rosenwald Collection, no. 115.

*far right:*
FIGURE 4. St. Lucius with an Ox and a Bear Harnessed to His Plow. Thomas Lirer, *Chronik von allen Königen und Kaisern* (Ulm: Conrad Dinckmut, 1486), Rosenwald Collection, no. 115.

FIGURE 5.
Landscape with Imperial Cities.
[Konrad Bote], *Cronecken der Sassen*
(Mainz: Peter Schoeffer, 1492),
Rosenwald Collection, no. 157.

subject simply eliminated. The normal relationship of landscape to figures can be seen in a similar woodcut from the same book, showing Saint Lucius, who has managed to harness a bear to his plow in place of the ox that the bear had killed (fig. 4). Whether or not the former view bore much similarity to the actual place, the castle and the terrain it dominated were given an illustration of their own without being upstaged by a narrative scene. The process of recasting the traditional landscape background into the main subject occurred, it would seem, because of the political and historical rather than scenic interest of the site.

An illustration of a landscape especially constructed for a similar purpose appears in Konrad Bote's *Saxon Chronicle* (*Cronecken der Sassen*), published 1492 in Mainz by Peter Schoeffer (fig. 5). Set within a continuous, steeply rising landscape are clusters of late medieval buildings identified by inscriptions as German cities and estates, such as Magdeburg, Lüneburg, Salzwedel, and Harzburg. An imperial figure, labeled Julius, oversees this terrain from a high, rocky place in the foreground. The telescoped arrangement of this political landscape should not have troubled a contemporary viewer who would have been accustomed to seeing paintings in which several episodes from one narrative were shown simultaneously within a single landscape, sometimes representing locations great distances apart.

Amid the many individual woodcuts of cities and lands in the *Nuremberg Chronicle* there is one illustration in which a dozen cities of the German Empire occupy a single panoramic landscape extending across facing pages of the folio-sized book (fig. 6). Each is identified by an inscription and coat of arms. Their disposition in the woodcut has nothing to do with their actual geographic relationship to one another. Instead they are located in three horizontal zones, designated from the bottom up as the Quatuor Rustica, Quatuor Ville, and Quatuor Civitates. Thus, in the lowest zone four cities—Cologne, Regensburg, Constance, and Salzburg—are each represented by no more than a few rural buildings, while at the top of the picture Augsburg, Metz, Aachen, and Lübeck appear as great walled cities with towers rising above the horizon. Each city is surrounded by a small area of land that is separated from its neighbors by rivers, streams, valleys, or roadways. During this period the land around a town was referred to as its landscape, meaning not a view but rather the adjacent rural area, which might even be politically organized with its

FIGURE 6.
Landscape with Imperial Cities.
[Hartmann Schedel],
*Liber chronicarum*
(Nuremberg: Anton Koberger,
23 December 1493), Northampton,
Massachusetts, Smith College
Library Rare Book Room.
Courtesy Smith College Library.
Photo by Stephen Petegorsky.

own privileges. This meaning still survives, for example, in the Swiss Canton of Basel Landschaft.[14] The small parcels of land in the woodcut are, of course, nothing so specific as this, but it is not unlikely that a contemporary viewer would have taken the composite organization of the whole scene as an expression of "landscapes" in this very sense. On the other hand, these multiple landscapes coalesce into one large one, which conveys pictorially the idea of the all-embracing empire. The process of representation inevitably transformed, or at least expanded, the meaning of *landscape*. Unlike the term *portrait* which distinguishes between the image and the person portrayed, landscape came to refer to both the place and the picture, so that even today, unless the context makes it clear, landscape can easily be taken to mean one thing or the other.

A shift from the territorial to the pictorial meaning of landscape together with a shift in emphasis from topography to a visual experience of the outdoor scene can be observed in any number of the city views from the *Nuremberg Chronicle*. Strasbourg is a particularly impressive one (fig. 7). Both the designer of the woodcut and the designer of the layout were thinking of ways to make the illustration measure up to the memorable skyline. Again the woodcut stretches across facing pages of the open book, but even then it cannot encompass the whole expanse of the walled city. The cathedral, dominating everything, protrudes above the border of the illustration and threatens to defy the limits of the page itself. As spectators, we stand off a way. The foreground between us and the city is occupied by rural land, Strasbourg's landschaft. There are no distinguishing features here but the bushy trees nevertheless block our view of much of the city wall. This is partly due to the relatively low eye-level of the picture which takes us through rather than over the intervening landscape. Our passage is guided by the two roads winding their way to the city gates, but our perception of the space before us also has much to do with the variation of light and shade falling among the overlapping trees and across the land. Attention to such optical phenomena goes hand in hand with the artist's interest in a particular view of the city. In other words, how we experience the scene matters almost as much as what is represented.

Although the topographical woodcuts of the early travel books and chronicles are intended to describe important, identifiable subjects, usually famous cities with certain outstanding features, it is significant that the focus of these woodcuts is not located right in the foreground. In this respect the woodcuts differ from virtually all contemporary paintings, whether involving landscapes or not. The customary subjects of these paintings were narrative scenes, devotional images, or likenesses of people, and the foreground was the place to look for the main subject. Since at least from the beginning of perspectival representation in western art, it has been as natural for us to read the foreground first as it is to read a page from the upper left. We expect to have the closest and best view of what is most important, and conversely we assume from our egocentric position that what finds itself closest to us must at that moment acquire special significance.

The one area of representation that defies the law of the foreground is landscape. When it does not, it tends to be like still-life—nature on stage for a human audience. A major concern of the landscape painter has been how to get beyond the foreground. His subject is not simply the specimens of nature but rather the terms of their existence: the space, the light, the terrain. The qualities of these things are not revealed by their proximity to the observer, and their poetry may even reside in their lying beyond reach. But as long as the foreground and the figural subject preserved their firm alliance, landscape would remain in the background both compositionally and metaphorically. In the guise of topographical scenes, book illustrations opened a breach in this alliance or, rather, kept it out of sight, for neither the figural subject nor the foreground holds sway in these pictures.

Playing down the importance of the foreground has implications for both sides of the picture plane. The foreground is an experience of the observer in place. Even when the appearances of the foreground seem to be in a state of flux, its dominant forms entreat a corresponding proximity on our part. With landscape, on

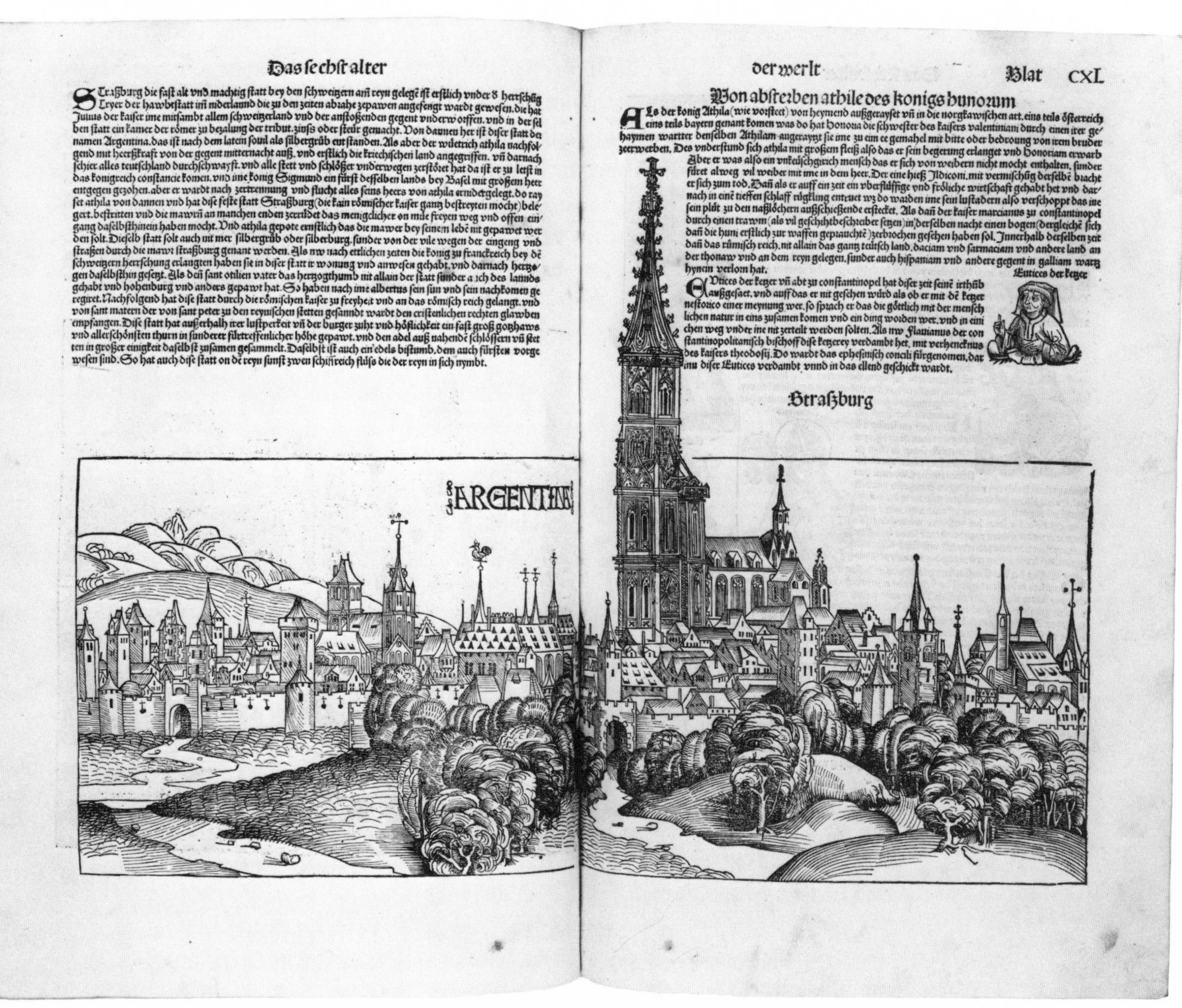


FIGURE 7. Strasbourg. [Hartmann Schedel], *Liber chronicarum* (Nuremberg: Anton Koberger, 23 December 1493), Rosenwald Collection, no. 166.

the other hand—and this applies to the topographical views we have considered—the spectator must relate to a world that stands back and maybe passes rapidly from sight. It is a world of the traveler. Reuwich's cities and those in the *Nuremberg Chronicle* are not viewed from within, but rather from outside the walls, as if upon approach from elsewhere. Our vantage point may indeed be stationary, but we take that position only in passing. The travel books and chronicles describe places where we are not but might go, and that, too, is how we see the landscapes.

The coming of landscape to art was more than the arrival of a new subject. As the meaning of the word itself evolved from designating a possessable place with a name toward signifying the view of such a place or some other whose name is inconsequential, so also did representations of landscape undergo a comparable evolution. The difference is that in the latter case the evolution was inherent in the representation itself. The woodcut illustration may have started out as a means of showing and identifying a specific territory under rule, but once shown it became a visually experienced object, transformed by its very nature into a modern landscape.

## NOTES

1. Elisabeth Rücker, *Die Schedelsche Weltchronik* (Munich: Prestel, 1973), which has a catalog of the cities and landscapes.
2. Charles Talbot, "Landscapes from Incunabula to Altdorfer," *Gesta* 15 (1976):321–26.
3. Otto Pächt, "'La Terre de Flandres,'" *Pantheon* 36 (1978):3–16.
4. London, British Library, Cotton Ms. Aug. A.VI. Ibid., pp. 7–8, pl. II and figs. 10, 15.
5. London, British Library, Cotton Ms. Aug. A.V. Ibid., pp. 4–5, pl. I.
6. Ibid., pp. 10–12.
7. Ernst H. Gombrich, "The Renaissance Theory of Art and the Rise of Landscape," in his *Norm and Form* (London: Phaidon, 1966), pp. 107–21. This article first appeared in the *Gazette des Beaux-Arts* 41 (1953):335–60, although it was written in 1950 for a Festschrift for Hans Tietze, the publication of which was delayed.
8. Ibid., p. 109.
9. Vitruvius Pollio, *Vitruvius: The Ten Books on Architecture*, trans. Morris Hicky Morgan (New York: Dover Publications, 1960), p. 150.
10. James E. Snyder, "The Early Haarlem School of Painting," *Art Bulletin* 42 (1960): 45, n. 32. See also his n. 8 here, p. 62.
11. E. His-Heussler, "Beiträge zur schweizerischen Kunstgeschichte," *Anzeiger für Kunde der Deutschen Vorzeit*, Organ des Germanischen Museums 1, n.s. 13 (1866):273.
12. Albrecht Dürer, *Schriftlicher Nachlass*, ed. Hans Rupprich (Berlin: Deutscher Verein für Kunstwissenschaft, 1956–69), vol. 1 (1956), p. 169.
13. Rainer Gruenter, "Landschaft: Bemerkungen zur Wort- und Bedeutungsgeschichte," *Germanisch-Romanische Monatsschrift*, n.s. 3 (1953):110–20. This article is reprinted in *Landschaft und Raum in der Erzählkunst*, ed. Alexander Ritter (Darmstadt: Wissenschaftliche Buchgesellschaft, 1975), pp. 192–207.
14. For this information I am indebted to Professor Hans Guggisberg and his research on the history of Basel.

KAREN S. PEARSON

# THE MULTIMEDIA APPROACH TO LANDSCAPE IN GERMAN RENAISSANCE GEOGRAPHY BOOKS

Therefore, good Germans, help me to bring to honor our country and place its beauties in the clear light of day. Do this and your descendants shall hold us in honor and affection. Scholars and artists! Do not hesitate to goad the lords of our land into action to have their domains described. Pass the word to other learned men whom my little work may not reach; you shall be esteemed for it. Cities of the German nation! Do not regret the Gulden or two you might spend on a description of your region. Let everyone lend a hand to complete a work in which shall be reflected, as in a mirror, the entire land of Germany with all its peoples, its cities, its customs.

Sebastian Münster, 1528[1]

The sixteenth century brought to Germany the awakening of a new geographical self-awareness. Sebastian Münster's plea, quoted above, voices a general preoccupation of German humanists with their native landscape. This interest found expression simultaneously in sixteenth-century German literature, cartography, and art. All three modes of representation were brought together in sixteenth-century geography books,[2] which integrated geographical description, maps, and views in a complementary fashion. The roots of this multimedia approach to landscape exist in the medieval and classical periods, but the most active development of the illustrated geography book occurred during the first half of the sixteenth century. Although refinement continued long afterward, the descriptive geography book with its artistic and cartographic illustrations had assumed mature form by the mid-sixteenth century.

The development of the illustrated geography book as a literary form was a group effort by German humanists, who shared a major interest in the history and geographical setting of the German people. The motivation for this collaboration among geographers, cartographers, and artists can be traced to a number of sources. An existing tradition of landscape representation in German literature, cartography, and art was reinforced and given new direction during the late fifteenth century by exposure to Italian and classical influences. For German scholars, the desire to emulate recent Italian writers of geographical description was mingled with antagonism aroused by the scanty and often slighting references to Germany in both ancient and recent literature. Scientific cartography had experienced a similar awakening in the fifteenth century with the rediscovery of Ptolemy's *Geographia*. The recognition of the faulty coverage of European countries spurred cartographers to improve their maps. The general Renaissance curiosity about man's natural surroundings became for German humanists a voyage of self-discovery marked by the stirrings of national pride. One of the sixteenth-century geographical authors, Martin Helwig, summed up their outlook when he asked, "considering how an animal knows its stall and barn, how a thinking man can hold up his head if he neither knows his fatherland nor wishes to know it."[3]

Those who contributed to sixteenth-century geography books represented diverse interests and occupations. Frequent travel and correspondence ensured continuing exchanges among members of the German humanist circle. The page of acknowledgments from Sebastian Münster's *Cosmographia*,[4] a list which mingles the names of ancient scholars with those of Münster's contemporaries, indicates his wide-ranging contacts. Humanists' interests were so varied that the same individual often made substantial contributions to several quite different fields of study. Although it is possible to make a basic distinction in the form of landscape depiction among geography (literary description), cartography (maps), and art (pictorial representation), these fields were not as well-defined in the sixteenth century as they are today.

For instance, a dual role as both geographer and cartographer was common. Sebastian Münster, for example, had studied Hebrew, mathematics, cosmography, and astronomy. He held the post of professor of Hebrew at the University of Basel. His chief geographic and cartographic works, the *Cosmographia* and a new edition of Ptolemy's *Geographia*, were done on the side.[5] Other humanist geographers were doctors, teachers, clergymen, or government officials by profession, men who set out to describe and map their home regions with the enthusiasm of dedicated amateurs.

In contrast, few geographers were also artists. This situation surely stems from differences in the way geographers and artists were trained and in the way their respective trades were practiced. The traditional university program of the trivium and the quadrivium exposed the geographer to the subjects of grammar, logic, rhetoric, arithmetic, geometry, music, and astronomy. A few of the geographer-cartographers may have had some artistic training. Konrad Türst, the author of a 1493 map of Switzerland, had studied goldsmithing; Wolfgang Lazius, a physician, etched his own maps of the Austrian region in the mid-sixteenth century.[6] An artistic background surely enhanced the ability to draw maps, but none of the geographers was known independently as an artist. Lazius, for example, consistently signed himself "Medicus et Historicus." Artists, on the other hand, came out of the separate workshop tradition where they received practical training in artistic crafts through apprenticeship. Books by artists tended to be technical treatises, such as Albrecht Dürer's cartography-related *Underweysung der Messung*,[7] rather than geographical descriptions of the physical landscape, its inhabitants and their customs.

Artists were often cartographers, however. Sixteenth-century German artists had been exposed through Italian contacts to the concepts of mathematical perspective, ideas closely related to the scientific construction of map projections.[8] Art and cartography were linked further in the production of surveying and astronomical instruments, a craft which combined scientific precision with decorative metalwork. Another area of contact was the woodcutter's workshop, where both artistic and cartographic illustrations were prepared for printing, often apparently by the same formcutters.[9] The best known example of dual activity in art and cartography is Augustin Hirschvogel, an artist who produced his first recorded map in 1539. Hirschvogel continued to work as both artist and cartographer until his death in 1553.[10]

Geographers sometimes sought out such artists or cartographers to execute the special illustrative material their volumes required. Bernhard von Breydenbach took along an artist, Erhard Reuwich, to sketch maps and town views for his account of his journey to the Holy Land (see fig. 2, p. 109).[11] Cuspinian (Johannes Spiesshaymer) planned to illustrate his history and geography of Austria with maps (unfortunately now lost) prepared by Stabius (Johannes Stöberer).[12] In other cases, the graphic material formed the core of the project, and geographical text was added as a supplement. For Martin Waldseemüller's 1511 map of Europe, his humanist friend Philesius (Mathias Ringmann) assisted with the explanatory text.[13]

The combination of geographical description and landscape illustration in the form of the illustrated geography book had numerous historical precedents. The mappae mundi produced in medieval Europe were usually manuscript illustrations, often placed with meaningful association to the text.[14] During the medieval period wayfinding maps and charts also developed in conjunction with text—in the form of written itineraries and sailing directions.[15] The joint presentation of maps and text was reinforced in the fifteenth century by the rediscovery of Ptolemy's second century A.D. treatise on geography and cartography. The Byzantine copies of his *Geographia* that made their way to Europe included sets of maps, which were widely copied along with the text.

Building upon the existing traditions of combining landscape description graphien van Pe. Apiano. i - Cāe: Fo.iiii.

telijck ter memorien de ordinantie eñ gelegenthz van verscheydē plaetsen. Daer om es dat gebruyck/eñ dat eynde der Geographiē des geheelen omgancks des werelts gelegentheyts aenschouwinge/als een ghe
heele ghelijckenisse des hoofts van eenen mensche met bequamer schil-
deryen beworpen ende ghemaeckt.

Geographie | Huer ghelijckenisse.

## Wat dat Chorographie es.

Chorographie (als de selue Wernerus seyt) die oock Topo-
graphie geheetē wordt/aenmerckt alleene sommige wtge
nomē plaetsen in hun seluen/eñ sonder comparatie der seluer onderlinghe/oft totten geheelen omganck der aerden/
want si bewijst alle dingen ende bycans de minste die in haer begrepen
zijn/als hauenen/ steden/volck/loopen van riuieren/eñ vele andere omtrent ligghende plaetsen/als timmeragien/huysen/torrens/vesten.etce.
Eñ dat eynde oft gebruyck der seluer sal veruult worden int makē der
gelijckenissen van eenigher plaetsen/ghelijck oft een schildere een oore
alleene/oft een ooghe alleene/teeckende ende schilderde.

Chorographie | Huer ghelijckenisse.

FIGURE 1. Geography and Chorography. Petrus Apianus, *Cosmographia* (Antwerp: G. van Diest for G. de Bonte, 1545), Rosenwald Collection, no. 1164.

with maps and other illustrations, the geography book took shape from the last decade of the fifteenth century through the middle of the sixteenth century. The progressive stages of this development can be illustrated by comparing three geographical works: Hartmann Schedel's *Liber chronicarum* (1493), Conrad Celtes's *Quatuor libri amorum* (1502), and Sebastian Münster's *Cosmographia* (1550).

The first substantial move toward the development of the illustrated geography book came with the *Liber chronicarum*.[16] Although the author, Dr. Hartmann Schedel, took his historical schema from the medieval chronicle, the work also has numerous modern features. The text was a motley composite from various sources, but a modern section on Europe was inserted by Hieronymus Münzer, the author's friend and fellow physician. A description of Sarmatia also appears at the end of the book. In addition, the book is amply illustrated with portraits, biblical and historical scenes, city and regional views, and maps. Most of the 116 city views are imaginary, repeated throughout the book to serve as pictorial captions to the text. However, the fact that about 28 of them were derived from actual sketches or prints represents an unprecedented shift toward realism.[17]

The illustrative scheme appears to be the result of close cooperation between Schedel and the artists Michael Wolgemut and Wilhelm Pleydenwurff, who were responsible for preparing both exemplars (layout copies in Latin and German) and woodblocks ready for printing.[18] A recent study of the Latin exemplar by Adrian Wilson has shown two-thirds of the text and some of the rough sketches to be in Schedel's hand.[19] This close involvement suggests that the author may also have directed the artists in planning the subjects and placing the illustrations. Other evidence of a tendency to link text and illustrations comes from Schedel's personal copy of the *Liber chronicarum*, in which a 1492 map of the Nuremberg area appears adjacent to two meditations on cities.[20]

When the landscape illustrations in the *Liber chronicarum* are considered as a group in relation to the text, it becomes apparent that they constitute an attempt to present a coherent program of illustrations at different levels of detail. The range of scales represented includes large-scale city views, medium-scale regional views, and small-scale maps of Germany and the world. This progression of scales matches the accepted (if somewhat loose) subdivisions of the field of geography during the sixteenth century, as based on the ideas of Ptolemy. They are shown in illustrations by Peter Apian for his *Cosmographia* (fig. 1). The city and regional views correspond with the branch of geography that Apian called "chorography," the detailed study of particular places. The smaller scale maps of Germany and the world, on the other hand, belong to the branch named "geography," whose task was to describe larger areas and the world as a whole. Although Ptolemy was referring to cartography, the German humanists interpreted his words to mean geographical description as well.[21]

However, the aim of illustrating the German landscape with an ordered sequence of large-, medium-, and small-scale representations has not been fully achieved in the *Liber chronicarum*. In this early geographical work, there is not yet a smooth transition in the method of depiction from one scale to the next. The

Cõstantinopel die kaiserlich vnd aller hohberümbst statt ist etwen dieweil sie noch klain was Bizãciũ vnd darnach Constantinopolis genant worden. dañ als der groß Constantinus im fürgenomen het den kaiserlichen stůl zu schickerlicher gegenweer wider die Parthos auß Rom in den orient zewenden. do ist er (als etlich geschihtbeschreiber setzen) gein Troiaden (do weylend Agamenon vnd ander kriechisch fürsten wider priamum ire gezelte geheftet haben) gezogen. vnd hat daselbst die grundfeste einer koniglichen statt fürgenomen. vnd doch dasselb auß vermanung christi vnsers hailands der ime in dem schlaff ein anders ort anzaiget den angefengten paw (des langzeit anzaigung bliben sind) vnuerbracht gelassen. vñ in Traciã gein Bisanciũ geschiffet die statt alßpaldt erweytert. newe zinnen aufgerichtet. hohe thürn gepawet vnd mit großtatigen gemaynen vnd sundern gepewen so hübsch vnnd schön gezieret das sie das ander Rom nit vnbillich genant werden möcht. Die alte geschihtbeschreiber die dise statt in irem plüenden wesen gesehen haben. dieselben statt mer ein wonung der götter auff erden dañ der kaiser geschatzt. Diser kaiser hieß dise statt das new Rom. aber nach dem gemaynen rüff ist sie nach irem erpawer Constantinopel genant bliben. Dise statt haben die nachkomen kaiser võ weil zu weil mit gemaynen vnd sundern fasthohen fürtreffenlichen gepewen also gezieret das die eilfern daselbsthin komẽde in verwündrũg diser stat scheinperkeit dieselben statt ein behawsung nit allain der tödlichen sünder auch der himlischẽ zesein vermaynten. Die mawrn diser statt warñ an höhe vnd dicke in der gantzen werlt berümbt vnd die vorwere schickerlicherweis bewaret. Sie schreiben dise stat dreyegket gewesen sein. an zwayen örtern rüret das meer daran. sie ist an mawrn zu gegenweer des schiffsturms geschickt. Das ander ort gegen dem lãd gelegẽ ist außerhalb der zinnen vnd vorweer mit eim großen graben beslossen. Dise statt hat aylff pforten die die zierde der statt fürzaigten. Außerhalb andern großmechtigen gepewen ist daselbst der tempel Sophie Justiniani des kaisers paw. in gantzer werlt gedechtnus wirdig etwen mit. iiiᶜ. briestern besorget. mit wunderperlicher arbait vnnd köstlicher materi aufgerichtet. Dise statt ist ein besuchung des gantzen orients vnd einige wonung des gelerteñ kriechischẽ lands gewesen. Daselbst sind drey große concili gehalten worden. Diser statt haben von irer wirdigkeit vñ wolstands wegen die Türcken neyd vnd gramschaft getragen. vnd darumb dieselben statt nach der gepurt cristi vnsers hails im. j[m]. xciij. iar mit großem gewalt belegert vnd darnach erobert. Nachfolgend habẽ die Gallier mit den venedigern dise statt. lv. iar besessen. darnach hat das edel geschlecht der Jenueser palealogorum genant dise statt von den Galliern an sich gebracht vnd inngehabt bis in dz. j[m]. iiiiᶜ. liij. iar. darin Machomet ottomannus



der Türcken kaiser die statt erobert vnnd zerrüdet hat. also ist dise aller edelste statt nach irer erpawung tausent hundert vnd dreyssig iar oder dabey in die hend der vnglawbigen komen vnd elter dañ Rom gestanden. Atharicus hat von erpawung der statt Rom im. j[m]. c. lxiiij. iar dieselben stat Rom zerrüdet. vnd doch dabey verpoten die kirchen der heiligen nit zeerstören. aber die wütend tobheit vnd vihisch vnsinnigkeit der Türcken hat nichtz hailigs. nichtz rayns in diser koniglichen statt gelassen. sunder die hailigẽ tempel daselbst dẽ schnödẽ machmetischen mißprauch vnderworffen. Wir lesen von vil wunderperlichen hohberümbten großmechtigẽ geschihten vnd taten der Thebanier Lacedemonier Athener Corinthier vñ vil gedechtnus wirdiger stett der doch ietzo kaum anzaigung irs gelegers auff erdpodem beschehen mag. aber allain dise stat. Cõstantinopel vbertrift auß so großem fal irs alters. die souil wunderperlicher gepew. souil waffen. souil schrift. souil vnd groß glori vnd ere gehabt hat das allain dise stat den schaden aller stett zevergleichen erscheint. vnd wiewol Cõstantinopel nach wẽdung des kaiserthumbs auff die Frantzosen in die hend der feind komen ist so sind doch nye die kirchen der hailigen zerprochen. noch die libraarey verprent. noch die clöster gantz berawbt worden. sunder die anzaigungẽ der alten weißheit zu Constantinopel bis in dis iar bliben. kein lateinischer mocht nit gelert gnůg gesehen werdẽ er het deñ etliche zeit zu Constantinopel gelernet. Von dannen her ist vns Plato gegeben. von dannẽ her sind vns die schriften vnd lere Aristotilis. Demostenis. xenophõtis. Thucididis. Basilij. Dionisij. Origenis vnnd vil andrer zu vnsern tagen geoffenbart. aber yetzo wirdet es anders gestalt vnder dem kaiserthumb der Türcken der grymmigen menschen der feind gůter sitten vnd lere. yetzo ist der fluss der lere abgegraben vnd der prunñ d weißheit versigen. Jch bekenn das bey den lateinischen an vil endẽ. als zu Rom Parys Bononia Padua Senis Perus Köln Wieñ Leiptzk Erfurt vnd anderßwo treffenlich hohschuln sind. aber dise sind als bachlein auß kriechischẽ prunnen geflossen. Wie aber dise statt vnder den gewalt des Türckischen kaisers vñ durch ine mit sturm vñ geschoss komen sey des alles beschiht hienach vnder kaiser Friderichen dem dritten beschreibung vnd anzaigung.

## Constantinopel

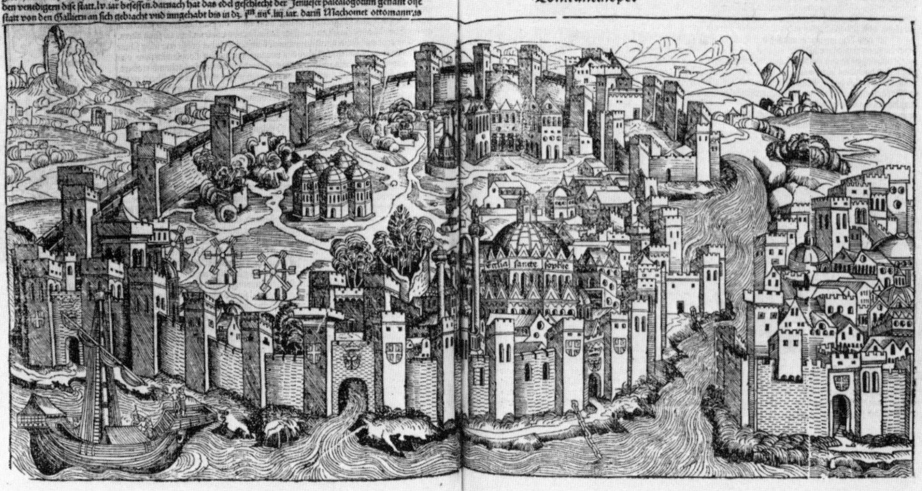

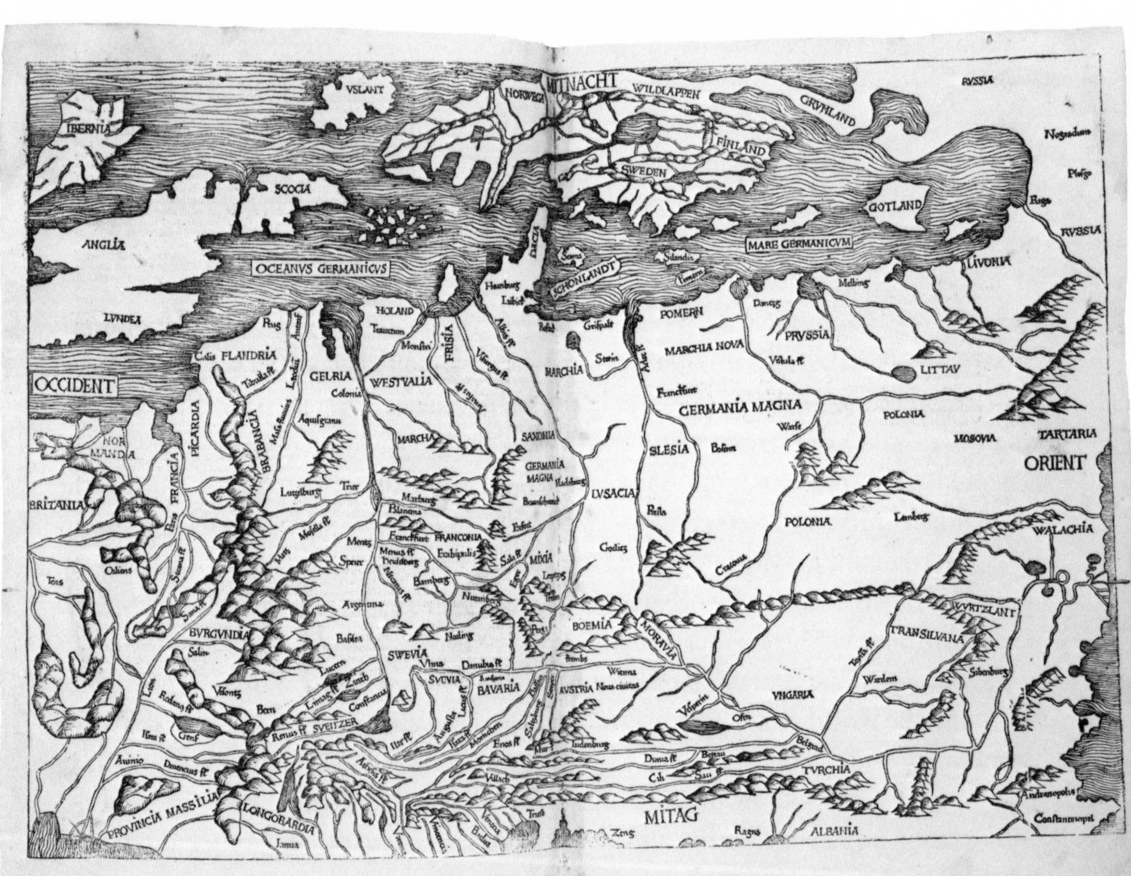

large-scale city views represent local landscapes seen from a single ground viewpoint—with rear streets and buildings hidden—or from a low vantage point—with street patterns visible (fig. 7, p. 115, and fig. 2). On the other hand, the small-scale maps of Germany and the world present a greatly reduced earth, seen from an infinite number of directly vertical viewpoints (figs. 3 and 4). There is a rough planimetric framework of rivers, coastlines, and town locations, but these two maps suggest little of the character of the terrain. At such small scales, the obliquely sketched mountains appear as molehills aimlessly trailing over the skin of the earth. Intermediate in scale between the city views and the maps, there are regional views which represent an incompletely realized effort to combine these two approaches—the pictorial realism of the low-level view with the planlike structure of the vertical view—in the form of the high oblique bird's-eye view.

*opposite page, top:*
FIGURE 2. Constantinople. [Hartmann Schedel], *Liber chronicarum* (Nuremberg: Anton Koberger, 23 December 1493), Rosenwald Collection, no. 166.

*opposite page, bottom:*
FIGURE 3. Map of Germany. [Hartmann Schedel], *Liber chronicarum* (Nuremberg: Anton Koberger, 23 December 1493), Rosenwald Collection, no. 166.

*below:*
FIGURE 4. World Map. [Hartmann Schedel], *Liber chronicarum* (Nuremberg: Anton Koberger, 23 December 1493), Rosenwald Collection, no. 166.

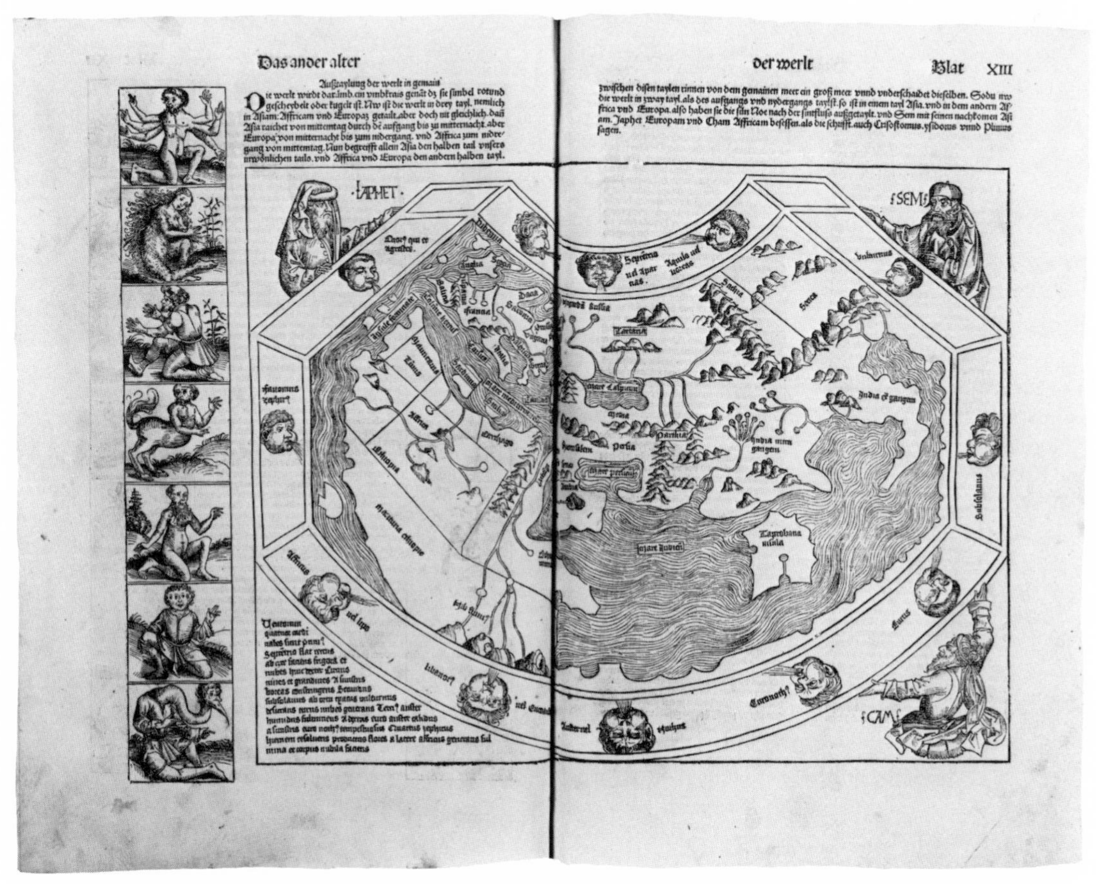

In the view of Sarmatia (modern Romania), for example, the artist has reduced and assembled local details into a composite regional view (fig. 5). Whether or not this represents an attempt to characterize the Sarmatian landscape along the Black Sea is open to question, but the approach definitely stems from the pictorial tradition of landscape representation. The impression of a coastal landscape is strikingly similar to part of a diptych, which shows the flooding of Holland in a dream of St. Elizabeth, painted ca. 1480 by the Master of Rhenen.[22] Both take the

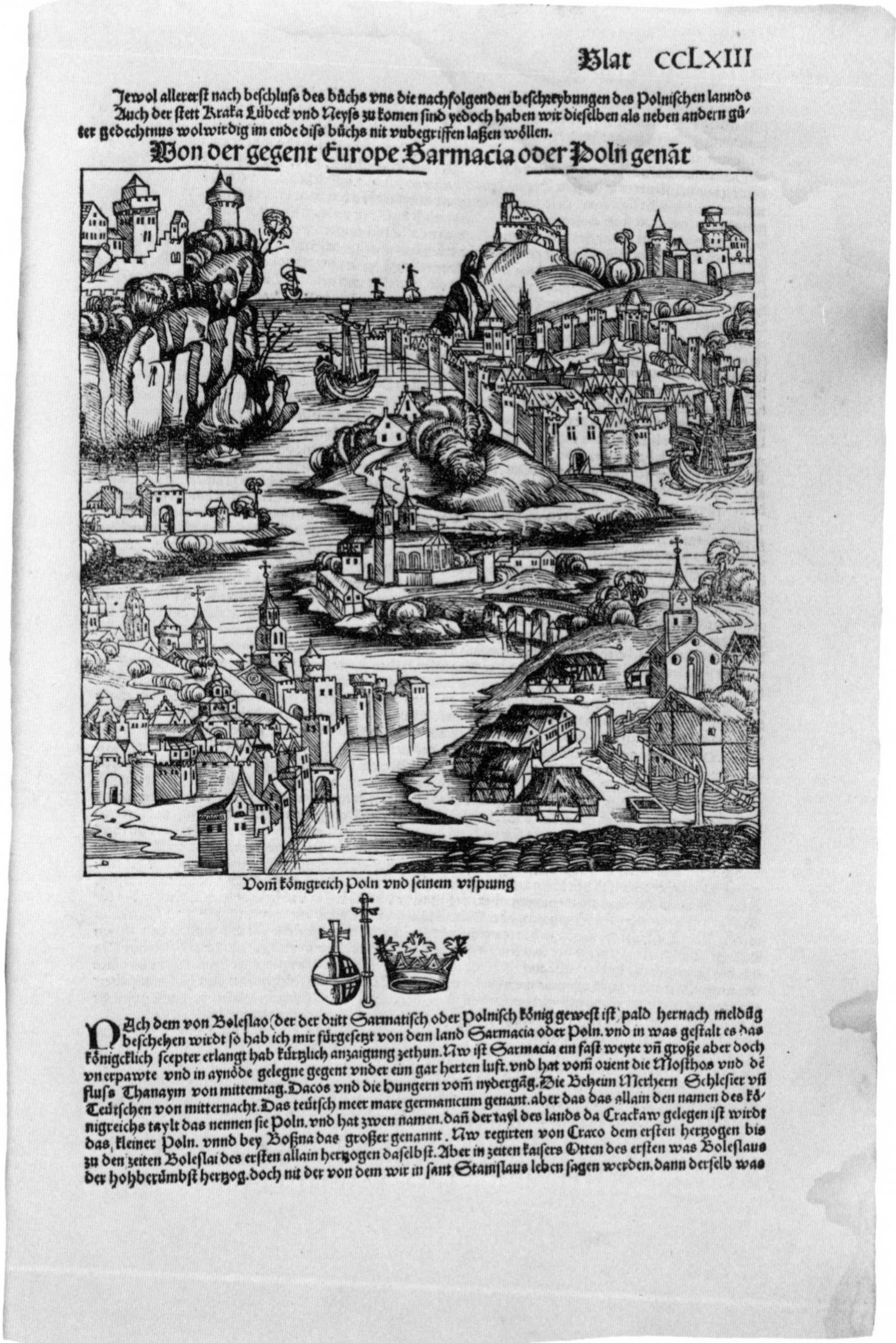

Blat CCLXIII

Jewol allererſt nach beſchluſs des bůchs vns die nachfolgenden beſchreybungen des Polniſchen lannds Auch der ſtett Kraka Lůbeck vnd Neyſs zu komen ſind yedoch haben wir dieſelben als neben andern gů-ter gedechtnus wolwirdig im ende diſs bůchs nit vnbegriffen laſſen wöllen.

**Von der gegent Europe Sarmacia oder Poln genãt**

Vom königreich Poln vnd ſeinem vrſprung

Nach dem von Boleſlao (der der dritt Sarmatiſch oder Polniſch könig geweſt iſt) pald hernach meldũg beſchehen wirdt ſo hab ich mir fürgeſetzt von dem land Sarmacia oder Poln. vnd in was geſtalt es das königcklich ſcepter erlangt hab kürtzlich anzaigung zethun. Nw iſt Sarmacia ein faſt weyte vñ groſſe aber doch vnerpawte vnd in aynöde gelegne gegent vnder eim gar herten luft. vnd hat vom orient die Moſthos vnd dẽ fluſs Thanaym von mittemtag. Dacos vnd die hungern vom nydergãg. Die Beheim Merhern Schleſier vñ Teũtſchen von mitternacht. Das teũtſch meer mare germanicum genant. aber das das allain den namen des kö-nigreichs taylt das nennen ſie Poln. vnd hat zwen namen. dañ der tayl des lands da Crackaw gelegen iſt wirdt das kleiner Poln. vnnd bey Boſſna das groſſer genannt. Nw regirten von Craco dem erſten hertzogen bis zu den zeiten Boleſlai des erſten allain hertzogen daſelbſt. Aber in zeiten kaiſers Otten des erſten was Boleſlaus der hohberümbſt hertzog. doch nit der von dem wir in ſant Staniſlaus leben ſagen werden. dann derſelb was

FIGURE 5. View of Sarmatia. [Hartmann Schedel], *Liber chronicarum* (Nuremberg: Anton Koberger, 23 December 1493), Rosenwald Collection, no. 166.

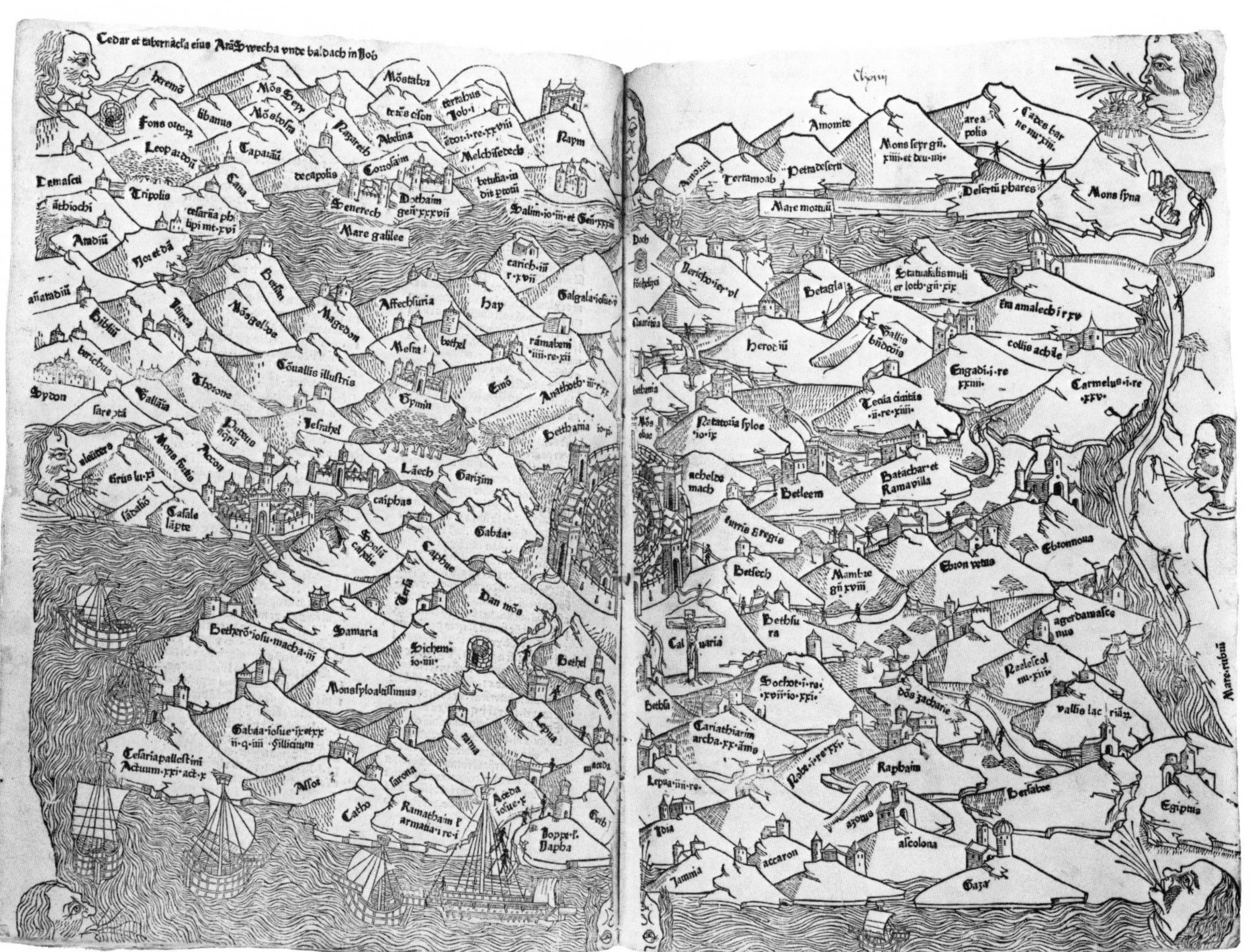


FIGURE 6. Map of the Holy Land. *Rudimentum novitiorum* (Lubeck: Lucas Brandis, 1475), Rosenwald Collection, no. 55.

same high oblique viewpoint, displaying the land as an overlapping succession of hills through which a river winds. Although the view of Sarmatia does not show identifiable places, the realistic intent of the earlier diptych is made clear by the labeling of the towns.

On medieval maps, terrain details were typically represented in similar pictorial fashion but positioned according to a symbolic rather than a realistic spatial framework. On the map of the Holy Land from the *Rudimentum novitiorum* (Lübeck, 1475), there is no pretense at planimetric arrangement or consistency of scale (fig. 6).[23] The organization of the map is based on Christian symbolism with Jerusalem at the center. Around the Holy City are arrayed the other places of the region, portrayed as clusters of obliquely viewed hillocks in bird's-eye-view fashion.

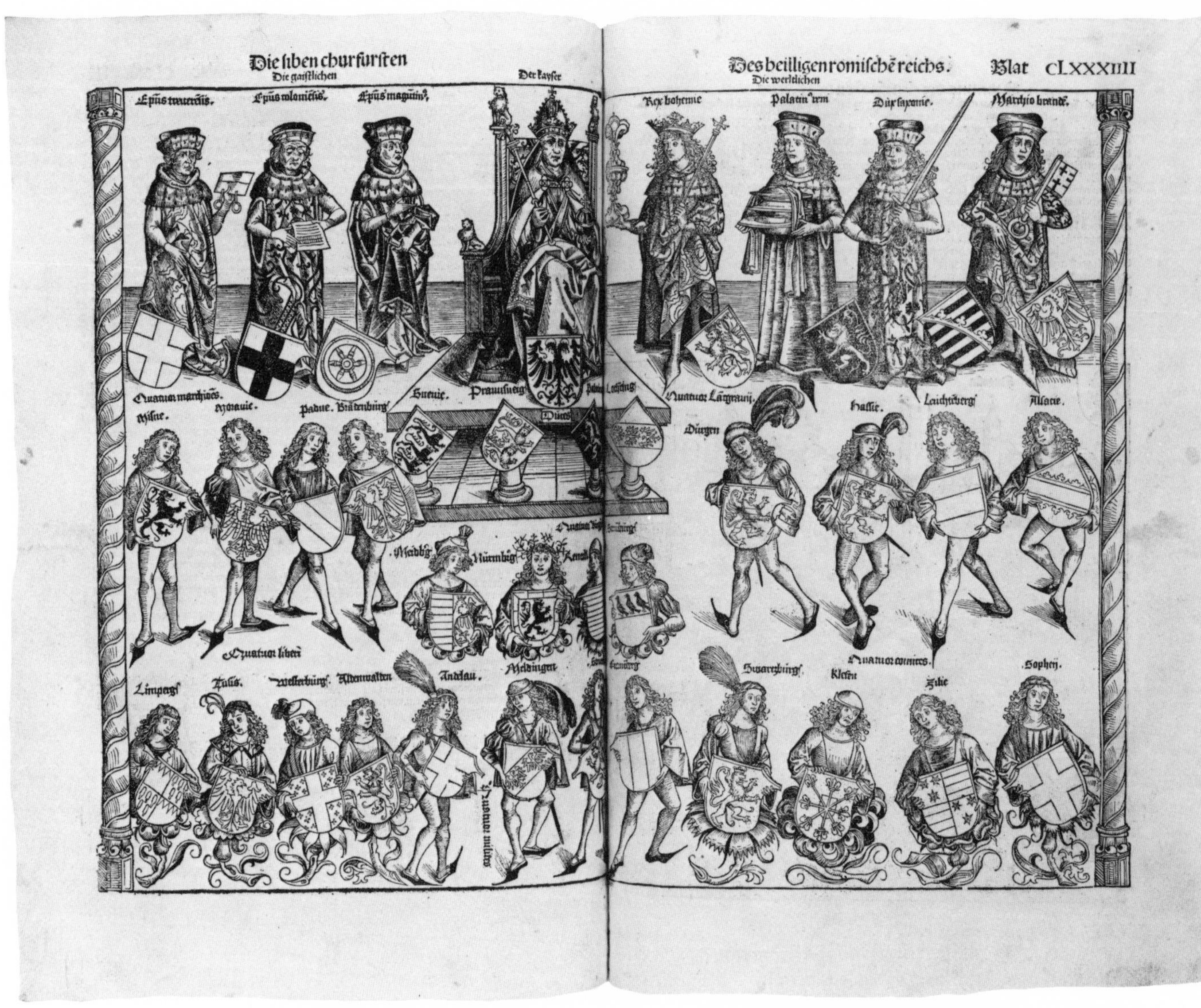


FIGURE 7. Electoral Hierarchy. [Hartmann Schedel], *Liber chronicarum* (Nuremberg: Anton Koberger, 23 December 1493), Rosenwald Collection, no. 166.

This pictorial treatment of a symbolic format has a direct equivalent in the *Liber chronicarum*—in a bird's-eye view depicting part of the electoral hierarchy of Germany. The page preceding the bird's-eye view diagrams the upper levels of this political institution with four symbolic representatives per level, according to the Quaternionen theory[24] (fig. 7). The emperor is enthroned at the upper center, and nobles, each holding his symbol of office, stand in rows beneath him. As space runs out toward the bottom of the page, the figures change from full to half length. This page lacks space for the three lowest levels of the political hierarchy, which instead continue in the bird's-eye view on the following two pages (see fig. 6, pp. 112–13). The rectangular view depicts a three-level hierarchy of urban places, arranged in rows of decreasing importance from top to bottom. Across the top are four walled and fortified civitates, in the middle, four large but unfortified villes, and at the bottom, four rustices, shown as small clusters of buildings. The composite view mixes apparent visual realism with a symbolic spatial framework.

Between the twelve-city view and the map of the German region added to the *Liber chronicarum* by Hieronymus Münzer, there is a complete break in approach. The map of Germany was probably based on a mid-fifteenth-century map either prepared or commissioned by the early German humanist Nicolas of Cusa. Although Nicolas of Cusa's sources of information (as well as his original map) are unknown, he did have ties to centers of astronomical activity in Germany and knowledge of classical authors by way of Italy.[25] The relatively accurate arrangement of rivers and coastlines on his map speaks for a connection to the tradition of scientific cartography. Yet the map of Germany, with its vertical viewpoint and rows of tiny, gumdrop-shaped mountains, completely lacks the apparent pictorial realism of the Sarmatia view or the composite twelve-city view.

The same observations hold true for the world map in the *Liber chronicarum*, which is based on a Ptolemaic conic projection. The map's similarity to the frontispiece map from the 1488 *Cosmographia* of Pomponius Mela suggests that both derive from a common source.[26] The gap between this scientific approach to cartography and the pictorial approach of the views had to be bridged before substantial progress could be made in the creation of medium-scale regional maps.

The time was ripe for this effort to begin in 1492 when Conrad Celtes addressed the University of Ingolstadt with innovative ideas for a teaching program (studia humanitas) in which the historical and geographical study of Germany was to play a large part.[27] Obviously inspired by the just published *Liber chronicarum,* Celtes signed a contract in 1493 with the financial backer of the Schedel work, Sebolt Schreyer, to "with all diligence, newly correct and put into another form the work, the Cronica, as it is now printed, together with a new Europa, and all other things belonging thereto and being necessary to it, such as shortening and expanding, as such may be necessary to benefit the work."[28] Celtes envisioned the publishing of a "Germania Illustrata," a book to be modeled on the *Italia illustrata* of Flavio Biondo, an Italian humanist. This work was intended to be a joint effort of German humanists. Even though the project remained an unfulfilled dream at his death in 1508, the solicitations of Celtes greatly stimulated efforts at regional description and mapping.[29]

Among Celtes's published writings, the *Quatuor libri amorum* of 1502 best demonstrates the progress in geographical writing and illustration due to his efforts.[30] Whereas the literary style and organization of the *Liber chronicarum* still owes much to the medieval chronicle, the *Quatuor libri amorum* consists of four classically inspired Latin poems, each personifying a different region of Germany as a woman. Closely tied to the text are four regional views of Germany, which clearly represent an attempt to integrate the pictorial and scientific approaches to landscape illustration (fig. 8). The innovative character of the views is almost certainly due to the editorial influence of Celtes, collaborating on the design of the book with the artist, presumed to be Dürer or a member of his school.[31] In each view from the *Quatuor libri amorum*, locally observed landscape details have been combined into a composite landscape seen from the high oblique, but there are marked differences with the Sarmatia view from the *Liber chronicarum*. In 1500 Erhard Etzlaub, a compass-maker and mapmaker in Nuremberg, had given Celtes one of his maps, probably the "Romweg" map.[32] The Etzlaub map, which was probably constructed from road distances given in itineraries, is a remarkably accurate map whose influences can clearly be seen in the Celtes views.[33] On both the map and the views, latitude and longitude divisions have been marked off along the borders. In addition, landscape features have been labeled and positioned, albeit roughly, according to their geographical coordinates. On the view of "Barbara Codonea" (northern Germany), the heart-shaped Bohemian forest, a further distinctive feature of the Etzlaub map and its derivatives appears at the bottom center of the view. This attempt to combine the scientific and pictorial approaches to landscape representation parallels Celtes's attempt to unite literary and mathematical humanism in a group called the Collegium Poetarum et Mathematicorum.[34] The views in the *Quatuor libri amorum* clearly stem from a desire to move beyond the purely pictorial assembly of characteristic details reflected by the Sarmatia view in the *Liber chronicarum*.

During the course of the sixteenth century, continued progress in both the pictorial and cartographic portrayal of landscape was to make possible a more successful integration of these approaches in the form of regional maps. Shortly after 1500 the Danube School made the landscape of southern Germany the independent subject of drawings, prints, and paintings. One of the characteristics of their work was the use of an elevated viewpoint to help create the effect of panoramic space. Another feature of landscape representation in German Renaissance art was the sketchlike abbreviation of landscape details, such as hills and trees. This was a graphic vocabulary which had originated in late fifteenth-century prints and which was further developed by both Albrecht Dürer and the Danube artists. The sketchlike treatment of landscape details could also be adapted, at somewhat reduced scale, for representation of terrain on regional maps. Examination of Augustin Hirschvogel's maps reveals a strong similarity to his landscape etchings in the schematic shorthand he uses for landscape details. Although other sixteenth-century German cartographers were not always artists, the preparation of their woodcut maps in the same shops as artistic illustrations surely resulted in the transfer of such stylistic characteristics to maps.

At the same time, the cartographic representation of Germany was being improved by the application of better surveying instruments and procedures to increasingly ambitious regional mapping projects. The introduction of triangulation, using distances and directions measured by field survey to locate features during map construction, enhanced the planimetric accuracy of the maps produced. A strong emphasis on personal knowledge of the terrain being mapped also contributed to the quality of maps. Displaying typical personal dedication, the Swiss historian, Aegidius Tschudi (then nineteen years of age), toured all over Switzerland on foot in 1524, climbing mountains and making sketches which later formed the basis for his excellent 1528 map of Switzerland.[35] The increasing realism of hillforms on maps of the period reflects the intensive observation by geographers of landforms.

Although much of the regional mapping was not done until the second half of the sixteenth century, Sebastian Münster was able to take advantage of many new sources like Tschudi's map when preparing the maps for his *Cosmographia* (fig. 9). The contrast with the *Liber chronicarum* is immediately apparent. Münster's text is better organized, with the section on Europe forming the core of the book rather than a last-minute addition. The effective writing of descriptive prose has been mastered, and, even though Münster's information comes from a variety of sources, he has been able to combine the material into a continuous narrative. Most striking, though, is the expanded role of the landscape illustrations. The illustrative program hinted at in the *Liber chronicarum* has been realized through the addition of medium-scale regional maps to fill in the gap between the large-scale city views and the small-scale maps.

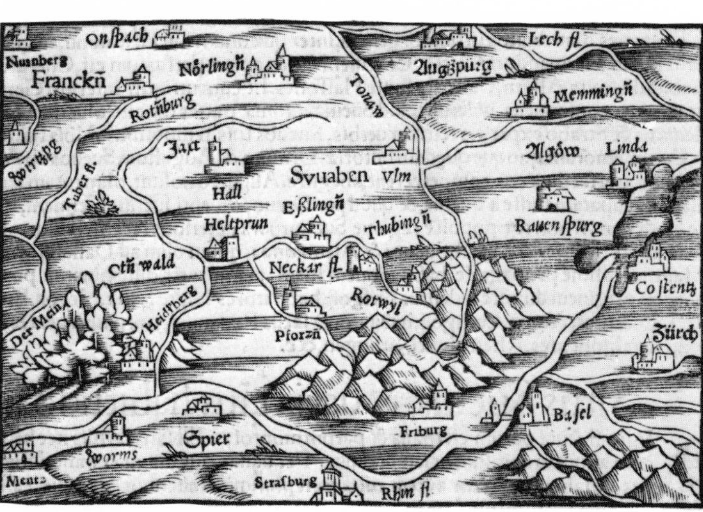


FIGURE 9. Suavia. Sebastian Münster, *Cosmosgraphiae universalis* (Basel: Henrichvm Petri, 1550), Library of Congress, Rare Book and Special Collections Division, G113.M7 1550.

FIGURE 8. Barbara Codonea. Conrad Celtes, *Qvatvor libri amorvm secvndvm qvatvor latera Germanie . . .* (Nuremberg, 1502), Rosenwald Collection, no. 592.

The important role played by the illustrations in the *Cosmographia* is clearly a result of Münster's efforts. Intensive biographical study has documented his active procuring and editing of both literary source material and illustrations.[36] He may also have had a hand in the arrangement of text and illustrations, although he was assisted by professional artists. In this regard, the lesser importance of illustrations in the first edition of the *Cosmographia* (1544) has been attributed partly to the fact that planned assistance from the artists Konrad Schnitt and Hans Holbein the Younger fell through when the former died and the latter moved to England. Only somewhat later did Hans Rudolf Manuel Deutsch, second son of the then better known Niklaus Manuel Deutsch, become involved as chief artistic collaborator.[37] Between 1544 and 1550, Münster worked intensively to improve the illustrative material, spurred on partly by the competitive threat of Johann Stümpf's *Gemeiner loblicher Eydgenoschafft Stetten, Landen und Völckeren Chronick*, which appeared in 1548.[38] As a result, the number of illustrations in the extensively revised 1550 edition of Münster's *Cosmographia* is greatly increased.

Near the beginning of the *Cosmographia*, the fourteen small-scale double-page maps have been placed in a section by themselves (fig. 10). Two maps of the

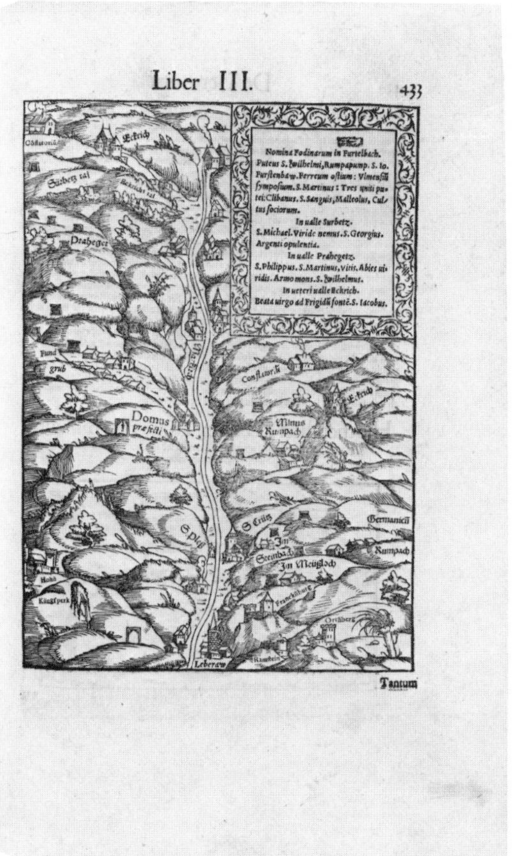


*opposite page:*
FIGURE 10. Germaniae. Sebastian Münster, *Cosmographiae universalis* (Basel: Henrichvm Petri, 1550), Library of Congress, Rare Book and Special Collections Division, G113.M7 1550.

*right:*
FIGURE 11. De argentisodina Leberthalensi. Sebastian Münster, *Cosmographiae universalis* (Basel: Henrichvm Petri, 1550), Library of Congress, Rare Book and Special Collections Division, G113.M7 1550.

world, one modern and one historical (according to Ptolemy), appear here, as well as maps of the continents and various European countries. These small-scale maps form a sort of reference section. Münster's intention that they be used with the text is made clear by his note at the beginning of the section on Europe, referring the reader to the maps.

In addition, Münster has incorporated in the body of the text fifty-two medium-scale maps of the regions being described. These maps are often quite small; only one-fifth are full-page size or larger, and the majority are one-half or one-third of page size. On these maps the coastlines and rivers form a cartographic base on which hills, mountains, forests, and towns are shown obliquely in pictorial form. It should be noted, though, that the cartographic niceties of scale and orientation are lacking in all but a few cases. Münster prepared his regional maps from whatever sources he could obtain, reducing and generalizing them for publication. Hence the considerable variation in the maps. His efforts at incorporating new cartographic material are commendable, although unfamiliarity with areas being mapped sometimes resulted in editorial errors.[39] He was performing the important service of making recent cartographic information generally available. Although the character of the pictorial representation varies with the quality of Münster's cartographic source and the type of landscape in the area shown, the best of them convey a real sense of the nature of the terrain, as the one titled "De argentisodina Leberthalensi" (fig. 11). On this map, the tree foliage reminiscent of the Danube School is also a reminder of the contributing influences of artistic style.

Finally, there are about a hundred city views in Münster's *Cosmographia*, about forty-nine of which are realistic. These, like the maps, were obtained by Münster from his scholarly contacts, whom he credits fulsomely. Considering the variety of sources, it is not surprising that the views, like the regional maps, vary considerably in appearance. Most of them (thirty-eight) are double-page views, in contrast to the much smaller imaginary views that serve as visual markers throughout the text. Only one-third of the realistic views are obviously ground-level views, while the remainder show the cities from low or high oblique viewpoints. The informative role of about two-thirds of the realistic views is enhanced by the inclusion of place-names, both on the view and in a legend. In addition, the orientation of

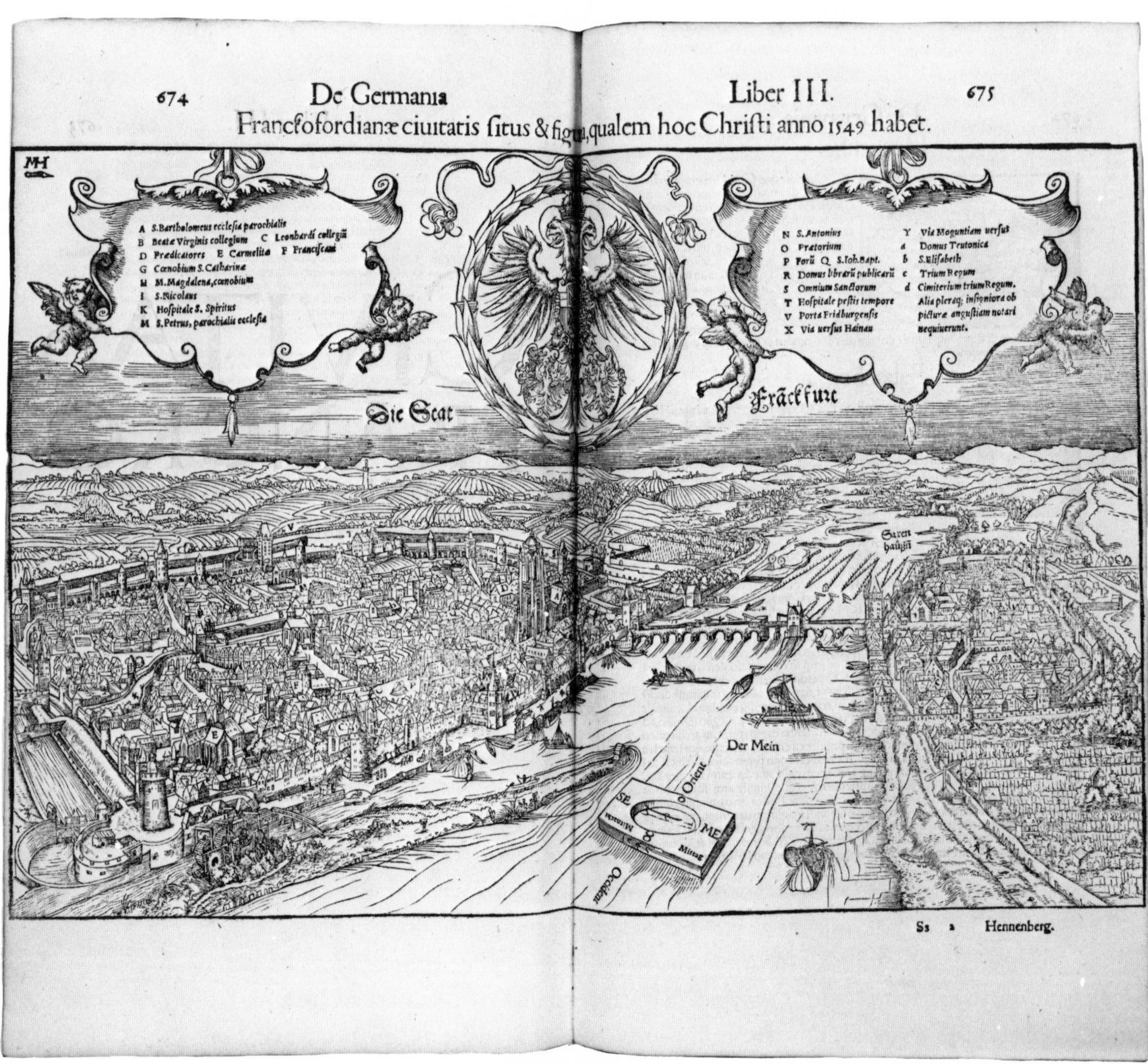


FIGURE 12. Francofordianae. Sebastian Münster, *Cosmographiae universalis* (Basel: Henrichvm Petri, 1550), Library of Congress, Rare Book and Special Collections Division, G113.M7 1550.

the view is indicated about half of the time. The view of "Francofordianae civitatis" shows streets in maplike fashion from the high oblique, for example. Both place-names and a legend have been used here, and directions are indicated by a decorative symbol shaped like a compass (fig. 12). The view of "Colonia Agrippina civitas" differs in that it is drawn from a point on the ground and therefore fails to show the street pattern in maplike perspective, but it does include place names, an extensive legend, and indication of orientation (fig. 13). Given these "cartographic" features, it seems clear that the city views constitute part of a related sequence of landscape illustrations at different scales rather than a completely separate mode of representation.

FIGURE 13. Colonia Agrippina. Sebastian Münster, *Cosmographiae universalis* (Basel: Henrichvm Petri, 1550), Library of Congress, Rare Book and Special Collections Division, G113.M7 1550.

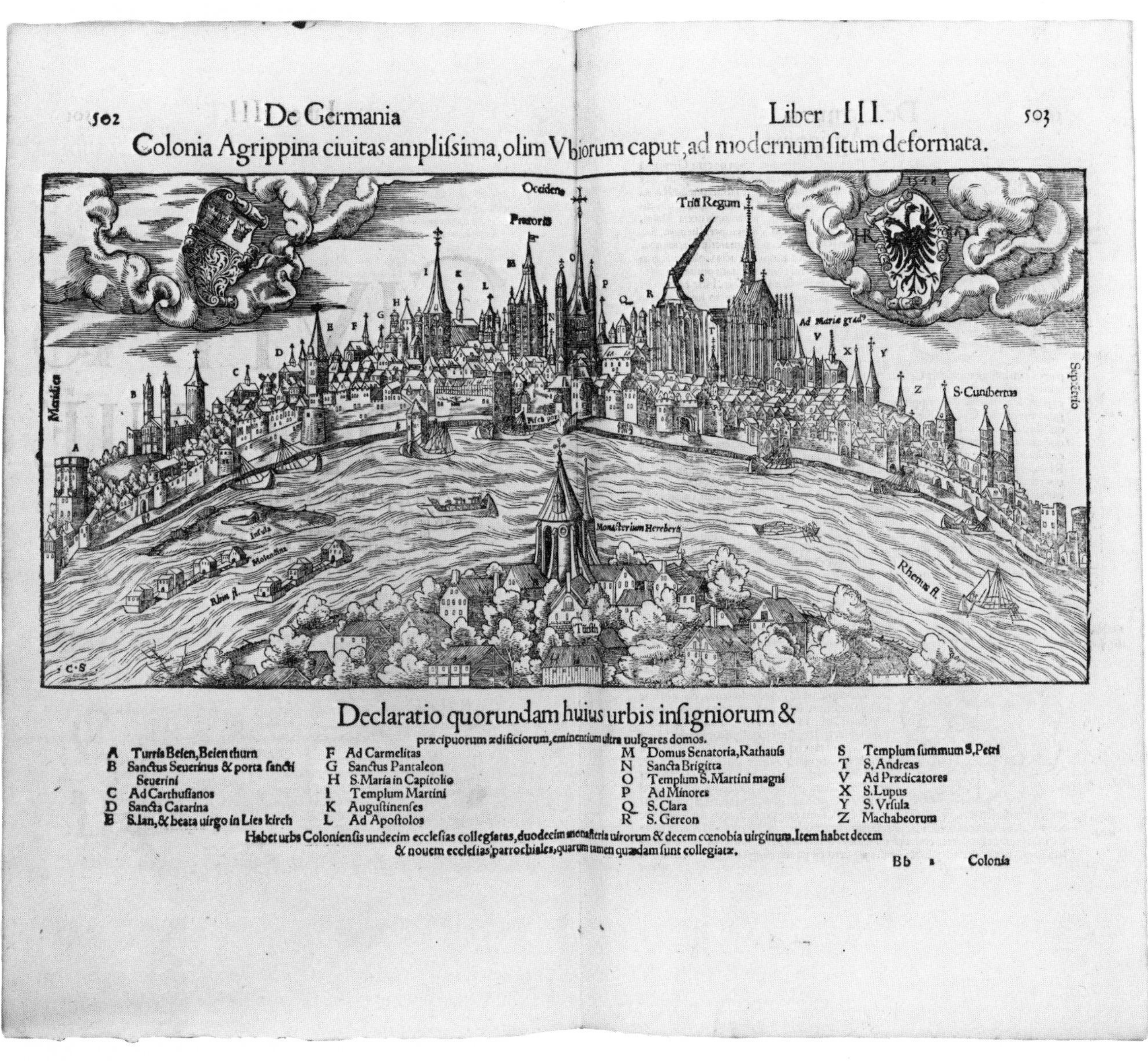

The major features of the illustrated geography book had come into being by the middle of the sixteenth century in Germany. One crucial characteristic was the combination of descriptive text with an ordered program of pictorial and cartographic landscape illustrations at different scales. For this form of landscape representation, modern geography owes a great deal to the efforts of the German humanists to record the German landscape on paper, or, as Sebastian Münster expressed it, to reflect the entire land of Germany as in a mirror. When these men developed a multimedia mode of landscape representation that would be applied in later times to other places, they achieved far more than they had set out to do.

## NOTES

1. Sebastian Münster, "Erklarung des newen Instruments der Sunnen . . . Item ein Vermannung Sebastiani Münster an alle liebhaber der künstenn, im hilff zu thun warer und rechter beschrybung Teutscher Nation" (Oppenheim, 1528), as translated in Gerald Strauss, *Sixteenth-Century Germany, Its Topography and Topographers* (Madison: University of Wisconsin Press, 1959), pp. 26–27.

2. Gerald Strauss, who has traced the historical development of this genre, calls it both "topographical-historical" and "geographical" in his "Germania Illustrata, Topographical-Historical Descriptions of Germany in the Sixteenth-Century" (Ph.D. diss., Columbia University, 1957), later published as *Sixteenth-Century Germany, Its Topography and Topographers*, cited above. The former term does have the advantage of sidestepping the varying meanings attached to the word "geography" in Renaissance Germany and also, suiting Strauss's purpose as a historian, accents the historical aspect. However, the terms *descriptive geography* or *regional geography* are commonly used by modern geographers to refer to this type of literature, past or present, and it is in this sense that the word *geography* will be used here.

3. This quotation comes from the explanation accompanying Martin Helwig's map of Silesia, 1564: "dieweil auch ein Vieh seinen Stall und Herburg kennet; Obs einem vernünftigen Mensch ehrlich sey, da er seyn eygen Vaterland nicht kennet, noch kennenlernen wil," as reprinted in A. Heyer, "Geschichte der Kartographie Schlesiens bis zur Preussischen Besitzergreifung," *Acta cartographica* 13 (1972):75.

4. Sebastian Münster, *Cosmographia: Beschreibung aller Lender durch Sebastianum Münsterum, in welcher begriffen aller Völcker, Herrschaften, Stetten, und namhaftiger Flecken herkommen . . . durch die gantze Welt, und für nemlich teutschen Nation . . .* (Basel, 1544) and *Cosmographiae universalis*, Book 4 (Basel?, 1550).

5. Karl Heinz Burmeister, *Sebastian Münster: versuch eines biographischen Gesamtbildes* (Basel and Stuttgart: Helbing und Lichtenhahn, 1969), pp. 131–33.

6. Leo Weisz, *Die Schweiz auf alten Karten* (Zurich: Buchverlag der Neuen Zürcher Zeitung, 1971), pp. 26 and 28.

7. Albrecht Dürer, *Underweysung der Messung mit dem Zirckel und Richtscheyt, . . . durch Albrecht Dürer, zusamen gezogen, und durch in Selbs, . . . an vil Orten gebessert* (Nuremberg: Hieronymous Formschneider, 1538).

8. Samuel V. Edgerton, Jr., *The Renaissance Rediscovery of Linear Perspective* (New York: Basic Books, 1975).

9. F. Grenacher, "A Woodcut Map: A Formcutter of Maps Wanders through Europe in the First Quarter of the Sixteenth Century," *Imago mundi* 24 (1970):31–41.

10. Leo Bagrow, "A. Ortelii Catalogus Cartographorum," *Petermanns Geographische Mitteilungen*, Supplement, no. 199 (1928):106–10; Yale University Art Gallery, *Prints and Drawings of the Danube School: An Exhibition of South German and Austrian Graphic Art of 1500 to 1560,*

prepared under the direction of Charles Talbot and Alan Shestack (New Haven: Yale University Press, 1969), pp. 88–93.

11. Bernhard von Breydenbach, *Peregrinatio in Terram Sanctam* (Mainz: Erhard Reuwich, 1486), Rosenwald Collection, no. 116.

12. Ernst Bernleithner, "Osterreich im Kartenbild der Zeiten," *Kartographische Nachrichten* 5 (1966):177–78.

13. Leo Bagrow, "Carta Itineraria Europae Martini Ilacomili, 1511," *Imago mundi* 11 (1954):149–50.

14. Marcel Destombes, "The mappamundi of the poem Alexandreios by Gautier de Châtillon (ca. A.D. 1180)," *Imago mundi* 19 (1965):10.

15. P. D. A. Harvey, *The History of Topographical Maps: Symbols, Pictures, and Surveys* (London: Thames and Hudson, 1980), pp. 133–52; Derek Howse and Michael Sanderson, *The Sea Chart* (New York: McGraw-Hill Book Company, 1973), p. 11.

16. Hartmann Schedel, *Liber chronicarum* (Nuremberg: A. Koberger, 1493).

17. Harvey, *History of Topographical Maps*, p. 83; Valerian von Loga, "Die Städteansichten in Hartmann Schedel's Weltchronik," *Jahrbuch der K. Preuss. Kunstsammlungen* 9 (1880):93–107 and 184–96.

18. Adrian Wilson, *The Making of the Nuremberg Chronicle* (Amsterdam: Nico Israel, 1976), p. 50.

19. Ibid., pp. 150–51 and 168.

20. Ibid., p. 216.

21. Strauss, *Sixteenth-Century Germany*, pp. 54–56.

22. Leo Bagrow and R. A. Skelton, *The History of Cartography* (Cambridge: Harvard University Press, 1966), pl. cxvi.

23. *Rudimentum novitiorum* (Lübeck: Luca Brandis, 1475). This view precedes the section of text on the Holy Land.

24. A. Werminghoff, "Die Quaternionen der Deutschen Reichsverfassung," *Archiv für Kulturgeschichte* 3 (1905):288–300.

25. Harvey, *History of Topographical Maps*, p. 146.

26. It has been suggested that the *Liber chronicarum* world map was copied from the one in Pomponius Mela (Von Loga, "Die Städteansichten," pp. 105–6; Wilson, *Making of the Nuremberg Chronicle*, p. 115), but the fact that the latter map is less detailed, much smaller, and markedly different in proportions makes an unknown common ancestor seem a more likely possibility.

27. Strauss, *Sixteenth-Century Germany*, pp. 19–21.

28. Wilson, *Making of the Nuremberg Chronicle*, p. 245.

29. Strauss, *Sixteenth-Century Germany*, pp. 17–25.

30. Conradus Celtes, *Quatuor libri amorum secundum quatuor latera germaniae . . .* (Nürnberg: Subprivilegio sodalitas Celticae, 1502).

31. Library of Congress, *The Lessing J. Rosenwald Collection: A Catalog of the Gifts of Lessing J. Rosenwald to the Library of Congress, 1943 to 1975* (Washington: Library of Congress, 1977), p. 114; Fritz Schnelbögl, "Life and Work of the Nuremberg Cartographer Erhard Etzlaub," *Imago mundi* 20 (1966):23.

32. Schnelbögl, ibid.

33. Harvey, *History of Topographical Maps*, p. 147.

34. Bernleithner, "Osterreich im Kartenbild der Zeiten," pp. 177–78.

35. W. Blumer, "The Map Drawings of Aegidius Tschudi (1505–1572)," *Imago mundi* 10 (1953):57.

36. Burmeister, *Sebastian Münster*.

37. Ibid., p. 120.

38. Ibid., p. 119; Johannes Stumpf, *Gemeiner loblicher Eydgnoschafft Stetten, Landen und Völckeren Chronick . . .* (Zurich, 1548).

39. K. Buczek, "Ein Beitrag zur Entstehungsgeschichte der 'Kosmographie' von Sebastian Münster," *Imago mundi* 1 (1935):35; and W. Horn, "Sebastian Münster's Map of Prussia and the Variants of It," *Imago mundi* 7 (1965):67–74.

J. H. PARRY

# DEPICTING A NEW WORLD

One of the most obvious uses of the talents of the landscape painter might seem to be that of giving the reading public a visual perception of newly discovered lands. For a brief space of years, in the second half of the eighteenth century and in the early decades of the nineteenth, there was indeed a close and fruitful collaboration between explorers, painters, engravers, book illustrators, and publishers. Many of the naval expeditions which, during those years, charted the Pacific, its coasts, and myriad islands, included painters as well as astronomers and botanists in their companies. Not all naval officers, it is true, cared to have these incongruous characters on board. Warships were always crowded, and a captain might well object to allotting precious space to artists and their gear. Bligh never carried them. Vancouver thought that among his officers and young gentlemen, some, "with little instruction," could learn to draw landscapes as well as charts.[1] He saw no need to ship "professional persons" for these duties. This was a pity, in view of the majestic splendor of the coasts he explored; surprising, too, since Vancouver had served as a midshipman under Cook and should have known better.

Many of his contemporaries did know better. Cook, himself, though not particularly interested, so far as is known, in art for its own sake, recognized the importance of recording what he called—loosely and compendiously—"landskip." He had painters with him on all his expeditions, took an interest in their work, and—though himself the least vain of men—sometimes affably sat (or rather stood) for his own portrait.[2]



Sydney Parkinson, William Hodges, and John Webber (artists who accompanied Cook) were not of course exclusively or even mainly engaged in landscape painting in the normally accepted sense. They were expected to make accurate drawings of plants and animals, to depict people, with their artifacts and their ceremonies, and in general to record what Cook called "remarkable occurrences"; anything, in short, from cannibals to kangaroos. They managed, nevertheless, to get in an astonishing amount of straightforward landscape work. They may not have been great artists, but they were highly competent, hard-working, and prolific. Some of their efforts, perhaps, convey impressions different from those originally intended. Polynesian young women performing their "wanton" dances become nymphs in Arcadian groves. Hodges's picture of a boatload of sailors hunting walrus for food and ivory off Alaska suggests irresistibly a well-armed Jacquerie invading the drawing room of the Athenaeum. Straight landscapes are more objective, and in painting them the artists—Hodges and Webber especially—were at their best. Webber captured admirably both the precipitous, icy hostility of Tierra del Fuego and the misty fragility of the Tahitian peaks. Such work was influential, and deservedly so, then and later. Between 1773 and 1784 a substantial part of it was reproduced in the form of engravings and published in London.[3] It enabled a fascinated European public to become familiar not only with the appearance of many Pacific peoples but with the landscapes in which those peoples dwelled. It is precious material for historians of discovery today.

The happy collaboration of explorers, painters, engravers, book illustrators, and publishers was characteristic of the age of Cook and his contemporaries and his immediate successors: of the Silver Age of maritime discovery, so to speak. It survived into the nineteenth century. The *Beagle* carried several artists in succession; fortunately for the records, for Darwin (to judge from the few surviving sketches among his papers in the Cambridge University Library) was no draftsman. Since the ship was primarily engaged in survey, the artists' principal duty—in Captain Fitzroy's opinion at least—was the preparation of coastal profiles for the Hydrographic Office, but they made sketches and watercolors as well, including landscapes, and some of those done by Augustus Earle and Conrad Martens have considerable charm.[4]

In the course of the nineteenth century the explorer-artist alliance largely broke down, for two main practical reasons. First, there was relatively little maritime exploration remaining to be done. Most of the major nineteenth-century expeditions were by land, in the interior of the great continents. Painters and other civilian specialists could usually be fitted into a ship, even a warship, if the captain did not object, but the leader of an arduous land expedition, using human porterage, could not easily take along an entourage of scientists and artists such as accompanied Cook and Bougainville. Second, artists were less needed, or apparently less needed. The invention of the camera and progressive reductions in its size and weight provided explorers with an easier and cheaper form of visual record.

In the present century, probably the most distinguished examples of paintings illustrating exploration were the watercolors done by Edward Wilson on the two

Scott expeditions to the Antarctic. These expeditions were, at least in part, maritime in character. Wilson, however, participated in them officially not as a painter but as physician and zoologist. His skill in watercolor was employed chiefly (and triumphantly) in precise depiction of birds. His haunting, icy landscapes were an uncovenanted bonus.[5]

The significant role of artists in the voyages of the Silver Age of maritime discovery contrasts with their almost total absence from the expeditions of the Golden Age, from the voyages of Columbus, Vasco da Gama, Magellan, and others who in the brief space of half a century or so demonstrated the worldwide unity of the sea, established direct maritime communication between Europe, East Africa, and Asia, and opened the vast new world of the Americas to Europeans. Here, one would think, was an immense area of new visual experience to be recorded, reproduced, and published. Yet no competent artist accompanied the expeditions. Those artists who drew or painted the results of exploration showed what their public expected to see rather than what the discoverers actually saw.

The many contemporary books and pamphlets describing the early discoveries are illustrated mainly by woodcuts. Some of these were the product of the stay-at-home artist's imagination, depicting topics that sent agreeable shivers of horror down the spines of the reading public of the time: savage people, their nakedness, their wild dances, their cannibal feasts, or else savage wild animals or the stock monsters of medieval fancy, giant gold-storing ants, cynocephali, monoculi, skiapods, pygmies, and hermaphrodites. Yet other illustrations were the result of another kind of cannibalism: the reuse of blocks made originally for illustrating other books that had nothing to do with discovery. Some woodblocks, and later some engraved plates, were used again and again. A well-known example is the famous Sadeler-Stradanus engraving of the building of Noah's Ark (fig. 1). It did duty on many occasions and was finally used by Theodor de Bry in 1594 to illustrate the adventures of Nicuesa on the coast of Veragua in 1510. De Bry, more concerned with verisimilitude than most of his predecessors, inserted a little shipwreck scene in the top righthand corner, to indicate the occasion of the busy housebuilding and shipbuilding that occupy the center of the plate.

In default of eye-witness paintings and drawings, the next best thing would be paintings and drawings based on eye-witness descriptions. Many journals and first-hand accounts of discoveries and conquests have survived. Some of the writers—especially among the Spanish conquerors of the Americas—were superb narrators of the events in which they participated, masters of simple literary artifice, of dry irony, and of dramatic suspense. For the most part, however, they possessed limited powers of description and narrow views of what they thought worth describing. They were practical men; neither intellectual curiosity nor aesthetic appreciation appear prominently in their writings. They were more interested in the works of man than in the works of nature, more interested in cultivated fields than in forests, more interested in the uses of things than in what they looked like.

Oviedo, whose *Historia general* is the best and most comprehensive early

FIGURE 1. Jan Sadeler, Building of the Ark, engraving, as adapted by Theodor de Bry to illustrate Nicuesa's adventures in Veragua. Theodor de Bry, *Grands Voyages*, part 4 (Frankfurt, 1594), Rosenwald Collection, no. 1309.

Olandus carauellam, & casas ædificare curat. XIX.

NIQVESA *noctu coorta tempestate, à suis abripitur. Qui centum millia deinde emensi vt eum inuenirent nec quidquam intelligerent, Olando, dum Niquesa rediret, summam Imperii deferunt. Is quo omnem sociis spem fugæ tolleret, naues fluctuantes temere ad littus ferri atq; allidi sinit: mox, nimis festinati consilii errore animaduerso, è fractarum nauium tabulis carauellam vnam ad subitos & necessarios vsus fabricari iubet. Inde casas moliri, Mayzum seminare cœperunt.*

*Indi*

account of the Americas, exemplifies these priorities of interest.[6] His descriptions of Indian artifacts are illustrated by crude woodcuts. They are somewhat diagrammatic, it is true—his dugout canoe[7] suggests a Victorian cast-iron bathtub rather than a vessel intended for actual travel over water—but nonetheless recognizable. He gives good accounts of the principal Amerindian food crops, again with woodcuts, and an appreciative description of the Peruvian llama, an animal which greatly took the fancy of the conquistadores. On wild animals and wild plants he is much less convincing, even perfunctory. Presumably he relied on descriptions given by Indians rather than observing for himself, and he rarely succeeds in conveying a clear impression of the plant or animal he is describing.

Nor have we from Spanish writings or, still less, from Spanish drawings clear visual impressions of the people of the New World. The ethnologist-missionary friars—Bernardino de Sahagún, Diego Durán, and, most distinguished of all in this respect, Juan de Tovar—all employed tlacuilos, Indian painter-scribes, to illustrate their manuscripts. The watercolor drawings these men produced are conventional, decorative, and, to European eyes, lifeless.[8]

It is odd that the only really lively and convincing drawings made by a European of Mexican Indians at the time of the conquest were made by a German. Hernando Cortés, when he visited Spain in 1528, took with him several Mexican notables and a troupe of acrobats and jugglers. The appearance of these people aroused great interest, and a series of watercolor drawings were made of them by Christoph Weiditz, medal engraver of Augsburg, who happened to be about the court on business unconnected with America. They are preserved in "Das Trachtenbuch des Christoph Weiditz," in Nuremberg.[9] It is odd, again, that so valuable a record should be tucked away in a collection of drawings of costumes.

The Iberian explorers of the New World, in short, were on the whole conspicuously insensitive to their visual surroundings and, as might be expected, they neither described nor painted, nor encouraged anyone else to paint, the landscapes they encountered. One thinks of Hernando Pizarro, the most articulate of the Pizarro brothers and the only literate one, on his way to the spoil of Pachacamac, riding along the eastern rim of the tremendous chasm known today as the Callejón de Huaylas, with the towering spires of Huascarán on his left and the rushing Santa river in its gorge far below him on his right. He says nothing of these splendors but merely grumbles from time to time about the malos pasos—the precipitous tracks, the rock-hewn steps, and the snow—that make the going hard for the horses.[10] Or one remembers Alvar Núñez Cabeza de Vaca, the man who walked from Florida to Mexico, a man of sensitive intelligence and great spiritual power: he was the first European discoverer, on a later expedition, of the Iguaçú Falls. In the journal of his expedition, that mighty cirque of cataracts is described simply as an obstacle to passage down the river, necessitating a tiresome portage.[11]

It may be objected that very few people in sixteenth-century Europe cared much for cataracts, mountains, or jungles. These were the romantic properties of a later, more prosperous, more comfortable generation. It is true, also, that landscape painting, engraving, and book illustration were all, in the early sixteenth century, in their infancy. Nevertheless, the visual indifference of the New World Spaniards seems extraordinary. They could not even—town-dwellers as they were by preference—describe the appearance of Amerindian towns. Bernal Díaz's excited account of his first sight of Tenochtitlan-Mexico is moving and evocative.[12] Don Bernal describes admirably his own feelings as he marched on the long straight causeway across the lake, but in describing the appearance of the city itself he takes refuge in analogy with a popular romance. He does not really succeed in telling us what the place looked like, and to this day we have no clear picture of it, except for archaeological reconstructions. Similarly, we know little of the appearance of Cuzco. There are a few early accounts of the architectural features of particular buildings, but apart from knowing that it had dressed-stone buildings, thatched roofs, and narrow streets, we have no clear visual image from contemporary sources of the city as a whole, or of the mountains that rim the high valley in which it lies.[13] The engravings of Cuzco in the Braun and Hogenberg *Civitates orbis terrarum* and in the De Bry *Grands Voyages* show it with the grid layout and the quadrangular wall of a Roman castra (fig. 2). The engravers had nothing better to go on.

FIGURE 2. Cuzco, engraving. Georg Braun and Franz Hogenberg, *Civitates orbis terrarvm* (Antwerp: Apud G. Kempensem, 1581–1618), Rosenwald Collection, no. 716.

FIGURE 3. Four Woodcuts. Amerigo Vespucci, *Quattuor navigationes* (Strasbourg: Johann Grüninger, 1509), New York, The New York Public Library, Rare Books and Manuscripts Division. Astor, Lenox and Tilden Foundations.

Few serious attempts, then, were made by Iberians (who of course were the people best informed in the matter) to present coherent visual impressions of the New World in the sixteenth century. Other Europeans, though less well-informed, did somewhat better. Some of the early Italian explorers in Iberian service recorded their impressions of the natural scene. Columbus was ecstatic, though vague, about the beauty of the Bahamas, Cuba, and Hispaniola. Of Vespucci's writing very little remains that is certainly attributable to him.[14] His manuscript letters suggest that he was a careful observer with a gift for recording what he saw. One of them contains a recognizably accurate description of the drowned coastlands of Guiana. The printed pamphlets attributed to him contain more tall stories, more titillating anecdotes of nakedness, cannibalism, and so forth, and much less serious description than the manuscript letters. They suggest vigorous embroidery by unscrupulous editors or publishers. They enjoyed a great vogue, however. They appeared in many editions and in several languages, and some of the editions, most notably those printed in Germany, are of interest for their elaborate illustrations.[15]

The 1509 Strasbourg edition of *Quattuor Navigationes*[16] has a series of vigorous woodcuts, showing the explorers' adventures, departing from Europe, arriving in the New World, and conversing with the natives (fig. 3). Most interesting of all, the human figures are set against carefully drawn landscapes. The European scene has the familiar conventional Renaissance landscape, with abrupt hills crowned with spiky castles. The American landscape is also abrupt, without castles, but with huts here and there and caves with naked people crawling in and out. The vegetation is sparse: there are a few spindly trees and what appear to be cacti. The scene might well have been drawn from a description of the arid terrain and xerophytic vegetation of the Goajira peninsula, which Vespucci is known to have visited in 1499. The landscape, however, was clearly only incidental to the action of the story. In the penultimate woodcut, an incautious European is shown in conversation with three personable young women, while a fourth, older and less attractive, steals up behind him with an upraised club. In the final scene he is being cut up and cooked.

Probably the earliest known attempt by a major European artist to depict the American scene is a panel painted by the early sixteenth-century Dutch painter Jan Mostaert, now in the Frans Hals Museum in Haarlem (pl. 6). It shows a well-armed European force advancing in determined order on a crowd of simple, unarmed people, in a dramatic mountainous landscape. The composition is of unusual interest for our purpose, because the invaders, and the ship which presumably brought them, are in relatively marginal positions. The beleaguered natives, their houses, their fields, and their cattle occupy the center of the foreground, and the whole incident is dwarfed by the landscape in which it is set.

The landscape has been variously identified with coastal Brazil, with central Mexico, and with the area, in what is now the Southwestern United States, visited by Francisco Vázquez Coronado in 1540.[17] The Brazil suggestion rests chiefly on the parrot perched on a stump in the foreground. The Southwest suggestion is more plausible. Mostaert cannot have seen any of the known written accounts of the

Coronado expedition, but he might conceivably have heard about it in conversation. The great rock in the center, with its horizontal striations and the ladders leading from ledge to ledge, does vaguely suggest a wind-eroded New Mexican mesa with cliff dwellings in its face, and the curious natural bridge formation on the right does somewhat resemble Window Rock in Arizona. On the other hand, the natives do not in the least resemble Pueblo Indians. They are naked, they are white, and the men are bearded. Their thatched huts are quite unlike the stone or adobe dwellings of the Southwest. Their cattle are peaceful dairy animals, not the shaggy wild bison described by Coronado and his companions. The distant view of the sea and the "window rock" formation were conventions often used in mannerist landscapes in Mostaert's day.

In short, though the painting was no doubt inspired, in part at least, by tales of New World discovery, there is no compelling reason to think that it depicts any particular historical incident or any particular landscape known to the painter through eye-witness description. More probably, Mostaert intended a general representation, of a tranquil pre-Lapsarian paradise in process of destruction by sophisticated brutality and greed.

Landscape often appears in sixteenth-century illustrated books about the New World as a background for drawings of primitive people. Benzoni's *Historia del Mondo Nuovo*[18] was the most popular of all general accounts of America in the sixteenth century. It contains more anecdote than description, but is lavishly illustrated with woodcuts of Indian artifacts and behavior, with some attempt at landscape background. Benzoni himself had traveled widely in the New World, but it is apparent that his illustrator had not. The woodcuts are evidently done from hearsay; the landscapes are perfunctory, and relentlessly European.

The German mercenary in Portuguese service Hans Staden did his amateur best to record the "wild, naked man-eating people" by whom he had been captured and almost, so he said, killed and eaten in Brazil. His account, with rough but appealing drawings of the Tupinambá, their dwellings, and their forest surroundings, apeared at Marburg in 1557 (fig. 4). A much more serious and more distinguished description of Brazil and Brazilians is the delightful *Histoire d'un voyage fait en la terre du Brésil*, written by Jean de Léry,[19] the Protestant theological student who in 1557 spent ten months with the unhappy Villegaignon colony, followed by a year living with Indians. The book has admirable descriptions and good illustrations. It is greatly superior in both these respects to the more popular, and even today better known, *Singularitez de la France antarctique*, by the Franciscan André Thevet.[20] In none of these books, however, does landscape amount to more than a few scattered trees as a decorative background. In a later generation the wild people, wild animals, and wild landscapes of Brazil were to receive distinguished attention from the artists and naturalists employed and encouraged by Prince Johan Maurits of Nassau, governor during the Dutch occupation of Pernambuco.[21] Willem Piso and George Marcgrave and Frans Post and Albert Eckhout provided the first full scientific and visual record of any part of America. Eckhout's paintings of Tapuya

Een notabel boec vandẽ le
uen ons heerẽ Jhesu christi

PLATE 5. Christ. *Een notabel boec vandē leuen Ons Heerē Ihesu Christi* (Delft: Jacobs Jacobszoen van der Meer or Christian Snellaert, 1488), Rosenwald Collection, no. 496.

PLATE 6. Jan Mostaert, West Indian Landscape. Haarlem, Frans Halsmuseum, on loan from the Dienst Verspreide Rijkskollekties, The Hague.

FIGURE 4. Staden in Captivity. Hans Staden, *Warhaftig Historia vnd beschreibung eyner Landtschafft der Wilden, Nacketen, Grimmigen Menschfresser Leuthen, in der Newenwelt America gelegen . . .* (Marburg: Andres Kolben, 1557), New York, The New York Public Library, Rare Books and Manuscripts Division. Astor, Lenox and Tilden Foundations.

Indians are remarkable for a detached, objective observation of primitive people.[22] Post has charming and informative landscapes of the coastal settlements. These men, however, came relatively late to an America already losing its maidenhead. Coastal Brazil was already, in Johan Maurits's day, the principal producer of sugar for the European market, and the Tapuya Indians, though wild enough, had become curiosities in a country increasingly run by Europeans and dependent upon imported Africans for its labor. The Pernambuco Dutchmen cannot fairly rank among the artists of discovery. The Golden Age of discovery by their time was losing its impetus, and the Silver Age was still a century away.

More significant for our purpose are the painters and observers who worked in the late sixteenth century in parts of America only recently opened to Europeans, still new and strange. Surprisingly, Englishmen were prominent among them. The English were newcomers to the New World, and their contributions to discovery in the sixteenth century were relatively insignificant; but once arrived there, they displayed—or some of them displayed—a keen interest in the natural scene and a sensitive visual appreciation of it, whether or not they had any technical skill as artists. Nuno da Silva, the captured Portuguese navigator, noticed that Drake always had sketchpad and watercolors by him.[23] Whoever heard of a conquistador with a sketchbook? Drake's concern, it is true, may have been purely practical: the charting of harbors and the sketching of coastal profiles. Da Silva did not describe his drawings, except to say that they "delineated birds, trees and sea-lions," and none has survived. What have survived, fortunately, are some of the drawings and paintings done by Jacques le Moyne in Florida and by the incomparable John White in the West Indies, Carolina, and (probably) Labrador (figs. 5 and 6).

The British Museum published the eighty-odd surviving White watercolors in two volumes of sumptuous reproduction in 1964.[24] Le Moyne has been less handsomely treated. Both men were practical colonizers as well as gifted artists. Le Moyne was with Ribault in Florida, and White was governor of the Roanoke settlement. Both enjoyed the patronage of Ralegh, le Moyne having removed to England "for religion" about 1580. Both made important contributions to the spread of reliable knowledge of the New World. When Theodor de Bry was planning

FIGURE 5. Hans Sloane, Frobisher's Men in a Skirmish with Eskimos at Bloody Point, 1 August 1577. Watercolor drawing after a lost original by John White. London, British Museum, Department of Prints and Drawings. Courtesy Trustees of the British Museum.

FIGURE 6. John White, The Manner of Their Fishing. Watercolor drawing. London, British Museum. Courtesy Trustees of the British Museum.

his *America*, he searched all over Europe for material on which to base engravings for the work, and the ubiquitous Hakluyt brought the drawings of White and le Moyne to his attention.

So it came about that in that vast and justly celebrated monument to European enterprise in the New World, the engravings of the native peoples of Mexico and Peru are based on inadequate written descriptions or hearsay, and present the features and attitudes of ancient Rome, but those of the simpler peoples of North America, some of them at least, are after the work of artists who were familiar with their subject at first hand, who observed with a clear eye, and painted with cool, if sympathetic fidelity. In general, we have a much clearer image of the more primitive peoples of America, including Eskimos, and of the landscapes in which they lived, than we have of the more sophisticated settled peoples there and the cities that they built. White and le Moyne were the artistic counterparts of explorers in the first European Age of Discovery, as Hodges and Webber were in the second.

## NOTES

1. George Vancouver, *A Voyage of Discovery to the North Pacific Ocean and Round the World . . . under the Command of Captain George Vancouver*, 6 vols. (London: Printed for J. Stockdale, 1801), 1:54.

2. Neither Hodges nor Webber was particularly gifted as a portrait painter, but both painted Cook, Webber more than once. The Hodges original has disappeared and is known only from engravings, which show a romantic Cook, wearing his own hair loose. Webber's portraits, one in the National Art Gallery, Wellington, New Zealand, and one in the Hull Trinity House, show a craggy, choleric Cook. They all contrast sharply with the formal Cook—rocklike, calm, and bewigged—of Nathaniel Dance's urbane portrait in the National Maritime Museum, London.

3. Official versions of Cook's journals—official in the sense of having the approval of the Admiralty—appeared as follows:

   a. John Hawkesworth, comp., *An Account of the Voyages Undertaken . . . for Making Discoveries in the Southern Hemisphere*, 3 vols. (London: Printed for W. Strahan and T. Cadell, 1773);

   b. James Cook, *A Voyage Towards the South Pole and Round the World . . . in the Years 1772, 1773, 1774, and 1775*, 2 vols. (London: Printed for W. Strahan & T. Cadell, 1777);

   c. James Cook, *A Voyage to the Pacific Ocean in the Years 1776, 1777, 1778, 1779, and 1780 . . .*, vols. 1 and 2 written by Captain James Cook, vol. 3 by Captain J. King and ed. John Douglas, 3 vols. (London, 1784).

All were illustrated by engravings after the work, respectively, of Parkinson, Hodges, and Webber. In particular, the sixty-odd plates accompanying the Douglas edition of the third voyage form a handsome folio volume in themselves. Webber himself supervised the work on these engravings. They are free from the neoclassical "editing" by Cipriani and others to which the work of Hodges was subjected.

4. Richard Darwin Keynes, ed., *The Beagle Record: Selections from the Original Pictorial Records and Written Accounts of the Voyage of H.M.S. Beagle* (Cambridge and New York: Cambridge University Press, 1979).

5. Edward Adrian Wilson, *Edward Wilson's Birds of the Antarctic*, ed. Brian Roberts (London: Blandford, 1967). Most of the paintings and drawings reproduced are in the Scott Polar Institute in Cambridge. Some Wilson watercolors, including landscapes, remain in private hands, unpublished. The writer is grateful to Miss Anne Trembath for the opportunity to see those in her possession.

6. Gonzalo Fernández de Oviedo y Valdés, *Historia general y natural de las Indias*, 4 vols. (Seville, 1547).

7. Ibid., folio lxi.

8. Jacques Lafaye, *Le Manuscript Tovar* (Graz: UNESCO, 1972), reproduces the drawings in the Tovar Ms. in the John Carter Brown Library at Providence and discusses similar drawings in the Durán Ms.

9. The Ms. of the "Trachtenbuch" is in the Germanisches National Museum at Nuremberg. A handsome facsimile edition was printed in 1927: Theodor Hampe, ed., *Das Trachtenbuch des Christoph Weiditz*... (Berlin: De Gruyter, 1927). This is now a scarce book. Some of the Indian drawings are reproduced in J. H. Parry, *The Discovery of South America* (London: Elek, 1979), pp. 165–68.

10. Hernando Pizarro's own account of his journey from Cajamarca to Pachacamac in 1533 is in a letter addressed to the judges of the audiencia of Santo Domingo, which is printed in Oviedo, *Historia general y natural* 3. 8. 15.

11. "The commentaries of Alvar Núñez Cabeza de Vaca," ed. and trans. L. L. Domínguez, in his *The Conquest of the River Plate* (London: Hakluyt Society, 1891), pp. 119 ff.

12. Bernal Díaz del Castillo, *The True History of the Conquest of New Spain*, trans. and ed. A. P. Maudslay, 5 vols. (London: Hakluyt Society, 1908–16), 2:37–38.

13. Of the Spanish party who rode into Cuzco with Pizarro in November 1533, only one—Pedro Sancho, his secretary—wrote a description. It is factual and fairly detailed, but lifeless and flat. Parry, *Discovery of South America*, p. 195.

14. Vespucci's surviving Ms. letters from Seville, Lisbon, and the Cape Verde Islands and the printed pamphlets attributed to him are collected in English translation in Frederick J. Pohl, *Amerigo Vespucci, Pilot Major* (New York: Columbia University Press, 1944).

15. For the intricate publishing history of the Vespucci pamphlets see José Toribio Medina, *Biblioteca Hispano-Americana*, 7 vols. (Santiago: Impreso y grabado en casa del autor, 1898–1907), 1:41 ff. and passim.

16. *Diss büchlin saget . . . ein Nüwe welt von wilden nackenden Leüten, vormals unbekant* (Strasbourg: durch Joh. Grüninger, 1509).

17. James Snyder, "Jan Mostaerts' West Indian Landscape," in Fredi Chiappelli, with Michael J. B. Allen and Robert L. Benson, eds., *First Images of America: The Impact of the New World on the Old*, 2 vols. (Berkeley: University of California Press, 1976), 1:495.

18. Girolamo Benzoni, *La Historia del Mondo Nuovo* (Venice: F. Rampazetto, 1565).

19. Jean de Léry, *Histoire d'un voyage fait en la terre du Brésil, autrement dite Amérique*... (La Rochelle: Pour Antoine Chuppin, 1578).

20. André Thevet, *Les Singularitez de la France antarctique, autrement nommée Amérique*... (Antwerp: Christophle Plantin, 1558).

21. Willem Piso, *Historia Naturalis Brasiliae, Auspicio et Beneficio Illustriss. I. Mauritii Com. Nassau . . . Guilielmi Pisonis . . . de Medicina Brasiliensi Libri quatuor . . . Et Georgi Marcgravi . . . Historiae Rerum naturalium Brasiliae Libri Octo . . . Cum Appendice de Tapuyis* . . . (Leiden: F. Hackium; Amsterdam: L. Elzevírium, 1648).

Kaspar van Baerle, *Casparis Barlaei, Rerum per Octennium in Brasilia*... (Antwerp: Gulielmi Pisonis, 1647).

22. See Thomas Thomsen, *Albert Eckhout, ein Niederländischer Maler, und sein Gönner, Moritz der Brasilianer* (Copenhagen: Levin og Munksgaard, Ejnar Munksgaard, 1938).

23. See Zelia Nuttall, *New Light on Drake* (London: Hakluyt Society, 1914), p. 303, for a translation of Nuno da Silva's deposition before the Inquisition, after Drake had put him ashore in Mexico.

24. Paul Hulton and David Beers Quinn, *The American Drawings of John White, 1577–1590, with Drawings of European and Oriental Subjects*, 2 vols. (London: Trustees of the British Museum; Chapel Hill: University of North Carolina Press, 1964).

JAMES CAHILL

# LATE MING LANDSCAPE ALBUMS AND EUROPEAN PRINTED BOOKS

If we consider the theme "landscape and the book" in relation to China, we think immediately of the landscape album, one of the principal forms in which Chinese paintings occur, especially in the later centuries, the Ming and Ch'ing periods. Some of these albums were simply collections of landscape pictures, without a unifying theme, but most had programs of some kind. Three landscape albums by the late Ming artist Chang Hung (ca. 1580–after 1650), painted during the period 1627–39, can serve to represent three of the programs possible by that time.

The album of paintings as a series of pictures having some unifying theme or program had come to popularity in the fourteenth century, although it was not unknown earlier. By the late Ming, the early seventeenth century, a great many subjects and types had evolved, but of these, only landscape themes concern us here. Chang's three albums exemplify three principal types: the album made up of landscape pictures in the manners of a series of old masters; the album of scenes viewed on a trip taken by the artist; and the album that explores, more or less systematically, the parts of some specific garden or scenic area. The first is a peculiarly Chinese form—a demonstration, even, by the artist of his engagement with the past history of Chinese painting. The other two have closer affinities with Western types of series pictures, and so offer greater possibilities of cross-cultural influence. Both of Chang's albums of these types in fact betray such influence clearly, as we shall see.

FIGURE 1. Chang Hung (ca. 1580 – after 1650), Landscape in the Manner of Hsia Kuei. Album of Landscapes in the Manners of Old Masters, dated 1636, Berkeley, California, Ching Yüan Chai Collection.

FIGURE 2. Chang Hung, Landscape in the Manner of Ni Tsan. Album of Landscapes in the Manners of Old Masters, dated 1636, Berkeley, California, Ching Yüan Chai Collection.

The album of 1636, originally of twelve leaves (one is now missing), is made up of pictures imitating the landscape manners of old masters from the tenth through the fourteenth century. Each stylistic source is identified in a written label (figs. 1 and 2). Some leaves appear to be based loosely on actual compositions by the old masters, while in others the "imitation" (for which the Chinese term is *fang*) is limited to the use of characteristic brushstrokes and type-forms for trees, rocks, and other components of the picture. Albums of this type enjoyed a vogue in China in the

FIGURE 3. Li Sung (late twelfth – early thirteenth century),
The West Lake at Hangchow. Section of a handscroll, Shanghai, Shanghai Museum.

seventeenth century. They are probably an outgrowth of the album of reduced-size copies of old paintings, made by artists for purposes of study and for preserving old compositions they had seen.[1] In the later form, the leaves are not based on particular old paintings but are done in a succession of more or less distinct old styles. This type suited the style-conscious approach of many seventeenth-century painters, permitting them to display their comprehensive grasp, both as artists and as connoisseurs, of the whole past of their art. The paintings that make up such albums are ideal landscapes. What the artists explore in them, leaf by leaf, is an art-historical realm, the dimensions of which are not in space but in time and style: the interaction or intersection of the time and style of the old master with that of the later one provides the coordinates that locate the picture within the art-historical realm.

Chang Hung's 1636 album is not typical of his output; he is usually less inclined than most other artists of his time to imitate the past. His album of 1639, titled "Scenes of the Yüeh Region," is free of allusions to old masters and is concerned with places, not styles. The eight leaves depict places that Chang viewed—and presumably sketched—on a trip he took into the old region of Yüeh, present-day Chekiang Province. Before considering this album we should look back briefly over the tradition of topographical painting in China.[2]

The study of topographical painting is impeded by the scarcity of good, identifiable, known, and published examples. There are several reasons for this scarcity. Landscape paintings of this kind, like other more or less functional painting in China, ordinarily ranked lower on the connoisseur's scale of value than landscapes of a more general, aesthetically motivated character. The bias against specific (and therefore limited) subjects in Chinese art theory strengthened the disinclination of Chinese collectors to take them seriously. Although famous artists sometimes painted them, they were typically the work of minor specialists, and for this reason also were less attractive to collectors, except when (as frequently happened) they were later provided with attributions to the masters and with spurious signatures.

For artists, too, topographical painting raised problems that many of them were reluctant to face. Chinese landscape painting in its later centuries was a highly conventionalized art, and the needs of depicting real scenery, with all its diversity and nonconformity to accepted compositional modes, were difficult to reconcile with that conventionalization. The artist could reduce the elements of the scene to a set of type-forms and arrange these into compositions that combined aspects of the particular scene with established patterns. Or he could create his own descriptive vocabulary, through observation and the alteration or "correcting" of the forms he inherited, and use this vocabulary for truer representations of what he saw. The latter course, besides running contrary to accepted notions of how painting should relate to nature, was by far the more difficult, and only a few Chinese artists undertook it. One of them, and one of the most distinguished, was Chang Hung.

Literary records and a few surviving works testify that artists of the Sung dynasty (906–1280) and earlier often depicted particular places, famous mountains or scenic spots. Judging from one of the finest extant examples, Li Sung's early thirteenth-century portrayal of the West Lake at Hangchow (fig. 3), the aim was not so much to describe in detail the actual appearances of these places as to render in artistic form a generalized impression that would remind the visitor of what he had seen. More properly topographical works, usually in handscroll form, take the character of picture-maps. Two examples in the Freer Gallery of Art, both probably

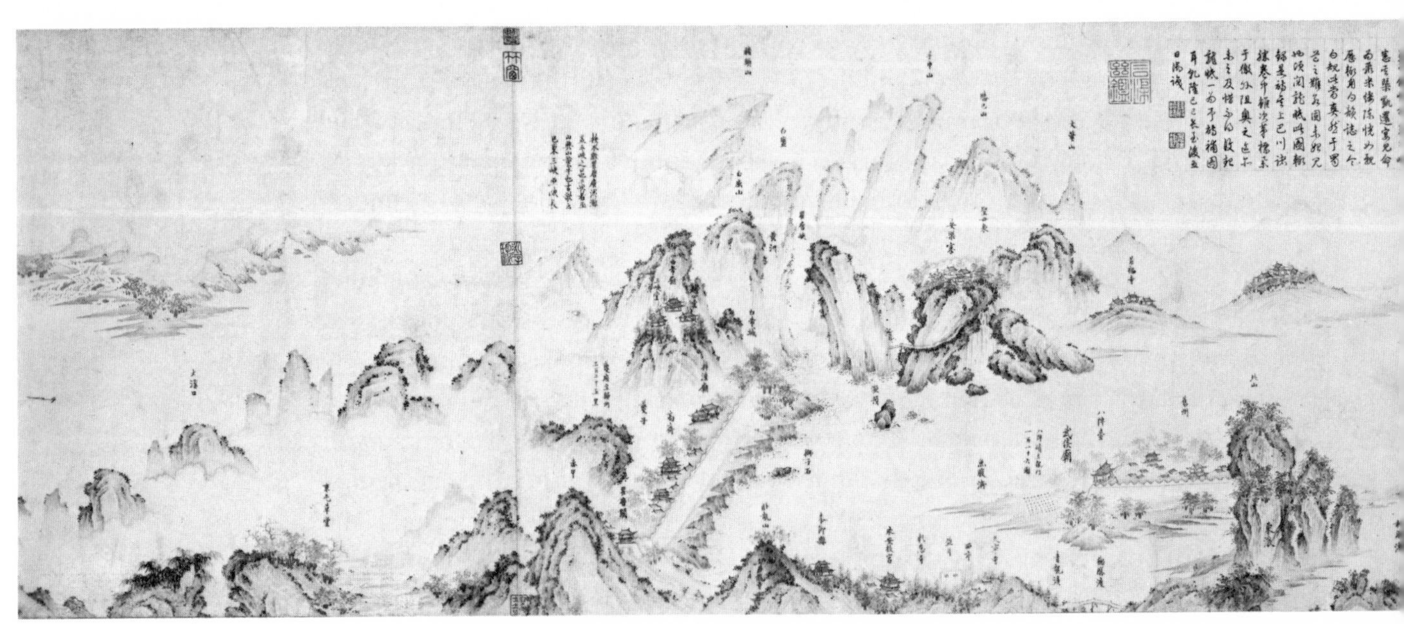

late Sung (thirteenth century) in date, offer schematic, telescoped panoramas of the upper Yangtze River (figs. 4 and 5). These are even less concerned with particularized appearances, or visual reporting. They locate the relative positions of large physical features of the terrain and landmarks, using conventional forms for mountains, groves of trees, and so forth, telling the viewer not how the place looks but how to get there and how to find his way around. Such scrolls, although they are (like these two) often attributed to famous masters, were probably done by minor artists who specialized in this genre. Even when a major master attempts a scroll of this type, such as Wu Chen (1280–1354) in his "Eight Views of Chia-ho" of 1344 (fig. 6), he assumes the same extreme of conventionalization, rendering rooftops and tree groves as conventional signs that mingle easily with the inscriptions and seals also disposed over the surface of the scroll.

*pposite page, top:*
IGURE 4. Anonymous, thirteenth century? Panorama of the Yangtze River. ormerly attributed to Chü-jan, tenth century. Section of a handscroll, Washington, D.C., Smithsonian Institution, Freer Gallery of Art. ourtesy of the Smithsonian Institution, Freer Gallery of Art, Washington, D.C.

*pposite page, bottom:*
IGURE 5. Anonymous, thirteenth century? Panorama of the Yangtze River. ormerly attributed to Li Kung-lin, eleventh century. Section of a handscroll, Washington, D.C., Smithsonian Institution, Freer Gallery of Art. ourtesy of the Smithsonian Institution, Freer Gallery of Art, Washington, D.C.

FIGURE 6. Wu Chen (1280–1354), "Eight Views of Chia-ho" (dated 1344). Section of a handscroll, formerly Taipei, Collection of Lo Chia-lun.

FIGURE 7. Wang Fu (1362–1416), "Eight Views of the Peking Region." Section of a handscroll, Peking, Historical Museum.

The handscroll of "Eight Views of the Peking Region" painted in the early fifteenth century by Wang Fu (1362–1416) is different in form. Instead of a panorama suggesting that all the parts occupy positions in a continuous space, it presents a series of separate pictures, alternating with passages of text (fig. 7). Here, too, the scenery in the paintings is subject to severe conventionalization. The type-forms of Wang Fu's own landscape manner only substitute for the schemata of the picture-maps—the artist shows no interest in making them more flexibly descriptive. Such conventionalization is not, now, peculiar to topographical painting but is characteristic of most Chinese landscape painting—the artists had by this time mostly relinquished any truly descriptive approach to the representation of the world around them. Wang Fu's paintings would not be much different if they did *not* represent actual places. They seem, in fact, to be conventional landscapes into which the painter has inserted a few identifying features such as temples and other buildings, bridges, and a gate.

A handscroll made up of separate scenes such as Wang Fu's introduces the possibility (by a simple change of format) of the topographical album, composed of a series of pictures of places related by geographical proximity or as parts of some larger topological unit. The earliest extant example of such an album dates from the late fourteenth century; it is the forty-leaf album of "Scenes of Hua-shan" (or "Scenes of Mt Hua") by Wang Li, now divided between the Shanghai and Peking Palace Museums (fig. 8). Here the artist's intent (as we know it from his inscription)[3] is to convey both the physical appearance of the awesome scenery and some sense of the effect it had on him—a dual aim that is, like the style, in harmony with Sung landscape traditions and in some part derived from them. Wang Li's scenes are based not on established compositional formulae but (presumably) on the physical properties of the Hua-shan terrain, as he recorded them in sketches. Nevertheless, the dominance of linear patterns and formal conventions keeps his paintings from being truly descriptive; he incorporates details specific to his subject, such as perilous hanging bridges and logs with projecting stubs of branches used as ladders for climbing up the cliffs, into landscapes rendered in this relatively traditional way.

Wang Li's Hua-shan album records a journey of exploration. Although by his time pilgrimage-ascents of this great Taoist mountain were not uncommon, it was still a wild place, difficult of access. In this, his album is unusual, perhaps unique,

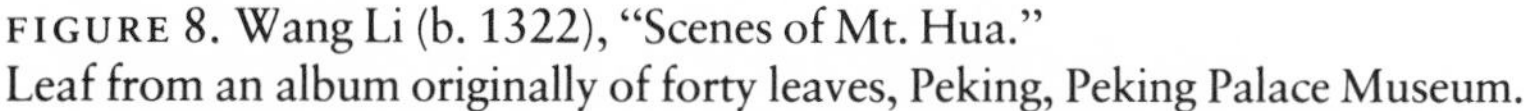
FIGURE 8. Wang Li (b. 1322), "Scenes of Mt. Hua."
Leaf from an album originally of forty leaves, Peking, Peking Palace Museum.

among surviving early paintings. More commonly represented were familiar, close-at-hand scenes. Artists of the Su-chou region often depicted these. A good example is Shen Chou's album of scenes of the Tiger Hill near Su-chou, painted probably in the 1480s or 1490s (fig. 9). The landscape here, in contrast to Wang Li's Hua-shan pictures, is human in scale and ordered by human presence; the Tiger Hill is presented more as a work of man than of nature. The style of the pictures accordingly transmutes the views into the formal system of a personal style, one in which differentiation and detail are minimized by the thick-line drawing and insistent patternizing. This is less a record of exploration than a pictorial remembrance of frequent outings to a familiar, nearby place. Designed for viewers who knew the place already, the pictures evoke without really describing.[4]

With the late Ming period, from the late sixteenth to the mid-seventeenth century, topographical painting becomes more abundant and more interesting. The

FIGURE 9. Shen Chou (1427–1509), Scenes of the Tiger Hill Near Su-chou. "Tiger Hill Album," Cleveland, Ohio, Cleveland Museum of Art. Courtesy The Cleveland Museum of Art, Purchase, Leonard C. Hanna, Jr., Bequest.

FIGURE 10. Sung Hsü (1525–1605), The Heavenly Stairs on Mt. Hua.
Album of Scenes of Famous Places, Berkeley, California, Ching Yüan Chai Collection.

artist's range of view seems to expand, extending to faraway places, and some of the ruling conventions give way to more direct and naturalistic manners of representation. An album painted around 1600 by Sung Hsü (1525–1605) depicts notable sights all over China, from Shantung in the northeast to Nan-ch'ang in the far southwest (fig. 10). Whether Sung Hsü actually visited all these places is unclear, but they are presented as if firsthand, like travel sketches, seen from some distance and drawn in a relatively informal way. In 1573, as we know from a record in a printed catalog, Sung painted the scenery of southern Anhui and Huang-shan (the Huang Mountains), where he had once journeyed, at the request of a patron from that region.[5] It is not impossible that these pictures are similarly based on memories, or sketches, of places viewed on trips.

Coming at last to Chang Hung's 1639 "Scenes of the Yüeh Region," we find that although confined geographically to a smaller area, they share with Sung Hsü's the character of pictorial reports. They are full of specific information. The compositions are unconventional, the brushwork looser. The style, while not entirely free of type-forms, seems to adapt relatively closely to the aim of showing how the scenery of Yüeh differs from that of other regions (figs. 11 and 12). Here we can be sure that the album records a trip made by the artist—he tells us so in his inscription, adding that what he saw in Yüeh didn't agree with what he had heard about it. "So when I returned home," he concludes, "I got out some silk and used it to depict what I had seen, because relying on your ears isn't as good as relying on your eyes."

The remark may sound ordinary to us, but it was not ordinary in Ming dynasty China. It is an untraditional assertion of the superiority of firsthand experi-

FIGURE 11. Chang Hung, Landscape with Waterfall. Album of "Scenes of the Yüeh Region" (dated 1639). Kyoto, Dr. Tadashi Moriya. Courtesy of Dr. Moriya.

FIGURE 12. Chang Hung, A Junk on the River. Album of "Scenes of the Yüeh Region" (dated 1639). Kyoto, Dr. Tadashi Moriya. Courtesy of Dr. Moriya.

PLATE 7. Chang Hung, A Bamboo Grove. "Scenes of the Chih Garden" (dated 1627), Berkeley, California, Ching Yüan Chai Collection. Photograph by Benjamin Blackwell.

PLATE 8. John Martyn, Hiacinthus Poeticus. *Pub. Virgilii Maronis Georgicorum libri quatuor*, edited by John Martyn (London: Printed for the editor by R. Reily, 1741), Rosenwald Collection, no. 1745.

ence over received information, and of visual over verbal description. Chang Hung seeks to convey in his album leaves more aspects of the experience of travel, visual and other, than earlier artists had done—the feeling of standing at the base of a high waterfall (fig. 11) or riding the rapids in a junk (fig. 12). Some leaves draw the viewer powerfully into the picture with strong diagonal recessions, such as a bridge joining near and far shores of a river (fig. 13), or, in another leaf, a zig-zag progression into depth reinforced by buildings diminishing in size (fig. 14).

Both aim and method were virtually unprecedented in China, but can be paralleled in European prints known to have been in China by this time, brought by Jesuit missionaries. The circumstances of the transmission of these to China, and the Chinese response to them, have been discussed elsewhere and need not be detailed here.[6] In particular, the great six-volume work on cities of the world, *Civitates orbis*

FIGURE 13. Chang Hung, River View with Bridge, a City on the Far Shore. Album of "Scenes of the Yüeh Region" (dated 1639). Kyoto, Dr. Tadashi Moriya. Courtesy of Dr. Moriya.

FIGURE 14. Chang Hung, A River Valley, a Walled City. Album of "Scenes of the Yüeh Region" (dated 1639). Kyoto, Dr. Tadashi Moriya. Courtesy of Dr. Moriya.

FIGURE 15. View of Campensis. Georg Braun and Franz Hogenberg, *Civitates orbis terrarum* (Antwerp: Apud G. Kempensem, 1581–1618), Rosenwald Collection, no. 716.

FIGURE 16. View of Gades. Georg Braun and Franz Hogenberg, *Civitates orbis terrarum* (Antwerp: Apud G. Kempensem, 1581–1618), Rosenwald Collection, no. 716.

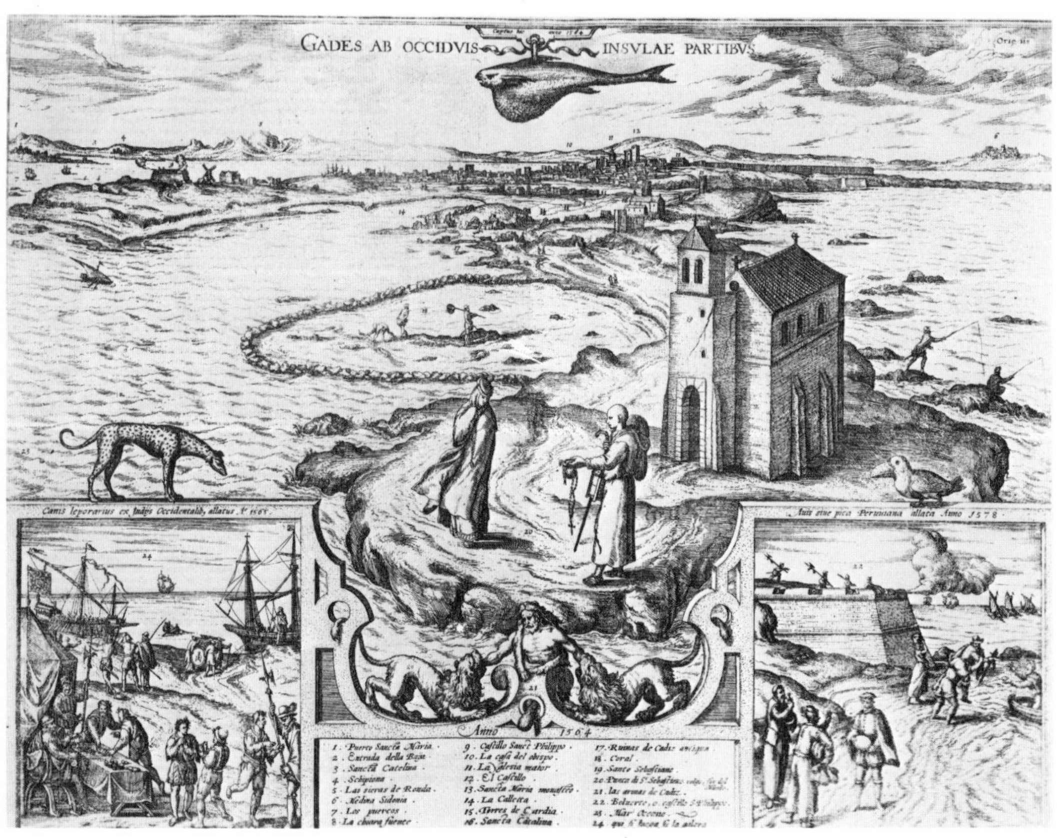

*terrarum*, compiled by Braun and Hogenberg and published in Antwerp from 1572, appears to have been a source of new ideas and motifs for Chang Hung and others (figs. 15 and 16).

Several aspects of the European engravings must have struck Chang and other artists of the time forcibly. First, the amount of specific topographical, ethnographical, and other information they contained—such as figures in characterizing costumes spotted around the pictures and buildings and other features that no doubt identified the place. Second, their capacity for pulling the viewer's gaze back into the picture by compositional devices for establishing sharp recessions and by placing the multiple focal points at different levels of depth. Finally, the testimony they provided of the existence of vast regions of strikingly diverse character, unknown to the Chinese, and of the fascination of departing from familiar scenery to search these out.

Chinese travels, as represented in art, had typically been like pilgrimages to known, notable places.[7] Going on such a pilgrimage is an act fundamentally different from setting out from the known into the unknown, without advance knowledge of what one will find. Artistic equivalents to the former are pictures that allude or remind; proper to the latter are pictures that describe and inform. Chang Hung's album of "Scenes of Yüeh" belongs to the latter type in both paintings and inscription. Although the places he visited were not very remote and by no means uninhabited, they were unknown to him. His journey was one of exploration, and he records it and validates it in his pictures, which are both descriptions and visual metaphors for the act of penetrating and observing a new region. Considering the clear occurrence in the album of representational techniques taken from the Western engravings, it seems likely that its whole approach was similarly affected by acquaintance with the Braun and Hogenberg series and other illustrated works of the kind. The Braun and Hogenberg pictures, themselves the products of an extraordinary Northern European project of exploring the inhabited world visually and transmitting knowledge about it through pictorial reporting, must have served as models and inspiration for similar projects by Chinese artists. Their means of presentation fitted Chinese proclivities and needs better than the Italian system of perspective, organizing the picture as though from a single vantage point, would have done.

A new interest in geographical investigation had in fact arisen in the late Ming, and it is generally considered to be the outcome, in some part, of contacts with the Jesuits. Matteo Ricci's map of the world was widely reprinted in China, and it drastically altered the Chinese conception of the world and China's place in it.[8] Explorations were undertaken of seldom-visited regions of China. The most famous traveler was Hsü Hsia-k'o, who made seventeen journeys, over thousands of miles, ending only with his death in 1640. He probably met the Jesuits and was affected by the writings they brought and by the new spirit of scientific investigation they stimulated, however briefly, in China.[9] Huang Hsiang-chien (1609–1673) traveled on foot to the remote regions of Yünnan province to bring back his aged father after the fall of Ming, and he painted pictures to record his journey that are similar in character to Chang Hung's.[10] Books with topographical pictures printed by wood-

FIGURE 17. Huang-shan (The Huang Mountains). *San-ts'ai t'u-hui* (1607), Berkeley, California, University of California, East Asiatic Library.

FIGURE 18. Huang-shan. *Ming-shan t'u* (*Pictures of Famous Mountains*) (1633). From Lo-chih Ho, *Ming-k'an ming-shan-t'u p'an-hua chi* (*Collection of Prints from the Ming Edition of "Pictures of Famous Mountains"*) (Shanghai, 1958).

FIGURE 19. Huang-shan. After a design by Hsiao Yün-ts'ung (1596–1673). *T'ai-p'ing shan-shui* (*Landscapes of T'ai-p'ing Prefecture*) (1648). From a Japanese facsimile reprint, undated.

block—local histories and accounts of famous mountains and scenic regions—appear in far greater number than before.

We can observe the reflection in art of the opening up of new regions in three such woodblock pictures representing Huang-shan, the Huang Mountains in southern Anhui province. In the 1607 *San-ts'ai t'u-hui* (a massive pictorial encyclopedia that itself exemplifies the late Ming urge toward a more comprehensive understanding of the visible world), Huang-shan is presented as a wild, uninhabited place (fig. 17). The bizarre, artistically unstructured shapes of the peaks are emphasized, and no way is indicated by which one could get from one part to another, excepting two paths that suggest the possibility of limited ascent of individual peaks. In 1606 the monk P'u-men built a Buddhist temple named the Tz'u-kuang Ssu there, and by the time of the 1633 *Ming-shan t'u* (*Pictures of Famous Mountains*), other temples had been built where travelers could lodge, and a regular route was established for pilgrims (fig. 18). Peaks, waterfalls, and venerable pine trees had been given names and designated as objects of contemplation, and these were often depicted in the middle decades of the century by artists of the area. In the *Ming-shan t'u* version of Huang-shan, the mountains have taken on intelligible structure and their relationships are clear. The landscape has been given order by human perception and artistic depiction. The picture of Huang-shan in the 1648 *T'ai-p'ing shan-shui* (*Landscapes of T'ai-p'ing Prefecture*) by Hsiao Yün-ts'ung (1596–1673) presents the mountain as still further humanized, reduced to comprehensible scale (fig. 19). A human structure has been superimposed on the physical terrain, changing its character and appearance. Hsiao even introduces a further cultural dimension by representing each of the scenes in the manner of a different old master, thus combining the two types of landscape albums into a single work that moves through both geographical and art-historical space.

Chang Hung's album of twenty "Scenes of the Chih Garden," finally, a work of 1627, is an even more striking example of the use of painting as a mode of visual exploration, and of his breaks with tradition. The tradition, for paintings of gardens, can be quickly illustrated with a sixteenth-century handscroll by some anonymous artist of Su-chou, portraying, probably, a garden in or near that city (fig. 20). Although we look over a wall and into buildings, the presentation of the parts of the garden does not serve to locate the viewer or allow any real penetration of the picture surface. The buildings, trees, and other objects, wherever situated, are seen from a constant angle. Most other Ming dynasty garden pictures follow essentially the same plan, in which the parts of the scene are spread out schematically in a garden equivalent of the picture-maps we saw earlier.

Chang Hung's album opens with a bird's-eye view of the whole garden (fig. 21). We are immediately aware that the picture is organized in a radically different way from its predecessors. The elevated vantage point is consistently maintained, and we look down onto and into a wall, a walled enclosure, boats, tree-lined dikes. Moreover, something approximating a natural scale for things seen at such a distance is attempted. The model must again be non-Chinese; it was probably one of the views of cities from Braun and Hogenberg's work, such as the View of Frankfurt (fig. 22). The oblique view was favored by Georg Braun because it gave the beholder a sense of seeing into all the streets and open spaces of the city. For Chang Hung it serves similarly to allow a detailed, part-by-part scrutiny of the garden.

FIGURE 20. Anonymous, sixteenth century (attributed to Ch'iu Ying, ca. 1510 – ca. 1552), A Garden in Su-chou. Section of a handscroll, Su-chou, Su-chou Museum.

FIGURE 21. Chang Hung, Bird's-Eye View of the Chih Garden. "Scenes of the Chih Garden" (dated 1627), Lugano, Switzerland, Franco Vannotti Collection (leaf 1). Courtesy of Dr. Vannotti.

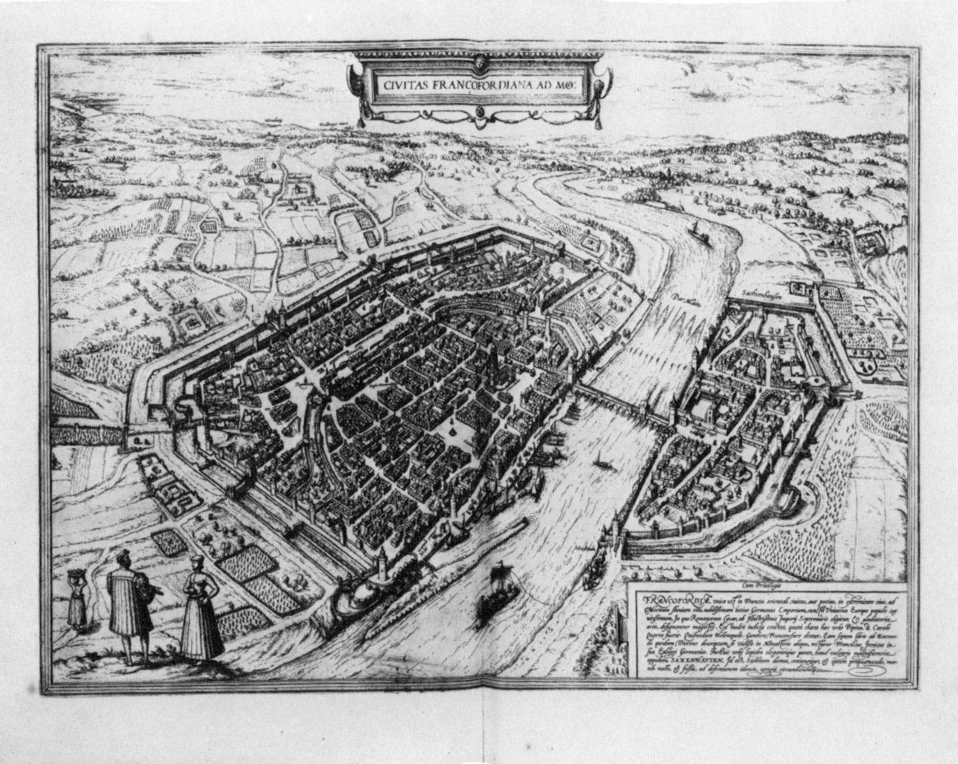


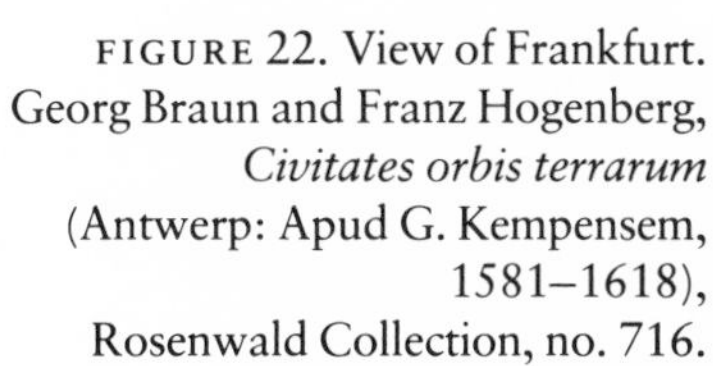

FIGURE 22. View of Frankfurt. Georg Braun and Franz Hogenberg, *Civitates orbis terrarum* (Antwerp: Apud G. Kempensem, 1581–1618), Rosenwald Collection, no. 716.

FIGURE 23. Chang Hung, Entrance to the Garden. "Scenes of the Chih Garden" (dated 1627). Berkeley, California, Ching Yüan Chai Collection.

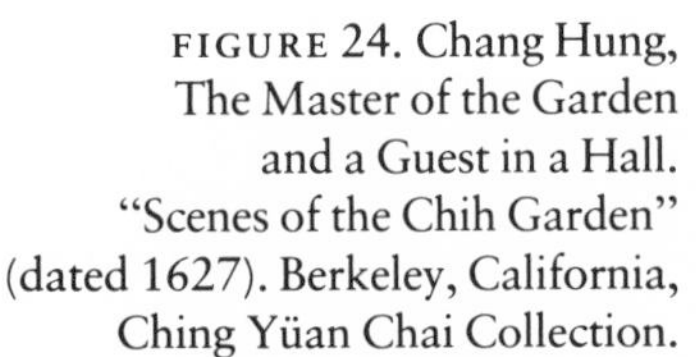

FIGURE 24. Chang Hung, The Master of the Garden and a Guest in a Hall. "Scenes of the Chih Garden" (dated 1627). Berkeley, California, Ching Yüan Chai Collection.

His whole project becomes clear, however, only when we turn to the leaves that follow.[11] With the second leaf (fig. 23) we descend almost to ground level and view closer-up the entrance to the garden, which we recognize immediately from its depiction in the opening leaf. We then move inside to see a bamboo grove separating two ponds (pl. 7). The scene is again recognizable, but so elucidated as to invite further exploration, which Chang Hung rewards with details tucked in unexpected places. From this point we move through the garden, as we turn the remaining leaves, seeing ponds and pavilions, covered walkways and rockeries. For some of the leaves, the angle of view changes, and we look across the line of sight established in the bird's-eye view. Throughout, the individual leaves confirm and amplify the information in the first leaf. The style is descriptive, differentiating surfaces and structures instead of assimilating them into types, avoiding conventions, bringing the viewer closer and closer to a complete visual understanding of the layout and physical appearance of the garden. We are always kept above the garden, gazing into it without quite entering. In one striking leaf (fig. 24) we look through cypress trees to see the master and his guest conversing in a large hall. Like the painter himself, we seem to be detached observers, participating only visually in the activities for which the garden is a setting. For the last leaf (fig. 25), we move outside the walls again; winter has set in, suggesting the passage of time during our progress through the garden's space.

FIGURE 25. Chang Hung, A Winter View of the Garden from Outside the Wall. "Scenes of the Chih Garden" (dated 1627). Berkeley, California, Ching Yüan Chai Collection.

Although this unprecedented plan might have been suggested to Chang Hung by series of woodblock pictures in Chinese local histories, which sometimes begin with a picture-map of a large area and then offer views of places or scenes within it, the whole approach seems inspired rather by the ideal of systematic investigation of the physical world introduced to China from Europe. The process of successive stages of visual penetration and of detailed, accurate representation so strongly conveyed by the paintings in this album seems a Chinese response to the representation method of the Braun and Hogenberg engravings and others brought by the Jesuits, which were so strikingly different from the conventions of their own tradition.

Potentially revolutionary though they were, these new ideas did not, in fact, sweep through Chinese painting and revolutionize it. Like the elements of European scientific thought that fascinated some Chinese in this same period, they met in the end with more resistance than acceptance. Western influence in Chinese painting continues into the eighteenth century and beyond, but takes other, odder forms. Engravings such as those in Nadal's *Evangelicae historiae imagines,* Ortelius's *Teatrum orbis terrarum* of 1579, and other European books that were known in China in the late Ming, inspired Chinese artist to use landscape imagery for visionary effects.[12] But the impact of these on later Chinese painting is beyond the scope of this paper.

## NOTES

1. One such album by the fifteenth-century master Yao Shou, reproducing compositions by artists of the preceding Yüan dynasty, may be the earliest extant example. See *Yao Kung-shou hsin-shang shan-shui ts'e* (*Album of Landscape Paintings Appreciated* [and copied] *by Yao Kung-shou*) (Shanghai: Wen-ming Publishing Co., 1924). The album, which consists of eight paintings and eight facing inscriptions, is currently in the Shanghai Museum. Another well-known album bears facing inscriptions by Tung Ch'i-ch'ang (1555–1636) dated between 1598 and 1627; the paintings are precise copies of old works judged by Tung to be masterpieces (Palace Museum, Taipei, MA 35). Several of the leaves in this album, as in Yao Shou's, are after paintings that can still be seen in the originals. An album of eight landscape paintings by Tung Ch'i-ch'ang himself, with leaves dated from 1621 to 1624, suggests a link between this type, which is composed of copies of particular old paintings, and the album of landscapes displaying the manners of selected masters without reproducing particular compositions by them. It contains leaves of both kinds. See Nelson Wu et al., *Jo i, Tō Kishō* (*Hsü Wei, Tung Ch'i-ch'ang*), *Bunjinga Suihen*, vol. 5 (Tokyo: Chuo Koron-sha, 1978), pls. 44–47.

2. A serious and thorough treatment of topographical painting in China would require a search of literary records as well as a consideration of the many extant paintings. The present account is no more than an outline of research projected for the future.

3. For a discussion of the album and a translation of a passage from Wang Li's colophon to it, see James Cahill, *Parting at the Shore: Chinese Painting of the Early and Middle Ming Dynasty, 1368–1580* (Tokyo and New York: Weatherhill, 1978), pp. 5–7.

4. A notable exception to these generalizations about sixteenth-century Su-chou painting is the sixteen-leaf album representing "A Journey to Mt. Po-yüeh" by Lu Chih (1496–1576), dated 1554,

in the Fujii Yurinkan, Kyoto. Two leaves have been published in *Yūrinkan seika* (Kyoto: Yurinkan, 1975), pl. 36. The album is discussed at length by Louise Yuhas in "The Landscape Art of Lu Chih," 2 vols. (Ph.D. diss., University of Michigan, 1979), 1:100–105, and 2:341–48. Yuhas is currently preparing a study of this album for publication. The problem of its authenticity and date is complicated by the existence of another version of the compositions, also in album form, attributed to another Su-chou master, Ch'ien Ku (1508 – after 1574), in the Palace Museum, Taipei (MA 19, unpublished).

5. Chin Yüan, *Shih-pai-chai shu-hua lu*, late eighteenth century, hsin-chi, pp. 3b ff.

6. See Michael Sullivan, *The Meeting of Eastern and Western Art; from the Sixteenth Century to the Present Day* (London: Thames & Hudson, 1973), pp. 44–46. See also chapters 1 and 3 of James Cahill, *The Compelling Image: Nature and Style in Seventeenth-Century Chinese Painting* (Cambridge: Harvard University Press, 1982), where some of the same comparisons are made as in the present paper, and the relationships discussed at greater length.

7. An exception to this statement might be seen in Wang Li's album of "Scenes of Mt. Hua"; although the mountain was long established as a holy place, the pictures seem exploratory in intent.

8. For Matteo Ricci's map of the world, see Joseph Needham et al., *Science and Civilization in China*, 5 vols. in 9 (Cambridge: University Press, 1954–80), 3:583–86. The stress that I place on the newness, for the Chinese, of the information and pictures brought by the Jesuits does not deny the notable achievements in exploration and cartography of the Chinese themselves, who in the early periods tended to be ahead of Europe in these regards. By the late Ming, the period of our concern, those achievements lay in the past and had been largely forgotten after a long period of relative isolationism.

9. Hung-tsu Hsü, *The Travel Diaries of Hsü Hsia-K'o*, trans. Li Chi (Hong Kong: Chinese University of Hong Kong, 1974), pp. 26–28.

10. For Huang Hsiang-chien's work, see *Loan Exhibition of Chinese Paintings* (Toronto: Royal Ontario Museum, 1956), no. 57 (a hanging scroll dated 1667) and an album of fourteen leaves dated 1656 in the former Richard Hobart collection, unpublished.

11. Chang Hung's "Chih Garden" album is now unfortunately divided into four parts. The Franco Vannotti collection, Lugano, has eight leaves; see James Cahill, ed., *The Restless Landscape: Chinese Painting of the Late Ming Period* (Berkeley: University Art Museum, 1971), no. 16. The Ching Yüan Chai collection, Berkeley, has six leaves, of which four are here published for the first time. A private collection, Washington, D.C., has four leaves, and two leaves are currently in the hands of a dealer. The reconstruction and study of the whole awaits the photographing of the now-missing leaves. We can hope that the album will eventually be reunited in a single collection, and viewable as the artist intended it to be.

12. These "visionary" landscapes in the late Ming period, painted by artists such as Wu Pin (ca. 1568–1626), and possible stimuli for their creation in European engravings, are treated in the third chapter of my *Compelling Image.*

# PART THREE

# THE ILLUSTRATION OF VERGIL IN PRINTED BOOKS

ELEANOR WINSOR LEACH

# ILLUSTRATION AS INTERPRETATION IN BRANT'S AND DRYDEN'S EDITIONS OF VERGIL

In his "Dedication of the *Aeneis*," John Dryden defines his aim in translating the work as that of making Vergil "speak such English as he would have spoken had he been living in England and in this present age."[1] Dryden's remarks outline the larger issues I want to raise in this essay, a large portion of which concerns itself with illustrations that appear in his translation of Vergil. The statement not only epitomizes those goals of poetic translation which Dryden pursued throughout his career, but it also suggests how closely the art of translation may approach that of illustration, both in its need to convey to the reader a coherent image couched within the understandable contemporary idiom and in its responsibility for preserving fidelity to the text. Both translation and illustration are forms of interpretive imitation.

In his 1658 "Preface to *Sylvae*: Or the Second Part of Poetical Miscellany," Dryden's figurative language virtually assimilates translation to the graphic arts.

> Translation is a kind of drawing after the life where everyone will admit there is a double kind of likeness, a good and a bad. 'Tis one thing to draw the outlines true, the features like, the proportions exact, the coloring itself tolerable, and another thing to make all these graceful by the posture, the shadings and chiefly by the spirit that animates the whole.[2]

This visual analogy exemplifies a major principle of Dryden's neoclassical poetics. Deeply imbued with the conviction of the intrinsic likeness of the "sister arts" of poetry and painting so common in seventeenth-century aesthetics, he finds within the terminology of painting a vocabulary to explain his own work in its double relationship to present and past. In insisting that the one true aim of artistic integrity in translation is to render the "spirit" of an author, he calls for a recreation of historical perspective most easily to be understood in visual terms. "The composition of a painter," he writes in his "Parallel of Poetry and Painting," the preface to his English version of du Fresnoy's *De arte graphica*, "should be conformable to the texts of ancient authors, to the customs and times. And this is exactly the same in poetry . . . we are to imitate the customs and times of these persons and things that we represent . . . to be content to follow our masters who understood Nature better than we."[3] From his formulation of these ideas during two months borrowed from his translating of Vergil, Dryden claims to have gained a better understanding of his literary task.[4] Although his work remains an imitation, still, "to copy the best author is a kind of praise if I perform it as I ought."[5] And it is precisely such efforts to recreate a sense of the past through the combination of fidelity to the text and individual interpretation grounded in the contemporary idiom that I wish to discuss in this paper.

These issues are of particular interest to me as a classicist in contrasting two of the most amply illustrated Vergilian volumes in the Rosenwald Collection: the Sebastian Brant 1502 edition printed in Strasbourg by Grüninger with text, commentaries, and woodcuts and the 1697 Jacob Tonson publication of Dryden's translation, *The Works of Virgil*, with engravings by Franz Cleyn and others.[6] Like most sets of illustrations in their period, each of these underwent more than one publication. I have selected these volumes for several reasons. In the first place, the multiplicity of the illustrations allows for the closely detailed rendering of single episodes with scope for fine points of interpretation, while the succession of so many scenes gradually builds toward a self-consistent visual essay on the poems. Often the correspondence of scenes chosen for illustration is remarkable and bears witness with a kind of objectivity of coincidence to the suggestive power which certain Vergilian passages exercise upon the visual imagination. In the second place, each of these editions conveys its own understanding of Vergil's poems as literature of the past.

Brant's *Opera* is not simply an illustrated text but rather a students' library in one volume. On each page the Vergilian lines are surrounded with explanations from five Latin commentators, ranging from the fourth-century grammarians Servius and Donatus to Domenicus Calderinus. Despite the anachronisms of costume and architecture in Brant's visual imagery,[7] he clearly did not want to present Vergil in the guise of a contemporary author but rather as one standing in need of historical illumination. In his verse preface he boasts to have surpassed every other Vergilian edition in the world by the fullness of his commentaries and illustrations,[8] and indeed, by the clarity of the latter, to have made Vergil available even to the unlearned. Although such claims are common among illustrated Renaissance books, this one is hard to accept at its face value since much of the subtle detail of Brant's woodcuts would certainly escape the spectator who could not read the text and seems, rather, calculated to appeal to one whose familiarity with the poems would allow him to appreciate precise visual allusions. In several cases, Brant's work incorporates details drawn from the commentators' interpretations. As a humanistic scholar, he is said to have placed the stamp of his own thorough knowledge of Vergil upon the book by providing master sketches for the illustrators.[9] Certainly the lengthy laus pictorum of his verse preface, which includes the words "has nostras quas pinximque ecce tabellas Virgilio" (these pictures, lo, which I have painted for Vergil), would imply such a contribution, but it is not definite proof. After their initial publication, Brant's woodcuts passed into the hands of a printer who worked for the family of Giunta and were several times reproduced between 1515 and 1552 in similar learned editions but with certain changes and omissions and a general blunting of their detail.[10]

Unlike Brant's illustrations, which were created for their edition, those appearing in Tonson's monumental Dryden volume had seen earlier publications, the first in John Ogilby's 1654 translation of the *Works.*[11] The text of this embellished volume was a revision of, and a great stylistic improvement over, a more humbly printed and somewhat wooden-jointed translation of four years earlier that Ogilby had not inappropriately termed the "shadow and cold resemblence" of Vergil.[12] In the preface of that first volume, the translator had expressed the hope of a more impressive publication, and his dedication of the 1654 edition acknowledges the generosity of those who supported his new version, "inlarged in volume and beautified with sculptures and annotations," for which the editor claims to have employed "the skill and industry of the most famous artists in their kind."[13] The marginal notes were in English, many of them based upon information given by the ancient commentators, and the plates themselves were reused a few years later for the publication of a Latin text.[14]

Although Dryden himself had earlier sneered at Ogilby's work as a prime misrepresentation of the "spirit" of an ancient author,[15] its many analogies with his own translation have been clear to scholars comparing the two texts closely.[16] For all their forty years' difference in time, Cleyn's illustrations are in no way inappropriate to Dryden's book, since the artist himself had worked within that same neoclassical mode that shaped the poet's philosophy and his practices and shows, both in his architecture and in his costumes, a comparable interest in reconstructing a sense of the past. Unlike Brant's illustrations, which pretend, at least, to be informational, the engravings are purely decorative. Their overt purpose is to increase the value and status of the book, but they reveal, nonetheless, a thorough knowledge of the poems, whether gained from the original or from translation, and show a definite interpretive approach.

The compositional format of Brant's illustrations is well suited to their declared purpose of providing information and wholly justifies his claim to have displayed Vergil's scenes clearly. The woodcuts follow two general patterns, the one quite simple, with emphasis on foreground figures against locational backdrops, the other a more spacious landscape style that makes use of the entire plate as a topographical setting for action with little perspective differentiation between foreground and background. Such complex patterning characterizes the majority of single illustrations accompanying each *Eclogue* and the introductory plates for the books of the *Aeneid*, but it occurs elsewhere in the epic as well.

Topographically expansive compositions in this mode are scarcely new in European illustration or in the traditions of German art. We find them in manuscript illustration, but also in the slightly earlier woodcuts of such artists as Dürer's teacher Hans Wohlgemut.[17] Grüninger's Terence edition of 1496, often attributed to Brant, had employed similar compositional formats for the title pages of its plays, although in that case they were merely elaborations of the urban setting of the comic stage to serve as showcases for statically posed figures.[18] The Vergilian illustrations, however, exploit to the fullest the possibilities offered by spacious topography for the combination of interrelated incidents within a single frame.

In the organization and distribution of figures, the style of these illustrations appears not unsimilar to that of continuous narrative, a pictorial convention that follows a single figure throughout a series of actions within a single, uninterrupted unit of space. The mid-fifteenth-century illuminated Vergil by the Florentine Apollonio di Giovanni presented the poems in this way, but di Giovanni's practices were shaped by his career in the painting of ornamental wedding chests, whose conventions demanded heroic legends fully unfolded in a narrative fashion.[19] Technically speaking, Brant's illustrations are not continuous narratives, since they neither repeat a single character within one frame nor employ the friezelike sequence characteristic of medieval versions of this style, but rather distribute incidents and details in a radial pattern over a topographical background organized in patterns of bird's-eye perspective.[20] What is most interesting about Brant's adoption of this style for Vergil is that bird's-eye, or cartographic (as classicists more commonly call it), perspective had so firm and longstanding a position in Roman artistic tradition that we are probably not misled in finding this mode of vision implied by many of the poet's own descriptive passages.[21] Appearing occasionally in the earliest extant illuminated Vergil manuscript, Vatican cod. 3225,[22] bird's-eye composition continues to be used within the traditions of medieval illumination, yet the direct influence of this background on Brant's work is dubious. Rather he would seem to have adopted what was, for him, a local and contemporary style as his own response to the text itself.

With its double potential for factual and symbolic representation, bird's-eye perspective lent itself well to Brant's aims of incorporating a multiplicity of detail. I find the style employed in his edition in three primary ways. First, it is used to give visual articulation to images that appear in the poems as imaginary images, thus organizing mental space as real space. Second, it serves to combine and compress several ramifications of a complex action within a single frame thus creating a panoramic narrative illustration. And, third, it is used to articulate a sense of the topographical or geographical range of certain passages by a symbolic combination of immediately visible objects with the distant or unseen.

Although some reminiscences of the extended landscape and multiple actions of the cartographic style appear in the illustrations of the 1560 French *Aeneid* paraphrase of Louis des Masures, such elements play no part in the engravings of Cleyn, whose style and taste show the influence of Rubens's baroque heroics and whose compositions eschew narrative for the dramatic concept of the frozen moment or tableau.[23] Whereas the Brant edition discriminates between the pastoral and heroic genres largely by the costuming and style of the figures, the later illustrations carry this discrimination over into settings as well in such a manner as to reflect the sophisticated rules of decorum then taking shape in neoclassical genre theory. Their focusing of dramatic moments depends largely upon their placing of figures in action, but it is often intensified by indications of emotion in gesture or countenance. Such emphases are much in keeping with Dryden's own literary pronouncements on heroic poetry, where an attention to the implied visual concepts of episodes or scenes betrays the manner in which the poet's thinking about narrative poetry had been influenced by his long career of writing for the stage.

But if action dominates the illustrations, background plays a large part in conveying their interpretation of the poems. Both singly and as an ensemble, the engravings in Brant's edition make us aware of a poetic interaction between the civilized and natural worlds, a concept whose perception in seventeenth-century art had been greatly enhanced by the work of such landscape painters as Poussin, with his combination of classical architecture and natural surroundings intended to approximate a Vergilian atmosphere. In the following pages, I shall explore the points I have outlined with reference to selected examples from the illustrations for the *Eclogues* and *Aeneid* in the two volumes.

In turning to these examples, I should observe that the style of each volume possesses its particular strengths and felicities that enable it to encompass certain features of Vergil's poetry, yet in each set of illustrations the two genres, pastoral and epic, call upon somewhat different resources of style. The pastoral poem, if we think of it in its artistic unity, does not easily lend itself to illustration since its formal organization as a fictive dialogue or a contest between two singers does not give prominence to any single dramatic action but rather serves as a framework for a series of poetic reflections or a multiplicity of vignettes to embroider a theme. As readers for many generations have discovered, the interrelationships among the sentiments or images of pastoral poems are often elusive; they have from time to time appeared either disarmingly simple or almost impenetrably complex, depending upon the reader's theoretical approach to interpretation. The introductory passages of each of Vergil's pastorals give us portraits of the bucolic singers within their

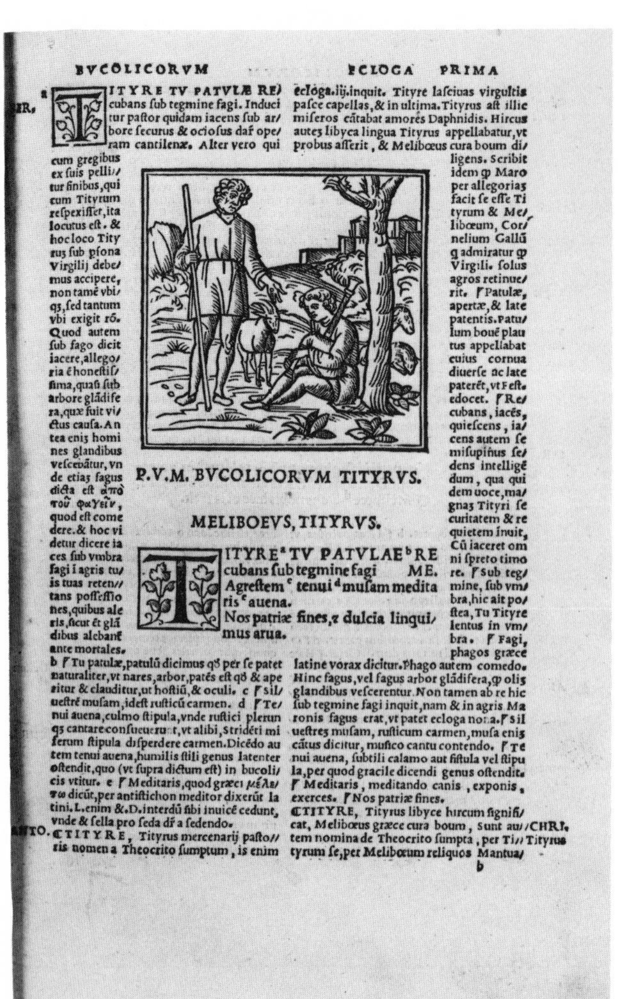

BVCOLICORVM ECLOGA PRIMA

P.V.M. BVCOLICORVM TITYRVS.

MELIBOEVS, TITYRVS.

TITYRE TV PATVLAE RECUBANS sub tegmine fagi ME.
Agrestem tenui musam medita
ris auena.
Nos patriae fines, et dulcia lingui
mus arua.

FIGURE 1. Tityrus and Meliboeus. Illustration for the first *Eclogue*, in *Bucolica*, *Georgica*, *Aeneis* (Venice: in aedibus G. de Rusconibus, 1520), Rosenwald Collection, no. 799.

milieu. The illustrator of Giorgio Rusconi's 1520 Venetian edition contented himself with just such an image of the speakers in the first *Eclogue* (fig. 1), an emblem, one might say, for the genre as a whole. But the Brant and Dryden volumes go further in creating introductory images specifically adapted to each poem. The freedom permitted by Brant's cartographic organization accommodates a symbiotic depiction in the illustrations of the pastoral singers and themes and motifs from their songs. By contrast, Cleyn's more limited focus elicits features of pastoral particularly attractive to its seventeenth-century theorists: the ease and relaxation of the singers, the pleasant atmosphere of their rural ambience.[24] His engravings do not so much illustrate the poems in their entirety as establish the mood in which each is to be read.

The difference appears very clearly in the two illustrations for the second *Eclogue*, a poem given to the traditional pastoral subject of unrequited love. Its singer is Corydon, a herdsman enamoured of the young Alexis whom the Eclogue Poet in his introductory words characterizes as *deliciae domini* ("the treasure of his master"). In Brant's illustration (fig. 2), Corydon sings amid a setting made up of images from his own courtship song. They are an eclectic mixture of the homely and the precious, of fact and fantasy, ranging from the harvesters and plowman, whose rural labors contrast with the lassitude induced by passion, to an imaginary, and here very meretriciously costumed Nympha, twining a flower garland. She is nothing like the classical notion of a nymph, but her incongruity within the rural setting is no greater than it is within the herdsman's song, where her basket of flowers is one of the improbable pleasures of the country that Corydon promises to Alexis.

The figures of drinking boars and a puffing wind in the upper lefthand corner are even more poetically evanescent than the nymph, for they are visual articulations of the metaphor by which Corydon expresses a fear of Alexis's scorn for his rural offerings. To quote Dryden's rather elegant translation:

> The boar amidst my crystal streams I bring
> And southern winds to blight my flowery spring.[25]

Beneath these figures appears a sequence of animals representing another poetic figure in Corydon's song, this one a justification of love which Dryden translates a little less felicitously:

> The greedy lioness the wolf pursues,
> The wolf the kid, the wanton kid the browse;
> Alexis you are chased by Corydon
> All follow several games and each his own.[26]

As a learned Vergilian, Brant must have been fully aware of the poem's commingling of real and imaginary images, since the commentator Servius, whose remarks appear in the margins, had clearly indicated that certain passages of the love songs were fantasies.[27] Thus we may assume that Brant created the composition as a deliberate evocation of the lover's extravagant state of mind. He has also brought out rather ingeniously Corydon's rustic character by giving him, in place of the traditional panpipe for his music, a large, unwieldy bagpipe. Although the tradition of the Italian bagpipe does, in fact, go back to antiquity, Vergil never suggests that these are what his pastoral characters play. The Eclogue Poet characterizes Corydon's futile verses as *incondita*. The term is pejorative in rhetorical vocabulary, and Servius explains it as *agrestia* ("countrified").[28] As the prettiness of Dryden's lines would suggest, the seventeenth century did not find Corydon's song uncultivated but rather the very model of pastoral blandishment, and Cleyn's engraving makes him a romantic figure, somewhat languid, with a handsome face and smooth lovelocks, in spite of his country dress (fig. 3). A contrast between amorous idleness and rustic labor is suggested by our glimpse through the densely shaded foreground grove into a sunny field beyond, where harvesters are at work, but the nature of Corydon's song is left to the text to explain. What we see here is pastoral that conforms to a theory, the simplicity of its characters to be understood not as a crude simplicity but rather as that of ideal shepherds in a golden age of myth.

At first glance, Brant's illustration for the first *Eclogue* seems not unlike that for the second (fig. 4), but this topography is not designed around fantasies. Instead, it has been drawn in very careful agreement with those descriptions that take shape in the dialogue between the poem's two speakers. Vergil's opening verses sharply

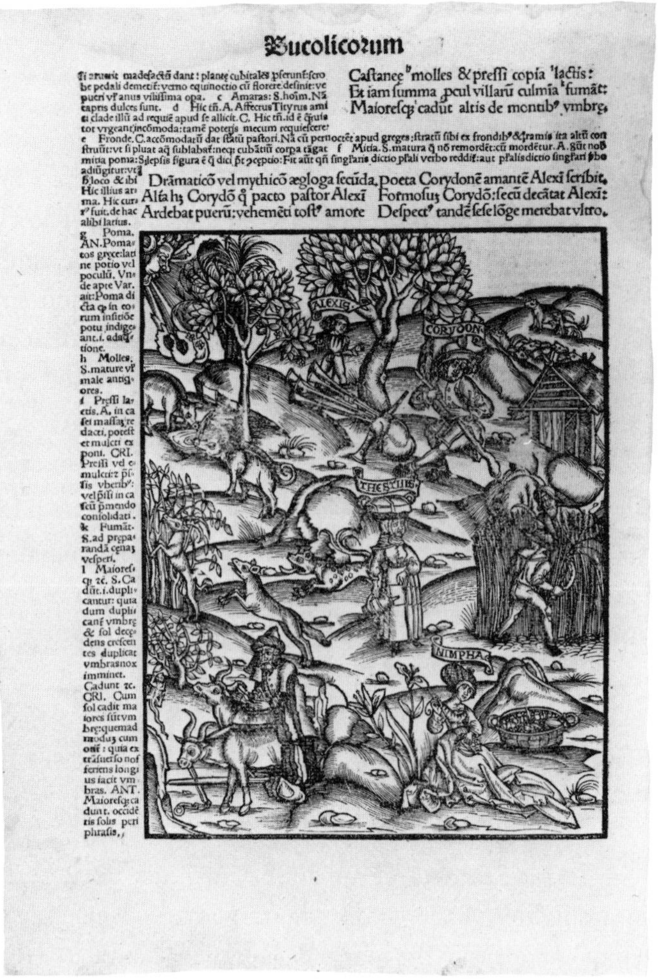

FIGURE 2. Corydon Surrounded by Images from His Song. Illustration for the second *Eclogue*, in Sebastian Brant, ed. *Opera*, by Publius Vergilius Maro (Strasbourg: I. Grieninger, 1502), Rosenwald Collection, no. 594.

contrast two men's fortunes: the carefree rural leisure of Tityrus, piping beneath a shady beech tree, and the distress of Meliboeus, who is leaving the farmland taken from him in the aftermath of civil war. For the Roman poet this was a bold venture which drew the hitherto autonomous world of pastoral into the sphere of contemporary Rome.

Commentators and critics have often thought of the *Eclogue* as a political poem, and sometimes as an allegory of Vergil's own experience.[29] No illustration can genuinely capture the effect of the poem's successive revelations. The reader is surprised to learn that Tityrus's good fortune is the result of a journey and has been conferred by a benefactor in Rome. In Brant's illustration this link between the pastoral sphere and the great world is suggested by the background images of two cities labeled Mantua and Rome. Tityrus had been surprised by his sight of Rome. Expecting no more than an enlargement of the familiar Mantua, he found instead that Rome "towered above other cities as the cypress over the pliant vines." The illustrator has attempted to capture the sense of this comparison in distinguishing Rome by domed buildings, a more foreign species of architecture, to set it apart from the Germanic Mantua. Of course the two cities are not to be taken for parts of the landscape literally before the eyes of the speakers. Their presence is symbolic and reflects the political consciousness of the poem.[30]

FIGURE 3. Franz Cleyn, Corydon Singing in a Beech Grove. Illustration for the second *Eclogue*, in *The Works of Virgil*, translated by John Dryden (London: J. Tonson, 1697), Rosenwald Collection, no. 1548.

FIGURE 4. The Meeting of Meliboeus and Tityrus. Illustration for the first *Eclogue*, in Sebastian Brant, ed., *Opera*, by Publius Vergilius Maro (Strasbourg: I. Grieninger, 1502), Rosenwald Collection, no. 594.

Argumēta Aeglogæ Primæ.

Publij Virgilij Maronis Mantuani opera
cū cōmētariis Seruii Mauri honorati grāmatici: Aelii Donati: Christofori Landini: Antonii Mancinelli & Domicii Calderini.

Argumentum ęglogę primę: quę Tytirus dicitur.
A patria fugiens Melibęus forte sub vmbra.
Tytrion inuenit cantantem carmina amicę.
Quapropter miratus ei sua damna recenset:
Auctoremq͡ȝ sui declarat Tytirus oci.
SEBASTIANVS BRANT
Sub fagi recubans Melibęum Tytirus vmbra
Solatur profugum: collataq͡ȝ munia laudat.

In the remainder of the landscape, Brant shows us Tityrus's farm as Meliboeus describes it. It is not, as the opening verses might suggest, a perfect paradise, but rather a small plot encroached upon by rocks and marshes. All the same, it is a place where master and flock may enjoy security *inter flumina nota* ("between familiar rivers"). Doves and pigeons make their sounds in the trees above; the leafcutter sings at his work while bees in the hedges drone the farmer to sleep. All these details suggest Tityrus's happy isolation from the troubled countryside, which the illustrator has made quite explicit in placing him on an islet bounded by streams. In the foreground his animals are in pens as if to demonstrate, as Meliboeus mentions, their safety from contagion by other flocks.[31] Two other details from Meliboeus's speeches fill out the composition but do not belong to the immediate scene: the one, in the background, the small farm with its thatched cottage which he has had to abandon,[32] the other, in the left foreground, two diminutive newborn kids left behind on a ledge of flinty rock.[33] The reader who is familiar with the poem will see this detail as a touch of pathos, but within the composition itself it is scarcely self-explanatory. Similarly, the factual nature of the illustration captures the pervasive sense of rural

FIGURE 5. Franz Cleyn, The Meeting of Meliboeus and Tityrus. Illustration for the first *Eclogue*, in *The Works of Virgil*, translated by John Dryden (London: J. Tonson, 1697), Rosenwald Collection, no. 1548.

realities that gives the poem its Roman tone but makes no attempt to convey the emotions of the speakers.

These emotions are the keynote of Cleyn's illustration (fig. 5), whose whole purpose is to dramatize through its contrast of action and repose that impassioned contrast between exile and security expressed by Meliboeus in the poem's opening lines. Meliboeus's figure is in motion, with his one hand straining the taut lead of his goat, who sprawls before him as if refusing to go further, while the other gestures backward to dramatize the unhappy words *nos patriam fugimus* ("we are fleeing from our fatherland").[34] By contrast, Tityrus's stolid posture of repose and especially his unresponsive, almost obtuse countenance looking blankly away from his interlocutor are in keeping with the self-complacency he displays in explaining his better fortunes throughout the poem. Only recently have classical readers begun to realize that he is not a wholly sympathetic character, yet his lack of charm seems subtly implied by this illustration. In the far distance are the farms, somewhat larger than the humble thatched cottage Meliboeus mentions, and the figures running excitedly in the farmyard would seem to dramatize the stirring up of the countryside into exile. The middle distance with its sharp, bare ledges and sparse trees shows the country Meliboeus has already traversed in his journey of exile. It is in fact to him and his story that the background landscape belongs rather than to Tityrus. Unlike Brant's illustrator, Cleyn has not followed Vergil's description exactly but rather has selected a few details to recombine in a manner that supports his dramatization of the emotional tenor of the interview. One may compare this graphic interpretation with Knightly Chetwood's remarks in his preface to Dryden's translation, one of the first explicit mentions of landscape in English pastoral criticism.

> A beautiful landscape presents itself to your view, a shepherd with his flock around him resting securely under a spreading Beech which furnished the first food to our ancestors. Another in quite different situation of Mind and Circumstances, the sun setting, the hospitality of the more fortunate shepherd *et cet.*[35]

Although one cannot credit Chetwood with much originality of visual imagination, he also seems to perceive a close bond between the physical and emotional character of the scene.

However acceptable or unacceptable to his theoretical definition of pastoral simplicity, no reader of any period could ignore the historical theme of the celebrated fourth *Eclogue*, and it is in their efforts to meet the challenge posed by this elusively visionary poem that the two illustrators most nearly coincide. From the Middle Ages, the birth of the unnamed child that gives the formal occasion of the *Eclogue* had been, to a greater or lesser degree, identified with Christ's Nativity. This tradition of the Messianic *Eclogue* persisted long after the actual belief that Vergil had prophesied Christ's birth, and well into the eighteenth century, when Alexander Pope's "Messiah" adopts Vergil's poetic organization for a Christian poem interwoven with imagery from the Book of Isaiah, whose similarities with that of the *Eclogue* Pope mentions in his notes.

FIGURE 6. Vergil and Asinius Pollio against a Background of Historical Symbols. Illustration for the fourth *Eclogue*, in Sebastian Brant, ed., *Opera*, by Publius Vergilius Maro (Strasbourg: I. Grieninger, 1502), Rosenwald Collection, no. 594.

Bucolicorum

poeta solus in laudem pollionis & Salonini filij. Aegloga quarta.

Pollio quarta tuas laudes & fortia facta: Altius hic canitur: celebratur Pollio: Cesar

Atq; Salonini fata immatura recenset. Alter: & hic secli venturi scribitur ordo.

Sicelides muse paulo maiora canamus.

Non omes arbusta iuuant: humilesq; myrice.

Sicelides muse. S. Asini⁹ Pollio dictor germanici exercitus: captis Salonis vrbe in Dalmacia: meruit laureā: deinde consulatū: & eodem anno suscepit filiū: quē a Salonis captis Saloninū vocauit. huic Virgili⁹ Genethliacon dicit: qui statim natus risit: qd parentibus omen fuit infelicitatis. Ipse enim inter primordia extinctus est. Sicelides grecum: nam latine Sicilienses facit: id est Theocriti. Nam Theocritū (qui Syracusanus fuit) imitat. AN. Sicelides. In antiquis etiam pluribus textibus: & in illo qui in summi pontificis bibliotheca maioribus characteribus scriptus est Sicelides per e nō per i: legi: quod grece dixit. illis enim Sicelia: nobis autē Sicilia dicitur. Celebratur hic Asinius Pollio qui orator & cōsularis: vt docet Eusebius: de quo latius in Alexi. Fuit historiarum & Tragediarum scriptor: qui & de Dalmatis triumphauit. Vnde Hora. Ode prima secundi voluminis ad eū scribēs. Cui laurus eternos honores Dalmatico peperit triūpho: Laudatur ibidē eūdē a prudētia: a dignitate honore: ab eloquentie viribus. Dicunt alii a Salona Dalmatie vrbe capta: susceptum filium Saloninum vocasse: qui & si parum vixit: hic tamē a Marone cum patre celebratur. sed laus ipsa talis est: q̄ sepe ad Augustum quoq; referenda ē: vt suo loco docebimus. preterea in Strabone legisse memini: Salone Salonarum. In Plinio Salona salone. Itaq; non recte Solone p̄lo. in prima syllaba dicit. Sicelides muse: q̄ sc; Theocrito syracusano fauistis: seu o Theocriti cantus & carmina. Sicelides. CRI. Deprecat errorē: si paulo sublimius quam pastoria res requirit canat. Dixit autem Sicelides & non Sicilides. Nam cum vsus sit patronymico nomie: quod potius grecum q̄ latinū est. deduxit ab eo quod est Sicelia: vt dicunt greci: & non Sicilia: vt dicunt latini.

b Paulo maiora. S. Non multo. Nam licet hec egloga discedat a carmine Bucolico: tamen aliqua operi apta inferunt. c Arbusta. AN. id est minima et humilia. C. Cū pprie arbustū sit locus cōsitus nouellis arborib⁹ q̄ ex seminario auulsa sunt: semina q; appellāt. voluit notare humiliores arbores. d Myrice. S. Virgulta humilia sunt. A.

FIGURE 7. Franz Cleyn, Vergil and the Family of Asinius Pollio with Symbols of the New Golden Age. Illustration for the fourth *Eclogue*, in *The Works of Virgil*, translated by John Dryden (London: J. Tonson, 1697), Rosenwald Collection, no. 1548.

In the 1544 Venetian reprinting of Brant's illustrations, the *Eclogue* is prefaced by a couplet from Ascensius that terms it a Christian genethliacon,[36] but Brant himself remains true to his classical learning and prints Servius's identification of the child as Saloninus, son of the consul of 40 B.C. who was born in the year of his father's consulship. The swaddled infant at the feet of Vergil and Pollio is duly labeled Saloninus (fig. 6). In Ogilby's edition, the poem is prefaced by four verses which appear to be an expanded translation of Ascensius's couplet,[37] and Cleyn's illustration captures the Messianic allusion rather subtly through a kind of visual metaphor (fig. 7). The family group whom Vergil addresses in his prophetic guise, complete with the magic wand of medieval necromancy, is at once Pollio's family and the parents of Jesus entering the temple. At the same time, the classical arch and colonnaded porch that give the setting for this group correspond to Vergil's own poetic elevation of the bucolic style to suit a historical theme: "paulo maiora canamus." In Brant's illustration the historical theme is also represented by the use of a nonpastoral architecture in the background.

In both cases, the illustrators have attempted to reflect the content of the poem by a selection of images from the prophecy that makes up its greater part. The birth of the child inaugurates a cycle of world renewal. The stages of his growth are attended by the development of a new spontaneity in nature and by recurrences of legendary events. Although some of Brant's images are not entirely clear in their significance, the upper lefthand corner shows the ships that will carry a second band of Argonauts and a new army of heroes to Troy.[38] With his greater emphasis upon the birth and the magical nature of the child, Cleyn limits his vision to those pastoral images that constitute Vergil's initial stage of natural transformation; grapes clustering on the wild thorn, fierce and tame beasts nuzzling with experimental affection, and, in the distance, a man raising his arms under a miraculous rain of honey from the oak.[39]

Aside from their concern for simplicity and for preserving the pastoral fiction, Cleyn's illustrations also show some consideration for variety in the development of the poem book. The issue is an interesting one to a literary critic, both from a historical and from an interpretive point of view. Even the ancient commentators had remarked on the variety of the pastoral scenes, which caused one of these scholars to speculate that Vergil had written no more than ten *Eclogues* because this number had exhausted the possibilities of invention.[40] Of these ten, we also hear that only seven are purely bucolic. The exceptions are poems four, six, and ten, presumably because of the prominent place that they give to historical figures.[41]

Possibly these comments had some influence on Brant, since his illustrations for the fourth and sixth poem include the figure of Vergil himself as poetic speaker and that of ten shows the historical figure, Cornelius Gallus, Vergil's fellow poet, whose love for a faithless mistress prompts his attraction to pastoral verse. But in other respects, Brant's illustrations show no great concern for variety; they are to be distinguished from one another chiefly by the fine points of their allusion to content in a manner quite in keeping with their concept of illustration as a visual realization of the text.

By contrast, the engravings, with their deliberate simplification of content and their focus upon the characters of the pastoral singers, also show self-conscious concern for the development of the book as an ensemble and resort to ingenious methods of varying the pastoral scene. Save for the difference in the number and nature of the singers, the illustrations of the first, second, and third poems resemble each other with their foreground groves and glimpses of a settled country landscape beyond. In the fifth poem, which might easily call for a similar setting, the illustrator has closed off his background and horizon by a bit of baroque paraphernalia which alludes to the traditional understanding of the poetic apotheosis of the shepherd Daphnis as an allegory of the apotheosis of Julius Caesar (fig. 8). Regardless of the validity of the interpretation, which has much to recommend it, this is certainly the least successful of the illustrations. The Ogilby translation which accompanied the original publication was a rather lame one:

> Daphnis admir'd beholding Jove's bright arch
> And stars and clouds beneath his feet to march.[42]

Dryden's, however, corresponds quite perfectly with an image strikingly reminiscent of the ethereal pretensions of the ceilings of Whitehall:

> Fair Daphnis wonders at strange courts above,
> Who clouds and stars beneath his feet beholds.

In illustrating the seventh poem, Cleyn makes his most conspicuous departure from the text and invents a dramatic situation entirely his own. Vergil's introduction presents four characters—two singers, a judge, and a spectator—but the illustration takes up the suggestion that this is a *magnum certamen* ("a great contest") and turns it into a rustic gathering of shepherds and picturesque shepherdesses who belong far more to the seventeenth-century tradition of the fête champêtre than to the atmosphere of Vergil's Roman pastoral.[43]

In recent years classical scholars have taken a particular interest in the design of Vergil's *Eclogue Book*, proposing one and another pattern of contrasts and parallels between its ten poems as the basis of its artistic unity.[44] Although a comparable interest in pattern does not occur in ancient or seventeenth-century discussions of the variety of the poems, still the repetitions and contrasts among Cleyn's portraits of the singers in their landscapes also suggest a perception of thematic interrelationships in the development of the book. As it draws toward its close, the background prospects show a subtle change from the rather domesticated countryside of the initial illustrations to scenery far more rugged and wild. The ninth poem, like the first, concerns the loss of farmland to Roman soldiers, veterans of the civil wars. The farm, however, is not the setting, which is rather a road leading somewhat ambiguously "to the city." The mood is not a cheerful one, and in Cleyn's rendition the gloomy cast of the dialogue seems reflected in the desolate and inhospitable surroundings through which the speakers are passing. For this poem he has invented his own milieu, but in the tenth (fig. 9) he follows Vergil's suggestions quite closely in picturing the steep and rocky landscape of Arcadia where the soldier poet Cornelius Gallus complains of his betrayal in love. To the contemporary reader it seems quite clear that Gallus is not physically present in Arcadia, but rather picturing in his mind the harsh crags and cold streams of its landscape.[45] Arcadia is a world created by his imagination to serve as the mirror of his unhappy state.

FIGURE 8. Franz Cleyn, Menalcus and Mopsus Sing the Apotheosis of Daphnis. Illustration for the fifth *Eclogue*, in *The Works of Virgil*, translated by John Dryden (London: J. Tonson, 1697), Rosenwald Collection, no. 1548.

FIGURE 9. Franz Cleyn, Gallus in Arcadia. Illustration for the tenth *Eclogue*, in *The Works of Virgil*, translated by John Dryden (London: J. Tonson, 1697), Rosenwald Collection, no. 1548.

The illustration brings out the alien character of the armed soldier amidst natural surroundings. Gallus is not, as Vergil has him, stretched prone on the ground in despair, but he sits brooding with a glance more dangerous than forlorn. Before him stand three pastoral interlocutors—Pan, Silvanus, and Apollo—who comment with critical amazement on the irrational character of his persistent love. Within Vergil's collection, this final poem serves as a self-conscious assessment of pastoral. Gallus's failure to find either satisfaction or long-lasting consolation within the fictional world he has created turns our attention sharply from realms of imagination back to reality. In the set of illustrations, the contrast between the intrusive

Liber Primus CXXI

De operibus Virgilij Sebastianus brant

Vita magis nulli eſt ſua cognita: docta Maronis
Quam mihi muſa: canens pergama; rura: capras;

Tetraſticon eiuſdem

Poſt nemora atq; greges culturam ruris: & vuas:
diſce & equos lector: mellificasq; feras.
Grandior oblectat ſi te hinc tuba parthenopea:
Diuigenum poteris perlegere arma ducum.

FIGURE 10. Musa mihi causas memora. Prefatory illustration for the *Aeneid*, Book One, in Sebastian Brant, ed., *Opera*, by Publius Vergilius Maro (Strasbourg: I. Grieninger, 1502), Rosenwald Collection, no. 594.

historical figure and his fantastic surroundings at once sets this poem apart from its predecessors and serves as a striking conclusion for the book.

In the *Aeneid*, the poet's vision of nature expands beyond the limited rural settings of pastoral, and even the Italian scenes of the *Georgics*, to encompass the entirety of the Mediterranean world, through which the hero wanders in search of his divinely decreed home. As is appropriate to Vergil's constant emphasis on Aeneas's longing for a new city to replace fallen Troy, the contrast between nature and civilization plays an important role in the epic, a role that has increasingly engaged the attention of contemporary critics in its association with the poem's themes of order and disorder in all aspects of man's social and emotional life.[46] The illustrations of both volumes show an instinctive grasp of the vital interplay between these two spheres. The majority of Brant's cartographic settings include some form of city, which often serves as the immediate location for actions, but again, as in *Eclogue* one, as a symbolic allusion to a more remote place. Save in the illustrations for Book Two, whose subject is the Greek invasion of Troy, Aeneas seldom appears within the confines of these cities but stands, rather, outside their walls and frequently at some distance. His exclusion, as it were, from walls, which so often serve as the symbol of his longing for a fixed home, quite effectively conveys the sense of restless exile that pervades the narrative. With his many architectural backgrounds, Cleyn does not hesitate to take Aeneas into cities which are often of a more monumental order than Vergil's descriptions would justify. In his work, the contrast between the spheres of nature and civilization appears occasionally in the juxtaposition of foreground with deep background vistas in a single image but more often as we turn from one to another illustration. Thus in Book Six Aeneas confronts the raving Cumean Sibyl within a handsome classical exedra decorated with colonnaded niches and statues, but in the succeeding illustrations we find him by the shores of Lake Avernus within that majestic ominous forest into which Venus has guided him to pluck the golden bough that is the mysterious token of a living man's admission into the realms of the dead.

In keeping with the difference in scope between single illustrations in the two books is the nature of their focus on the poem's actions. Whereas Brant's inclusive, informative style captures the narrative complexity of its episodes, Cleyn, by selecting significant dramatic moments, calls the reader's attention to a series of high points, such as major speeches or critical turns of the plot. Following Vergil's words very closely, Brant gives Book One a prefatory panorama (fig. 10). The first person voice of the epic speaker which opens the poem is made explicit in the figure of Vergil himself writing to the dictation of the Muse that passage following upon "Musa mihi causas memora" which searches into the background of the brooding wrath of Juno that pursues the hero throughout the poem.[47] The Muse's pointing finger indicates Carthage, whose future destruction by the offspring of Troy is known to the Fates, and also to scenes of old grudges strongly remembered: Jove's elevation of the Trojan Ganymede; the humiliating Judgment of Paris. This, then, is an exploration of Juno's mind within the convenience of a fictive landscape.

Cleyn's first engraving, by contrast, plunges the reader in medias res with the storm that drives Aeneas's fleet off course from the Sicilian coast to Carthage (fig. 11). Swelling waves and pitching vessels make a stirring, if conventional, composition. In this first appearance the hero himself is recognizable by no pronounced physical distinction but only by the posture of appeal that accompanies his desperate outcry to the gods. In Brant's equivalent illustration, it is again mythology, rather than drama, which predominates to trace a history of the storm from Juno's royal visit to Aeolus's prison of the winds (fig. 12). The winds' grotesque faces peer outward from their womblike cavern (Vergil's "loca feta furentibus Austris")[48] breathing decorative swirls. Rain falls from the clouds in this tempestuous region,

FIGURE 11. Franz Cleyn, Aeneas's Ship Tossed by Storm. Illustration for *Aeneid* 1. 87–101, in *The Works of Virgil*, translated by John Dryden (London: J. Tonson, 1697), Rosenwald Collection, no. 1548.

but below it, the disturbance to Aeneas's fleet seems minimal. The ships float placidly in a rippled sea with Aeneas's upturned face the only sign of distress.

The frequent coincidence to be found in Cleyn's and Brant's choices of episodes or moments for illustration is its own tribute to those passages where Vergil presents his most vivid suggestions to the imagination, but it also makes the differences between their two approaches easy to assess. Occasionally their productions are similar. Both, for example, depict the Trojans' first encampment on the African shore where Vergil gives Aeneas his first show of leadership in providing food and moral comfort for his men. With their interest in visualizing the safe harbor, whose twin enclosing peaks and deep recess Vergil describes with precision, and likewise the reassuring bustle about the homely necessities of fire and food, these illustrations have much the same tone. In both cases Aeneas and his comrade Achates are onlookers, rather than participants, in the actions depicted. A greater difference appears in the pair that represent Aeneas's encounter with his disguised mother Venus

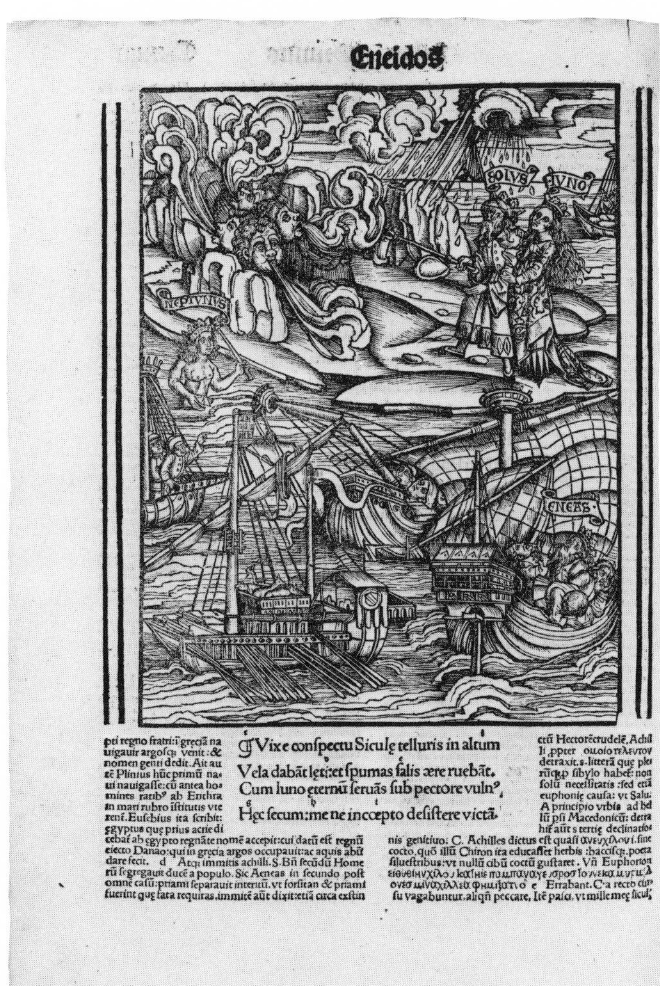


FIGURE 12. Juno Persuades Aeolus to Release the Storm Winds upon Aeneas's Ship. Illustration for *Aeneid* 1. 50–101, in Sebastian Brant, ed., *Opera*, by Publius Vergilius Maro (Strasbourg: I. Grieninger, 1502), Rosenwald Collection, no. 594.

FIGURE 13. Aeneas's Progress toward Carthage. Illustration for *Aeneid* 1. 305–401, in Sebastian Brant, ed., *Opera*, by Publius Vergilius Maro (Strasbourg: I. Grieninger, 1502), Rosenwald Collection, no. 594.

as he makes his way through the unknown African wilderness to Carthage.[49] Here both illustrators have clarified the scene by including the image of the still invisible city, but each has given it a different function within his composition. Brant's conventional image of the walled city, in combination with the ships moored by the shore, provides a factual location for the meeting (fig. 13). Emphasis is on promises of Aeneas's future safety, of which the reader knows far more than the hero himself. Above the city appears the figure of Mercury, whom Jupiter has dispatched to create a hospitable welcome for Aeneas in an enemy land.[50] In the foreground is the sign that Venus invokes to raise the spirits of her son: fourteen swans escaping pursuit by an eagle and settling safely on the earth.[51] Far more particularized than Brant's emblematic city, Cleyn's image of Carthage (fig. 14) borrows suggestions from a later descriptive passage to show the citizens engaged in various tasks of construction, yet his emphasis is not upon Vergil's theme of civic harmony but rather on the ambiguities of the present moment.[52] Her virginal hunting costume scarcely cloaks

FIGURE 14. Franz Cleyn, Aeneas's Meeting with Venus. Illustration for *Aeneid* 1. 325–34, in *The Works of Virgil*, translated by John Dryden (London: J. Tonson, 1697), Rosenwald Collection, no. 1548.

the voluptuous form of the love goddess who, all the same, resists Aeneas's instinctive identification of her divinity until after the tale of Carthage has been told. When Venus does, at last, reveal herself, her revelation is small comfort to her son but leaves him, rather, with his own uncertainty made more painful by such capricious deception. Cleyn's contrast between the armed heroes and the woman's voluptuous coyness aptly renders Vergil's sense of the wanton frivolity the gods can exercise. The distant Carthage has its own significance as a foreshadowing of the difficult emotional adventure that Venus is about to bring upon her son.

A further example of the different emphases procured by Brant's narrative and Cleyn's dramatic orientations appears in a pair of analogous representations of

FIGURE 15. Ascanius's Wounding of a Stag Provokes the First Skirmish of the Latin War. Illustration for *Aeneid* 7. 475–539, in Sebastian Brant, ed., *Opera*, by Publius Vergilius Maro (Strasbourg: I. Grieninger, 1502), Rosenwald Collection, no. 594.

the prelude to Aeneas's Italian wars. Upon the arrival of the Trojans in Latium, Ascanius wounds a deer, the pet of the king's shepherd's daughter, which his dogs have started after their senses had been quickened by the influence of a demon from the underworld.[53] The hue and cry raised by the grieving mistress stirs up the men of her family and neighboring Italian farmers to arms. In Brant's picture (fig. 15) an ample farmhouse indicates the shepherd's important position; a thick wood and rustic bridge convey the settled life into which Ascanius's action intrudes. Sylvia greets her wounded pet with visible indignation. At the left foreground her brothers collect their arms for vengeance while the demon Allecto, who has stirred up the dogs, smiles fiendishly from her seat on the roof. Into this landscape, whose rural atmosphere conveys the quality of Vergil's event, Brant has also incorporated its consequences in the first skirmishes of the Latin War. His composition is full of chaotic activity, moving simultaneously in several directions and within several separate moments of time. In the center of the picture Ascanius stands still, holding his hunting bow, but the right bank of the stream is already strewn with the bodies of dead men as more warriors of both parties emerge from the forest.

Cleyn's illustration (fig. 16) is similarly filled with motion, but all of it unified within that split second of the chase when Ascanius's arrow strikes its mark. The deer is a noble creature, so powerfully drawn that its thick flower garland and silly ribbons scarcely detract from the majesty of its form in flight. A very young Ascanius leans forward on his galloping horse with an intensity that precisely matches Vergil's phrase *eximiae laudis succensus amore* ("on fire with a passion for signal praise").[54] In this image of boyish energy caught up in the Roman drive for honor, Cleyn has

FIGURE 16. Franz Cleyn, Ascanius Wounds a Stag. Illustration for *Aeneid* 7. 483–99, in *The Works of Virgil*, translated by John Dryden (London: J. Tonson, 1697), Rosenwald Collection, no. 1548.

FIGURE 18. Franz Cleyn, Aeneas, Evander, and Pallas at Pallanteum. Illustration for *Aeneid* 8. 102–74, in *The Works of Virgil*, translated by John Dryden (London: J. Tonson, 1697), Rosenwald Collection, no. 1548.

FIGURE 17. King Evander Receives Aeneas at Pallanteum, the Site of Rome. Illustration for *Aeneid* 8. 364–65, in Sebastian Brant, ed., *Opera*, by Publius Vergilius Maro (Strasbourg: I. Grieninger, 1502), Rosenwald Collection, no. 594.

captured the full symbolic value of Vergil's Ascanius, the link between Aeneas and Roman empire. To this, however, he has added the bitterly twisted form of the infernal Allecto running alongside the hunter with the maddened dogs to disfigure with irony the young man's heroic sport.

Among the most compelling events of the poem is the narrative of Aeneas's visit, in quest of an alliance, to King Evander at Pallanteum, a legendary Arcadian settlement by the Tiber on the future site of Rome. Into his account of this wilderness community, itself created by exiles in Italy and maintaining with dignity the old traditions of peace and simplicity from the Italian age of Saturn, Vergil has woven thought-provoking images of the modern world of Rome in its gilded splendor. Thus Aeneas's visit becomes a meeting point for the several levels of historical and legendary time at play within the poem and an occasion for the evaluation of Roman civilization by its own legendary ideals.[55] Brant rises to the challenge of this scene with one of his handsomest landscapes (fig. 17). Although it bears no resemblance whatsoever to the real topography of Rome and the Tiber, still the strong lines of its monumental cliffs and dolmens, its thick trees and winding stream, create that very atmosphere of noble simplicity by which Vergil stirs his reader's imagination to thoughts of a vanished past. In addition to Aeneas's greeting of Evander and his son Pallas, the details include a sacrifice to Hercules on the edge of the forest and, for the ultimate mark of simplicity, cattle grazing on the Palatine Hill. The setting is most appropriate to Evander's advice to Aeneas:

> aude, hospes, contemnere opes et te quoque dignum
> finge deo, rebusque veni non asper egenis.[56]

In Dryden's edition (fig. 18), a very different landscape emphasizes a different aspect of Vergil's narrative: the brooding sense of time that haunts the interassociation of Pallanteum and Rome. Although Evander appears somewhat the primitive monarch in his short tunic and rough, if rich, fur cast over one shoulder, the monumental buildings behind him belie the sense of simplicity. Beside him stands Pallas in full armor with a thoughtful look and restless air that captures Vergil's account of the deep impression the heroic visitors have made upon the young prince and his longing to enter into the world of great deeds.[57] Stylistically, the architecture of the middle ground is somewhat nondescript, its crenulated towers suggesting, if anything, medieval structures so rare in Rome, but the hills of the far distance offer a prospect of ruined arches and towers. These are the once flourishing citadels of the founding deities Janus and Saturn, whose broken walls Evander points out to Aeneas, for indeed his own simple community has been established upon the ruins of a great past: "reliquas veterumque monumenta virorum."[58] One is in fact reminded of the ruins of the great palaces of the Palatine as Piranesi has presented them through seventeenth-century eyes. In no other illustration do we, perhaps, grasp so clearly the sense of the complex interweavings of time within the *Aeneid* and its extension even beyond Augustan Rome into the world of the illustrator and his audience.

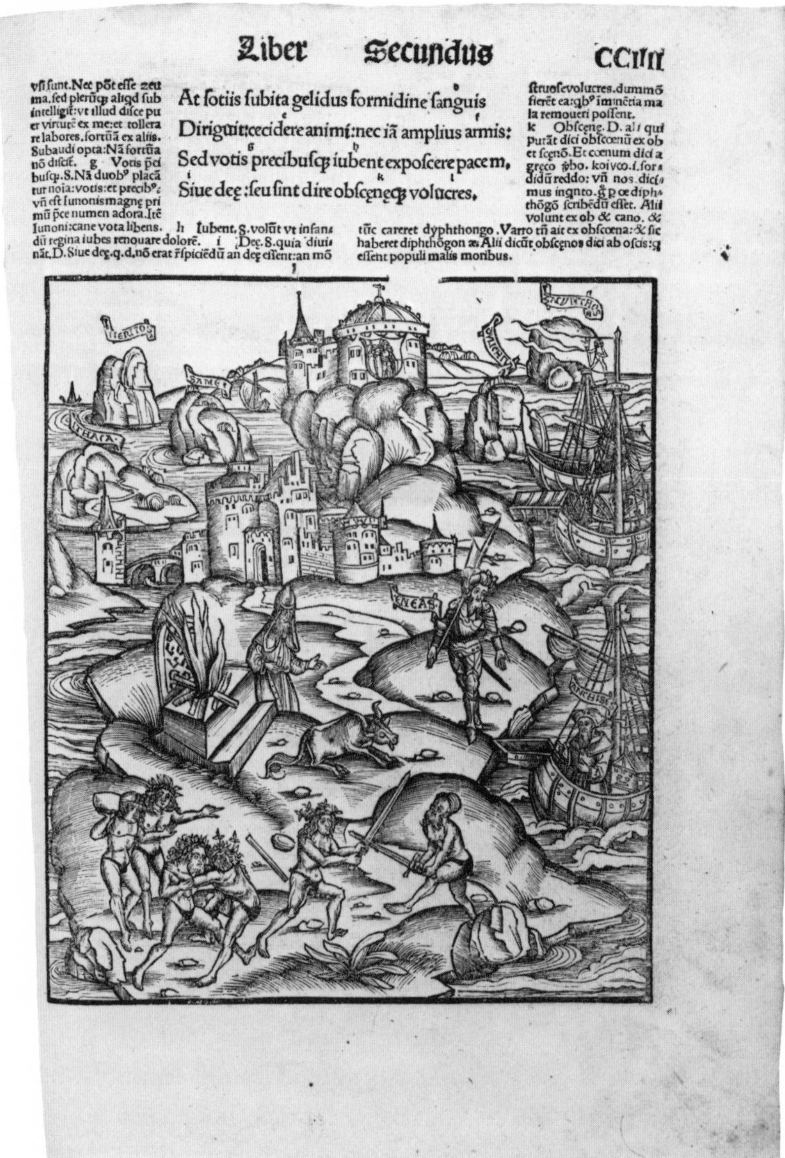


FIGURE 19.
Aeneas's Mediterranean Journey.
Illustration for *Aeneid* 3. 267–89,
in Sebastian Brant, ed.,
*Opera*, by Publius Vergilius Maro
(Strasbourg: I. Grieninger, 1502),
Rosenwald Collection, no. 594.

Equal, however, to the extension of the *Aeneid* throughout time is its extension in geographical space. In comparison with the *Odyssey*, whose actual and mythical places remain as vague in their spatial interrelationships as they are vivid in description, the *Aeneid* directs itself to an audience sufficiently informed by maps and by the experience of travel to be able to follow with interest the factual details of the poet's geography.[59] In addition to its encompassing the complex movements of narrative action, Brant's cartographic style is particularly well suited to give visual form to this aspect of Vergil's work. Geographical illustrations are thus naturally frequent in Book Three, the book of Aeneas's Mediterranean journey. These are not exactly maps, but rather abstract topographical designs. The picture that accompanies Aeneas's account of his sailing through the Cycladic islands gives no authentic order to the small, stark peaks whose names the poet mentions in a kind of traveler's catalog, but instead arranges them to create a frame for the central promontory of Leucate (fig. 19). Here we see the Trojans' landing, their sacrifice, and their triumphant celebration of games on the shore of Actium. The event prefigures Augustus's historical victory at Actium, but it is for the Trojans an immediate expression of their joy in a safe passage through a dangerous course:

> iuvat evassisse tot urbes
> Argolicas, mediosque fugam tenuisse per hostis.[60]

The surrounding illustrations are not unsimilar. Their succession one after another throughout the book answers to Vergil's rapid shifting of place and provides an imaginative sense of the range of Aeneas's wanderings.

By contrast, Cleyn's more narrowly focused compositions rarely provide a sense of wandering through distance, and when they do only vaguely suggest it through the use of background seascapes, as when Aeneas, on the Thracian coast, plucks a bleeding twig from Polydorus's unmarked grave and pauses in wonder, his figure outlined against a panorama of hills and farflung shores.

When Brant turns, however, to another and less factual kind of topographical design to chart Aeneas's course through the underworld, his combined fancy and tendency toward precision turn his illustrations to diagrams. The overtones of mystery and the ritual of initiation implied by the descent into Hades have never failed to capture readers' imaginations. Homer had described the land of the shades beyond the shore of Ocean as the "mouldering home of Hades" at the junction of two great rivers. His hero does not move physically through its spaces but rather stands at the border where the dead flock drink the sacrificial blood that permits communication with the living. For Aeneas, however, who must here, as elsewhere, travel a physical distance in answer to his father's call to seek him in the Elysian Fields, Vergil makes the underworld a mapped topography, preserving Homer's slight architectural suggestion by allusions to a threshold and entrance recalling those of a Roman house but extending the road far beyond through a series of secretive groves and forests to the flowering Elysian meadows where souls await rebirth.

Three separate diagrams of the underworld appear in Brant's Book Six: the one representing its threshold crowded with monsters, the second, the regions inhabited by persons who died before their time, and the third, those inner depths of Tartarus through which Aeneas does not actually pass, since the road to the Elysian Fields turns off to the right, but which the Sibyl describes for his curiosity in all their traditional lurid detail. The subject held an understandable fascination for Brant's period, with its high consciousness of sin and death. (One need only think of Dürer's woodcuts for the *Apocalypse* published a few years after the Vergil.)[61] He has approached it in his characteristically informative fashion, combining that sense of chaotic, tortured activity to be seen in contemporary paintings of damnation with a scheme based upon the categorical order Vergil gives to Aeneas's experience of the successive regions of the dead.

In the first and third of these diagrams, the illustrator has allowed his Bosch-like fantasy full play, filling out Vergil's suggestions and adding a few figures of his own. The threshold of Hades is remarkable for the beauty of its design, presenting an intermixture of fantastic creatures—Gorgons, Eumenides, Harpies, the Hydra, Chimera, and hundred-armed Briareus—in a great swirling writhing pattern of grotesque forms. The region of Tartarus is dominated by a rather exact rendition of a Vergilian construction, a great fortress surrounded by a triple wall and afire from the waters of Phlegeathon. In the Sibyl's account this fortress actually contains the torture ground of the damned, but Brant has placed their strained and scourged bodies in the courtyard, catalog fashion, before the reader's eyes.

FIGURE 20. Diagram of the Campi Lugentes, with Women Who Died for Love in the Foreground. Illustration for *Aeneid* 6. 443–44, in Sebastian Brant, ed., *Opera*, by Publius Vergilius Maro (Strasbourg: I. Grieninger, 1502), Rosenwald Collection, no. 594.

The region of untimely deaths is a place of a rather different order, less violent if also less picturesque (fig. 20). The rivers of the underworld flow through this territory dividing it into a series of islands, each with its own category of departed souls: infants who died in their cradles, persons condemned by false charges of crime with Minos, their judge, and after them, a region of guiltless suicides, who remain nameless in Vergil but for whom the illustrator has supplied the names of Cato, Mithradates, and Socrates. On the largest of the islands, completely filling the foreground, is the region to which Vergil gives the greatest attention, the Campi Lugentes, peopled by women who died for love. With only one stark tree supplied as a prop for the death of Phaedra, Brant's illustration has none of that sense of secretive shame implied by Vergil's description:

> secreti celant calles et myrtea circum
> silva tegit.[62]

Rather the heroines are crowded together in our full view, each one shown in some identifying gesture: Evadne casting herself into a pyre, Phaedra preparing her noose on the tree, Pasiphaë stroking the bull, Eryphyle imploring her son, and Procris prostrate with her spear wound. Dido, who kneels in the far right corner of the island, her breast conspicuously pierced by a sword, seems a very insignificant member of this group in spite of the fact that her moving last interview with Aeneas is the major incident in Vergil's account of the Campi Lugentes. So much of a catalog, in fact, is this piece, that the spirit of the commentator seems to have overridden all narrative concerns: Aeneas is not seen in progress through the region at all but stands with the Sibyl at its far borders.[63]

Ogilby's comparable illustrations represent an entirely different strain in Vergil's narrative, making the underworld journey an event full of mystery and melancholy romance. In place of factual diagrams, he concentrates on the emotional aspects of the journey, placing these within impressive, gloomy landscapes of mountains and trees. Thus on the threshold we see the lurking shadowy demons that guard the outer approaches: centaurs, Briareus, and the Hydra. But their forms are less grotesque than Brant's and the emphasis is upon the Sibyl's encouragement of Aeneas to gather his spirits and go forward. A moment later, in defensive terror, he will attempt to draw his sword, but his guide will dissuade him with words on the folly of expending his energy in vain battle against shadows and dreams.

This threshold scene is followed by a series of encounters with figures from Aeneas's past: the shades of Palinuris, his lost helmsman, of Dido, and finally of Deiphobus, Helen's last Trojan husband. The choice of these encounters takes on particular interest from a significant modern discussion of their interrelationships as the emotional high points of the underworld journey representing a series of events left unresolved in Aeneas's personal history, each of which still exercises a heavy pull upon his thoughts, but from which he must turn away as from all ties with the past.[64] These events, as the scholar Brooks Otis has argued, make the underworld journey a journey into Aeneas's own mind.

As a background for these emotionally charged scenes, Cleyn takes full advantage of Vergil's descriptive suggestions, especially in drawing thick groves of trees through which the shades of the dead seem visibly to flutter with an erratic unsteady motion. The women of the Campi Lugentes glide like sylvan nymphs through the myrtles (fig. 21). Dido scarcely seems to pause in passing Aeneas and receives his futile apologies with no more than a silent, reproachful glance. The figures in the ultima arva of dead heroes act out Vergil's narrative with particular precision. In the background the shades of Greek warriors are fleeing into the forest at the hero's approach, while the Trojans gather about him with wonder. In questioning the pathetic Deiphobus, Aeneas hears a final story of Trojan disgrace in the account of his humiliating mutilation by Odysseus and Menelaus, but the Sibyl hurries him onward as if to emphasize the moral imperative of his abandoning his vain nostalgia for persons and places of his past. In all of these eerie, yet fully realized scenes we are aware of Cleyn's particular ability to capture the bond between images of the natural world and the emotional qualities of the poem.

This contrast between an informative and a dramatic handling of scenes which are so much at the thematic and emotional core of the *Aeneid* leads me again to some of the larger contrasts between the two books. At the outset, I spoke of the two volumes as constituting self-coherent visual essays on the text of Vergil's poems, and I wish in conclusion to return to this point by considering the way in which continuity among the illustrations is fostered by their visual conceptualization of the hero. Once again Dryden's critical pronouncements speak for his period. "An heroic poem," he wrote at the commencement of his dedication, "is undoubtedly the greatest work the soul of man is capable to perform. The design of it is to form the mind to heroic virtue by example . . . all things must be grave, majestical and sublime."[65] Two particular aspects of the ancient epics were among the chief sources of their sublimity: the dignity of the hero and the dignity of the epic language. In his comparison of poetry and painting, Dryden again uses the language of the visual arts to define the preeminence of the hero in these works:

> The posture of a poetic figure is, as I conceive, the description of his heroes in the performance of such and such an action . . . as of Aeneas who has Turnus under him. Both the poet and the painter vary their posture according to the action or passion which they represent, but all must be great and graceful in them. The same Aeneas must be drawn a suppliant to Dido with respect in his gestures and humility in his eyes, but, when he is forced in his own defense to kill Lausus, the poet shows him compassionate and tempering the severity of his looks with a reluctance to the action which he is going to perform.[66]

Having chosen to translate the *Aeneid* as the crowning work of his poetic career, Dryden calls out all the resources of his moral and aesthetic criticism to argue for the worthiness of Aeneas with particular attention to his superiority as a hero of virtue or pietas over the vicious Agamemnon and Achilles.[67] Earlier, in his "Discourse Concerning Satire," he had raised the question of the appropriateness of heroic poetry to the contemporary world, asking in particular whether a poet who owed his

FIGURE 21. Franz Cleyn, Aeneas Addresses Dido's Shade in the Campi Lugentes. Illustration for *Aeneid* 6. 440–70, in *The Works of Virgil*, translated by John Dryden (London: J. Tonson, 1697), Rosenwald Collection, no. 1548.

moral allegiance to Christian concepts of virtue could ever recreate the glory of the pagan heroic ideal.[68] In his dedication, he finds the compromise to settle these doubts by defending Aeneas for virtues of compassion, responsibility, and gentleness that border upon Christian morality, yet are none of them incompatible with valor. Especially important in his arguments is Aeneas's role as a leader of his people, which makes him the prototype of the Roman Augustus, a figure blending history into myth.[69]

Such remarks help us to appreciate the visual role of Aeneas in these illustrations as a figure deliberately posed to capture the attention and admiration of the reader in the same manner as the hero of the text. In fact, the Aeneas of Brant's text is quite far from any classically grounded conception of the Roman hero. The illustrator has given him the white hair, beard, and dress of the sage elder. His poses and gestures display very little emotion and his face scarcely changes from scene to scene. His costume, however, does change from kingly dress in scenes of peace, hospitality, or diplomacy to knightly armor for battle. Brant's images are in no way incompatible with Vergil's text, for the poet never breaks the illusion of mythic antiquity by

FIGURE 22. Franz Cleyn, Aeneas and the Harpies. Illustration for *Aeneid* 3. 245–58, in *The Works of Virgil*, translated by John Dryden (London: J. Tonson, 1697), Rosenwald Collection, no. 1548.

specific description of Aeneas's clothing. Certainly he does not wear the toga. He has a cloak ready for hunting, a robe for sacrifice, and armor for battle, but the full details of his costume remain vague enough to place him somewhere between the Homeric world and Rome.

In the seventeenth-century version, however, Aeneas's costume is a major aspect of his identity and remains consistent throughout most scenes. He travels in armor, an armor that appears to be reconstructed from the artist's observation of classical statuary with a certain Renaissance contour to the massive, but elegant, plumed helmet that sets off his face. This costume especially, so alien to primitive forests or the Campi Lugentes, procures that sense of a meeting of two worlds in landscape scenes which I have described. Even more notable than the hero's costume is his face. Vergil, in fact, never describes the physiognomy of Aeneas, although he says much of his emotions, and it is in their supplying of these necessary particulars of facial structure that we find one significant difference between Ogilby's and Dryden's publications of the Cleyn illustrations.

In his 1654 appearance, Aeneas has the features and expressions of an homme gallant; his flowing Cavalier looks are complemented by the twisted Gallic moustache of the Restoration court. When we compare these pictures with their 1697 counterparts, we find that Aeneas's countenance has undergone great alteration. The nose is Roman and beaked; the muscles hard, the lip clean shaven, the mouth tightly set. The elegance of the courtly monarch has given way to the gravity of the national leader, and, indeed, the substitution of this new facial type, at once more Roman and more expressive, in a number of critical instances greatly alters the visual tone of the book. The changes are not wholly consistent; in several of the Dryden illustrations, the old face remains. It is, for instance, the courtly Aeneas who confronts a flock of charmingly grotesque Harpies in both books (fig. 22).

But in the meeting with Venus outside Carthage, the hero's serious face contrasts a ruler's concern with the frivolity of his mother. In greeting Andromache at Hector's false tomb, Aeneas wears a shaded countenance with deeply grooved lines compatible with the emotional weight of longing for lost Troy that he shares with his fellow survivors. At Cumae he addresses the mad Sybil with a look of surprise and awe. Even asleep on a bank of the Tiber after the outbreak of the Italian War, the hero still manifests his anxiety in the tightly drawn muscles that reflect Vergil's description of his disturbed thoughts. At the end of his journey to the site of Rome, he receives the armor of Venus with an eager glance and gleaming eye. In the last stages of the Italian War, the expression of the wounded warrior held back from the battle is downcast. Especially, however, in the hero's underworld meeting with Dido, there is a notable change from the careless cavalier of 1654, who seems ready to pursue his flirtation even under such unfavorably altered conditions (fig. 23), to the man of emotion and concern (fig. 21). Although we lack certain information, it might

FIGURE 23. Franz Cleyn, Aeneas Addresses Dido's Shade in the Campi Lugentes. In John Ogilby, ed., *Publii Virgilii Maronis Opera* (London: T. Roycroft, 1658). Bloomington, Indiana, Indiana University, Lilly Library. Courtesy of the Lilly Library.

seem that Dryden had some responsibility for the ennobling of the face of his hero, an alteration wholly consistent with his theoretical ideals of epic. Thus, indeed, illustration would seem to assume the role of interpretation. The image of the hero not only recreates an understanding of the past but also places the illustrated volume on the verge of contemporary judgments of the *Aeneid.*

## NOTES

*I wish to thank Mr. John Y. Cole, executive director of the Center for the Book, for the arrangements and hospitality of the symposium and Mr. William Matheson, chief of the Rare Book and Special Collections Division, for his assistance in providing photocopies, slides, and other bibliographical assistance. I am also grateful to Professor Annabel Patterson of the University of Maryland for her conversational and bibliographical suggestions for further investigation of the work of John Ogilby.*

1. "Dedication of the *Aeneis,*" in John Dryden, *Essays of John Dryden*, ed. William P. Ker, 2 vols. (New York, 1961), 2:228.
2. "Preface to *Sylvae*: or The Second Part of Poetical Miscellanies," in Dryden, *Essays*, 1:252.
3. "A Parallel of Poetry and Painting," in Dryden, *Essays*, 2:139.
4. Ibid., p. 117.
5. Ibid., p. 139.
6. Sebastian Brant, ed., *Opera,* by Publius Vergilius Maro (Strasbourg: I. Grieninger, 1502), Rosenwald Collection, no. 594; and John Dryden, trans., *The Works of Virgil: Containing His Pastorals, Georgics, and Æneis* (London: J. Tonson, 1697), Rosenwald Collection, no. 1548.
7. Arthur M. Hind, *An Introduction to a History of Woodcut: With a Detailed Survey of Work Done in the Fifteenth Century*, 2 vols. (London: Constable and Co., 1935), vol. 2, *Book Illustration and Contemporary Single Cuts*, p. 342, remarks that "Brant did not escape abuse from his contemporaries for the anti-classical fantasy of his illustrators' works."
8. Brant, *Opera*:

   Perlege virgilios quotquot bone lector in orbe
   Comperies toto: me quoque confer eis
   Spero equidem dices me longo alios superare:
   Videris atque ante hac nec mihi ubique parem.

9. Gilbert R. Redgrave, "The Illustrated Books of Sebastian Brant," *Bibliographica* 2 (1896): 47–61.
10. Harvard University Library, Dept. of Printing and Graphic Art, *Catalogue of Books and Manuscripts*, compiled by Ruth Mortimer (Cambridge: Belknap Press of Harvard University Press, 1964–), part 2, *Italian 16th Century Books* (1971), pp. 727–28.
11. John Dryden, *The Poetical Works of Dryden*, ed. George R. Noyes (Cambridge, Mass., 1909), pp. 418–19.
12. John Ogilby, trans., *The Works of Publius Virgilius Maro* (London: A. Crook, 1650).
13. John Ogilby, ed., *The Works of Publius Virgilius Maro*, translated, adorned with Sculptures and illustrated with annotations (London: Thomas Warren, 1654).

    Indeed the chief artist, Francis Cleyn (or Clein), was a man of no small prestige, having executed commissions for James I and Charles I and decorated houses for members of the British nobility before he became the illustrator of Ogilby's translations (*Dictionary of National Biography*, 1st ser., s.v. "Cleyn, Francis").
14. *Publii Virgilii Maronis Opera per Johannem Ogilvium edita* (London: T. Roycroft, 1658).
15. "Preface to *Sylvae,*" in Dryden, *Essays*, 1:253.

16. L. Proudfoot, *Dryden's Aeneid and Its Seventeenth Century Predecessors* (Manchester, Eng.: Manchester University Press, 1960), pp. 126–37.

17. Wohlgemuth in the 1491 Koberg edition of *Schatzbehalter oder Schrein der Wahren Reichthumer des Heils und ewiger Seeligkeit.* See Richard Muther, *German Book Illustration of the Gothic Period and Early Renaissance (1460–1530)*, trans. Ralph R. Shaw (Metuchen, N.J.: Scarecrow Press, 1972), p. 58 and pls. 118–19.

18. Muther, *German Book Illustration*, pp. 72–74 and p. 438, pl. 135.

19. Ellen Callman, *Apollonio di Giovanni* (Oxford: Clarendon Press, 1974), pp. 39–51.

20. Peter H. von Blanckenhagen, "Narration in Greek and Roman Art," *American Journal of Archaeology* 61 (1957):78 ff.

21. The Roman artistic tradition is discussed in Peter H. von Blanckenhagen and Christine Alexander, *The Paintings from Boscotrecase*, Mitteilungen des Deutschen Archaeologischen Instituts, Roemische, Abteilung, supp. 6 (Heidelberg: F. H. Kerle, 1962), pp. 54–57.

22. J. de Wit, *Die Miniaturen des Virgilius Vaticanus* (Amsterdam, 1959), pl. 6, fig. 10; pl. 8, fig. 14; pl. 12, fig. 19; pl. 13, fig. 21; pl. 16, fig. 28; pl. 19, fig. 33; pl. 21, fig. 36; pl. 22, fig. 39; pl. 26, fig. 47.

23. *L'Eneïde de Virgile* (1560) is Rosenwald Collection, no. 1068. Reuben A. Brower, "Visual and Verbal Translation of Myth: Neptune in Vergil, Rubens, Dryden," *Daedalus* 101 (1972):155–82, discusses from the point of view of a literary critic the interrelationship of Rubens's heroic historicism and Dryden's visualization of Vergilian scenes, and suggests, pp. 172–73, an influence of Cleyn's Rubensian baroque style upon Dryden's conceptualization of figures from Greco-Roman mythology.

24. The development of continental theories of pastoral and pastoral poems in the late sixteenth and early seventeenth centuries is discussed by James Edmund Congleton, *Theories of Pastoral Poetry in England, 1684–1798* (Gainesville: University of Florida Press, 1952), pp. 13–36.

25. Brant, *Opera, Eclogue* 2. 83–84.

26. Ibid., lines 91–94.

27. Servius, *Servii Grammatici qui feruntur in Vergilii Bucolica et Georgica Commentarii*, ed. Georg Christian Thilo (Leipzig, 1887; reprint ed., Hildesheim, 1961), p. 27, ad vs. 58.

28. Servius, p. 18, ad vs. 4.

29. Remarks in Servius, *Commentarii*, p. 2 and p. 4, ad vs. 1, provided the basis of the longstanding tradition of identifying Tityrus with Vergil.

30. E. H. Gombrich, *Art and Illusion: A Study in the Psychology of Pictorial Representation* (Princeton, N.J.: Princeton University Press, 1960), pp. 68–71, mentions the stereotyped drawings of a Teutonic medieval walled city variously labeled Damascus, Ferrara, Milano, and Mantua in Hartmann Schedel's *Nuremberg Chronicle*, a representation which, as Walter J. Ong, S.J., *The Presence of the Word: Some Prolegomena for Cultural and Religious History* (New York: Clarion Books, 1970), p. 53, puts it "was not of a visually apprehended reality but of an orally processed one . . . a kind of a visual commonplace on 'the city' or 'citiness.'" The cities in Brant's illustrations are of exactly this abstractly symbolic kind.

31. *Eclogue* 1. 56–59.

32. *Eclogue* 1. 68–70.

33. *Eclogue* 1. 14–15.

34. *Eclogue* 1. 4.

35. Knightly Chetwood, "Preface to the *Pastorals* with a short defense of Vergil against some of the Reflections of Monsieur Fontanelle," in Dryden, *Works of Virgil*, no pagination.

36. *P. Virgilii Maronis Opera, nunc recens accuratissime castigata cum XI acerrimi iudicii virorum commentariis* (Venice: Giunta, 1544), facing p. 24:

Quarta Sibyllini repetens oracula cantus
Atque: Genethliacon modulans collaudat Iesum.

37. Ogilby, *Works of Publius Virgilius Maro*, p. 19.

38. *Eclogue* 4. 34–36.

39. *Eclogue* 4. 18–30.

40. "Excerptum e vita Donatiana," in *Vergil Landleben: Bucolica, Georgica, Catalepton*, ed. Johannes and Maria Götte (Wartzburg: Heimeran Verlag, 1970); *Vergil-Viten*, ed. Karl Bayer (Wartzburg: Heimeran Verlag, 1970), p. 322, 65; "Vita Philargyii I," in *Vergil-Viten*, p. 312.

41. "Vita Donatiana," p. 322, 68.

42. The "Argument" in Ogilby, *Works of Publius Virgilius Maro*, p. 25, is a slightly ambiguous quatrain on the death of princes; the identification of Daphnis and Caesar is mentioned in the notes.

43. *Eclogue* 7. 16.

44. A survey of such discussion, along with new proposals, appears in the most recent study, John Van Sickle, *The Design of Virgil's Bucolics* (Rome: Edizioni dell'Ateneo & Bizzarri, 1978), pp. 15–38.

45. Eleanor Winsor Leach, *Vergil's Eclogues: Landscapes of Experience* (Ithaca, N.Y.: Cornell University Press, 1974), pp. 158–70.

46. The pioneering, and still influential study is Viktor Pöschl, *The Art of Vergil: Image and Symbol in the Aeneid*, trans. G. Seligson (Ann Arbor: University of Michigan Press, 1962).

47. *Aeneid* 1. 12–33.

48. *Aeneid* 1. 51.

49. *Aeneid* 1. 314–417.

50. *Aeneid* 1. 297–304.

51. *Aeneid* 1. 393–401.

52. *Aeneid* 1. 417–40.

53. *Aeneid* 7. 475–539.

54. *Aeneid* 7. 496.

55. Michael C. J. Putnam, *The Poetry of the Aeneid: Four Studies in Imaginative Unity and Design* (Cambridge: Harvard University Press, 1965), pp. 129–36.

56. *Aeneid* 8. 364–65.

57. *Aeneid* 8. 121–25.

58. *Aeneid* 8. 356.

59. Theodore M. Andersson, *Early Epic Scenery: Homer, Virgil, and the Medieval Legacy* (Ithaca, N.Y.: Cornell University Press, 1976), pp. 54–55, comments on the geographical stage of the poem.

60. *Aeneid* 3. 282–83.

61. William Waetzoldt, *Dürer and His Times*, trans. R. H. Boothroyd (London: Phaidon Press, [1950]), pp. 29–47.

62. *Aeneid* 6. 443–44.

63. The details of these women's deaths are not, in fact, given in the *Aeneid*, but Servius, ad *Aeneid* 6. 445 ff., tells each story at length and Brant illustrates, as it were, the commentator instead of the poem.

64. Brooks Otis, *Vergil: A Study in Civilized Poetry* (Oxford: Clarendon Press, 1964), pp. 291–97.

65. "Dedication of the *Aeneis*," in Dryden, *Essays*, 2:154.

66. Note "A Parallel of Poetry and Painting," ibid., p. 140.

67. "Dedication of the *Aeneis*," ibid., p. 179.

68. "A Discourse Concerning the Original and Progress of Satire," ibid., pp. 30–31.

69. "Dedication of the *Aeneis*," ibid., pp. 179–80.

RUTH MORTIMER

# VERGIL IN THE ROSENWALD COLLECTION

In Venice in 1501, Aldus Manutius chose Vergil as the classical author to introduce his new printing type, subsequently called italic letter. The same choice was made by John Baskerville in England in 1757 in his effort to make the printed book a work of art. This essay is concerned with the relationship of Vergil to the printed book, as demonstrated in the illustrated editions of all three works—the *Aeneid*, the *Eclogues*, and the *Georgics*—collected by Lessing J. Rosenwald. These editions number only seventeen catalog entries of the more than twenty-six hundred listed in *The Lessing J. Rosenwald Collection*,[1] but closely examined and compared among themselves they can be seen to represent major developments in the philosophy and techniques of book illustration through five centuries.

With Vergil, we have a good chance to study the balance of text and picture in the illustrated book and the development of sequential illustration as an art form. In general, I will use for this study John Dryden's translation of 1697, published in London under the imprint of Jacob Tonson, for the English quotations; the Dryden version is a midpoint in the illustrated editions and a high point in English literary style.[2] I want to open, however, with a passage from a twentieth-century translation, that of Allen Mandelbaum. From Book Two of the *Aeneid*:

> At this, indeed, I saw all Ilium
> sink down into the fires; Neptune's Troy
> is overturned: even as when the woodsmen
> along a mountaintop are rivals in
> their striving to bring down an ancient ash,

hacked at with many blows of iron and ax;
it always threatens falling, nodding with
its trembling leaves and tossing crest until,
slowly, slowly, the wounds have won; it gives
one last great groan, then wrenches from the ridges
and crashes into ruin . . .[3]

What this passage tells us, among other things, is that Vergil's own visual sense is so powerful and complex that his works present certain clear challenges for an illustrator.

The earliest edition of Vergil in the Rosenwald Collection (the only copy in an American library) is a French prose paraphrase of the *Aeneid*, dated September 30, 1483, printed at Lyons by Guillaume Le Roy.[4] This book moves Vergil's story into the popular tradition of the French romance, as the *Roman de Troie* or the *Roman d'Enéas*, and adds an explicit instructional element. The long explanatory title offers the text as a translation and suggests that the fall of Troy be seen as a lesson in the art of defense. Ulrich Gering, one of the first printers in Paris, completed the printing of a Latin Vergil in 1478. This French version, destined for a different kind of reader, was the work of the first printer established at Lyons.

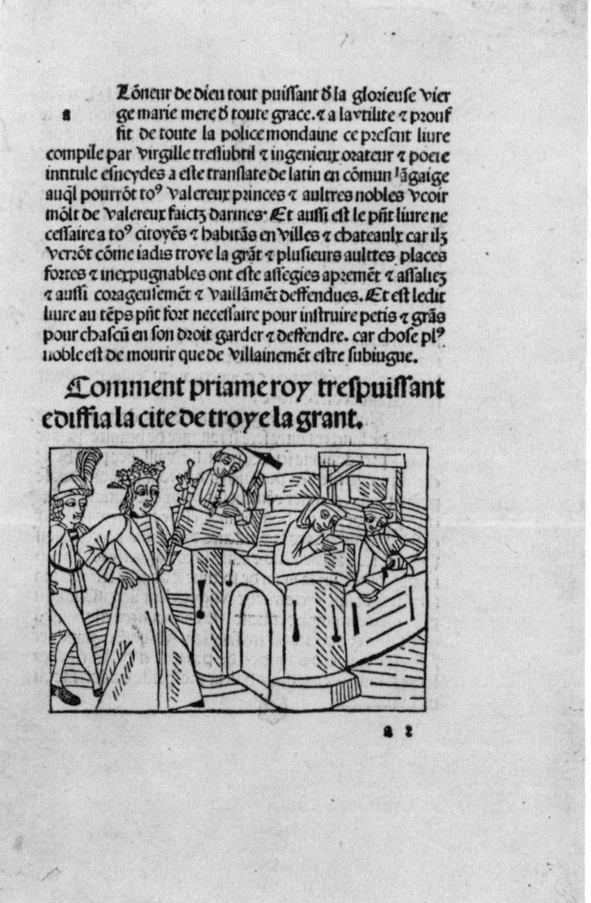
Lõneur de dieu tout puissant đ la glorieuse vier
a ge marie mere đ toute grace. ⁊ a la vtilite ⁊ prouf
fit de toute la police mondaine ce present liure
compile par virgille tressubtil ⁊ ingenieux orateur ⁊ poete
intitule eneydes a este translate de latin en cõmun lãgaige
auql pourrõt toꝰ valereux princes ⁊ aultres nobles veoir
mõlt de valereux faictz darmes. Et aussi est le pñt liure ne
cessaire a toꝰ citoyẽs ⁊ habitãs en villes ⁊ chateaulx car ilz
verrõt cõme iadis troye la grãt ⁊ plusieurs aultres places
fortes ⁊ inexpugnables ont este assegies apremẽt ⁊ assaliez
⁊ aussi corageusemẽt ⁊ vaillãmẽt deffendues. Et est ledit
liure au tẽps pñt fort necessaire pour instruire petis ⁊ grãs
pour chascũ en son droit garder ⁊ deffendre. car chose plꝰ
noble est de mourir que de villainemẽt estre subiugue.

**Comment priame roy trespuissant ediffia la cite de troye la grant.**

a 2

FIGURE 1.
Priam Supervising the Building of Troy.
Publius Vergilius Maro, *Aeneis*
(Lyons: Guillaume Le Roy, 30 September 1483),
Rosenwald Collection, no. 381.

Guillaume Le Roy worked in association with Barthélemy Buyer for almost a decade before he began printing on his own.[5] His *Aeneid* is the earliest dated book under his name alone, and it is set in a new type font to mark his new status. In the book, there are sixty-one large woodcuts, of which three are repetitions. The illustrations begin with Priam supervising the building of Troy (fig. 1). The style of the woodcuts is generally open and naïve, with parallel-line shading and some solid black details. Through these woodblocks the story is simplified and made even more immediate. To good effect, the block cutters introduced a certain amount of pattern, such as waves curling under ships or floors of triangular tile. The blocks are not technically accomplished, but they do dominate the page. Following Priam's Troy, another architectural subject is Dido building Carthage. The anonymous artists have put considerable emphasis on the plight of Dido, which is specific to the *Aeneid*, rather than on battle scenes, which could be applied to other texts.

> Arma viru[m]que cano: troi[a]e qui prim[us] ab oris
> Italiam fato profugus: lauinaq[ue] venit
> Littora: multum ille et terris iactatus et alto
> Vi superum: s[a]eu[a]e memore[m] iunonis ob iram.[6]

> Arms, and the Man I sing, who, forc'd by Fate,
> And haughty *Juno*'s unrelenting Hate;
> Expell'd and exil'd, left the *Trojan* Shoar:[7]

The most influential sixteenth-century illustrated edition of Vergil comes at the very beginning of the century, in 1502.[8] It is a scholarly folio edition of the complete works, printed at Strasbourg, with a lively program of woodcuts, a visual commentary concurrent with the five printed commentaries of Servius Maurus Honoratus, Tiberius Claudius Donatus, Cristoforo Landino, Antonio Mancinelli, and Domicius Calderinus, and the continuation by Mapheus Vegius.[9] The printer, Johann Grüninger, produced in the fifteenth century a key edition of Terence,[10] and the animation of his Terence informs the Vergil as well. The text was edited by Sebastian Brant. The page layout places a passage of Vergil's text in roman letter in the center, surrounding it by commentary in two columns of small roman. The title page has a full-page woodcut of Vergil with members of his circle, and with the muse Calliope directly behind and above his head. The text woodcuts, again by anonymous artists, are in five sizes: double page, full page, three-quarter page, half page, and one-third page. To demonstrate some of the characteristics of these blocks and form a basis for comparison with later editions, I have chosen Book Two of the *Aeneid* and the episode of the Trojan Horse.

> Instar montis equum diuina palladis arte
> Aedificant: sectaq[ue] intexunt abiete costas.[11]

> And by *Minerva*'s Aid a Fabrick rear'd,
> Which like a Steed of monstrous height appear'd;
> The Sides were planck'd with Pine, . . .[12]

The horse and its construction are described by Vergil. The illustrator is presented with the problem of the size of the horse in relation to the size of the men inside it and to the size of the walls of Troy. In the hands of some illustrators, the horse is realistic, suggesting bronze, marble, or even flesh rather than wood. R. G. Austin's commentary for Book Two reviews the speculation on the appearance of the horse, including the application of gemstones and movable parts.[13] Some suggestions bring to mind a structure such as those illustrated in Roberto Valturio's *De re militari* (a text represented in the Rosenwald Collection by two fifteenth-century manuscripts, as well as by a hand-colored copy of the 1472 Verona edition),[14] but the sixteenth-century illustrators in general saw the horse as votive sculpture, as the Trojans wished to see it, rather than as machinery of war. The 1502 edition has a sequence of five blocks at this stage of the narrative. The fantasy element is evident in the relative size of the men climbing into the horse in the first block (fig. 2). In three successive blocks, the horse almost appears traced, since the outline and position on the block are identical, and the scene shifts around it. This is a small economy of production in a book where there are no repeated illustrations, and it is a small sophistication of design in keeping the horse immobile in the Trojan turmoil.

The key feature of the 1502 illustrations is, as noted, animation, and the word is applicable almost in the modern sense of cartoon animation, achieving movement from still pictures. They follow the text so closely that Laocoön, for instance, moves from the righthand scene to the left, changing places with the Priam-Sinon group, while the Laocoön serpents move from left to right. The buildings in the background are agitated by changing angles. The blocks are *readable* in the light of the text. The exuberance of the Strasbourg artists is given full rein in the one double-page block, which depicts Dido's decorated temple in Book One. The treatment is sympathetic to the scene as Vergil's demonstration of the powers of pictorial representation.

Repetition of woodblocks was a common sixteenth-century practice. Equally common was the dissemination of a series of successful illustrations through a number of editions by copying or by transference of the blocks themselves. The two Venetian sixteenth-century editions of Vergil in the Rosenwald Collection are examples of this approach to book illustration. The 1544 Giunta edition[15] has eleven text commentators, but its illustrations are the blocks from the 1519 Giunta edition, which are reduced copies of the Strasbourg subjects. The blocks for the 1520 Giorgio Rusconi Venice edition originated with Bernardino Stagnino in 1507 and were transferred from one printer to another.[16] Whereas the Strasbourg edition began with a cut centering on Vergil and his muse, the Rusconi edition emphasizes patronage with a block showing Vergil kneeling to present the *Aeneid* to Augustus, with Maecenas and the *Georgics* and Caius Asinius Pollio and the *Eclogues* at either side.

The 1560 Lyons Vergil, after the Rosenwald Collection Strasbourg and Venice *Opera* folios, is a single text, the *Aeneid*, and in translation, the French of the poet Louis des Masures.[17] This is the first edition of the complete des Masures text, by the finest of sixteenth-century Lyons printers, Jean de Tournes. The translation was published in parts, the first two books by Chrestien Wechel in Paris in 1547, the first four books (with four woodcuts) by de Tournes at Lyons in 1552, and Books Five through Eight (unillustrated) by de Tournes in 1557.[18] Compared with the 1483 Le Roy volume from Lyons, the language of the text is here highly refined and the lines of the illustrations are extraordinarily complicated. The French text is in italic letter and the Latin text is printed as small italic marginalia.

The illustrations are woodcuts, one to a book. The scenes are attributed to the Lyons artist Bernard Salomon, who never signed his work for de Tournes but is believed to have been closely associated with the printer in the production of a number of sensitively illustrated books. Elsewhere in the volume, the woodcuts show open landscapes with multiple scenes, but the Trojan Horse scene for Book

Eneidos

Que ſecũdo eneidos libro cõtineãt. ouidi⁹.
¶Cõticuere omnes: tũc ſic fortiſſimus heros
Fata recenſebat troie, caſuſq; ſuorum:
Fallaces graios: ſimulataq; dona mineruę
Lacontis pœnã, et laxantem clauſtra ſinonẽ
Somnũ quo monit⁹ acceperat hectoris atrũ:
Iam flãmas cœli: troum patrięq; ruinas.
Et regis priami fatum miſerabile ſemper:
Impoſituq; patrẽ collo: dextraq; prehenſũ
Aſcanium: fruſtra tergum comitante creuſa.
Ereptã hanc fato, ſocioſq; in monte repertos.


FIGURE 2. Men Climbing into the Trojan Horse. Publius Vergilius Maro, *Opera*, ed. Sebastian Brant (Strasbourg: I. Grieninger [i.e., Grüninger], 1502), Rosenwald Collection, no. 594.

67

# LE SECOND LIVRE DE L'ENEÏDE DE VIRGILE.

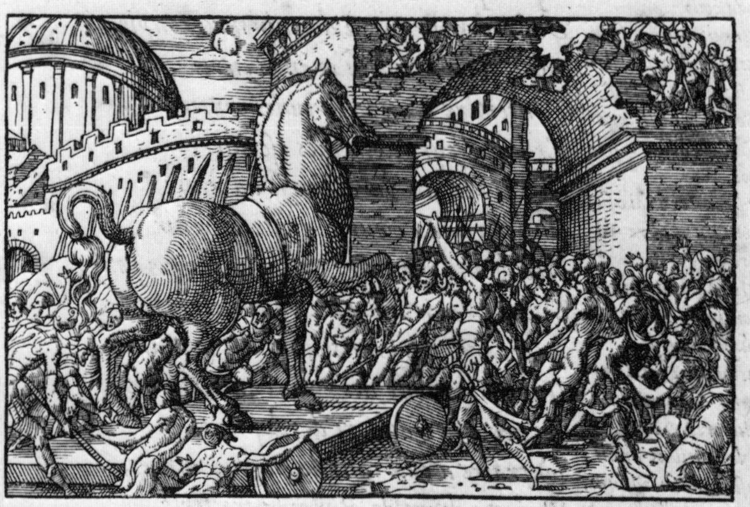

*Hacun ſe teut, & pour ouir ces choſes*
*Tous ententifs tenoient leurs bouches cloſes.*
*Le pere Enee à l'heure s'avança*
*Sur le hault lict, & ainſi commença:*
*Tu me contrains, Royne de grand' valeur,*
*Renouveller une eſtrange douleur,*
*Qui veux ouir, comme en ruïne & proye*
*Les Grecs ont mis les richeſſes de Troye,*
*Et ſaccagé le regne lamentable,*
*Ce que j'ay vû (miſere ineſtimable)*

*Conticuere omnes; intentiq; ora tenebant.*

*Inde toro pater Æneas ſic orſus ab alto:*

*Infandũ regina iubes renouare dolorẽ,*
*Troianas vt opes, & lamentabile regnum*
*Eruerint Danai, quæ que ipſe miſerrima vidi*

e 2 *Et*

FIGURE 3. Bernard Salomon (attributed to), Trojan Horse. *L'Eneïde de Virgile* (Lyons: I. de Tovrnes, 1560), Rosenwald Collection, no. 1068.

Two is crowded in the foreground with the energies of all figures concentrated on the struggle at the gates and on the walls (fig. 3). The rest of the block is architectural detail, the Troy Priam was building in a simpler fashion in Le Roy's first woodcut. The horse is led in the gates with raised foreleg as though prancing through.

> Et si fata deum: si mens non leua fuisset.
> Impulerat ferro argolicas foedare latebras.
> Troiaq[ue] nu[n]c stares priamiq[ue] arx alta maneres.[19]

> And had not Heav'n the fall of *Troy* design'd,
> Or had not Men been fated to be blind,
> Enough was said and done, t'inspire a better Mind:
> Then had our Lances pierc'd the treach'rous Wood,
> And *Ilian* Tow'rs, and *Priam's* Empire stood.[20]

The passage quoted is a response to the warning of Laocoön, which presented the first clear opportunity to reject the horse. The story of the Trojan Horse is told by Aeneas after the fact. The outcome was well known to Dido and her court and to the sixteenth-century reader likely to own this book, but the cumulative tensions and conflicting emotions before the deadly release of the soldiers from within the horse are still dramatic. Grüninger's 1502 illustrator worked along with Aeneas, picking up every suggestion of visual significance for the hidden menace in the horse. Salomon had to tell the whole story at once and chose the moment of no return, of practical action turned festive, although the observer knows it to be the Trojans' fatal error. Salomon's selection of 12 Vergil blocks coincides with his design of 178 blocks for the 1557 Ovid, *La metamorphose d'Ovide figuree*,[21] in which Ovid is turned into an emblem book with summary verse legends.

The Lyons woodcuts commissioned by Jean de Tournes mark the height of technical achievement in the sixteenth-century woodcut. The amount of detail compressed into the relatively small area of the block, filling part of a quarto or octavo page, encouraged a new audience to make demands that finally could be satisfied only in the medium of copper engraving. By the end of the sixteenth century, the copperplate was employed for any book illustration with claims to originality. The 1648 Paris edition of the *Aeneid*, Books One through Six, in the Rosenwald Collection is a French translation by Pierre Perrin printed by the widow of Pierre Moreau.[22] It is typical in having an added engraved title page and including a series of engravings within the text. The problem with the baroque book is that the illustrations and the text, in intaglio and relief, had to be printed on different presses and at different times. Thus the illustrations became materially and conceptually separated from the text.

The use of the copperplate was largely responsible for the development of summary illustration for a narrative, a group of scenes on one plate as preface to a single book of the text, similar to the summary arguments frequently provided for classical texts and epic poems. This grouping is by no means unique to the copperplate, but it is suited to it. More figures tended to be crowded onto the plate, and there were regular intervals at which the illustrations could be interleaved with the text. On engraved title pages, the text of the title was engraved as well and was essentially calligraphic. Pierre Moreau was a writing master who in 1640 designed four new types to simulate the effect of a handwritten page. His widow used his calligraphic types for this *Aeneid*.[23] The Latin and French appear on facing pages and the notes are in a side column that occasionally extends under the text.

The engravings, signed in part by Abraham Bosse, cover two-thirds of the page, with the prose argument beginning below and continuing on the facing page. The copperplates have picture-frame borders and ribbon labels with titles for the dominant scene from the book. The engraved ribbon titles are in letters similar to those of the script type of the text. In the beginning of Book Two, the engraving of the sack of Troy has Aeneas, Anchises, Ascanius, and Creusa in the foreground. The Trojan Horse dominates the left side and, although quite realistic, is completely capable of carrying an army of men of the size of the figures on the ground below. Bosse is the first of the artists we have seen to take a long view of the siege commensurate with the length of Vergil's description, and the prospect gives him the opportunity to draw building after building engulfed in flames and to send ordered troops marching through the streets. His illustration for Book Six is memorable for its ranging of the ghostly shades in the underworld in groups reminiscent of battle formations.

The artists of the *Aeneid* must find a way to handle the continual presence and intervention of the gods in the narrative. The *Bucolica, Georgica, et Aeneis* volume printed by Pierre Didot at Paris in 1798 in the Rosenwald Collection is illustrated with twenty-three plates by various engravers after designs ascribed to A. L. Girodet and François Gérard. The Rosenwald Collection copy[24] is accompanied by a portfolio of forty-five proofs before letter of twenty-two of the plates and two original pen-and-ink and wash drawings by Girodet. The drawings are for Book Three and Book Nine. Both of these drawings represent moments in the story when the gods appear. The Book Three drawing shows Aeneas's vision of his household gods, as they instruct him to leave Crete. The drawing for Book Nine depicts the triumph of Ascanius in his first participation in battle (fig. 4). Book Nine, beginning and ending with Iris sent to assist Turnus, results in a council of the gods in Book Ten. In the drawing, Ascanius stands in the light of Apollo and the other battle figures are darkened. A few lines later in the text, Apollo assumes the human form of Butes, squire to Anchises, for the protection of Ascanius.

The 1798 Paris edition, for which the Rosenwald Collection copy and accompanying portfolio make it possible to retrace the steps in illustration from drawing to proof to finished plate, could be juxtaposed with another Vergil *Opera* of the same decade in the collection, the 1793 Parma edition printed by Giovanni Battista Bodoni.[25] Both are monumental folios; the Paris is fifty centimeters in height, the

FIGURE 4. A. L. Girodet, Triumph of Ascanius. Drawing for the *Aeneid*, Book Nine. Publius Vergilius Maro, *Bucolica, Georgica, et Aeneis* (Paris: Petrus Didot, 1798), Rosenwald Collection, no. 1715.

FIGURE 5.
Florian, after Adolphe Giraldon, Layout for Opening of Fifth *Eclogue*. *Les Eclogues de Virgile* (Paris: Plon-Nourrit, [1906]), Rosenwald Collection, no. 2132.

Parma forty-four. Both are limited editions, the Paris of 250 copies, the Parma 200. But Bodoni's edition has no illustration, and the effect of a luxury Vergil is produced entirely by type: solid capitals for titles, lines leaded extensively, wide margins, and the occasional use of a simple spiral rule.

> Dicite qua[n]doq[ui]de[m] i[n] molli co[n]sedimus herba:
> Et nunc om[n]is ager: nu[n]c om[n]is parturit arbos:
> Nu[n]c fronde[n]t sylu[a]e: nu[n]c formosissim[us] annus:[26]

> Sing then; the Shade affords a proper place;
> The Trees are cloath'd with Leaves, the Fields with Grass;
> The Blossoms blow, the Birds on bushes sing;
> And Nature has accomplish'd all the Spring.[27]

The single nineteenth-century Vergil in the Rosenwald Collection is a Firmin Didot translation of the *Eclogues* with passages of Theocritus, printed by Didot in Paris in 1806.[28] This is a printing curiosity, its only illustration not an illustration of Vergil but an imitation of the olive tree device of the sixteenth-century Estienne family of printers with the motto changed from a quotation from St. Paul to one from Horace. It is an engraving printed by at-press adjustments at the same time as the text, to prove that it could be done. Apparently it could, but to no great advantage to the printer, and the medium for illustrating the next Rosenwald Collection *Eclogues* a full century later was wood engraving.

Twentieth-century illustrators turned from the *Aeneid* to the *Eclogues* and the *Georgics*, interested less in national origins, epic, and the daily life of the gods than in an escape into a supposedly idyllic country life. Taking the *Eclogues* first, because it was Vergil's first work, we find substantial material in the Rosenwald Collection for comparisons between twentieth-century views of the text.

For the 1906 Paris edition illustrated by Florian after Adolphe Giraldon, the Rosenwald Collection has a full working layout (fig. 5).[29] The Rosenwald Collection copy of the book itself is number 7 of 20 copies on Arches with a separate suite of all the wood engravings on japon. (The full edition was 336 copies.) The type was designed by Giraldon as well as the illustrations. The prospectus describes the illustrations as consciously comprising three elements, views of the countryside ("éternel décor"), details of plants and objects of country life, and representations of the gods of Rome. The Rosenwald Collection layout volume contains pencil drawings, pen-and-ink sketches, watercolor drawings, color samples, proofs of the wood engravings with color separations, and correspondence between the wood engraver and the artist. The primary emphasis is on landscape. In the layout, the landscape beginning each *Eclogue* is a full-color painting, whereas the border connecting it to the text page is still often in the sketching stage. The plants and animals, the objects of country life, are secondary and are introduced into the sequence of text borders, and the gods of Rome are set apart formally as portrait medallions.

Two of the twentieth-century illustrators of the *Eclogues* in the Rosenwald Collection chose to work with woodblocks, and their return to wood for printing illustration seems peculiarly appropriate to the celebration of wood in Vergil's text. Michael C. J. Putnam, describing in his book on the *Eclogues* the prizes for the singers' competition in the third *Eclogue*, notes that the prize cups carved with plants and figures are of beechwood, the wood usually used for practical objects.[30] The ornamentation is variously symbolic of the poet's craft, and hence the specific object works on several levels to complicate our perception of the shepherd-singers. This is not really a celebration of the simple life but of a life responsive to art. This question of putting wood to the service of art is also part of Putnam's gloss on the second *Eclogue*: the shepherd teaches the trees to memorize his refrain.[31]

The private press movement drew upon the study of manuscript illumination and illustrated incunabula. The 1906 *Eclogues*, with its color and its page borders, echoes the illuminated manuscript. The medium for the 1906 edition was wood engraving, with the shading provided by the width of the line cut into the woodblock. The blocks were not cut by Giraldon himself but after his designs. Aristide Maillol as sculptor cut his own blocks, and his most characteristic illustrations are woodcuts in fifteenth-century style, the image in black line of equal value with the type. The Maillol *Eclogues* is a true livre d'artiste, where an artist known for his work as painter or sculptor turns to book illustration; the illustration medium is original, not reproductive; and the edition is necessarily limited, divided by the use of special papers or the addition of extra prints or a suite of proofs to some copies.[32]

The illustration of Vergil occupied Maillol for more than thirty years. Maillol editions of the *Eclogues* in the Rosenwald Collection are *Eclogae*, the Latin and German text, and *Les Églogues de Virgile*, the Latin and French text, both printed in 1926. Maillol's *Suite des bois originaux pour illustrer les Géorgiques de Virgile*, a suite for the edition of the *Georgics* Philippe Gonin published in Paris in 1950, is also in the collection.[33] The project originated with Count Harry Kessler at his Cranach

FIGURE 6. Aristide Maillol, Drawing for Vergil's *Eclogues*. *Les Eglogues de Virgile* (Weimar: Cranach Presse, 1926), Rosenwald Collection, no. 2089.

Presse in Weimar. Maillol was involved at every stage, even to the making of the paper on which the editions were printed. It is well to look at both the *Eclogues* and the *Georgics* to understand fully Maillol's interpretation of Vergil. The Rosenwald Collection copy of the French *Eclogues* has a set of original sketches that offer a special insight into Maillol's method of working with the text.

Throughout the two works, the woodcuts vary in Maillol's use of the black line. Some blocks are shaded, some have no shading at all, and a few have larger surface areas printed solid black. Although the livre d'artiste is by its nature experimental, the artist usually experimented with mixed media within a book, not with differing styles in one medium. The *Georgics* printer, Philippe Gonin, publishing the work after Maillol's death, quotes at the end of Book Four Maillol's description of working on the blocks and his desire for simplicity without caricature.[34] Maillol, as a sculptor, celebrates the *Eclogues* in terms of the human figure in the landscape, visualizing the speakers of the Vergilian dialogue. The soft line of the sketches is solidified in the woodcuts (cf. figs. 6 and 7). One drawing in the set is fully shaded and finished in terms of the corresponding woodblock. Three other drawings approximate a finished block in the volume. The others, particularly those depicting

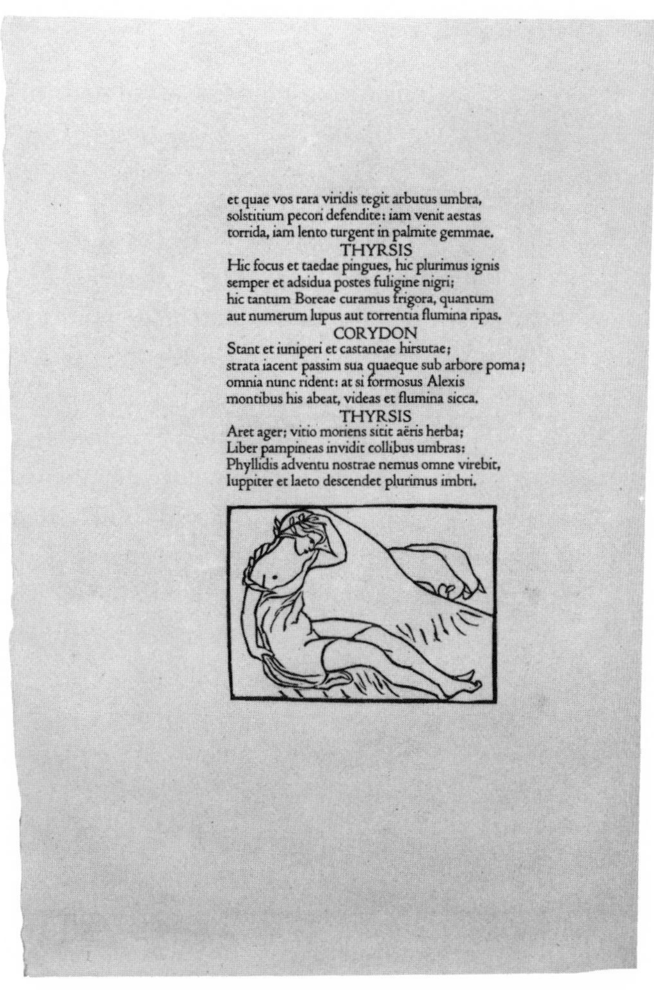

et quae vos rara viridis tegit arbutus umbra,
solstitium pecori defendite: iam venit aestas
torrida, iam lento turgent in palmite gemmae.

THYRSIS

Hic focus et taedae pingues, hic plurimus ignis
semper et adsidua postes fuligine nigri;
hic tantum Boreae curamus frigora, quantum
aut numerum lupus aut torrentia flumina ripas.

CORYDON

Stant et iuniperi et castaneae hirsutae;
strata iacent passim sua quaeque sub arbore poma;
omnia nunc rident: at si formosus Alexis
montibus his abeat, videas et flumina sicca.

THYRSIS

Aret ager; vitio moriens sitit aëris herba;
Liber pampineas invidit collibus umbras:
Phyllidis adventu nostrae nemus omne virebit,
Iuppiter et laeto descendet plurimus imbri.

FIGURE 7. Aristide Maillol, Pastoral Figure. *Les Eglogues de Virgile* (Weimar: Cranach Presse, 1926), Rosenwald Collection, no. 2089.

the female figures, enter into the woodcuts less directly—at times with only part of a pose. One female pose reworked in these sketches is related to the Maillol-Kessler watermark in the paper made for the printing of the *Eclogues*.

The third twentieth-century edition of the *Eclogues* is a new translation by Paul Valéry with color lithographs by Jacques Villon, bearing the Paris imprint of Scripta & Picta, published in 1953.[35] The lithograph has been closely associated with the livre d'artiste from the time of Ambroise Vollard's publication in 1900 of Verlaine's *Parallèlement*, illustrated by Pierre Bonnard.[36] Bonnard and Matisse were the masters of the lithograph in the illustrated book, using the medium to break into and out of the type area of the text. Villon, applying large swatches, almost patchwork, of bright color, creates a completely modern carnival atmosphere. This is a shock-treatment Vergil, not to everyone's taste, but it is not an unreasoned Vergil. The *Eclogues* have their own harsh lights and flashes of color. The prophetic fourth *Eclogue* has an arresting image, as brilliant as Villon's interpretation, in the sheep growing fleece of purple and gold. The Villon illustrations are described in the book as printed from 320 stones. The "Didot" type was especially designed for this volume. Again, the desire for a *new* Vergil.

> Quid faciat l[a]etas segetes quo sidere t[e]rram
> Vertere moecenas: . . .[37]

> What makes a plenteous Harvest, when to turn
> The fruitful Soil . . .[38]

To follow the fortunes of the illustration of the *Georgics*, it is necessary to return to the 1502 Strasbourg edition. The poet himself is very much present in the woodcuts for the Grüninger *Georgics*, where he is either seated at an ornate desk at the side of what is otherwise a rural scene or pointing out features of the scene to Maecenas. This is completely in line with the text, which, unlike that of the *Eclogues*, has a consistent voice and authority. The first woodcut contains the figures and details of the Book One invocations, even to the new sign in the zodiac proposed for Augustus (fig. 8). The sign itself—a crown enthroned—is the artist's invention.

The illustration of the *Georgics* in John Dryden's English translation of the complete works of Vergil is a series of genre scenes. Dryden had been translating Vergil in parts and publishing sections since 1684. It was Jacob Tonson who initiated the plan for publishing a complete translation supported by subscription.[39] There were two subscriber lists. A five-guinea subscription was a subscription to the illustrations, and each subscriber was assigned to a particular illustration with his own coat of arms added to the foot of that copperplate. The work is described on the title page as "Adorn'd with a Hundred Sculptures." Little of the subscription money was needed for illustrators, however, since Tonson borrowed from the preceding great Vergil project, John Ogilby's edition of 1654, the illustrations by Franz Cleyn. The Ogilby Vergil was a tall and impressive folio, with the plates dedicated to individuals. Even the advertisement of Tonson's volume as adorned with sculptures

FIGURE 8. Invocation Woodcut, for the *Georgics*, Book One. Publius Vergilius Maro, *Opera*, ed. Sebastian Brant (Strasbourg: I. Grieninger [i.e., Grüninger], 1502), Rosenwald Collection, no. 594.

originated with Ogilby. Apart from the new subscribers' coats of arms, other slight alterations were made for Tonson, but the plates carry most of the original dates and signatures untouched in the reworking of the surface. Wenceslaus Hollar was the engraver employed by Ogilby on the better plates in the series.

Both Johann Grüninger's 1502 *Georgics* and the 1697 Tonson *Georgics* were part of *Opera* volumes in which the illustration was affected by the narrative techniques of the *Aeneid*. No illustrated edition of Vergil's models for the *Eclogues* and the *Georgics*, Theocritus, Lucretius, and Hesiod, appears in the Rosenwald Collection until the John Flaxman Hesiod of 1817, in which the engravings are the work of William Blake.[40] It is quite possible that without the pressures on the illustrator to match the *Aeneid*, the potential for illustration in the *Georgics* would not have been recognized as early as 1502.

FIGURE 9.
André Dunoyer de Segonzac,
Landscape.
Publius Vergilius Maro,
*Les Géorgiques* [Paris, 1947],
Rosenwald Collection, no. 2194.


An eighteenth-century project for a translation of the three works was begun by the botanist John Martyn, but he published only the *Georgics* and the *Eclogues*, and his notes for the *Aeneid* were left to be published after his death. He intended to provide natural history annotations throughout, and his *Georgics* of 1741, printed for him by R. Reily in London, is an edition that figures in the history of botanical illustration and in the history of color printing.[41] The Latin text is printed in one to fifteen lines per page (many pages have only a single line) with English notes in two columns below. Martyn quotes and corrects Dryden in some passages. Martyn's is a prose translation, but he criticizes Dryden's interpretation of "quo sidere" in Book One, line 1, as unpoetical. The subscriber list printed in this edition includes William Cowper, John Dyer, Edmund Halley, and Sir Hans Sloane.

There are twelve copperplate illustrations, printed separately from the text, five of them printed in color. This is a transitional volume, in which the color plates are among the early English experiments in the use of mezzotint for book illustration. Copies were issued with hand-coloring added to black-printed plates and to the color-printed plates to heighten the color detail. The application of color to the printed book is profitably studied in terms of botanical illustration, where it is possible to start with the coloring of individual copies of the earliest herbals and where color has the virtue of being scientific rather than being purely for enhancement. The Rosenwald Collection copy of the *Herbarium* of Apuleius Barbarus, assigned to Joannes Philippus de Lignamine in Rome and dated ca. 1483–84 (contemporary with the Le Roy Lyons Vergil), has its woodcuts hand-colored.[42] Specific to eighteenth-century English interest in color-printing processes, the Rosenwald Collection includes Jakob Christoffel Le Blon's *Coloritto; or, The Harmony of Colouring in Painting, Reduced to Mechanical Practice* [London, 1725].[43] Color was important to John Martyn, and he had used mezzotint color earlier in his *Historia plantarum rariorum.*

Martyn's illustrations for the *Georgics*, aside from a few maps and pictures of farming implements, are representations of single plants mentioned by Vergil. Martyn's discussion of "ferrugineos hyacinthos," the "Hiacinthus Poeticus,"[44] illustrated in a two-color mezzotint with hand details (pl. 8), extends in notes from page 351 to page 354. He includes both explanations for the letters *AI* on the petals—Apollo's lament for the boy Hyacinthus, or the flower rising from the blood of Ajax and marked with the first two letters of his name. This is the flower that is referred to in Vergil's third *Eclogue* as "A Flow'r, that bears inscrib'd the names of Kings:"[45] and Martyn shows it again in the plate of mixed flowers in his 1749 *Eclogues.* He identifies it as a Martagon (*Lilium floribus reflexis*). Although a scientist, Martyn takes account of legend as part of the real texture of the poem.

The 1947 Paris edition of the *Georgics* with etchings by André Dunoyer de Segonzac is one of the majestic livres d'artiste of the twentieth century.[46] There are 119 etchings, with touches of drypoint and aquatint. The Rosenwald Collection copy is one of 50, of the edition of 250, with a suite of the etchings. The text is in Latin and French (the translation by Michel de Marolles) on facing pages. The beginning and end of each book have a half-page etching for each language. The plates for these were larger than the paper used, so that no plate mark is interposed between the image and the text. Within each book, the etchings are full page, with a plate mark, but are printed on the text sheets, not as loose plates. All are printed to face the Latin text. The French text on the next opening faces the blank verso of the illustration. The real artistry is in the balance of the italic letter of the Latin text with the etching. The most original illustrations are those for Book One, where the sense of light and space on the page is extraordinary. Here Vergil's text deals with man's ability to read signs and portents in the universe. The etchings are long vistas, beginning with grains or grasses in the foreground and stretching across fields to an expanse of sky (fig. 9). Most of the human figures are seen as minute specks in the distance, dwarfed by the landscape and the larger order of nature.

A stylistic link between the *Georgics* and Vergil's last work, the *Aeneid*—which operates both in the original and in translation—is the continual suggestion by poetic simile of correspondences between the natural world and man. In the *Georgics*, Book Four, the militaristic life of the bees is one example. The world of nature is the focus, and man might understand it better with reference to human artifice. In the *Aeneid*, the hero is the focus, and crucial moments in the action are extended by similes involving wind, water, trees, or wild beasts. In Book Two of the *Aeneid*, no illustrator could depict, to Vergil's effect, Laocoön as an ox at the altar, Pyrrhus as a crested snake, or Hecuba and her women as a flock of doves. The artist can put both Laocoön and the ox into one scene, but how can he superimpose one image on the other, make the vital connection that the poet does. No illustrator can approach Aeneas's horrified vision of Troy, beginning, in Dryden's translation, "Thus when a flood of Fire . . ." and ending, "the Seas are bright / With splendor, not their own; and shine with *Trojan* light."[47] Aeneas listens to the roar of the city as the shepherd to the mountain torrent. In the poem, the two figures become one; in a picture, they will not merge in the same way. The artist reading Vergil must identify the material that *can* be illustrated, stop the progression of words at a certain point, and arrest the reader's attention. Along with the *Eclogues* and the *Georgics*, the *Aeneid* has been retranslated in the twentieth century, but it has not yet been comparably illustrated. However, even as this essay was being presented for discussion at the Rosenwald symposium, Allen Mandelbaum and the artist of his forthcoming Dante translation, Barry Moser, began work on an illustrated *Aeneid*.

The impulse toward illustration is similar to the impulse toward poetry. It involves the concentration of ideas in imagery, the selection of detail, the imposition of order and form. At his best, the artist expands the text as the poet extends the limits of language. The book artist is working with wood, with copper, or with stone, under that necessity of invention identified by Vergil in a passage in the *Georgics*, Book One:

> *Jove* added Venom to the Viper's Brood,
> And swell'd, with raging Storms, the peaceful Flood:
> Commission'd hungry Wolves t'invest the Fold,
> And shook from Oaken Leaves the liquid Gold.
> Remov'd from Humane reach the chearful Fire,
> And from the Rivers bade the Wine retire:
> That studius Need might useful Arts explore;
> From furrow'd Fields to reap the foodful Store:
> And force the Veins of clashing Flints t'expire
> The lurking Seeds of their Coelestial Fire.[48]

> So thought and experiment might forge man's various crafts
> Little by little, asking the furrow to yield the corn-blade,
> Striking the hidden fire that lies in the veins of flint.[49]

# NOTES

1. Library of Congress, *The Lessing J. Rosenwald Collection: A Catalog of the Gifts of Lessing J. Rosenwald to the Library of Congress, 1943 to 1975* (Washington: Library of Congress, 1977).

2. John Dryden, trans., *The Works of Virgil: Containing His Pastorals, Georgics, and Æneis* (London: J. Tonson, 1697), Rosenwald Collection, no. 1548.

3. Publius Vergilius Maro, *The Aeneid*, trans. Allen Mandelbaum (Berkeley and Los Angeles: University of California Press, 1971), 2. 843–53.

4. Rosenwald Collection, no. 381. See Frederick R. Goff, *Incunabula in American Libraries, Third Census* (New York: Bibliographical Society of America, 1964), V-200.

5. British Museum, Department of Printed Books, *Catalogue of Books Printed in the XV$^{th}$ Century Now in the British Museum*, part 8 (London: Trustees of the British Museum, 1949), pp. 232, 236.

6. Publius Vergilius Maro, *Opera*, ed. Sebastian Brant (Strasbourg: I. Grieninger [i.e., Grüninger], 1502), *Aeneid* 1. Rosenwald Collection, no. 594. I will use this edition for the Latin lines quoted in this essay.

7. Dryden, *Works of Virgil* (1697), *Aeneid* 1. 1–3.

8. Theodore K. Rabb, "Sebastian Brant and the First Illustrated Edition of Vergil," *Princeton University Library Chronicle* 21 (1959–60):187–99.

9. Vergilius Maro, *Opera* (1502).

10. Publius Terentius Afer, *Comoediae* (Strasbourg: Johann [Reinhard] Grüninger, 1496), Rosenwald Collection, no. 175.

11. Vergilius Maro, *Opera* (1502), *Aeneid* 2.

12. Dryden, *Works of Virgil* (1697), *Aeneid* 2. 19–21.

13. Publius Vergilius Maro, *Aeneidos liber secvndvs* (Oxford: Clarendon Press, 1964), pp. 34–36, summarizing a longer article, and p. 80, note to line 150.

14. Rosenwald Collection, nos. 6, 7, and 218.

15. Publius Vergilius Maro, *Opera nvnc recens accvratissime castigata, cvm XI acerrimi ivdicii virorvm commentariis* (Venice: Apud Ivntas, 1544), Rosenwald Collection, no. 842.

16. Rosenwald Collection, no. 799. See Harvard University, Library, Department of Printing and Graphic Arts, *Catalogue of Books and Manuscripts*, 2 parts in 4 vols. (Cambridge: Belknap Press of Harvard University Press, 1964–74), part 2, *Italian 16th Century Books*, 2 vols. (1974), 2: nos. 524–25.

17. Publius Vergilius Maro, *L'Eneïde de Virgile* (Lyons: I. de Tovrnes, 1560), Rosenwald Collection, no. 1068.

18. Harvard University, Library, Department of Printing and Graphic Arts, *Catalogue*, part 1, *French 16th Century Books*, 2 vols. (1964), 2: no. 540.

19. Vergilius Maro, *Opera* (1502), *Aeneid* 2.

20. Dryden, *Works of Virgil* (1697), *Aeneid* 2. 70–74.

21. Rosenwald Collection, no. 1060.

22. Rosenwald Collection, no. 1393.

23. Daniel Berkeley Updike, *Printing Types, Their History, Forms, and Use: A Study in Survivals*, 3d ed., 2 vols. (Cambridge: Belknap Press of Harvard University Press, 1962), 1:207–8.

24. Rosenwald Collection, no. 1715.

25. Rosenwald Collection, no. 1599.

26. Vergilius Maro, *Opera* (1502), *Eclogues* 3.

27. Dryden, *Works of Virgil* (1697), *Eclogues* 3. 81–84.

28. Publius Vergilius Maro, *Les Bucoliques de Virgile, précédées de plusieurs Idylles de Théocrite, de Bion et de Moschus . . .*, trans. Firmin Didot (Paris: F. Didot, 1806), Rosenwald Collection, no. 1883.

29. Publius Vergilius Maro, *Les Églogues de Virgile* (Paris: Plon-Nourrit, [1906]), Rosenwald Collection, no. 2132.

30. Michael C. J. Putnam, *Virgil's Pastoral Art: Studies in the "Eclogues"* (Princeton, N.J.: Princeton University Press, 1970), pp. 124–26.

31. Ibid., p. 92.

32. There have been two major exhibitions focusing on the livre d'artiste. The first was at the Museum of Modern Art in 1936, "Modern Painters and Sculptors as Illustrators," with a catalog by Monroe Wheeler. The second, "The Artist and the Book, 1860–1960," at the Museum of Fine Arts, Boston, in 1961, was significantly broader in scope. Its catalog was compiled by Eleanor M. Garvey, with an introduction by Philip Hofer. Both catalogs define the range of works qualified to be called livres d'artiste.

33. Publius Vergilius Maro, *Eclogae* (Weimar: Cranach Presse, 1926), Rosenwald Collection, no. 2088; *Les Églogues de Virgile*, trans. Marc Lafargue (Weimar: Cranach Presse, 1926), Rosenwald Collection, no. 2089. Aristide Joseph Bonaventure Maillol, *Suite des bois originaux pour illustrer les Géorgiques de Virgile* (Paris: P. Gonin, [194–?]) is Rosenwald Collection, no. 2200.

34. Publius Vergilius Maro, *Les Géorgiques*, 2 vols. (Paris: Philippe Gonin, 1950), 2: 153–54.

35. Publius Vergilius Maro, *Les Bucoliques de Virgile*, trans. Paul Valéry (Paris: Scripta & Picta, 1953), Rosenwald Collection, no. 2212.

36. Paul Marie Verlaine, *Parallèlement* (Paris: A. Vollard, 1900), Rosenwald Collection, no. 2125.

37. Vergilius Maro, *Opera* (1502), *Georgics* 1.

38. Dryden, *Works of Virgil* (1697), *Georgics* 1. 1–2.

39. Harry M. Geduld, *Prince of Publishers: A Study of the Work and Career of Jacob Tonson* (Bloomington: Indiana University Press, 1969), pp. 66–81.

40. John Flaxman, *The Theogony, Works & Days, & the Days of Hesiod* (London: [Longman, Hurst, Rees, Orme & Brown, 1817]), Rosenwald Collection, no. 1837.

41. Publius Vergilius Maro, *Pub. Virgilii Maronis Georgicorum libri quatuor. The Georgicks of Virgil*, ed. and trans. John Martyn (London: Printed for the editor, by R. Reily, 1741), Rosenwald Collection, no. 1745.

42. Apuleius Barbarus, *Herbarium* [Rome: Joannes Philippus de Lignamine, ca. 1483–84], Rosenwald Collection, no. 237.

43. Rosenwald Collection, no. 1741.

44. *Georgics* 4. 183.

45. Dryden, *Works of Virgil* (1697), *Eclogues* 3. 164.

46. Publius Vergilius Maro, *Les Géorgiques*, trans. Michel de Marolles [Paris, 1947], Rosenwald Collection, no. 2194.

47. Dryden, *Works of Virgil* (1697), *Aeneid* 2. 408–22.

48. Dryden, *Works of Virgil* (1697), *Georgics* 1. 197–206.

49. Publius Vergilius Maro, *The Georgics of Virgil*, trans. C. Day Lewis (London: Jonathan Cape, 1940), 1. 133–35.

## ELFRIEDE ABBE

# AN ARTIST LOOKS AT THE *GEORGICS*

The purpose of this essay is to present the point of view of an artist toward the *Georgics* of Vergil. In a general perspective all the arts are interrelated, and in the *Georgics* the visual aspect is inseparable from the other elements of the poem. The following endeavors to account for some of the impressions and means that evoke a visual response in the imagination (fig. 1).

One day while browsing in a library I came upon a whole shelf of the *Georgics*. Never having read the work, and retaining a profound respect for the author of the *Aeneid*, I took down one of the books, an English translation. A reading of several others revealed inevitable discrepancies in meaning and interpretation. Artists tend to be pragmatists, and no matter what their contemporaries or predecessors have done, each individual claims the right of independent exploration. Having determined to illustrate and print the *Georgics*, I saw no other way to a unified production than to work out my own version of the text, trying to stay as close to the original meaning as possible and at the same time maintain a rhythmical phrasing.

The illustrations I did are technically wood engravings, since they were cut on end-grain wood with gravers. The terms *wood engraving* and *woodcut* are not interchangeable. Woodcuts are cut with knives, chisels, and gouges on a plank, the tools mostly following the grain, whereas in engraving the wood fibers are standing vertically, and the gravers move around among them. Woodcut is of ancient origin, but wood engraving did not develop until the eighteenth century and evolved from the technique of metal engraving. I transfer a simple line drawing directly to the uncoated surface of the wood block, the bare wood being a pleasant and congenial surface on which to work. After much of the design is cut, the block is rolled with black printing ink for better visibility and is then finished.

Acquaintance with the poem proved to be much the same as with any genuinely great work in any medium; the closer the examination, the more one sees and the more interesting the work becomes, as, for example, in studying a painting for its brushwork, rendering of detail, the artist's manner of treatment, and so on, one always makes new discoveries yet always returns to a contemplation of the whole with increased wonder.

To one who thinks visually, the reality of the images in the *Georgics* is predominantly arresting. It becomes apparent that Vergil's realities are created from sound, action, and form rather than by the descriptive means of color and atmosphere as we know them in modern literature. The ancients were more perceptive of inherent qualities of things and seem to have ignored the superficial. Homer's phrase "the wine-dark sea" more effectively conveys a sense of the heaviness and quality of sea water than would accurate descriptions of color or other conditions.

FIGURE 1. Spring Plowing.

FIGURE 3. Shepherd under Oak.

FIGURE 2. Mice and Burning Stubble.

It is from the interweaving of concise verbal expression and the cadences of the lines, which have the evocative qualities of music, that Vergil's images arise and from which the scenes and episodes draw their moods and their compelling vividness of immediacy. The abstract musical element which prevails in the poem one enjoys for itself, but Vergil also introduces specific natural sounds. One is reminded of Beethoven's Sixth Symphony, in which a similar device appears. In the *Georgics* we hear the murmur of the freshet over smooth stones, the thud of hoofs and the master's hand clapping the horse's neck, the harsh buzz of the horsefly, the crackling flames in the burning stubble, and the vine tender singing among the farthest rows (fig. 2). As the shepherd and the flock take refuge in the shade, the midday heat seems intensified by the shrill cicada rending the air (fig. 3). Like form and action, sound is a physical thing, although not usually thought of as such, and Vergil perhaps used it unconsciously.

FIGURE 4. Heifer before Storm.

FIGURE 5. Storm.

As an example of mood, in Book One the sense of vague uneasiness that precedes the storm is hardly less dramatic than the storm itself. The raven croaks, and the girls at their spinning anxiously watch the lamp. The heifer suspiciously sniffing the air tells without words that the wind is coming from an unusual direction (fig. 4). The calm explodes into rushing action, and sound again becomes a major element in the scene (fig. 5). After the storm comes the concert of birds and at moonrise the cry of the owl.

In the fluctuations of mood in the *Georgics*, despair and hope, resignation and effort, fortitude and cheer succeed one another. Contrasted with such sad episodes as the cattle plague and the tale of Orpheus and Eurydice are the jovial harvest and vintage festivals of the country people. Suddenly starting out of the depths, the upbeat carries us into the fast-moving present, a race, a fire in the olive orchard, the killing of a poisonous snake, a fight between rival bulls (figs. 6 and 7).

FIGURE 6. Horse Race.

FIGURE 7. Kids.

In Vergil's benign purpose of improving the condition of the tiller of soil, his humanity includes the animals that share the life and hardships of the peasant. Besides the larger passages in Book Three, which is devoted to the care of animals, there are grains of humor through the poem which bespeak a kindliness even toward creatures of a more remote nature; for example, in what may be proverbial expressions, he refers to the "ant who fears an indigent old age" and to "garrulous frogs." There is kindly humor in the description of the cow, in which Vergil says that he does not object "if she refuses the yoke, is hasty sometimes with her horn, is tall throughout her whole length, and sweeps her hoofprints with the tip of her tail as she walks." Here are conveyed the cow's basic obligations, her temperament and dignity.

Metaphor is a primitive but highly effective device for achieving concreteness. An example is Vergil's passage on laying out a vineyard, in which he compares the rows of vines to lines of soldiers: "Just as before a mighty battle . . . the squadrons in battle array stand marshaled on the open plain, and far and wide the whole field shimmers like the sea with gleaming bronze." Rather a grandiose metaphor for a vineyard, but nevertheless elegant, and it does convey the idea of the spacing. In the episode of the fighting bulls, one falls upon his adversary like a great wave roaring and tumbling on the rocks (fig. 8).

Some of the strongest images are called up by fewer than half a dozen words, as in the line from Book Two, *casus abies visura marinos* ("the fir that shall know the perils of the sea"). We recognize in a flash the tree as the mast of a ship (fig. 9). The words "iamque ministrantem platanum potantibus umbras" are an interesting means

FIGURE 8. Fighting Bulls.

FIGURE 9. Fir Trees.

of making the size of a shade tree apparent by the presentation of a little scene under its boughs.

The unembellished directness of the Latin language originally did not lend itself to poetry of the quality of the Augustan Age, but from Greek studies the later Roman writers gradually evolved a richer, more fluent language. Vergil's poetry retains the inherent strength enhanced with grace. The *Georgics* derives its basic validity from the familiarity and attachment that Vergil had for his subject, but the highly concentrated and effective expression is the result of conscious deliberation. Vergil limited himself severely. He is said to have dictated early in the morning as impulse prompted, then spent the rest of the day in editing and condensing the meaning into the smallest compass. This habit of composition in the arts, the will to express the most by the least means, has always been a challenge, and the achievement a proof of intellectual vigor. The succinct brushwork of a Chinese painting, the

FIGURE 10. Helmets and Bones.

FIGURE 11. Plow at Sunset.

strict limitation of form in haiku, the small number of actors in a Greek tragedy, the severe conditions imposed by the media of sculpture are all of a similar nature. Restrictions also require a strong sense of organization, which was characteristic of the Roman mind.

Vergil was conscious of his genius, and the sustaining power of this awareness and of his absorption in his art impelled him onward at the same height and constancy through many years. Coupled with this resolution and knowledge of inner power was a contradictory self-depreciation and sense of futility. It is tempting to draw a parallel between his temperament and that of Michelangelo, whose work has been described as embodying a kind of brooding sorrow, and who regarded himself as an unworthy servant, although fully aware of his great and unique power.

Owing as much to the melancholy element in Vergil's temperament as to external causes, darker strains intermingle with the serenity that characterizes the main theme of the *Georgics* (fig. 10). Sorrow over the past and fervent prayers for the future of the world, irony toward misguided worldliness, unrealized philosophic and scientific aspirations inspired by Lucretius, nostalgia for the Golden Age. These instances of somberness lend a deeper tone and meaning to the poem. Such abstract elements do not readily lend themselves to illustrative treatment, yet they influence the feeling and thought of the listener. Beautiful in themselves, these passages are actually subsidiary themes. Vergil's inward compulsion to weave them into the poetic fabric arose partly from the depth of his nature but also from a cultural consciousness. One feels that his true satisfaction as a poet lay in elemental reality. Country bred, the son of a small farmer, strongly attached to the land, he was most at home in meadow and woodland, orchard and garden, with the abundance of details that delight every lover of the earth (fig. 11).

In the *Georgics* the celebration of the simple rural life with its daily tasks from season to season and the rewards of an ethical existence devoted to hard work constitutes the great theme. Influenced by this consideration, it was on the main fabric alone that I concentrated in the visual rendering of my edition of the work; also in part because of a subjective affinity for nature and folk ways, and partly because the strong medium of the woodblock seemed most suitable to this concept. The principal theme is timeless and universal, whereas styles of philosophical, scientific, and religious thought come and go.

The universality of the *Georgics* actually helped to preserve the work in a number of early copies, for it was readily adopted into the practical teachings of the early Christian church, to which Vergil's dignity and gentle and ethical spirit strongly appealed. Bede and Augustine revered Vergil, and his works were taught in church schools as much for style as for content. The simple processes of planting and tilling, caring for sheep, cattle, and gardens were the lives of the monks and peasantry in the Dark Ages (fig. 12). The *Georgics* was one of the lights from a great past that shone into an obscure future. The early church fathers wisely adopted from the past whatever things were useful and good, pagan though they were. The marching tunes of the Roman legions became in fact the hymn tunes of the early church. Vergil was quaintly characterized as a Christian who was born too early.

In closing this part of the dissertation, it should be said that much of the foregoing may be subjective. In its universal qualities, the *Georgics* is in a sense the possession of each individual who approaches it. The number of editions in the Rosenwald Collection, ranging from the sixteenth to the twentieth century, creates a spectrum of the greatest variety in style and treatment.

FIGURE 12. Bee Yard.

In art or nature the whole is always greater than the sum of its parts; the totality of the *Georgics* as a great work originally motivated my production. In pursuing the project, however, I became aware of the many plants that are mentioned in the poem, herbs, trees, agricultural crops, and wild vegetation (fig. 13). Some were pleasantly familiar, others of obscure identity. The subject was irresistible, once curiosity was aroused, but to fragment the poem by the intrusion of mainly factual material was unthinkable. The study of the Vergilian plants had to take form in a completely different book (fig. 14).

There is more romanticism in plant exploration than is generally admitted. If a botanist writes a flora of the Greek islands or of North Africa or the Fijis, one may justifiably suspect that he likes the Greek islands or is fascinated with North Africa or the Fijis. The attraction of the *Georgics* and of Italy were a part of the motivation for this project. Nevertheless, the need for modern research to bring the Vergilian plants to life for the reader was obvious. A few commentaries had been written before 1920, with names, descriptions, and some conjectural identifications, but unless the reader had more than average botanical knowledge, the information was of little use. To arrive at a truthful representation, my procedure was to determine the identity of each plant as accurately as possible by comparisons of the earliest existing descriptions, appraisal of the opinions of commentators, and application of

FIGURE 14. Double-Page Spread. Reprinted from Elfriede Abbe, *The Plants of Virgil's "Georgics,"* Illustrations copyright © 1962 by Elfriede Abbe. Copyright © 1965 by Cornell University. Used by permission of the publisher, Cornell University Press.

FIGURE 13. Plane Tree Leaves.

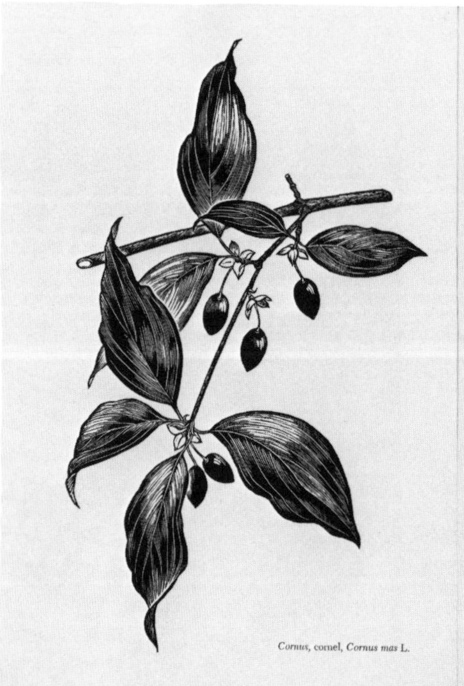

*Cornus*, cornel, *Cornus mas* L.

DOGWOOD FAMILY, *Cornaceae*

CORNUS

Cornel, cornelian cherry — *Cornus mas* L.

Fr. *cornouiller* — Ger. *Kornelle, Kornellkirsche*

It. *corniolo, crognolo*

prunis lapidosa rubescere corna [II.34]

Stone-pitted cornel cherries redden on [stock of] plum. [See *Prunus*.]

et bona bello
cornus [II.447–448]

Cornel useful in war. [Spears were made of the wood.]

Theophrastus. 3.12.1–2: A male and a female kind of *kraneia*. Wood of male tough like horn, no pith. Fruit sweet and fragrant. [*C. mas* L.]

Dioscorides. I.172: Krania. Cornus is a strong tree bearing a fruit like ye Oliue.

Pliny. 16.25.42, 16.38.73: *Cornus mascula* has no pith (*medulla*). One of the toughest woods. 16.26.43: Cornus enim circa solstitia reddit primo candidum, postea sanguineum. (At the summer solstice the fruit is white but later turns red.)

Columella. 12.10.3: Corna, quibus pro olivis utamur. (Cornel berries which we use as olives.)

[*C. mas* is common in Europe from France to central Italy. The flowering dogwood cultivated in the United States is *C. florida* L. and is native here. The "female" plant mentioned by the ancients is *C. sanguinea* L., so named for its red twigs. Its wood is soft, the fruit bluish-black and sour.]

153

*far left:*
FIGURE 15. Squill.

*left:*
FIGURE 16. Cowpea.

historical and scientific context. Once identified, the plants had to be found, drawn, and engraved. With the aid of a grant from the Hunt Institute of Botanical Documentation at Carnegie-Mellon University, I embarked on the project in Europe in 1961.

The most fruitful sources of early botanical works proved to be the Biblioteca medicea-laurenziana in Florence, the Herzog August Bibliothek in Wolfenbüttel, Germany, the Bibliothèque nationale in Paris, and the Biblioteca Apostolica Vaticana in Rome. The works consulted there and elsewhere constitute the bibliography of my *Plants of Vergil's Georgics*, published by Cornell University Press in 1965. Fifty sets of the wood engravings on Japanese paper were published separately by me in 1962.

To mention a few of the works in the bibliography, among the most interesting are Albertus Magnus's *Tabula Tractuum Parvorum naturalium . . . de vegetabilibus et plantis* (Venice, 1517); Thomas Martyn's translation and commentary on the *Georgics* (Oxford, 1819); and the unique Carolingian manuscript "Capitulare de villis." The last is also the oldest, written in the ninth century as an inventory of the imperial gardens. It includes the lily, squill, walnut, hazel, cherry, pear, cowpea, and poppy mentioned by Vergil (figs. 15 and 16).

The works of Albertus Magnus contain remarkably lively and graphic descriptions of plants and besides treat of plant structures and parts unnoted by early writers, except by Theophrastus, a pupil of Aristotle. Albertus's concept and perpetuation of Aristotelian philosophy probably influenced his way of looking at plants.

Thomas Martyn's commentary is an informative work which pulls together exceptionally well the fields of botany, agriculture, and the classics. Martyn was professor of botany at Cambridge, author of several botanical works, and editor of the ninth edition of Philip Miller's *Gardener's Dictionary*. He also wrote *A Chronological Series of Engravers* (Cambridge: Printed by J. Archdeacon for J. Woodyer, and sold by J. Beecroft, London, 1770) which is in the Rosenwald Collection.[1] The 1741 edition of his Vergilian commentary, translated by his son, John Martyn, is also in the collection.[2]

One "old English farming book," Thomas Hale's *A Compleat Body of Husbandry* (London: T. Osborne, 1758), I consulted and included in the bibliography principally to indicate the influence that by their literary prestige ancient classical writings on agriculture long exercised over the agricultural practices of Europe. Even the same weather signs that appear in the *Georgics*, and that Vergil originally found in the works of Hesiod, are described by Hale.

Of other major works consulted, several are available to scholars in the Rosenwald Collection. These include the *Herbarium* of Apuleius Barbarus (Rome: Joannes Philippus de Lignamine, ca. 1483–84);[3] Bartholomaeus Anglicus's *De proprietatibus rerum*, of which there are three editions in the collection;[4] *Ruralia commoda* of Pier de' Crescenzi (four editions);[5] Pliny's *Historia naturalis* (Venice: Johannes de Spira, 1469); *Regimen sanitatis Salernitanum* (Louvain: Johann de Paderborn, Westphalia, [1484–85]);[7] and Servius's commentaries on the *Georgics* (1502 and 1520).[8]

The pursuit of references and of the actual plants went on simultaneously. Two of the oldest plant collections in existence were examined, first the herbarium of Andrea Cesalpino (1519–1603) in the Istituto Botanico of the University of Florence. The sheets on which the plants are mounted form three large volumes bound in red leather. Each sheet bears the name of the specimen written by Cesalpino in Latin, Greek, and Italian. A dedicatory letter to his patron in the same beautiful script and dated 1562 apears at the beginning of the first volume. The other collection was the herbarium of Hieronymus Harder (d. 1599 in Ulm) in the Naturhistorisches Museum, Vienna. The plants were collected between 1576 and 1594, many of them in the Tirol.

For the plants, my sources were botanical gardens, public, private, and institutional, and the countryside of southern Europe, explored by car. Of the botanical gardens, the most rewarding was the ancient monastery herb garden that is now part of the grounds of the Istituto Botanico of the University of Padua.

Olive and chestnut were found on the heights above Florence, butcher's broom (fig. 17) and laurel (fig. 18) in the city gardens. Cypress trees were everywhere but first seen as windbreaks against the mistral in the vineyards of southern France. On the roadsides down the Rhone valley grew holly-oaks (fig. 19), so dark and dense

FIGURE 17. Butcher's Broom.

FIGURE 18. Laurel.

FIGURE 19. Holly-Oak.

FIGURE 20. Acanthus.

FIGURE 21. Strawberry Tree.

that at first sight I thought they were holly. Acanthus (fig. 20) lined the edges of pools and fountains, and wild thyme carpeted rocky hillsides. Shrub-clover, Spanish broom, and Vergil's *Arbutus* (fig. 21), the strawberry tree, were found near Rome.

The region familiar to Vergil in his childhood and early youth now presents an aspect quite different from its character near the beginning of the Christian era. The whole plain of the Po, economically the foremost region of Italy in modern times, is so intensively cultivated that wild vegetation occupies only small scattered areas. Very little of the land is devoted to pasturage, whereas in Vergil's time this was one of its principal uses. Vergil praises the pasturage of the lands "that unhappy Mantua has lost" following the distribution of land to the victorious army after the civil war; he dwells especially on the quick renewal of the grass in its moist and fertile environment, even after being grazed down. From a practical view this description simply indicates an earlier phase in agricultural development. Intensive cultivation has prevailed only since the two World Wars, for even as late as the early twentieth century some of the plain was wooded, and the marshy areas east of Ostiglia and around Mantua, which appear on the mural maps of 1581 in the Vatican Gallery, had not yet been drained. Vergil speaks of the desirability of draining marshes, evidently a problem of the countryman of his time. Today the plain is one vast vegetable garden crossed by innumerable canals and drainage ditches, and except along the river banks the only trees are poplars and plane trees, planted for shade, borders, and windbreaks.

The delta of the Po has, of course, also changed. The sixteenth-century Vatican maps show Ravenna, which is south of the delta, as closer to the sea, the mouth of its harbor protected by land bars. The great forest of *Pinus pinea* (Vergil's "utile lignum navigiis pinus")[9] (fig. 22) is designated on the maps as "Pineta di Porto et Classe." In Roman times Ravenna was an important seaport, and in the first century Augustus enlarged the harbor to accommodate the Adriatic war fleet. At present in Ravenna are visible the ruins of Theodoric's palace, which until the beginning of the twelfth century was situated on the shore. Today Ravenna is twelve kilometers from the sea, and the famous forest is much depleted.

The Prealpi Bresciane and the Prealpi Benacensi Occidentali were familiar to Vergil, for he mentions the "mighty lakes," Larius (Como) and Benacus (Garda). Beyond Brescia, which is about twenty-five kilometers west of Lago di Garda, appear rocky peaks and in the foreground steep hills wooded with hazel, birch, and ash, and higher up with oak and chestnut. Vergil advises the beekeeper "to bring thyme and pine from the high mountains."[10] Thyme covers many rocky areas, and the pine in this case is Scotch pine, *Pinus sylvestris* L. (fig. 23).

FIGURE 22. *Pinus pinea.*

FIGURE 23. *Pinus sylvestris.*

FIGURE 25. Hazel.

FIGURE 24. *Aster amellus.*

In Book Four Vergil mentions the river Mella for which *Aster amellus* (fig. 24) is named, one of the important bee plants of the *Georgics*. He says it is gathered by shepherds near the winding stream. The Mella rises at the 2,000-foot level north of Brescia near Lago di Garda and flows past Brescia to meet the Oglio, a tributary of the Po, about twenty kilometers from Bozzolo. Northward, the channel of the Mella is narrow and deep in the rock bed, its banks overgrown with hazel (fig. 25) and birch. Between Brescia and Sarrezzo it becomes shallow and gravelly and is bordered by willows and alders.

Another of Vergil's rivers is the Mincio, on which Mantua is situated. The Mincio flows from the southern tip of Lago di Garda to the Po. In its upper reaches it resembles the Mella, but it is a more vigorous, swift-flowing watercourse. Around Mantua the Mincio originally widened and formed swampy areas. With the aid of dams it has been divided into three shallow lakes. The ancestor of one of the dams appears in the Vatican maps and probably originated as a means of approach to the shore. Mantua was a strong fortress because of its natural moat.

Except for bits of landscape and people working in the fields, to one haunting the region of Vergil's youth and the true birthplace of the *Georgics* for traces of the past, there seemed a disappointing lack of features to carry one's imagination back to the time. But one day, on entering the village of Bozzolo, I came unexpectedly upon an impressive Roman arch. It was much weathered and served as part storehouse, for the usual fagots and pole wood were stacked inside, but it was massive and reminiscent of the Arch of Titus. Three aged village women in black dresses noted my amazement and, smiling shyly, came near to speak to me. They were proud of their *porta romana* and pleased that a stranger stopped to look at it.

## NOTES

1. Rosenwald Collection, no. 2583.
2. Publius Vergilius Maro, *Pub. Virgilii Maronis Georgicorum libri quatuor. The Georgiks of Virgil*, trans. John Martyn (London: Printed for the editor, by R. Reily, 1741), Rosenwald Collection, no. 1745.
3. Rosenwald Collection, no. 237.
4. Bartholomaeus Anglicus, *De proprietatibus rerum* (Lyons: Johannes Siber, [after 26 January 1486]), Rosenwald Collection, no. 394; *De proprietatibus rerum* (Haarlem: Jacob Bellaert, 24 December 1485), Rosenwald Collection, no. 488; and *Bertholomevs De proprietatibvs rervm* (London: T. Bertheleti, 1535), Rosenwald Collection, no. 1225.
5. Pietro de Crescenzi, *Ruralia commoda* [Speyer: Peter Drach, 1 October 1493], Rosenwald Collection, no. 164; *Ruralia commoda* (Paris: Jean Bonhomme, 15 October 1486), Rosenwald Collection, no. 390; *Ruralia commoda* (Louvain: Johann de Paderborn [Westphalia], 9 December 1474), Rosenwald Collection, no. 512; and *La Manière de empter & planter en iardins, plusieurs aultres choses biẽ estrãges & tres-plaisantes* (Lyons, 15—), Rosenwald Collection, no. 1090.
6. Rosenwald Collection, no. 212.
7. Rosenwald Collection, no. 532.
8. Publius Vergilius Maro, *Opera* [cũ cõmẽtariis Servii Mauri Honorati grãmatici: Aelii (i.e., Tiberii Claudii) Donati, Christofori Landini, Antonii Mancinelli & Domicii Calderini] (Strasbourg: I. Grieninger, 1502), Rosenwald Collection, no. 594; and *Bvcolica, Georgica, Aeneis, cvm Servii commentariis cvratissime emendatis*... (Venice: G. de Rusconibus, 1520), Rosenwald Collection, no. 799.
9. *Georgics* 2. 442–43.
10. *Georgics* 4. 112.

# NOTES ON THE CONTRIBUTORS

ELFRIEDE ABBE is a sculptor and graphic artist at Manchester Center, Vermont 05255. She has exhibited frequently and examples of her work are included in many permanent collections in America, including the Library of Congress and the National Gallery of Art, and abroad. Her numerous publications include hand-printed woodcut books of *Æsop's Fables* (Ithaca, N.Y., 1950), *Prometheus Bound* (Ithaca, N.Y., 1952), and *The Georgics of Virgil* (Ithaca, N.Y., 1966), and she wrote and illustrated *The Plants of Virgil's "Georgics"* (Ithaca: Cornell University Press, 1965).

JAMES CAHILL is Professor of the History of Art, University of California, Berkeley, California 94720. He has published widely on Chinese and Japanese painting, including a recent volume of the Charles Eliot Norton lectures: *The Compelling Image: Nature and Style in Seventeenth-Century Chinese Painting* (Cambridge: Harvard University Press, 1982). Two volumes of his five-volume series on later Chinese painting have appeared to date: *Hills beyond a River: Chinese Painting of the Yüan Dynasty, 1279–1368* (Tokyo and New York: Weatherhill, 1976) and *Parting at the Shore: Chinese Painting of the Early and Middle Ming Dynasty, 1368–1580* (Tokyo and New York: Weatherhill, 1978).

SANDRA HINDMAN is Associate Professor of the History of Art, The Johns Hopkins University, Baltimore, Maryland 21218. Her special field of interest is later medieval art of northern Europe, on which she has written articles and reviews in the *Art Bulletin*, the *Journal of the Warburg and Courtauld Institutes, Speculum*, and elsewhere. She has also published *Text and Image in Fifteenth-Century Illustrated History Bibles* (Leiden: E. J. Brill, 1977) and coauthored, with James Douglas Farquhar, *Pen to Press: Illustrated Manuscripts and Printed Books in the First Century of Printing* (College Park: Art Dept., University of Maryland, 1977).

BARBARA G. LANE is Associate Professor of Art at Queens College of the City University of New York, Flushing, New York 11367. Her publications include articles in the *Art Bulletin, Oud-Holland*, and the *Journal of the Warburg and Courtauld Institutes* on problems involving early Netherlandish painting and manuscript illumination. Her books include *Hans Memling* and *Jan van Eyck*, both in Die grossen Meister der Malerei series (Frankfurt am Main: Ullstein, 1980).

ELEANOR WINSOR LEACH is Professor of Classical Studies, Indiana University, Bloomington, Indiana 47405. In addition to a book entitled *Vergil's Eclogues: Landscapes of Experience* (Ithaca, N.Y.: Cornell University Press, 1974), she has written widely on issues of interpretation as they relate to art and literature of the classical and medieval periods. Her frequent essays have appeared in the *Journal of the History of Ideas, Ramus, Arethusa,* and *Latomus.*

RUTH MORTIMER is Curator of Rare Books and Assistant Librarian, as well as Lecturer in Art, at Smith College, Northampton, Massachusetts 01063. In addition to review articles, she has written widely on the history of printing, including a four-volume corpus for Harvard College Library Department of Printing and Graphic Arts, the *Catalogue of Books and Manuscripts*, in two parts, *French 16th Century Books* and *Italian 16th Century Books* (Cambridge: Belknap Press of Harvard University Press, 1964–74).

KEITH P. F. MOXEY is Associate Professor of Art, University of Virginia, Charlottesville, Virginia 22903. He is the author of a volume on iconoclasm and the arts in the sixteenth-century Netherlands, *Pieter Aertsen, Joachim Beuckelaar, and the Rise of Secular Painting in the Context of the Reformation* (New York: Garland Press, 1977). He has also published articles in the *Journal of the Warburg and Courtauld Institutes* and *Simiolus.*

JOHN HORACE PARRY is Gardiner Professor of Oceanic History and Affairs, Harvard University, Cambridge, Massachusetts 02138. In addition to numerous articles and reviews, he has written ten books that range from *The Spanish Theory of Empire in the Sixteenth Century* (Cambridge: The University Press, 1940) and *The Age of Reconnaissance* (New York: Praeger Publishers, 1963) to *The Discovery of the Sea* (New York: Dial Press, 1974) and *The Discovery of South America* (London: Elek, 1979).

KAREN S. PEARSON is Cartographer, Department of Natural Resources, State of Alaska, Division of Geological and Geophysical Surveys, P.O. Box 80007, College, Alaska 99701. Her special fields of interest are in fifteenth- and sixteenth-century German cartography and nineteenth-century European and American cartography. Her publications include an exhibition catalog, with T. Murphy, on *Portraits of the World: an Exhibition of World Maps from the Period of the Great Discoveries*, for an exhibit at the Sheldon Memorial Art Gallery, University of Nebraska, Lincoln, in 1981, as well as articles in *Imago Mundi* and *The American Cartographer.*

DIANE G. SCILLIA is Adjunct Assistant Professor of Art at Virginia Wesleyan College, Norfolk, Virginia 23502. Her articles, focusing on problems related to manuscript illumination and panel painting in the northern Netherlands, have appeared in the *Art Bulletin* and *Oud-Holland*.

JAMES SNYDER is Professor of Art and Curator-in-Residence of the Hobson Pittman Memorial Gallery, Bryn Mawr College, Bryn Mawr, Pennsylvania 19010. He has published widely on fifteenth- and sixteenth-century Netherlandish art, including articles in the *Art Bulletin*, *Oud-Holland*, and elsewhere. He has also written two books on Hieronymus Bosch: *Bosch in Perspective* (New York: Prentice Hall, 1973) and *Hieronymus Bosch* (New York: Excalibur Books, 1980).

CHARLES TALBOT is Professor of Art, Smith College, Northampton, Massachusetts 01063. His field of interest is graphic art of the later medieval and northern European periods, about which he has published articles, reviews, and catalogs. These include *Prints and Drawings of the Danube School: An Exhibition of South German and Austrian Graphic Art of 1500 to 1560* (New Haven: Printed by the Carl Purington Rollins Printing-Office of the Yale University Press, 1969), *Dürer in America: His Graphic Work* (Washington: National Gallery of Art, 1971; and New York: Macmillan, 1971), and *From a Mighty Fortress: Prints, Drawings, and Illustrated Books from the Age of Luther at Coburg*, a catalog for an exhibit at the Detroit Institute of Arts and the National Gallery of Canada, Ottawa, 1981–82.

# INDEX

This index lists names of authors, printers and publishers, artists and engravers, historical figures, and other individuals mentioned in the text; selected titles of printed books; and titles and locations of manuscripts and works of art.

For full bibliographical data on Rosenwald Collection imprints, the reader is referred to *The Lessing J. Rosenwald Collection: A Catalog of the Gifts of Lessing J. Rosenwald to the Library of Congress, 1943 to 1975* (Washington: Library of Congress, 1977).

*The text type of* The Early Illustrated Book *is Linoterm Sabon, a typeface originally designed for hot metal by Jan Tschichold. It was set by The Stinehour Press, Lunenburg, Vermont. The display type, Weiss Initials, Series I, which was designed by Emil Rudolf Weiss for hot metal, was set by Haddon Craftsmen, Inc., Scranton, Pennsylvania. Color separations were done by Prolith International, Beltsville, Maryland. The text and illustrations were printed on 70 lb. Mohawk Superfine text, softwhite, eggshell finish, and the color illustrations on Warren's 80 lb. Lustro Offset Enamel, dull, cream, by Garamond / Pridemark Press, Inc., Baltimore, Maryland. The book was bound in Holliston Roxite C and Elephant Hide by Nicholstone Book Bindery, Inc., Nashville, Tennessee.*

*The book was designed by Adrianne Onderdonk Dudden.*